Praise for *Science Under*

"Today, good conse⸺ ⸺ ⸺ ⸺ty, and courage in the scientific community have too often been rewarded by back-alley attacks of the worst sort. Todd Wilkinson, one of the finest western journalists (and, regrettably, no relative), has ably documented an indispensable and extraordinary chapter in the history of the modern West."

—**Charles Wilkinson, Moses Lasky Professor of Law
at the University of Colorado, and author of
Crossing the Next Meridian and *The Eagle Bird***

"This book champions the scientists and other employees of natural resources agencies who buck the system that supports them because they care more for biological truth and interspecific justice than job security. A few of these people have become well known, but most we never hear about. They are stamped into the ground by the commodity industries—aided and abetted by the Wise Use movement, our own government, and our own tax dollars. If enough people read this book, perhaps we can take back the real America from those who care only for profit."

—**Reed Noss, President-elect, Society for Conservation Biology,
former editor, *Conservation Biology***

"Todd Wilkinson has written an important and riveting book on the war being waged by politicians and commodity groups on truth, nature and the American West. Read this book to learn how the crooks have turned the lives of public resource managers into utter hell."

—**Tom McGuane, novelist, rancher, and conservationist**

"Full of stories of courageous men and women bravely told, *Science Under Siege* introduces us to America's "Combat Scientists," biologists, hydrologists, grizzly trackers, rock hounds, and cave-diving detectives who are struggling to understand and protect our nation's natural resources.

"In often vivid prose author Todd Wilkinson reveals these whistleblowers' fears and frustrations: fears over what their science is discovering, and frustration over having their life's works attacked by government bureaucrats more interested in protecting oil companies and real-estate developers than the public that pays their salaries.

"*Science Under Siege* is not always a pretty story, but it's one everybody who cares about our landscape, our future and the future of our democratic freedoms ought to read. This book is a sling-stone for every David prepared to take on a Goliath."

—**David Helvarg, author of *The War Against the Greens***

"A courageous, relentlessly readable book based on superb reporting. ... This is an important, chastening book."
   —*Audubon*

"*Science Under Siege* is a remarkable project, both daunting and inspiring. It details almost too clearly one of the most elemental tenets of our time, or any other time: That truth has its own specific and considerable power, and that because of this, we cannot help but be tempted to shape and bend it, to buy it and sell it. Wilkinson's book makes the case that this is a human certainty, a flaw, a weakness being manipulated more than ever by the ever more massive corporations and their elected senators and representatives, with dire results for the dwindling public wildlands."
   —Rick Bass, *San Fransicso Chronicle Book Review*

"An inspirational and eye-opening work for those interested in environmental issues." Selected as an Outstanding Academic Book.
   —*Choice*

"Powerful and important and thoroughly well-documented. ... One hopes that the outrage Wilkinson expresses in this book will go far toward restoring the competence and integrity we all expect and must relentlessly demand of our government in all of its functions."
   —*Amicus Journal*

"A scorching and compelling account of the harassment experienced by government scientists who become whisleblowers."
   —*The Salt Lake Tribune*

"In riveting detail, Wilkinson tells eight stories of 'combat biologists' daring to question the environmental protocols of their superiors in agencies such as the Bureau of Land Management, the U.S. Forest Service and Fish and Wildlife Service. ... Wilkinson shows that as the clear-cutting of America's forest land goes, so goes the habitat of the fish and the grizzlies—and of humans as well."
   —*Publishers Weekly*

"*The War Against the Greens* meets *Profiles in Courage*."
   —*Wildlife Conservation*

Science Under Siege

Science
Under Siege

The Politicians' War on Nature and Truth

Todd Wilkinson

Foreword by David Brower
Introduction by Jim Baca

Johnson Books
BOULDER

For my parents, Dick and Mary,
but especially for my wife, Jeanne

Published in the United States by Johnson Books, a division of Johnson Publishing Company, 1880 South 57th Court, Boulder, Colorado 80301.
E-mail: books@jpcolorado.com

9   8   7   6   5   4   3

Cover design: Debra B. Topping
Front cover photograph copyright © Branson Reynolds

Library of Congress Cataloging-in-Publication Data
Wilkinson, Todd.
    Science under siege: the politicians' war on nature and truth /
Todd Wilkinson; foreword by David Brower; introduction by Jim
Baca.
        p.   cm.
    Includes index.
    ISBN 1-55566-210-2 (cloth: alk. paper).—ISBN 1-55566-211-0
(paper: alk. paper)
    1. Environmental responsibility—United States—Case studies.
2. Environmental degradation—United States—Case Studies.
I. Title.
GE180.W55   1998
363.7—dc21   98-12458
                                                                 CIP

Printed in the United States by
Johnson Printing
1880 South 57th Court
Boulder, Colorado 80301

 Printed on recycled paper with soy ink

Contents

Foreword

David Brower

WHY DO SO MANY government agencies seem continually prone to make the wrong decisions? As you read through *Science Under Siege: The Politicians' War on Nature and Truth*, the reasons become readily apparent. I trust the stories will move you as they have moved me.

During the middle of the New Deal, U.S. Supreme Court Justice William O. Douglas told Franklin Roosevelt that government agencies more than ten years old should be abolished. After that point, they become more concerned with their image than with their mission.

To me, that's the problem with many of our land management agencies—the Forest Service, the Fish and Wildlife Service, the National Park Service, the Bureau of Land Management, the Bureau of Reclamation, the Corps of Engineers. They have lost their bearings and forgotten who their customers are. Their directors no longer listen to the people.

One of the great regrets of my life has been a failure at certain moments to prevent ecological harm from proceeding, despite having been lucky enough to have critical truths revealed to me in advance. Today, one such truth is the obscenity of Lake Powell—a spectacular reservoir swamped by billions of gallons of backed-up Colorado River water. This unnecessary reservoir conceals a place that was one of the most beautiful on the face of this earth. When I look across Lake Powell, I do not see the genius of human creativity; I can think only of the human addiction to destroying wild places and the species, besides our own, that inhabit them.

Yes, we could have saved Glen Canyon. It was Sierra Club policy to protect such places. The directors elected not to, and my courage collapsed. Forty years later they voted to rescue it from oblivion. This decision could lead to sparing the earth from similar disasters now lurking in minds that can't stand the sight of flowing water. The late Joe Penfold compared such people to beaver.

After sixty years of working in conservation, I conclude that there are two kinds of science: One is purchased, manipulated, and dispensed at industry's whim. The other cannot be bought. This science is amplified in Todd Wilkinson's important book; unfortunately, it is science out of fashion with those who control Congress, corporations, and the land management bureaus.

Here is a one-liner that reveals a bias of mine: "A fact is a fragment of information isolated from context." Good science lives on facts, of course, but seeks to understand the interrelation of fragments, admits what is not known, thinks about consequences, and can be guided by the whole context. Bad science is best described by mathematician-pianist Tom Lehrer: "'The rockets go up, and where they come down / Is not my department,' said Wernher von Braun."

When the first atomic bomb was detonated at Alamogordo and the fireball lasted longer than predicted, two leaders of the Manhattan Project who had developed the bomb were witnesses. Harvard's James Branch Conant said to Vannever Bush, "My God, we've done it?"—meaning that the bomb would ignite the atmosphere and the world would end. Fortunately, his assumption was incorrect. Fortunately, too, those scientists thought hard about the atomic bomb's consequences.

The researchers and developers of Glen Canyon Dam did not think hard enough about the loss of beauty; water; recreational pollution; the strength of Navajo sandstone; or downstream consequences to the Grand Canyon, Arizona, Nevada, Southern California, and Mexico. Grandeur, wildness, and good judgment have now bypassed two generations unseen.

Having once intended to be an entomologist, and having known a good many scientists, I am glad they are with us, especially those willing to admit or feign fallibility—of which there were a few who took advantage of the Cosmos Club founded in Washington, D.C., in 1869 by John Wesley Powell to help politicians understand places like the Grand Canyon. I settled for becoming a combat intelligence officer in the Mountain Troops in World War II. We were taught that for your position to prevail, you had to first consider the enemy's capabilities—not just anticipate them but be ready to react. We should have called it *anticipatory retaliation,* a term I learned years later from a Broadway play after having practiced it in Italy's North Apennines. The public needs to marshal its own anticipatory retaliation on behalf of the good scientists who have no defense against their suppressors.

With so little left of the '90s, can we help the coming decade be one of pause and reorganization, giving science and, more profoundly, technology a place but not command? I would like it to be a decade of concentrating on ameliorating the extant human-caused disturbances of the universe before hastening to see how much more disturbing the universe is willing to put up with. I would like it to be an era of not waiting until it is practical, or until one is called upon, to be ethical about confessing uncertainties, biases, and conflicts of interest. Of admitting that people who question the status quo may even be right and are responding honestly to their different drummers. Of realizing that the public pays the cost of the mistakes that may benefit the political scientists who err. Of permitting the intelligent lay public to be less brutally laid, and to be intelligently listened to. Of giving scientists with whistleblower tendencies a chance to survive the prevailing institutions that prefer status to quo, disdain perspective, and seem to enjoy the larcenous quality of the economic and population growth as presently practiced. Of an abyss awaiting the violators of natural laws and order. Of sustainable ecosystems, of the ecological conscience that was keeping the planet afloat before we decided the Industrial Revolution was the way to go.

My son, Kenneth, whose work I admire the way a father should, wrote, "Science is fragile. It depends, like the rule of law, on the cooperation and integrity of the people involved. It is not impossible that science, though it leads the way, will be our weak link, the first institution to fail under the pressures of the complex new age it has helped us usher in. Perhaps the end will announce itself as scattered breakdowns in scientific integrity—little cancer cells of myth in the body of science."

Consider the cancer cells in the body of Glen Canyon Dam, and the weak link—the inability to think hard enough about consequence, the absence of the boldness Goethe admired: "Whatever you can do, or dream you can, begin it. / Boldness has genius, power, and magic in it."

$\sim$

I remember too well my own lack of enough boldness to keep the Sierra Club bold in 1956, what we lost when clear thinking and

whistleblowing, neither encouraged nor protected, were not politically correct.

Forty years later the missing qualities have been discovered, thanks
to the noble efforts of the Glen Canyon Institute. To cure the cancer
of the dam, the Bureau of Reclamation needs to rethink and debate
and recognize better data. But they've had an infatuation with dams.
Their expertise has been lent around the world. Some 30,000 big
dams have been built around the world in my lifetime. Ecosystems
have been destroyed on an idea which once ran rampant, that dams
are unmitigated benefits. But we now know better and in fact we
knew long ago but we did not listen to scientific dissent. What we
need to do is think like a river and rethink the whole damn business.

Thirty years ago, these were my thoughts as the Bureau of Reclamation considered damming the Grand Canyon and the Army
Corps of Engineers feared this would lead to the Bureau's coveting
the Columbia River: "The only answer ... that might work would
be to have a board of review composed of eminent scientists who
should not be connected with any government bureau either directly or indirectly. The big problem with the Reclamation—as with
the Army Corps of Engineers and to a lesser extent other agencies—
is they are the ones who do the planning, who carry out the plan,
and who are the final judges as to whether it is a good plan. I am
and always have been against this type of setup, but it is a very popular one with Congress. It makes it easier for pork-barrel projects
when there is enough political pressure behind them. We know that
truth will come out, and that when several government agencies that
are keepers of the expertise are not allowed to speak freely, people
will speak freely in their stead."

We need this kind of scrutiny applied to our public land agencies
and the decisions they make based on shady science. Sadly, we live
in an age of scientific suppression. For example, even now, after all
of the facts have been strung together to be irrefutable, we have people practicing bad science, telling President Clinton he should not
take global warming seriously. We are perched on the brink of a new
millennium, but more importantly, to mix a metaphor, we have
reached a road sign that says, "Dangerous Curve Ahead." This curve,
the most dangerous on the highway, goes by a different name in scientific circles. There it is called the exponential curve of cause and
effect. The problem with exponential curves is that they start out

slowly, they travel along the bottom of a chart, and they induce you not to worry. But as unforeseen factors accumulate, as exponential forces coalesce, they eventually send the lines rocketing off the wall, over the edge, or whatever image you prefer.

There will always be scientists who come up with bad decisions because they get paid well and have no conscience. For the professionals who suffer from doubt and have a heart, I have one word: Persevere. For the rest of you, who value wildness, who support good science by exercising your influence in our democracy, you are a great hope for tomorrow. We need a government institution that can encourage the use of whistles, or equivalent alarms, to help the big corporate CEOs and their big investors to worry about what their actions cost the earth and our future.

The whistleblowers and brave advocates for nature described in this book help us fulfill that obligation. I know no better person to serve as a standard-bearer than Rachel Carson. She did her homework, minded her English, and cared. *Silent Spring*, an epic feat in scientific whistleblowing, should be placed on the shelf with your Bible; and if you don't own a Bible, put it on the shelf anyway, right up there with Aldo Leopold's *A Sand County Almanac*. Find a good shelf for this book too.

My friend Starker Leopold was a gifted scientist who sought answers and learned what to do with them. Buy a trumpet, he would say, not a cubbyhole. The truth is out there. Let good science, flavored with compassion, light our way.

Acknowledgments

THIS BOOK IS intended to be about many things—suppression of personal liberty, dysfunctional bureaucracies, soul-searching science, and the conservation of nature—but it is foremost about people who aspire to public honor and goodness while working under conditions of unspeakable duress. There are heroes inhabiting the following pages, and thousands of others not mentioned, who confront a crisis of conscience every day. They opt for the difficult, lonely path of truth over capitulation. This book is for them and their families.

I offer special gratitude to my bighearted, fearless editor at Johnson Books, Stephen Topping, and my agent, Carol Mann in New York, for their encouragement and shepherding. I also wish to thank the other members of the Johnson team: Barbara Johnson Mussil, Mira Perrizo, Richard Croog, Marc Young, Stephanie White, and David Sias.

Here, too, I must recognize a group of others who indirectly contributed to this book. Insightful editing is the bedrock of writing, and over the years I've been blessed to work with several fine editors at various publications who have made my words stronger. Among them (and with special thanks for persevering with me through the past five years as this book came together) are Scott Armstrong, Dave Scott, and Mark Sappenfield at the *Christian Science Monitor;* Tom Shealey, Jim Gorman, and Michele Morris at *Backpacker;* Chip Blake at *Orion;* Ed Marston, Betsy Marston, and Paul Larmer at *High Country News;* David Seideman at *Audubon;* Linda Rancourt and Sue Dodge at *National Parks;* Mark Wexler at *National Wildlife;* Anne Studabaker, Anne Collier, Tony Bogar, Chris Bergonzi, and Ken Beaulieu at *Continental Magazine;* Dawn Stover at *Popular Science;* Deb Behler and Joan Downs at *Wildlife Conservation;* Ed Smith, Lori Krieger, and Billie Stanton at the *Denver Post;* Rebecca Hakala Rowland, Bob Koenke, and the staff of *Wildlife Art;* James Deane at *Defenders;* Angus M. Thuermer Jr. and Michael Sellett at the *Jackson Hole News;* David McCumber and Allen Jones at the *Big Sky Journal;* Kathleen James Ring and Lynn Prowitt *at Snow Country;* Michael

Frank at *Diversion;* Jean Weiss at *Women's Sports and Fitness* (and previously at *Jackson Hole Magazine*); Giselle Smith at *Seattle;* Phil Monaghan at *Outdoor Life;* Matt Rasmussen at the *Inner Voice;* Chuck Weschler at *Sporting Classics;* Tom Webb at the *Bear Essential;* Carter Walker at the *Tributary;* and the editors who publish my weekly column, "The New West." To any I've missed, I apologize.

Thanks to the publications *High Country News* and *National Parks* magazine, where portions of the chapter "Latter-Day Frogs" previously appeared. Profound appreciation to those who shared in the creative rearing of this book, who read the text, offered moral support during moments of doubt, or just made me laugh out loud during times of serious reclusion: Rick Peterson, Dan Swanson, Nancy Verling, Kent Ullberg, David Quammen, Ted Kerasote, Ed Dobson, Tim Crawford, Mike Finkel, Anne Sherwood, Tim Sandlin, Pete Geddes, John Baden, Marie Harland, Annette Alderson, the folks at Highland Montessori, Mark Shuman, Dennis Glick and the Chubacabras, Steve Fuller, Louisa Willcox, Doug Honnold, Mark Peterson, Jeff Ruch, George Berklacy, Mo Ganey, Elaine Sevy, Floyd DeWitt, Tom Graf, Rocky Barker, Bert Harting, Tim Clark, Will Snider, Bill Kerr, Tom Wolf, Ron Cooper, Bob Crabtree, Ross Parker, Ray Rasker, Chip Rawlins, Mike Francis, Gary Ferguson, Matt Reid, Curtis Freese, Lizzie Grossman, Michael and Eleanor Carter, Sheila and Dan Hart, Michele and Andy Ransick, Kevin and Terri Carter, and my brother, Steve.

Thanks also to David R. Brower and Jim Baca, earthly defenders, never yielding, who have taught us the meaning of stewardship by example and who believed in this project from the start. Thanks to those who instilled me with accumulated confidence to be a science writer: Juanita Fallbeck, Margaret Nelson, Don Kaddatz, the Danielson and Wilkinson clans, and my friends in Mora and Bozeman; my mentors in the St. Olaf Paracollege and political science departments; my colleagues at the *Manitou Messenger;* Bob Phelps and Dan Jorgensen at the St. Olaf News Service; Diane Banis, Joe Reilly, Paul Zimbrakos, and colleagues from the City News Bureau of Chicago; Scott Richardson at the *Northfield News;* and Terry Tempest Williams, Don Richard Eckelberry, Wade Weber, Bob Beck, and Roger Nieboer.

I am also grateful to three organizations that provide a haven for scientific whistleblowers and public employees who are besieged by their superiors and politicians to make unscrupulous compromises. They are Davids daily taking on Goliaths—the Government Accountability Project (GAP), Forest Service Employees for Environmental Ethics (FSEEE), and Public Employees for Environmental Responsibility (PEER). There is more information on each organization in the Epilogue.

Thanks to my friend David Kuchar, who is a source of daily inspiration; and to a compadre with whom I shared nature long ago, Ken Smith. Finally, two notes of personal citation: to the late Jim Syring, who taught me how to better live, and to the late Paul Kirchner, whose guidance went a long way. None of you are forgotten.

Introduction
Fighting those who would sell our Natural Heritage

Jim Baca

EVERY SINGLE DAY dedicated employees venture out into the public lands of the United States to carry out their responsibilities to the owners who happen to be us—you and me—the taxpayers. Every single day they face an onslaught of obstacles to performing their duties.

What are these obstacles? They range from U.S. senators, western governors, entrenched exploitative industries, so-called Wise Use groups, and a deliberate lack of funding to uncommitted political appointees and meek second-level managers. What a life! What a war zone!

I have a decade of experience in public land management from the perspective of elected and appointed political offices. I have watched a consistent and well-orchestrated attack by commodity groups (which author Charlie Wilkinson at the University of Colorado calls "the lords of yesterday") upon our public land managers. These aggressors, who are striking out against the taxpayer and the environment, have been incredibly successful in scaring the pants and skirts off many members of our congressional delegations and western state houses. After all, it is these groups that fund the campaign war chests for the lapdog politicos.

The stories that writer Todd Wilkinson tells so well in this book are important because they expose the kind of organizational repression and silencing that has gone on behind closed doors. These problems are paralyzing the government's ability to uphold the law and do its job of acting in our best interests. We are in a position to either lose our natural heritage or help rescue it by listening to the people whose stories are found on the following pages. I believe this book should be required reading for every one of our public servants who works in federal and state land management arenas as well as any concerned citizen who wants to gain an intimate, behind-the-scenes look at the world of scientific whistleblowing.

Over the years I have found that most of our land science professionals, while sometimes lacking tact and personal charm, merely want to do the right thing to preserve our water, soil, forests, and air and the species that inhabit them for future generations. That is their job, and that is *the law*.

And yet, as we begin to understand more about the complicated interworkings of ecosystems, these scientists have come under mounting pressure to "fix" their findings for political and economic reasons. Courage is the one quality a successful public land manager displays under fire. It takes real courage and conviction to go head to head with the local rancher, logger, and miner who live in the same small town as the public land manager. Often the people who wear agency badges must regulate users of public land who are well connected and are prepared to make their lives hell. Often the manager and his or her family face banishment from the social fabric of a community. Why? For the simple reason that the principals of stewardship are being followed and upheld.

In the 1990s our public land employees face an even greater danger at the hands of radical Wise Use and militia groups in the West. Threats are common in the current atmosphere, and leaders in Washington have not been too keen on standing up for their own employees. There is a misconception that these radical groups have a lot of voting power and that giving them their way is a politically savvy thing to do—a dangerous miscalculation indeed.

Add to this a nearly complete abdication of important scientific decisions by the executive branch of government to senators, Congress, and western good-ol'-boy governors, and you can see the perilous terrain the public land scientist works in. Even small, everyday decisions on matters such as stocking rates on grazing allotments can end up on some senator's desk as the issue of the month. Most likely the senator gets what he or she wants, and to hell with the science.

The alarming concern now is that things are not going to get any better anytime soon for our public land employees, certainly not without the public rising up in support of science. The new majority that first gained control of Congress in 1994 has created a consistent pattern of overriding good stewardship in favor of exploitation of public lands everywhere. The new majority is on a slash-

and-burn juggernaut against the budgets of our science and land management agencies.

Where does this leave the embattled employees of the Bureau of Land Management, the Forest Service, the Environmental Protection Agency, the National Park Service, and the Fish and Wildlife Service as well as other scientific professionals in both federal and state agencies? In the unenviable position of being asked to do with fewer resources for research and day-to-day operations, all the while watching the health of the land deteriorate under shortsighted leadership in the congressional and executive branches of government.

The public land manager now faces greater challenges than ever in protecting the health of fragile ecosystems. Someone, somewhere, will have to start thinking about where the next 120 million Americans will live in the next century. Will it be in the delicate western and eastern ecosystems where our water supplies are already at risk and overappropriated? Will it be beside forests and fish and wildlife populations that already are staggering from poor management? How will pivotal decisions be made if our cadre of environmental scientists has been neutralized by bad politics and appeasement?

So, what can each of us do? Start by supporting the local land manager. These dedicated public servants stand between us and those who would destroy our children's future. They are on the front line of the battlefield leading to our nation's ecosystems, which Americans of the next century will inherit from us. Read the riveting stories that Todd Wilkinson has assembled and let them move you to action. Most importantly, God bless the defenders of our natural heritage—the people we hire to work for us.

Jim Baca is the current mayor of Albuquerque, New Mexico, and the former national director of the Bureau of Land Management, appointed to the post by President Bill Clinton. A whistleblower himself, he was ousted by Secretary of the Interior Bruce Babbitt in 1994 after arousing controversy for going to the defense of field scientists and trying to bring constructive reform to his own agency. Baca is also the former commissioner of the New Mexico Department of State Lands, a natural resource consultant, and a popular national lecturer on public lands management and government reform.

Prologue
Remembering the Spirit
of Rachel Carson

*God offers to every mind its choice between
truth and repose. Take which you please: you
can never have both.*—Ralph Waldo Emerson

IN TEN YEARS OF TRACKING grizzly bears across the boulder-strewn, glacier-gnawed interior of Yellowstone National Park, biologist David Mattson grew accustomed to witnessing the remains of backcountry cabins that had been ransacked by powerful bruins. Typically, the aftermath he encountered looked something like this: stout rustic doors pried from their hinges; floor planks splintered to pieces; window glass strewn across the floor; the contents of cabinets, once sealed safely under lock and key, plundered by the forearms of six-hundred-pound ursids.

The physical damage aside, what eventually settled in upon Mattson during his solo forays into grizzly country was a psychological tentativeness, a stutter-step of apprehension that made him less willing to take risks. After all, he had a family back home to think of. He was obliged to be responsible. But for the man considered the nation's premier expert on Yellowstone grizzly bear ecology, the bone-chilling sensation of invasion, violence, and trauma meeting him on the stoops of wilderness cabins was nothing compared to the jolt he received when he reported to work for the U.S. government.

Upon arriving at the office one cold winter morning, Mattson discovered that someone had rifled through his personal files at the headquarters of the federal Yellowstone Interagency Grizzly Bear Study Team in Bozeman, Montana—the nerve center for bear research in one of America's largest and last wild ecosystems. The intruder had seized eight years' worth of field data, deleted key documents from Mattson's computer, and turned his files upside down.

1

The scene, Mattson said, looked as if a grizzly had torn through the premises.

Initially, he was perplexed. Only later did he learn that the raid was carried out at the direction of his own government superiors, who had decided they did not want Mattson's criticisms or his bleak forecast for the survival of Yellowstone's famous bears to reach the public. A scientific dissenter, David Mattson ultimately was forced out of his job for threatening to blow the whistle on federal policies that he believes could doom the grizzly to extinction in the next century.

While Mattson's story often elicits startled expressions from the lay public, it does not stand alone, nor is his case a matter of fiction. Today in the United States, hundreds of other "combat scientists" are under fire by political forces that have conspired to ensure that their knowledge never sees the light of day. These dissidents carry on a public fight boldly commenced more than thirty years ago by a U.S. Fish and Wildlife Service biologist who bridged the division between science and advocacy. In 1962, with the completion of her classic book, *Silent Spring,* Rachel Carson alerted the world to the insidious effects of DDT and other harmful biocides. But what few young readers probably realize is that her ground-breaking treatise and literary triumph came at a high personal cost. Almost from the moment her research began, the chemical companies that manufactured DDT and other toxic agents mobilized to discredit Carson's work.

Paul Brooks, the longtime editor of natural history at Houghton Mifflin, which published Carson's exposé, recalled the backlash she endured from chemical companies and members of Congress who were in denial, erroneously insisting that a ban on DDT would ruin American agriculture and allow back-yard patios everywhere to be overwhelmed as breeding grounds for killer bugs. Carson certainly was not the first scientific whistleblower, and she "knew very well that she would be attacked by the chemical industry," Brooks wrote in an introduction to *Silent Spring.* "It was not simply that she was opposing indiscriminate use of poisons but—more fundamentally— that she had made clear the basic irresponsibility of an industrialized, technological society toward the world. ... Hundreds of thousands of dollars were spent by the chemical industry in an attempt to discredit the book and to malign the author. She was described as an ignorant and hysterical woman who wanted to turn the earth over to the insects."

The record now is clear that big business did all it could do to deny the message of *Silent Spring* by blatantly denying that toxic chemicals were killing millions of birds and other creatures essential to the web of life on earth. Carson's persecutors were steadfast in their defiance all the while that America's national wildlife symbol, the bald eagle, and another beautiful raptor, the peregrine falcon, were two birds among many whose populations were cast into a downward spiral from widespread DDT spraying. Numbers don't lie.

In league with those who portrayed Carson as a raving lunatic gone over the edge were congressmen who received hefty campaign contributions from the firms that made the poisons. These politicians trumpeted the virtues of toxic pesticides in the same way that certain elected leaders in the 1990s have denied that cigarette smoking is addictive or causes lung cancer. They are the "dittoheads" who stridently reject the notion that manufactured chemicals are causing depletion of the ozone layer and that the world's mantle of biological diversity is crashing around us at a rate unprecedented since the age of dinosaurs.

Fortunately, Rachel Carson's science and her unyielding commitment to doing what is right prevailed, but her friends said the stress heaped upon her by those who attacked *Silent Spring* hastened her early death. Although she died before full vindication arrived with the official banning of DDT in 1972 (and the official listing of both bald eagles and peregrine falcons under the Endangered Species Act), Carson, as a forerunning combat scientist, won an important skirmish in the war for the environment. She showed generations of women and men that ecologically based science and conservation advocacy were not mutually exclusive. She believed that scientists who fail to act on what the information tells them have no soul. And, despite resistance from her superiors in the Fish and Wildlife Service, an agency she eventually left, she spoke out when it would have been far safer and politically prudent to retreat in silence.

It was this image of Rachel Carson that led me one autumn morning to a cavernous meeting hall outside Washington, D.C., where hundreds of Carsonesque idealists had gathered to stage a convention of whistleblowers. The assembly, sponsored by a nonprofit group, Public Employees for Environmental Responsibility (PEER), became my first formal introduction to the growing army of biologists, earth scientists, and public land managers who have risked their careers to expose threats to our environment.

Converging at personal and professional peril were not merely a few anonymous faces in a crowd. I saw hundreds of scientific and natural resource workers, young and old; Democrats and Republicans; some at the beginnings of their careers, others well into retirement; people united by their desire to proudly wear the uniforms of their agencies and follow the laws of the land; still others with a grudge to bear.

Before you plunge any deeper into these words, I offer an admission. Truth be told, at the outset of this journey I had doubts about whistleblowers. I expected to encounter whiners whose stories pressed the limits of believability. Instead, in street clothes, sans departmental badges and uniforms, Carson's spiritual descendants came from every region of the country. Here were some of the "jackbooted government thugs" decried by Rush Limbaugh and his radical-militia followers; the people who should be brought down with a rifle shot to the head, according to G. Gordon Liddy; the renegades who grew up believing, apparently ignorantly, that it is a virtuous calling to be a natural resource scientist working on behalf of other citizens.

Although there are many Wise Use evangelists in our democracy who would like us to assume otherwise, the tyranny of repression in the workplace is not solely the device of Third World despots or former communist dictators. A campaign of stifling attacks on the essence of scientific truth is present and thriving both within the ranks of the nation's largest employer, the federal government, and among natural resource agencies in most of the fifty states.

Yes, in the beginning I was skeptical. I went to the nation's capital with a view skewed by what I had heard about the people who break rank and question authority because the bureaucracies no longer work. Maybe you too cling to the same stereotype. Be honest. What kind of person comes to mind when you hear the term *whistleblower?* Invariably, the pejorative perception of the average whistleblower is of a burned-out, disgruntled, antisocial, troublemaking martyr. Castigated as insubordinate nonconformists, outlaws, and snitches, they are civil servants of whom their superiors say it is best to ignore. "Don't listen to the whistleblowers," a spokesperson for the U.S. Forest Service said. "They represent the fringe; they're renegades with a bone to pick," added a public relations specialist at the U.S. Department of the Interior. "*If you print what they say,* it may be difficult for you, Mr. Wilkinson, to get our cooperation on stories you write in the future," warned another federal flak.

I had begun this book with an open mind, but the insinuation of reprisal left me more than a little nonplussed. I wondered: If they could threaten me for merely writing about whistleblowers, what were they actually doing to people such as grizzly bear biologist David Mattson? What are the motives behind the posturing? Who are the brash rebels that state and federal agencies are so vigorously attempting to keep quiet and alienated? Over the course of many months, the answer crystallized. As I spent years researching the alleged transgressions of embattled scientists, it became more and more evident that the whistleblowers aren't the ones breaking the laws. They are the heroes who deserve to have their stories told on *60 Minutes.*

Had Rachel Carson lived, it is likely that she too would have come to Washington that day, encouraging others to bravely heed a call to action, ignoring the far easier path of lying in repose. Certainly she would be appalled by the current attempts of some elected officials in Congress to overturn the ban on DDT, clearcut our remaining forests through salvage logging, suck dry our last wild rivers, play fast and loose with the facts regarding the importance of biological diversity, downplay global warming, and weaken environmental laws that have made the United States an international beacon for protection of clean air and water.

The federal workers inspired by the spirit of Carson are right now, at the end of a millennium, trying to create a voice for the last great bears in the northern Rockies, the wilderness caves of southern New Mexico, the giant cedars of Oregon, the last free-flowing rivers in Arizona, the tiny stalks of rare wildflowers in the Appalachians, the frogs of Utah, the tortoises of California's Mojave Desert, and the ancient bull trout of the Northwest. Risking their careers and livelihoods, they have taken on corrupt politicians and bureaucrats wedded to logging and mining companies, industrial polluters, the livestock industry, water developers, and energy conglomerates that have left ecological destruction in their wake.

Perhaps the real tragedy is that whistleblowers such as the people whose stories are told in the following pages are drawn to public service (and often punished) for loving the natural resources they were hired to care for *on our behalf*. For doing their jobs, they are portrayed as radicals. "Scientists in the civil service bureaucracy face the type of job-related repression common in the Soviet Union before glasnost," suggests Washington, D.C., attorney Thomas Devine. At no time in the history of humankind, Devine says, has there been a greater imperative for assessing where our scientific compass is leading us. Yet the suppression of combat scientists continues under both Democratic and Republican regimes. For several years Devine has been a chief ally to whistleblowers through his job as legal director of the Government Accountability Project (GAP), a nonpartisan, nonprofit organization that offers legal representation to government and corporate whistleblowers. More than anyone else in the United States, he has chronicled the means by which agencies punish employees who challenge the status quo, even when their ideas would make government work better. He is so well versed that on several occasions Congress has called him to testify as an expert witness.

Not long ago, Devine coauthored a report for GAP titled "The Whistleblower's Survival Guide: Courage Without Martyrdom," which spells out the very real liabilities of going public with revelations. Whistleblowing is not for the faint of heart; it comes with the inherent risk of self-destruction. GAP alone has defended two thousand whistleblowers against retaliations and firings over the past three decades and has counseled as many people against whistleblowing because of the consequences. One U.S. Justice Department worker suggests that "suffering through whistleblower retaliation teaches you a lot about your own strengths and weaknesses, about what really matters in life, about who your friends are, and about what human beings are capable to doing to each other in even the most civilized of settings. It is a life-altering experience."

According to Devine, the following methods are routinely used to quash scientific dissent and promote shunning by peers of those who advocate environmental protection. Keep them in mind, for they surface time and again in the following pages.

- *Tactic One: Make the dissenters the issue instead of their message.* "The first commandment for this brand of 'political science' is to obfuscate the dissent by attacking the source's motives, professional competence, economic credibility, sexuality, or virtually anything else that will work to cloud the scientific issues," Devine says.

- *Tactic Two: Isolate the scientific dissenter.* "Here the technique is to transfer the 'troublemaker' to a bureaucratic Siberia, both to make an example of them and to block the employee's access to information," Devine says. At the U.S. Forest Service, National Park Service, Fish and Wildlife Service, and Bureau of Land Management (BLM), "the most popular reprisal technique has been to reassign employees from active environmental monitoring projects in the field to headquarters desk jobs where they don't receive any assignments and are monitored by bureaucratic babysitters."

- *Tactic Three: Place the dissenter on a pedestal of cards.* A common practice is to give the whistleblower an assignment but make it impossible to complete it in a timely or professional manner. "This technique involves appointing the dissenter to solve the problem and then making the job impossible through a wide range of techniques, undercutting any realistic possibility of actually achieving reform," Devine says. "The finale then is to fire the employee for being incompetent when the problem is not solved."

- *Tactic Four: Create trumped-up charges against the person the agency wants to silence.* "The technique here goes well beyond merely defeating a whistleblower. In order to prove to others that no one is safe, the goal is to make the most outrageous charges possible," Devine says. "For example, a dissenter who is renowned for being a gentleman may face sexual harassment charges. A soft-spoken, self-effacing individual will be branded a loud-mouthed egomaniac."

- *Tactic Five: If you can't make conditions miserable enough so that the whistleblower quits, eliminate the job.* A common practice is to lay off dissenters even as the agency is hiring new staff.

- *Tactic Six: If intimidation doesn't work, prosecute them.* Attack whistleblowers for "stealing" the information they use to expose corruption, even if they collected or prepared the information themselves. This tactic is often used in the corporate world. Remember the lawsuits brought by tobacco companies against former employees who turned whistleblowers? The foundation for this tactic is similar to the premise of the British Official Secrets Act: The government purports that it alone owns all the information it generates or possesses, regardless of whether the public paid for the information and has a right to scrutinize it.

- *Tactic Seven: Substitute "democracy" for the scientific method.* Employ the bureaucratic equivalent of mob rule: A group of peers who will not challenge the dysfunctional status quo and who are loyal to corrupt managers outvotes the whistleblower in management decisions and thereby subdues him or her. A more subtle variation of this tactic is to misuse peer review as a discrediting tactic by packing the allegedly "objective" panel with people who have a particular bias.

- *Tactic Eight: Don't allow a written record of anything you say to the person you wish to intimidate.* At the same time, issue an informal gag order against the dissident with the warning that if they seek outside help, they will be punished. Managers seasoned in the art of intimidation carefully restrict any threats they make to oral dialogue and hearsay. Such intimidation is supported by applying verbal peer pressure, holding meetings behind closed doors, and carrying out harassment over the phone. The point is that it is difficult to accuse someone of wrongdoing if there are no paper trails and no corroborating witnesses.

If Americans knew what was happening behind closed doors to loyal civil servants, Devine says, they would be shocked. Why should we be concerned? Since 1986, whistleblowers in every segment of the federal bureaucracy have saved citizens billions of dollars by exposing waste and fraud in the spending of public tax money. Their chief tool is an amendment to the federal False Claims Act that allows individuals to file suit on behalf of all citizens. Originally enacted during the Civil War to thwart profiteering by nefarious suppliers of shoddy goods to the Union Army, the code today is aimed squarely at contractors from the private sector who try to swindle the government. The lawsuits allow whistleblowers to share between 10 and 30 percent of the money recovered by government attorneys. Perhaps the seminal example is the former corporate official who earned $22 million in a case involving a Department of Defense contractor.

In the natural resource agencies specifically, scientists have raised red flags over looming problems that, if not fixed now, could have grave economic and social implications for the generations of tomorrow. Often, however, such reformers are muzzled by draconian bureaucratic structures resistant to change.

When Howard Wilshire, a distinguished, decorated senior geologist with the U.S. Geological Survey, angered Wise Use movement proponents by documenting the impacts of off-road vehicles on the fragile desert environment of the Mojave, his own agency tried to discredit him and have him fired. When U.S. Forest Service fisheries biologist Al Espinosa said that overcutting the Clearwater National Forest was eviscerating habitat for half a dozen species of trout and salmon, he was met with racial epithets and intimidation by government managers friendly with the timber industry. When Utah herpetologist David Ross started compiling a report on the status of rare spotted frogs along the Wasatch Front, the state's entire nongame division, which reviews the status of threatened and endangered species, was eliminated, apparently at the behest of developers.

In 1989 the Government Accountability Project was influential in convincing Congress to pass what is known as the Whistleblower Protection Act, a code designed to protect the rights of public employees who challenge bad land management practices or blow the whistle on fraud and corruption. It supplemented another code that was already on the books, the Civil Service Reform Act of 1978, which makes it illegal for a federal agency to act against individuals who expose violations of laws, waste, fraud, or abuse. In addition, there are whistleblower provisions built into laws such as the Clean Water Act. As well as these laws, over eighty professional societies now have codes of ethics to accomplish similar ends. Furthermore, there are nearly three dozen federal and state laws forbidding retaliation against dissenters, and at least twenty-six states have adopted the "public policy" exemption to the "at will" doctrine, which permits dissenters to sue for punitive damages if they have been harassed or fired by their bosses.

A rampant problem with government, as with politicians, is incentives. Loyal servants who act in the public's best long-term interest are often punished while those who perpetuate dysfunction and shortsighted solutions are rewarded. "The best explanation I have seen of whistleblowing appears in Vaclav Havel's long essay,

'The Power of the Powerless,'" wrote Ed Marston, publisher of the award-winning environmental journal *High Country News.* "Havel, now the playwright-president of the Czech Republic, was at one time sent by the former Communist regime to the countryside, where he worked in a brewery. Most of the employees were putting in their time according to the Soviet formula—'we pretended to work and the government pretended to pay us.' But one man was passionate about the work, and frustrated by the rotten grains, the malfunctioning refrigerators, and the other obstacles to producing a good beer. So he went over his superior's head with suggestions and complaints. The higher-ups backed the brewer's immediate superior, and the man who only wanted to make good beer was punished."

It is Marston's opinion that Havel's experience serves as a powerful metaphor for the conditions greeting civil servants in this country. "Our natural resource laws are like the old Soviet-bloc constitutions—meant to be genuflected to but not obeyed," Marston observed. "Civil servants who attempt to implement the Endangered Species Act, for example, quickly learn that their agencies exist to subvert the law, and its spirit, rather than to follow it. The 'power' Havel refers to in his essay was not the ability of dissidents to organize and seize the government. The power Havel respected was that of the brewer: a man who insisted on doing a good job, on living his life as truthfully as possible. He was a man who shook up and began the transformation of the regime by resisting the organized lying and the demoralization that results when people must live a lie."

And that's all the whistleblowers in *Science Under Siege* want to do: re-create a system that, metaphorically speaking, is capable of producing good beer.

Before he was hired as president of Defenders of Wildlife, Rodger Schlickeisen was chief of staff for U.S. Senator Max Baucus, a Montana Democrat who often turned to government scientists to inform his vote on such landmark laws as the Clean Water Act, the Clean Air Act, and a host of other important bills. Were it not for the brave environmental scientists cast from the mold of Rachel Carson, Schlickeisen says, Americans would be breathing dirtier air, drinking contaminated water, eating dangerous food, dying at younger ages, getting by with a poorer quality of life, being exposed to dangerous nuclear power plants, and looking out upon a landscape with fewer pristine views to inspire them. On Capitol Hill, Schlickeisen saw from the inside how the lawmaking process functions, and he says that science is a moral compass for making the right choices. "My response to those lawmakers and heads of industry and especially the bureaucrats who choose to ignore the preponderance of science is to remind them that really, when it comes to planning for our children's future, science is the only game in town. When you're dealing with things as complex and long range as environmental impacts that affect all of us, science is the light that tells us where we should go," Schlickeisen says.

Science is not just under repression; the attack is akin to the burning of books that occurred in Nazi Germany. Our elected leaders are marshaling a campaign of ignorance against the American public. The authors of the Contract with America are unabashedly beholden to industry lobbyists who are waging an all-out war to weaken key environmental laws, mobilizing to gut the budgets of environmental regulatory agencies, obliterating vanguard agencies such as the National Biological Service that protect the nation's wealth of diverse species, and arranging sweetheart deals with special interest constituencies to ensure that private industry makes a profit at the public's expense. What's wrong with this picture?

Ironically, during George Bush's term in the White House, the president appointed a thirty-nine-member scientific advisory board to identify pressing issues relating to the global environment and human welfare. Conservationists protested that certain biologists were deliberately left off the panel at the behest of Republicans. Nonetheless, in the October 1990 report delivered to William Reilly, then director of the Environmental Protection Agency, there was overwhelming consensus that four problems loomed large, demanding immediate attention: (1) loss of species, that is, biological diversity; (2) loss of species habitats; (3) depletion of the ozone layer; and (4) global warming. "Say what you want, but this was Bush's scientific blue-ribbon advisory board, for heaven's sake," Schlickeisen says. "This wasn't some kind of agenda spearheaded by Beltway liberals. These were credible scientists respected across the board who reached the same conclusion. The only people who tried to refute the findings or claim that we are not in the midst of an environmental crisis were those trained in political science."

Schlickeisen adds that the report came with a troubling corollary: At least in the cases of global warming and ozone depletion, because they are caused by technology, the assumption is that technology also can solve the problem and rescue humanity in a reasonably short period of time. This idea may or may not be true. After all, loss of biodiversity as manifested in the disappearance of myriad plant and animal species is not a problem that can be fixed quickly, if ever. Humankind can't engineer the essence or the biological knowledge encapsulated in a grizzly bear, or a California condor, or a bull trout. "In the context of any time frame that's meaningful to man," Schlickeisen says, echoing the conclusions of E. O. Wilson, an evolutionary science professor at Harvard University and two-time winner of the Pulitzer Prize, "the loss of biodiversity means passing a point of no return. Once a species disappears, it's gone forever."

Today one of the most endangered species in America is the scientific whistleblower. Why should we care? If we as citizens stand idly by and tolerate the repression of government scientists in the public workplace, then where does the repression end? If it can happen here, among people whom we rely upon to tell us the truth about the health of our environment, it can happen anywhere: in our own offices; in our homes and schools. "There is as yet no ethic dealing with man's relation to the land and to the animals and plants which grow upon it," wrote Aldo Leopold a half century ago in *A Sand County Almanac*. "The land relation is still strictly economic, entailing privileges but not obligations." The same problem continues to haunt us, but scientists at the forefront of reform find themselves under attack by the old guard of public land users.

If anyone has doubts about how pervasive the problem of silencing reformers is, talk to Jim Baca, former director of the Bureau of Land Management, who wrote the introduction to this book. Baca, recently elected mayor of Albuquerque, New Mexico, was relieved of his command by Clinton appointee Secretary of the Interior Bruce Babbitt for putting science above political science and for telling the public that the free lunch was over for miners and ranchers on public lands in the West.

Is it any wonder that the grim experience of combat scientists reinforces the paranoid attitudes about government held by the militia movement? Myron Peretz Glazer and Penina Migdal Glazer suggest that the phenomenon of whistleblowing is only a recent "movement" born of increasing frustration and mistrust of the federal government and large companies. "Whistleblowers, or ethical resisters, are a historically new group," the Glazers wrote in their ground-breaking book, *The Whistleblowers—Exposing Corruption in Government and Industry.* "No doubt there were earlier workers who exposed practices that would harm the public, as there were thousands of workers who went on strike to improve their own wages and circumstances. But only in the period since the 1960s has there been a continual stream of employees who do not act primarily out of self-interest but concentrate on exposing policies that could endanger or defraud the public."

And yet Louis Clark, director of the Government Accountability Project, suggests that contrary to their adversaries' characterization of them, whistleblowers are not radical products of the 1960s. Most are conformists who won the rank of Eagle Scout, went to church on Sunday, marched in the high school band, were raised on "family values," served their country in the military or Peace Corps, consider themselves to be politically conservative, and entered government service not to get rich but to make a difference. "My observation is that '60s people tend to be cynical when they take a job," noted Clark in an interview with Robert A. Rosenblatt of the *Los Angeles Times.* "They expect that corners will be cut. But people who blow the whistle are very different. If something goes against their professional standards, they just won't accept it." Clark himself heeded a higher calling before taking the helm of GAP. Before obtaining a law degree, he was a Methodist minister urging congregations to follow the right path.

Theoretically, whistleblower laws are supposed to act as a shield of protection, but as Tom Devine of GAP suggests, they have done little to stop agencies from purging combat scientists who disagree with the findings of their superiors or resource-extraction industries. What exists on paper can be profoundly different from conditions that honest professionals confront in the field when politicians are breathing down their necks. The message is a chilling one, percolating down from the top brass through the rank and file. If you are a government employee and choose to exercise free speech that does not mesh with resource-extraction notions or, heaven forbid, get involved with a conservation group on your own time, there is usually a hired-gun politician who will apply pressure on your superiors to have you struck down. When Devine testified before a special U.S. House of Representatives subcommittee looking into

First Amendment rights (and violations of those rights) of federal workers, he pointed to a clear pattern of quashing dissent that started in earnest with the presidency of Ronald Reagan. Make no mistake, no single political party has a monopoly on the ability to manipulate science or flout environmental laws for political gain. "Increasingly during the last ten years, government scientists have not had the freedom to follow the scientific method," Devine told members of Congress on Capitol Hill.

"The increasing intolerance is ironic, because at first glance the last decade appears to have introduced a refreshing trend toward the protection of freedom of scientific dissent, even when that dissent is not popular on the job." Devine noted that although each whistleblower case is unique, patterns continually arise. "The point of all these ploys," Devine said, "is to overwhelm the whistleblower in a struggle for self-preservation—of career, family, bank account, and even sanity—until the point of dissent is forgotten or put behind weightier survival priorities."

Speaking before the national meeting of the American Association for the Advancement of Science in 1996, Vice President Al Gore criticized the Republican majority in Congress for scientific suppression. "Congress is saying we don't know and we don't want to know" about scientific matters, he declared. "They are approaching science with the wisdom of a potted plant. Most approach science with policies appropriate for Fred Flintstone."

But Michael McCloskey, the national chairman of the Sierra Club, says the hopes for more progressive land management once pinned to the Clinton administration by environmentalists and scientists remain unfulfilled. "There are still a lot of old Reaganite types who have burrowed into the bureaucracy. They're still around in key positions, and the Clinton folks have not weeded them out, nor have they rotated them into less influential positions to minimize the damage they can inflict on science-based management decisions," McCloskey says. "Has anything substantive changed? We've seen very little evidence of it. The old guard still is in power, and they are sending signals down the line that being proenvironment and creating a conservation-minded climate within agencies comes with liabilities. Look at what happened to Jim Baca at the BLM. The agencies, unfortunately, are loaded with these people who now hold fairly high positions of power. They were the enforcers of the political appointees of the previous administrations. Rather than being brash, they are probably a little more subtle about their attitudes and messages, but achieving the same ends."

It's the same old game with new faces, says Andy Stahl, executive director of the Forest Service Employees for Environmental Ethics (FSEEE) in Eugene, Oregon, and a former grassroots activist with the Sierra Club Legal Defense Fund and the National Wildlife Federation. Stahl had an important role in spearheading conservation efforts for the northern spotted owl and salmon that led to major, court-ordered decreases in the volume of timber harvested on national forest lands in the Pacific Northwest. He asserts that the Forest Service and U.S. Fish and Wildlife Service could easily have averted titanic conflict—as well as great social, economic and ecological hardship—if the agencies had listened to their best scientists who sounded the alarm over habitat destruction years before. "Speaking out," Stahl notes, "is still regarded as traitorous activity. We've progressed little from what are regarded as the repressive years of the 1980s."

With much ado being made these days about the partisan battles in Washington, D.C., a compelling example of the dysfunction of government is the smokescreen used by the Forest Service to snuff out concern over the controversial salvage logging program from its own elite corps of firefighters, the smokejumpers. Five smokejumpers traveled to Washington to offer their expert opinions about timber industry–backed proposals to log huge swaths of living trees to prevent future forest fires. They told their superiors that cutting more trees might actually exacerbate dangerous fire conditions and cause widespread ecological harm that already is dimming the prospects of survival for many species, from salmon and grizzly bears to raptors and toads. Their testimony echoed the warnings of prominent ecologists such as Reed Noss, Thomas Lovejoy, Michael Scott, and E. O. Wilson. After the smokejumpers delivered their presentation to members of Congress, they were "called on the carpet," Stahl says, and "read the riot act" by Forest Service bureaucrats because those words weren't what the timber industry wanted to hear. The lesson was that where there are smokejumpers risking their necks on Capitol Hill, there usually is political fire. Poignantly, President Clinton signed the controversial Emergency Salvage Timber Sale Program into law despite a national outcry that included the Forest

Service's own scientists and environmental groups backed by a large percentage of the independent scientific community. "What was offensive to the bureaucracy was that [the smokejumpers] were speaking out. Never mind that there were a lot of people, including scientific experts from the Clinton administration, that agreed with them," Stahl says. Not only did the bureaucracy castigate them, but several U.S. senators and congressmen sought to have them disciplined for their temerity. "It doesn't matter what side of the ideological fence you sit on," Stahl says. "If you are not a faceless bureaucrat who chooses not to make waves, you'll suffer for it."

Democrats who self-righteously berate Republicans over the legacy of James Watt should not be fooled. When Clinton was swept into two terms in the White House, it was on a platform of change augured by a commitment from the "environmental" Vice President Gore to reinvent government and restore the integrity of science. When Republicans took control of Congress, it similarly was with a pledge to bring change and transform government bureaucracies so that they are more accountable to the people.

"I look around for evidence that things are changing, and I still see taxpayer-run agencies that resemble the very types of government that we condemned in Eastern Europe during the Cold War," offers Stahl. "One wonders, is it a problem of evil people, or is it one of an evil institutional system? I've seen some of each, but more often than not what I've seen are boring people acting stupidly and ignorantly because of the institutions they work for. We the people in part made these institutions by condoning the way they do business, and now it will be up to us to bring about meaningful change. In a democracy, a person shouldn't have to worry about losing his job for speaking the truth."

Undoubtedly, Rachel Carson and the combat scientists in this book would agree.

Confessions of the Timber Beast

*A new truth does not triumph by convincing
its opponents and making them see the light
but rather because its opponents eventually
die and a new generation grows up that is
familiar with it.*—Max Planck

A PALPABLE BUZZ hangs in the meeting hall. Caffeine is being
drained by the gallon. In the Washington, D.C., suburb of Bethesda,
Maryland, the trees are burnished with the utopian botanical shades
of an autumn morning. But don't be fooled.

All around, anonymous faces are half lit and the audience is antsy
while it waits for the featured motivational speaker to appear. On
the day's agenda are two presidential cabinet secretaries, a handful of
other high-ranking government officials, and a bevy of federal
whistleblowers who have chosen this day to "come out" as scientific
dissidents. It will be a defining moment in their careers, for better or
for worse, when they cross the line knowing they can never go back
to what they were. Most, I learn later, carry the blessings of their
families and friends. It's a good thing.

Although today's program is impressive, it ranks as a warm-up to
the main attraction. When the man of the hour makes his entrance
after milling about in the hotel lobby bear-hugging his adherents,
he does so through a back door to a flush of whispers. Stocky, physically diminutive, losing hair on top, remarkably ordinary-looking
but already a recognizable legend, Jeff DeBonis moves toward the
dais bearing the stigma of a hell-raiser.

He does not disappoint.

His eyes gleaming, DeBonis softly describes the loving years with
his former employer, the U.S. Forest Service. The devoted vows of
fealty, the honeymoon, the period of estrangement, and the eventual
realization that the marriage had gone south. His voice strengthens.

17

As the room turns quiet and spectators are pulled to the edges of their seats, he talks emotionally about his personal struggle against alienation and depression. Tears well up among some of the on-lookers. A woman seated next to me nods affirmatively. She embraces a man on her other side. Solidarity within a convention of whistleblowers.

Although he does not specifically apply the metaphor of an abused spouse, DeBonis relates that he had to leave the Forest Service—the institution that portrays itself as "the Family"—because it was the only way he could get out and still have a soul.

"Why are we holding this conference?" DeBonis asks the crowd. "We are here because it hurts. It hurts to work for once proud agencies that no longer serve the public trust—agencies that have lost sight of their original missions. These agencies have turned into instruments of mismanagement, instruments of political pork barrels, instruments of environmental destruction, and instruments of repression against ethical employees.

"The hope here today comes from the fact that we are no longer isolated individuals trying to battle giant powers that are behind our agencies," he says. "What we are really talking about here is grass-roots social and organizational change." In short, a revolution.

For nearly five years I had tracked DeBonis's unflinching exploits and had interviewed him by telephone on half a dozen occasions for stories I'd written in national newspapers and magazines. My first face-to-face interview with him came in 1993 at a conference sponsored by Public Employees for Environmental Responsibility (PEER), an organization he founded. The conference was novel because it attracted hundreds of whistleblowers, a phenomenon that some federal agencies claim does not exist.

Several months earlier DeBonis had led a highly publicized revolt against an agency long synonymous with Smokey the Bear. He was credited with starting a holy war between the true believers of industrial forestry in the Forest Service and a breakaway group of young Turks ready to join an insurrection against one of the most venerable public land icons in the world. For his part in this revolution, DeBonis found himself both on the receiving end of death threats and near canonization.

This day, his fiery broadsides earn him a standing ovation. A couple of days later, owing to the way celebrities of the moment are courted in Washington, D.C., he receives an invitation to meet with the staff of Vice President Al Gore, whose motto is the reinvention of the federal government—making the bureaucracy work better, getting rid of old deadwood, trying to hold stolid politicians more accountable. (Granted, this invitation occurs before Gore and his boss, the president, come under attack by congressional Republicans for their allegedly unethical fund-raising practices and alleged she-nanigans in the White House.)

After his meeting, I ask DeBonis how he broached the topic of restoring integrity to the Forest Service, a concept that has report-edly loomed on the fringes of Gore's radar screen. I am hardly pre-pared for DeBonis's retort—advice given to the person who in the year 2000 could become the most powerful government leader in the world. DeBonis tells me he has a rough blueprint in his head and made it known to the vice president. If Gore made him czar of the Forest Service (a whimsical notion admittedly far-fetched), he would manage the agency the same way it has treated the landscape these past fifty years. Without hesitating, DeBonis says he would begin his reforms by toppling the agency, which oversees 192 mil-lion acres of forested countryside (a piece of nature equal in size to Texas and nearly 9 percent of the nation's total surface area), and then he would launch into a bold plan to facilitate its rebirth. Tak-ing a cue from his mentors in forestry school, he would commence by swinging his ax blade at the base of the oldest, most seasoned deadwood in Washington, D.C., clearcutting the ancient Forest Service pillar called "multiple use," and working his wedge deeper into various stages of management succession; then, with satisfac-tion, he would cry, *"Timber!"* as an old American institution fell.

Were anything still left standing, he would slash and burn what the old guard has considered to be the primary paradigm of the agency's mission since the end of World War II—supplying timber as the land's commodity. The people who would keep their jobs after the initial purge, he says, would be the Forest Service workers who have demonstrated a proclivity for thinking green and challenging their superiors. He would reward dissidence.

Otherwise, DeBonis would spare no one on the thirty-thousand-person payroll. From the Forest Service chief to the local district rangers, each employee would be handed temporary walking papers. Commercial logging on all national forests would cease. Portions of the tens of millions of dollars now being spent by taxpayers each year to subsidize the construction of logging roads so that private companies can make a profit would be funneled instead into a massive landscape restoration plan. The civil servants who have managed to maintain their personal integrity and ethics would be invited to reapply for a position in the new Department of Public Lands, a cabinet-level hybrid of the Forest Service, Bureau of Land Management (BLM), and National Park Service whose leader would report directly to the president. To return to the point of what DeBonis believes is responsible public land stewardship, he would keep swinging the blade until he reached the bare roots of an agency planted a century ago by Gifford Pinchot and promoted by Theodore Roosevelt.

DeBonis says the act of killing the Forest Service in order to save it has become an option only because the agency, despite pledges made by recent chiefs, has shown itself incapable of implementing reform due to internal resistance. He has no aspersions to cast upon current Forest Service Chief Mike Dombeck, but he is convinced that the revolution must come from the bottom instead of the top, sweeping through like a wildfire. Dombeck is taking the call for devolution seriously.

As one might imagine, such talk scares the bark off old Forest Service loyalists and timber lobbying groups, which is why DeBonis, almost a decade after he left the agency, still commands a Bunyanesque reputation as a heretic. The man once written off as a subversive has emerged in the minds of many conservationists and agency reformers as a Lech Walesa of American public lands management. If I had any doubts about the effectiveness of his impact, they were eliminated when the Sierra Club, with its 600,000 members, announced recently that it, like DeBonis, was advocating a temporary end—at least for a few human generations—to all corporate logging in national forests.

~

The story of Jeff DeBonis is ironic because just two decades ago he was considered one of the most notorious architects of massive tree felling in the inland West. During a career that spanned thirteen years, DeBonis had a role in delivering billions of board feet of lumber into the laps of local timber mills in the Pacific Northwest and shipping raw American wood to Japan. His decisions brought down tree trunks a millennium old, killed fish, displaced grizzly bears and spotted owls, carved up mountainsides into tidy rectangles of visual blight, and cost taxpayers at least tens of millions of dollars in losses through publicly subsidized road construction. Of course, he helped dole out thousands of short-term, unsustainable jobs for loggers, but ultimately, he says, his complicity in perpetuating the myth of an endless timber supply helped put them out of work. Today he is doing penance for those sins as guilt gnaws at his conscience. What torments DeBonis's enemies is that they cannot ignore the fact that his previous existence as a proud "timber beast" exudes credibility. In Forest Service parlance, a timber beast is an agency employee, usually educated in industrial silviculture, who proudly, aggressively, and without shame or consideration of ecological factors carries out massive tree cutting. Most, were they not on the government payroll, would be working for private timber companies.

There are no pat dictionary definitions of timber bestiality, DeBonis says. There are only the broad landscapes that serve as their canvases. Timber beasts are like dinosaurs in the twilight of the late Jurassic period, seeing the environment around them changing but not yet realizing they are already extinct as a species. Their time has passed, their glory faded, and their only hope of survival is to adapt to the wind of enlightenment or be transformed into fossils. Most would rather fight than switch. "It's a harsh reality," DeBonis says, telling me that it is not his intention to sound sanctimonious. "The Forest Service that entered this century is very different from the agency leaving it. I have met thousands of Forest Service employees who love what they do, who want more than anything to contribute something meaningful, but they are concerned about the direction the agency is taking them. They did not take a job to be manipulated by the timber industry. They swear allegiance to the public interest, not to corporate board rooms. Loyalty to upholding high ideals and principles is one thing, but loyalty based on fear and intimidation has no place in a free and open democracy. It's almost funny, but rule by tyranny has become an accepted part of the Forest Service's process of decisionmaking. For many people who wear the green uniform, the working environment is like living in East Germany before the Berlin Wall fell."

Arguably, not since the turn of the twentieth century, when Gifford Pinchot laid out the multiple-use ideals for how public forests should be managed—to yield the greatest good for the greatest number of people over the longest period of time (Pinchot also said that everything in a forest is for sale)—has a fiery civil servant so affected the esprit de corps of the Family.

"Someone had to deliver a wake-up call, and fortuitously, Jeff was the one," says Dave Iverson, a Forest Service economist stationed in Ogden, Utah, and the board chairman of a group DeBonis founded, Forest Service Employees for Environmental Ethics. "He provided a spark of light like a Vaclav Havel or a Nelson Mandela or a Lech Walesa," Iverson says. "There's almost something magical about a spiritual leader like Jeff. Someone like him might come around only once in a lifetime. When the history of the U.S. Forest Service is written a hundred years from now, there will be a chapter about him."

DeBonis started his revolution by quietly shaking up the organization at its roots. He did it by committing the ultimate sacrilege: talking openly about the Family's incestuous relationship with the timber industry. His transformation started in the late 1980s, and his efforts were then, as they are now, aimed at breaking down the walls of what reformers call the Iron Triangle—a triad of power formed by old-guard Forest Service bureaucrats, the timber industry, and lackey politicians, mostly from Alaska and states in the Pacific Northwest.

"Jeff is unique in the sense that he remained an activist reformer while at the same time he was one of them," Iverson explains. "To a certain extent, every time bureaucrats in the Forest Service look him in the eye, even today, they see a part of themselves staring back, and it scares them. They have a crisis of conscience. It makes them think about how far their own values have been compromised. It's like brothers fighting each other in the Civil War. Each has a cause they think is worth dying for. The point that disturbs the Forest Service to no end is that it can't completely refute what Jeff is saying. He was a timber-sale planner, and he too had been a true believer in harvesting trees. Heck, he marked sales for the agency by tying red ribbons around the trunks of old-growth trees. He was a guy who decided how big the clearcuts would be and where the trunks would fall."

By many, DeBonis is greeted as a messianic trailblazer; to others he remains the bad boy who shamefully turned against the system that produced him. His delinquency, however, is shared with esteemed company. The forerunner of American ecology, Aldo Leopold, struggled with the same ethical dilemmas and ultimately departed from the Forest Service as a nonconformist under similar terms, as did naturalist Olaus Murie at the National Biological Survey, Rachel Carson at the U.S. Fish and Wildlife Service, and thousands of scientists whose own conversions are not so widely known.

Ralph Waldo Emerson wrote, "Courage charms us, because it indicates that a man loves an idea better than all things in the world, that he is thinking neither of his bed, nor his dinner, nor his money, but will venture all to put in act the invisible thought of his mind." DeBonis's courage, and thus his charm, originates with the idea that open discussion is the heart of Family values.

~

In the early 1980s, Gloria Flora formed a singular, unflattering impression of DeBonis, a perspective that should disarm the majority of critics who portray him as a dyed-in-the-wool extreme *environmentalist*. "Jeff was a timber beast; by that I mean he was quite focused on getting the cut out at almost any cost," Flora says. "I have to admit, he was very good at his job."

Flora is a rarity and, according to agency insiders, a rising star who could, if she survives the bureaucracy, someday lead it. She has climbed through the ranks to become a full-fledged forest supervisor (top manager) of Montana's Lewis and Clark National Forest. She is one of a handful of women to hold upper-management positions in the agency. In 1997 she risked her career by announcing a decision that shocked the powerful American energy industry. Listening to her constituents, the American public, Flora decided to withdraw a significant portion of the eastern face of the Rocky Mountains from oil and natural-gas drilling, citing the need to safeguard grizzly bears, wild places, and Native American spiritual sites. "Land management decisions are not public referendums," Flora explains. "We don't put issues out to a vote, but of the 1,500 comments I received from forty-nine of the fifty states, 80 percent of the people who wrote a letter were opposed to development." Similarly, the *Great Falls Tribune* commissioned an independent poll of Montanans that showed opposition to drilling outpaced support by a ratio of two to one.

Prior to Flora's decision in Montana, Chevron and FINA (a pair of energy companies), two of the largest leaseholders in the Lewis and Clark National Forest, were going after an estimated 3.6 trillion cubic feet of natural gas—even though there was a glut of gas on the market, low prices, and no commercial incentive to drill. Flora characterizes her decision as not so much the loss of opportunity as a deferral of options to the future, when technological advances will make energy development more compatible with wildlands that are in increasingly short supply. There was a time not long ago when such a decision would have meant the instant end of her career. Among her defenders is Forest Service Chief Dombeck. Her professional persistence may be tied to his longevity in that position. Under the supervision of previous Forest Service administrators in Washington, D.C., people like Flora have been vulnerable to career-ending retaliation.

"I for one am very excited by what I see going on in the Forest Service," Flora says. "We as an agency—thanks largely to concerns from the nation—were able to sit up and say, 'Wait a minute. We have choices.' We have an obligation to be involved in civil dialogue, whether it involves rabid environmentalists or those who subscribe to the hog-and-log mentality of resource extraction. But the larger and most important question is, how can we redeem our responsibilities as citizens and caretakers of local communities and finite resources? I think we need to look at decisions in a bigger picture, and I must tell you that I am very concerned when we base decisions solely on economics, solely on jobs and commodity values. I view natural resources in the national forest as our national natural capital. This is our savings account. If we're not investing in our natural capital as the human population grows, we're taking out more of our collective savings account than is being put back in."

Back when her path first crossed DeBonis's, he was working in the Troy Ranger District of the Kootenai National Forest in northwest Montana and she was the resident landscape architect. It was her job to minimize the aesthetic ravages of logging created by DeBonis and other timber-sale specialists. DeBonis, she said, kept her on the run because he took an aggressive approach to logging and chastised those who stood in his way.

Timber-sale planners are the folks who draw the boundaries of logging areas, including clearcuts, and assert them across a healthy forest. They are the symbols of "multiple-use" management that environmentalists most loathe. Slick in his delivery, DeBonis went out into the communities, told conservationists at public hearings not to worry, that everything would be all right, then the next morning handed out red flags and cans of spray-paint. He told agency timber crews to help logging companies mark the biggest trees, often those guarding the edges of rivers. He ordered the rest slashed and burned. Collaborating with road engineers, he mapped bulldozer routes to make way for lumberjacks and logging trucks to commence the liquidation. He admired his handiwork when entire drainages were completely denuded.

The route to quick praise from DeBonis's superiors was always the same: across sloping hills; flattening primeval canopies; stripping the landscape down to the flanks of streams if that's what it took to yield the prescribed volume of timber. DeBonis was proud to make the logging company executives smile, and when they did Forest Service officials and the politicians who funded the agency grinned too.

Flora has never positioned herself as an environmentalist, and still doesn't. But what DeBonis did sometimes gave her second thoughts about her future in a Forest Service uniform. Scores of colleagues share her trepidation.

"I wouldn't say my relationship with Jeff was acrimonious, but our discussions got testy at times," she says. "We had disagreements over the appropriate way to harvest timber. He got his methods straight out of forestry school. In Jeff's mind, cutting trees was supposed to take precedence over everything else. He was very thorough and efficient in his dedication to maximizing the production of board feet. Often he got his way, and that's what the foresters admired about him."

Promoted into key decisionmaking positions, DeBonis achieved a level of prestige in being a timber beast. Flora says she had to take it upon herself to try to keep him from giving too much away. In the midst of heated debates, it was DeBonis who told her that if the agency were going to err, it would be on the side of turning fir, spruce, pine, and cedar into two-by-fours and pulp. Had he kept his mouth shut, there is no telling how far he might have gone. One place he went after Montana was the Nez Perce National Forest in north-central Idaho, where he worked alongside Gloria Flora again. Having flown over the degraded remains of his logging program in Montana, and heeding the cautions of colleagues such as Flora, DeBonis by this time had tempered his views. The timber beast exhibited signs of taming his previous indifference to ecosystem health, but he was afraid to share his doubts with other members of the Family. The violence of destruction he had perpetrated caught up with him, manifested in his gut, and he started feeling like a man who grows up hunting big game for blood sport but upon reaching the twilight years of his life realizes that a deer perhaps has more aesthetic qualities running free than it does as a trophy on the den wall.

Flora knew DeBonis was battling his conscience. She could read the struggle in his face. "Jeff was a very responsible person trying to weigh multiple use against what was good for the ecosystem," Flora says. "He no longer saw trees as strict commodities." DeBonis admits that he realized the horror of his work when he walked through the aftermath of clearcuts. Fellow timber beasts had warned him against revisiting hillsides that had been logged over.

For five years, DeBonis worked under Nez Perce supervisor Tom Kovalicky, another dissident in the making. "Jeff was doing his own soul searching, and he had several reputations depending upon what he was doing," Kovalicky tells me. "As a human being at large when it came to visiting with people, he was very outgoing and up front, compared to a lot of Forest Service employees who are loners. He was quick to help out on civic projects with the local people. The community loved him.

"On the job," Kovalicky adds, "Jeff slowly turned into a mild activist. He would quote people like Aldo Leopold at staff meetings to remind us we were there to be stewards." Indeed, in *A Sand County Almanac,* Leopold wrote as a foreword, "We abuse land because we regard it as a commodity belonging to us. When we see land as a community to which we belong, we may begin to use it with love and respect. There is no other way for land to survive the impact of mechanized man, nor for us to reap from it the esthetic harvest it is capable, under science, of contributing to culture. That land is a community is the basic concept of ecology, but that land is to be loved and respected is an extension of ethics."

Kovalicky says DeBonis started to show care in crafting timber sales that he could be proud to come back and see in the first half of the next century when he is an old man. The quality of his efforts earned numerous awards and cash bonuses—one of the primary ways the Forest Service shows its gratitude to employees for continuing to get the cut out. "What he refused to tolerate were bad manners by other people who had a single-minded vengeance. He got very angry at folks who championed their special interest cause, like timber, at the expense of other uses, such as recreation, hunting, and wildlife. His anger extended to staff, rangers, and even me if it looked as if we were front-loading the process, as in the case of timber, which usually won out. I always had an open-door policy, and we discussed his belief that the hierarchy of how decisions were made needed to be changed. In his arguments, he would try persuasion before condemnation. He wasn't narrow-minded."

Kovalicky also witnessed DeBonis's spirited warrior side, his self-righteousness, and, in the minds of timber companies, his hypocrisy. "If he were pushed up against a wall, he would come out fighting, pounding tables," Kovalicky says. "Jeff's definitely a Type A personality. He is not one to lay around waiting for things to happen. He stirs things up. He's a very intense fellow and has a tendency, at times, to put you on the edge or make you feel uneasy. That said, his planning for timber sales was always professional, and he would accept responsibility for his own mistakes, which is something most people don't. The problem with mistakes in timber sales is that they sit there in your face for your lifetime, over the lifetime of your kids and your grandchildren after that."

During his tenure, under a slogan of "Admit your mistake and fix it but never repeat it," Kovalicky faced just one major environmental challenge in a timber sale in the Nez Perce that caused activists to lay their bodies in front of bulldozers. Still, thanks to the tenacity of DeBonis and others, the forest produced a consistent average of eighty million board feet a year, compared to the one hundred million board feet demanded by Idaho's congressional delegation. Environmentalists say the volume was still far too high to support biodiversity, and today DeBonis agrees. He laments the slowness of his awakening.

Kovalicky and DeBonis say there is a hysterical notion promulgated by the timber industry that needs to be debunked: the claim that complying with environmental laws is antithetical to logging and jobs. Applying the laws as Congress originally intended can actually generate efficiency in timber sales. "I would tell my staff to become proactive and honest with everything they did," Kovalicky says. "The reason we had the National Environmental Policy Act [NEPA] was to force agencies into full disclosure of their intentions. There's no question the current efforts to harvest trees in the 1990s are an attempt to circumvent the law." Kovalicky and DeBonis say that four politicians in particular—Congresswoman Helen Chenoweth, U.S. Senator of Idaho Larry Craig, and Congressman Don Young and Senator Frank Murkowski of Alaska—have fostered an environment of lawlessness. DeBonis says that by ordering the Forest Service to continue supplying trees to keep mills in business, though science suggests that this approach is shortsighted and destructive, they are forcing agency personnel into an ecological equivalent of the notorious My Lai massacre.

Deforestation often has been presented in the media as a phenomenon of tropical rainforests in foreign lands far away. DeBonis, who worked as a Peace Corps volunteer in El Salvador and a contractor on behalf of U.S. Aid for International Development in Ecuador, says that depiction is nothing more than an imperialistic fallacy to divert attention from the real deforestation in North America, which dwarfs the cutting of trees in the tropics.

After World War II, the harvest of timber from U.S. national forests increased almost two-and-a-half-fold over prewar levels, and the growing patchwork of clearcuts that emerged in the 1960s, continuing through the early 1990s, convinced managers that exhaustion of the forest supply was inevitable. It led to the passage of the Multiple-Use Sustained Yield Act of 1960, a law that presaged even more foresighted laws put on the books during the Nixon and Ford administrations.

DeBonis alludes to the National Forest Management Act (NFMA), which passed into law in 1976. The benchmark national code instructs the agency to ensure that logging is done without a deleterious effect on other resources. Here the notion of sustainable yield comes into play as a guiding principle, mandating that foresters view trees not as finite commodities to be liquidated but as a potentially endless resource if managed conscientiously.

"The Forest Service ... has both a responsibility and an opportunity to be a leader in assuring that the Nation maintains a natural resource conservation posture that will meet the requirements of our people in perpetuity," the NFMA says. In other words, forever.

The Forest Service's yardstick has been "allowable sale quantity," or ASQ. As defined by the Forest Service, the ASQ represents an estimate of the maximum volume of timber that can be sold from each forest over a ten-year period without harming other values.

Generally, many foresters in both the private and public sectors say that ecologically friendly yields of timber would be roughly half to three-fourths of the designated ASQ, which most concede was inflated. At best, ASQ was supposed to be the absolute ceiling that could not be surpassed; it was never intended as a yearly goal for production, but over the past twenty-five years the timber industry, leveraging its political forces, has turned it into exactly that. It's like driving a car as fast as it will go, expecting the engine to hold out. Pretty soon the engine dies.

Under the administration of Ronald Reagan, members of Congress in the big timber states began blackmailing the Forest Service by rewarding the agency with adequate funding (which included programs for endangered species, landscape restoration, and maintenance of such things as hiking trails and campgrounds) only if the ASQ was met. In time, funding for these other services was siphoned off into timber production.

John Mumma, the regional forester responsible for meeting timber quotas in Montana and Idaho, had received complaints from Idaho's congressional delegation about Kovalicky's recalcitrance in elevating the output of timber in the Nez Perce on the basis that such elevation couldn't occur without breaking environmental laws and harming wildlife habitat. Eventually, Mumma received a directive from then Forest Service Chief F. Dale Robertson to fire Kovalicky. There was no doubt that the people behind the memo were U.S. Senators James McClure and Steve Symms, both of Idaho, and U.S. Representatives Larry Craig of Idaho and Ron Marlenee of Montana. Mumma refused, exposing himself to retaliation. Later he resigned in disgust when conservative Republicans arranged for his transfer to a desk job in Washington as discipline for not selling more trees, as demanded by the timber companies, which, in turn, supported the politicians' political campaigns. Mumma, who now is director of Colorado's state department of wildlife, exposed the political meddling and was widely hailed by environmentalists for being candid.

"John Mumma had dirt on a lot of people, but he decided not to spill it all because he knew it would erode public confidence in the Forest Service and he loved working for the agency. Rather than take down the agency, he fell on his sword. To be honest, I should say that he neither chastised nor championed me," Kovalicky says. "Although he was known for his micromanagement, and he certainly micromanaged the hell out of the region, he didn't do it to the Nez Perce. He respected the strength of this forest because it had a strong constituency that worked with us to do what was right by the resource."

That didn't stop now retired Senator McClure, Idaho's archenemy of conservation and the current chairman of the ultraright National Endangered Species Act Reform Coalition, from attempting to intercede. Nor has it stopped McClure's successors. McClure sought not only to intimidate Kovalicky on timber issues but to pressure him to drop an investigation of one of the senator's own staffers. Kovalicky claims that his law-enforcement specialists caught Carl Haywood, an aide to Senator McClure, stealing trees from the Nez Perce in the late 1980s, but the Forest Service refused to prosecute because political strings were pulled. Haywood, who owned a private logging company, denied deliberate wrongdoing.

"What Haywood and his private logging company did was move the boundary fence between the national forest and private land in a remote area where they didn't think they would get caught. They were removing old-growth ponderosa pine. Our own survey crews saw what they were doing. Boy oh boy, talk about a smoking gun, but the Forest Service didn't want to hear anything about it. It was too sensitive—signing off on the prosecution of Haywood by high-level Forest Service bureaucrats could have negatively influenced their careers. You can imagine what ran through my mind. Here I was, a forest supervisor charged to protect a national forest on behalf of the American public, and I couldn't get a hearing because it involved a senator's aide."

Kovalicky says the case was sent to Mumma at the regional level, who passed it along to the agency's national headquarters in Washington. Rather than pursuing it as a criminal matter, Kovalicky recommended treating it as a civil case to spare McClure embarrassment. But again, the case went nowhere with the top Forest Service brass. "I guess you already know the rest of the story," Kovalicky says. "It shows the depth of power that politicians have, which is why I have little faith that the logging occurring during this decade and into the next will be conducted above board."

Indeed, each Congress since 1994 has drafted proposals to "streamline" NEPA, the Endangered Species Act, NFMA, and other laws; all of these proposals have components that would restrict the right of citizens to appeal questionable management actions.

Andy Stahl, executive director of Forest Service Employees for Environmental Ethics, says agency officials and certain members of Congress have lost their moral and ethical bearings. "We all know that it is wrong to steal national forest timber. If the Forest Service discourages investigations of timber theft, perhaps to protect the agency's public image, it does not take great ethical insight to realize the agency's action is improper."

Until he retired, Kovalicky says, he was harassed by people in McClure's office—specifically Haywood—who pushed him to cut 120 million board feet of trees in exchange for being left alone and the guarantee that the timber program would be funded. His "cooperation," he was told, would earn him favorable reviews from his superiors. Each time, he refused.

"If you do what they say without asking questions, you will move along with rewards and promotions for being obedient," Kovalicky says. "But it places you in an awkward situation because you give up your soul and pride. Either you're with them advocating the breaking of laws or you're considered an enemy. The first thing they do to discredit you is say you've lost your objectivity."

The Forest Service obviously had sufficient confidence in his skills to make him supervisor, but his refusal to turn the Nez Perce over to the logging industry ended his career. "There is an administrative practice of shunning that is not an organized strategy, but it exists. It's like the old Quaker method of shunning that punishes members of the community by making them outcasts and breaking their spirit. They don't officially demand that you change your behavior, but you get the message. Once I refused to cut more trees [beyond what was sustainable]," Kovalicky says, "I never got any more cash bonuses from the agency and I always managed to have a less than perfect report card from the assistant chief, James Overbay. Despite all the hoorah I caused internally, I say with pride that we were one of the few forests to continue to get logs out because we weren't hamstrung by appeals from environmental groups for attempting to cut too much. It's the overambitiousness that got the Forest Service, the timber industry, and the politicians into trouble in the first place. They brought it on themselves by promising more than could be delivered."

Esprit de corps, pride in the Family, blind allegiance, he says, died during the Reagan and Bush years in an atmosphere of distrust and watching one's back. Ethics were abandoned as forest supervisors were thrust into survival mode. A fracturing of mission occurred throughout the rank and file. DeBonis bore witness as he was promoted.

~

The Willamette National Forest was for many years the largest producer of timber in the lower forty-eight states. Within the Forest Service, being moved from the clearcuts of the inland West to the Willamette is akin to a ballplayer advancing from the minor to the major leagues. The forest has been a showcase for industrial logging, and it just happened to be the location of DeBonis's next and final assignment.

According to one agency insider, the Forest Service had not given up on DeBonis's ability to "make the right decision in the eyes of the timber industry." The transfer was intended to put DeBonis's education to good use and perhaps to restore his religion as a born-again timber beast. However, the gambit backfired.

On the desk of Willamette National Forest supervisor Michael A. Kerrick, someone had attached a makeshift sign that said, "A billion or bust!" jokingly referring to the minimum number of board feet Kerrick had promised the timber industry he would deliver. Unfortunately, DeBonis says, Kerrick took the joke seriously. For much of the 1980s, the Willamette was indeed cutting nearly a billion board feet annually (averaging between six hundred and eight hundred million a year), more than the combined yield of ten inland national forests. An impressive but ultimately devastating figure even for then, it represented 25 percent of the production of all the forests in the Pacific Northwest (Oregon and Washington), which altogether were cutting 4.5 billion board feet a year. Many of the raw logs were shipped to Japan. Today four billion board feet is the cut amount for the whole national forest system. DeBonis would like to cut that number to zero and give the public woodlands a rest. He winces when asked whether the treatment of the Willamette was the kind of silviculture he learned in forestry school.

The impetus behind the liquidation of western public forests has been endlessly written about of late, but here, again, is a little history. Logging companies in the Pacific Northwest that exhausted the trees on their own private reserves normally operate on eighty-year rotations, that is, they have to wait eighty years before the next generation of trees is ready for harvest. Over the past forty years, national forests—public lands—have bought those companies time with higher volumes while they waited. Stewardship obviously isn't a top priority on land the timber companies don't own, DeBonis suggests.

"It didn't surprise me that once Jeff left the Nez Perce and went to a forest like the Willamette, the magnitude of the clearcuts would disturb him because they would sure leave an impression on anyone," observes Gloria Flora. "As a forest planner, he realized he didn't like the direction that his career was taking him. I could see how he tried to bring his enlightened knowledge forward. When it was not well received, it was difficult for him to remain subservient. Jeff is a very strong-willed person. He probably decided what he needed to do was approach it from a different angle." Jeff DeBonis was about to become a whistleblower.

In the Forest Service today are hundreds of employees biding their time, waiting to retire. Their will is broken. They are tired and burned out, realizing they can no longer make a difference. They have given up. Another agency professional who, like DeBonis, questioned what he saw was Jay Gore, a Forest Service resource specialist who coordinated a report on the spotted owl that was massaged to suit political directives aimed at cutting more trees. Today he is the National Forest Service coordinator for grizzly bears. The Willamette, Gore says, was the first forest geared to maximize timber production in the short term. "In Vietnam we bombed a lot of villages with the attitude that you had to destroy them in order to save the inhabitants," Gore says. "On the Willamette we had to destroy the forest in order to appreciate it." Gore regards DeBonis as a hero for declaring that enough is enough.

"You had people who came out of the forestry schools in the 1950s and '60s, as Jeff did from Colorado State University, and they were trained in the mechanized, tree-farm-type forestry. Their goal was to weed out diversity of trees and create monocultures, much like a wheat farmer in Kansas approaches a field. Foresters like Jeff looked at the landscape and realized that if you put one species back in you will get maximum yield, even though you kill the diversity of the forest to do it. Those people who rose through the ranks are the timber beasts. They are the old-guard foresters that Jeff eventually butted heads with."

Like Leopold before him, DeBonis came out of the closet as a conservationist shortly after his stint in the Willamette began. He confesses, "Three years into my job when I was in Montana, I was sucked into the idea of being a gonzo forester. I denied my intuition that their mandate was to do bad things. Then a biologist by the name of Ernie Garcia, who had worked on the Gifford Pinchot Forest, came to the Kootenai, specifically the Troy Ranger District, as the first wildlife biologist we had ever had. He arranged to give a talk to us timber guys. He told us we were not meeting the law by putting sales in prime grizzly habitat. At first I was part of the effort to silence him, belittle him, and intimidate him. Today when I look back, I am ashamed. I realize that I was just like the people I am fighting. I was sucked into the abusive mindset. Eventually a flash of enlightenment went off in my head. Although I was only three years into my career, it took me another nine to act on what I had learned."

According to Dave Iverson, the fellow agency dissident who has chosen to try to reform the Forest Service while remaining in the Family, DeBonis encountered "future shock" (also known as "westside shock," a reference to the west side of the Cascade range) after he arrived in Eugene. "It all clicked in Oregon," Iverson says. "Jeff had the same conversion that Paul did on the way to Damascus, but it was a different kind of gospel."

DeBonis says the Forest Service knew that levels of logging were unsustainable, and the timber companies knew it too. His supervisors wanted him to craft iron-clad sales that could skirt the growing number of legal challenges from environmentalists to stop the cutting. Rather than pursuing full-blown environmental impact statements and opening the process to public review, DeBonis was told to prepare internal environmental assessments, as he always had done, that could expedite logging in short order. In the meantime, he was hearing the emerging field reports from fisheries and wildlife biologists who said that ecosystem health was in a critical situation. He had a flashback to Garcia's warning.

On weekends DeBonis spent hours hiking through mile after mile of clearcuts and talking with colleagues who were similarly shaken by their complicity in landscape-level destruction. "I realized I could no longer live a lie," he says. "Some of those landscapes appeared as if they had been nuked. I couldn't continue to go along with their farce that clearcutting was having no discernible effects on wildlife, fisheries, and rivers. I wasn't then, and still am not, opposed to logging, but I am opposed to logging like that. Clearcutting isn't forestry."

To mix a metaphor, Iverson says the difference between leaders and followers is defined by whom they regard as their keeper. "After he expressed loyalty to the household, i.e., upholding the agency's legal commitment to stewardship and professional ethics, rather than offering obedience to the bureaucratic masters and the timber industry, he was never accepted again," Iverson says. "Once you cross the line you're labeled an outsider, a pariah in your own home, which in this case is the local district."

The events that cast DeBonis into his current role were largely spontaneous. Though still a forest planner, he attended a regional conference on logging and then penned a short memorandum that would come to be known as his manifesto and call to arms. "We, as an agency, are perceived by the conservation community as being an advocate of the timber industry's agenda. Based on my ten years with the Forest Service, I believe this charge is true," DeBonis wrote. "I also believe," he added, "along with many others, that this agency needs to re-take the moral 'high-ground,' i.e., we need to be advocates for many of the policies, goals, and solutions proposed by the conservation community."

As an agency, and as a resource manager, the Forest Service must embark upon a long-term perspective, embracing the original ideas of sustainability as outlined by Pinchot and then clarified by Leopold, he continued. "Our mission and goals, as an agency, are much closer to those of the conservation community than to those of the timber industry. It is time to start perceiving the conservation community as our allies and partners in developing a strategy which will contribute to an ecologically sustainable lifestyle for the 21st century."

DeBonis stirred up a hornet's nest when he pressed the keyboard on his computer and instantaneously beamed out his opinions to untold numbers of fellow Forest Service employees—including then Forest Service Chief F. Dale Robertson—who were tied together by the agency's version of the Internet. Called the Data General, or DG, it was the Forest Service's private national electronic mail system and had long been used as a tool to indoctrinate employees. Although DeBonis had boldly stepped where no civil servant had gone before, he wrote a disclaimer that bemused the rank and file but rankled his superiors who otherwise might have had grounds to ensnare him with charges of insubordination. "Note," he typed, "the opinions expressed are those of the Author's and don't necessarily reflect official Forest Service policy."

Just as DeBonis suspected, it did not take long before a copy landed in the hands of timber industry executives, inciting a predictable response. A. Troy Reinhart, executive director of Douglas Timber Operators in Roseburg, Oregon, wrote a letter to DeBonis's superiors and dispatched a carbon copy to Robertson suggesting that the Forest Service pursue immediate disciplinary action and take steps to ensure that "such rhetoric is not repeated." There was no vagueness in the demand. Reinhart wanted DeBonis fired.

Reinhart claimed DeBonis's assessment sounded like a membership recruitment solicitation for the radical environmental group EarthFirst! How dare he blaspheme the "professionalism" of the Forest Service and the integrity of the timber industry by implying the two were in bed together? The system that had created the repentant timber beast now turned against him. "Douglas Timber Operators is concerned that an employee with these ideas can in good faith prepare timber for sale," Reinhart fumed. "It very well may be that his judgment is clouded by his misconceptions and lack of understanding of the real issues. Steps should be taken to insure that a high quality job of timber planning [read: logging] is being performed. Also necessary disciplinary actions should be taken against this employee as well as others who undertake this action. In light of the fact Mr. DeBonis feels the agency is an advocate for the timber industry, and must break that mold, and reclaim the 'moral high ground,' a formal reprimand is most surely necessary."

DeBonis responded by suggesting that Reinhart's reaction "only served to reaffirm my suspicions that timber industry spokespeople find it hard to communicate lately without a healthy dose of misleading propaganda and disinformation. ... It's said that desperate times make for desperate actions, and your letter certainly reflects desperation," he wrote back. "However, I suspect the desperation has less to do with log supply than it does with the fact that the truth hurts."

Shortly thereafter, DeBonis was warned that he shouldn't walk alone in small towns and national forest lands outside of Eugene. He was no longer invited to parties thrown by some of his fellow timber-sale planners, and his superiors offered him stern stare-downs in place of salutations and high fives.

"There's no descriptive way to describe it other than telling you the scale of cutting on the Willamette and other coastal forests is

ferocious and intense. I knew I was in deep when I was told repeatedly to alter environmental documents. My supervisor called me
into his office and said the district forest ranger who oversees implementation of timber sales was upset with my thoroughness, that
by mentioning concerns and developing a cumulative-effects model
I was essentially writing appeals for environmentalists. That's when I
realized the system didn't work, that the agency will only do the
right thing if it is challenged in court or believes it will be exposed.
It can't make the right decision voluntarily, on its own. It is unable
to scrutinize itself."

Dan Heinz says the pressure on dissenters today is worse than it
has ever been because timber interests inside the agency have their
backs against the wall. Heinz started working full time for the Forest Service in 1958 in the San Isabel National Forest in Colorado
and then had a hitch in the Black Hills National Forest in South
Dakota. "At cocktail parties when I got into the Forest Service, we
would talk about justifying every tree we took out. When I left, we
were fighting to leave any tree in the forest," Heinz says of his several decades of service.

Heinz's own version of "future shock" occurred in the 1960s and
1970s, when he was flown to help fight forest fires in the Forest
Service's Region One, which included thirteen forests in Montana
and Idaho—the same ones DeBonis would try to tame in the 1980s.
"I remember flying over the Bitterroot [National Forest], and I was
aghast that our agency would do anything like that," he says of seeing the clearcuts that caused national outrage and spawned the eventual creation of NEPA and NFMA.

In 1979 Heinz, a wildlife and range specialist, was transferred to
the Deerlodge National Forest headquartered in Butte, Montana,
where he experienced the results of decisions by forest planners such
as DeBonis on the ground. "I just saw things come unraveled during the Reagan years," he reflects. "Responsible timber targets that
had been the backbone of good stewardship eroded. I got disillusioned and refused to wear my uniform. I loved my job and never
stopped loving the Forest Service, but when the opportunity came
for an early retirement I took it because the good guys were out-
numbered."

Heinz needed to channel his pent-up frustration. When the Family paying his retirement wouldn't listen, he cautiously shared what
he knew after environmentalists sought him out. "When you become

disillusioned, it is a traumatic thing to go through. It's like finding out your teetotaling father is a closet alcoholic. The lack of integrity was rotting up the core and the agency had a polished image on the outside, but it was decaying from within. It still is."

DeBonis's emergence could not have happened at a better time, he says. "He's everything positive that goes with the term *idealist*. So many whistleblowers, i.e., people who turn against an agency, are labeled as kooks. He's an exception in that generality," he says. "DeBonis is brilliant, quick on his feet. But like any revolutionary, he has his warts. Somehow that makes him that much more authentic. I've never met anybody like him, and I've been around for a while."

In the months after DeBonis's memo appeared, he was contacted by hundreds of fellow Forest Service employees who wanted to speak out but were afraid. The groundswell convinced him later to found the Association of Forest Service Employees for Environmental Ethics (AFSEEE), dedicated to defending agency personnel who are denied free speech or forced to break federal laws by doctoring documents or failing to consider the impact of logging on other resources.

The formation of AFSEEE represented a watershed for another reason. It brought to the fore a U.S. Supreme Court case known as *Pickering v Board of Education* (391 US 563, 1967). *Pickering* is to whistleblowers' rights what *Brown v Board of Education* represents to the Civil Rights movement. In *Pickering,* the Supreme Court laid out a "balancing test" that weighed the interest of an employee in speaking out on matters of public interest against the interest of the public employer in getting a job done in an orderly and productive way.

Without question there was compelling public interest—saving tax dollars, protecting endangered species and public resources—to justify DeBonis's whistleblowing. Under *Pickering,* the Forest Service had the legal power to silence him only if it could prove that his actions were impeding the function of the agency—a burden it could not meet. In fact, another related case, *Connick v Myers* (103 US 1684, 1983) also asserts that dissenting employees are protected if their activity relates to matters of public concern. "If we can assume that timber harvest issues are of public concern (a fairly safe assumption)," wrote Steve Kreisberg, representing the National Federation of Forest Employees, in a letter to DeBonis, "management must then demonstrate that your expressions on timber harvest issues interfere with Forest Service programs."

Kreisberg added, however, that DeBonis needed to be careful. "It is easier to tell you what you cannot do than it is to tell what you can do," Kreisberg wrote. "Do not advocate a work stoppage, or a refusal to carry out a management imposed timber management proposal. You can most definitely join organizations and even take an active part in non-partisan groups. You can write Congress, industry and environmental groups. However, you should never allow any group to exploit your connection to the Forest Service. In the public eye, you must only be known as citizen DeBonis."

Ed Marston, publisher of the environmental journal *High Country News,* was among the first in the mainstream media to devote significant ink to DeBonis's cause, and some credit *High Country News* with saving DeBonis's neck by making it impossible for the Forest Service to muzzle him through internal administrative channels. Marston has his own take on DeBonis and the groundswell he started: "They [DeBonis and others who joined him] are simply trying to do good work and to implement natural resources values the United States had codified into law over the last twenty years. As they see it, they are in step with the law and with the times, and their agencies are not in step.

"[They] are not saints," he adds. "They are not perfect. But they are, for the most part, people willing to give up security and comfort in order to live their lives with a measure of truth. Their quest for truth and ethical existence has brought them into conflict not just with their agencies and with powerful economic interests but also with the materialistic values of society at large—values that are turning the West into a devastated land."

In spite of DeBonis's influence in creating a forum for whistleblowers, and in spite of court cases protecting free speech, the Forest Service has a track record of besieging those who dare to question the wisdom of the big timber establishments. There are, at present, hundreds of workers and thousands of their sympathizers—spread across 155 national forests and grasslands managed by the agency—who have suffered for their candor. For years the agency actually had a provision that legally forbade Forest Service employees from challenging bad timber sales. It gave managers the authority to seek retribution against dissenters, and it had a chilling effect.

Under enormous public scrutiny, the Forest Service only reluctantly abolished the regulation in 1998 as part of a precedent-setting
settlement with a forester working in Alaska's Tongass National Forest. Mary Dalton, a fifteen-year veteran assigned to the agency's Sitka
office, had challenged a timber sale proposed for a section of Bara-
nof Island in 1996. As a resource specialist, Dalton carefully analyzed
the likely effects, determining that clearcutting steep slopes in the
sale area would cause sedimentation in streams from erosion, possible landslides, and habitat damage for fish, brown bears, and deer.
Dalton's research, however, was purposely left out of the environmental review process mandated by federal law. She then formally
appealed her supervisor's decision to rubber-stamp the sale, and for
that she received a thirty-day suspension and a forced transfer to the
Coronado National Forest in Arizona, near the Mexico border,
thousands of miles away. Seeking assistance from FSEEE and PEER,
Dalton filed a grievance to have the disciplinary action rescinded.
Both FSEEE and PEER also used the case to highlight the hostile
conditions experienced by Forest Service whistleblowers who try to
hold the agency to compliance with federal laws. Dalton's lawsuit
specifically asked the court to strike down the Forest Service regulation barring employees from appealing bad timber sales, arguing
that it violated their right to free speech.

The case attracted attention from the highest levels of the Forest
Service and Department of Agriculture in Washington, D.C. Confronting a public backlash, Forest Service officials promised to abolish the regulation and finally create an official outlet for such appeals
to be heard. "What it means now is Forest Service employees can
appeal a decision they don't agree with," says Tavia Hollenkamp, a
Forest Service spokeswoman in Juneau. "The Forest Service recognizes a mistake was made and that we're righting it."

Even so, Andy Stahl, the FSEEE executive director who provided
legal support for Dalton, says the Forest Service capitulated only because it had no other choice. After all, although Dalton's suspension
was rescinded, the agency still got away with getting rid of her
through the forced transfer. Shipping her off from the Tongass follows a now unofficial agency policy of punishing the messenger
who says the impacts of industrial forestry are wrong. The Tongass
remains a battleground where the Forest Service has resisted meaningful reform. It is known as a last playground for timber beasts un-

willing to change their ways. "I don't think the Tongass is mature enough to have an employee of Mary Dalton's quality working there," FSEEE's Stahl says. "She knows that now. Maybe she can return someday when the Tongass has matured and grown up, but not right now."

Meanwhile, the logging trucks roll on, hauling their booty from places that should not be cut, and would not be cut, if the Forest Service listened to its biologists and conscientious foresters such as Mary Dalton.

~

Healthy forests, in theory at least, maintain stable populations of flora and fauna. Yet from 1977 to the mid-1990s, 192 species whose habitat consists partly or wholly of national forest lands found their way onto the federal Endangered Species List, representing a 278 percent increase in the number of imperiled animals or plants over the previous two decades. Assessing what this means for the overall health of the forest habitats in which these species are found is virtually impossible because the Forest Service has little data on the great variety dependent on national forests. Ironically, some of the very species in trouble are those that the Forest Service identifies as "indicator species" whose declines are supposed to provide advance warning to foresters that their activities are harming the environment. This warning system has been a dismal experiment.

"Indicator species are the tip of the iceberg when they are in trouble," DeBonis says. "For example, in the Northwest old-growth forests, including those where salvage logging is now occurring, there may be as many as twenty other species which are threatened in addition to the spotted owl. The agency is purposefully and knowingly overcutting our national forests to meet the demands of the timber industry and shortsighted politicians."

The reason for the declines in species and the general lack of information is that the purse strings of the agency are controlled by a powerful group of western senators and congressmen who have refused to provide funding for assessing the biological costs of timber sales and other development proposals to native wildlife. Furthermore, money that has been appropriated has often been diverted from wildlife programs that might have demonstrated cause for concern.

Months after she was elected to Congress, neophyte politician Helen Chenoweth of Idaho—a no-apology apologist for the Wise Use movement—attended an "endangered salmon bake" and said she didn't understand the fuss over trying to save salmon habitat from logging. Chenoweth flat-out told a reporter that she couldn't take the fish seriously as an endangered species. "How can I, when you can go and buy a can of salmon off the shelf in the [supermarket]?" Such attitudes were the driving force behind the Western Forest Health Initiative, also known as Public Law 104-19, also known as the salvage logging bill, also known as the logging without laws bill, which was signed into law by President Clinton in 1995. The premise is that forest fires can be prevented by chopping down old and decaying trees before they are set ablaze by lightning. This bill, however, resulted in hillsides of green trees being toppled as well. Killing the forest in order to save it from fire is the agency's idea of promoting ecological health. DeBonis says the approach is nothing more than a ruse.

From 1989 to 1993, the volume of unharvested timber under contract to logging companies on federal lands decreased from eleven billion board feet to almost four billion board feet, making the timber industry eager to find another source of logs. Breathing new life into the already failed notion of sustainable logging, Law 104-19 was especially harmful because it made salvage logging immune from provisions of the Endangered Species Act, the National Environmental Policy Act, and the National Forest Management Act.

What's happening today with logging from the east side of the Cascades to the western slope of the Rockies is the boldest assault yet on the last intact forests of the lower forty-eight states. Overnight, targets for timber yield as a result of the salvage logging rider and subsequent timber quotas demanded by Western Republicans almost doubled, and the war over spotted owls shifted inland from the Washington, Oregon, and California coasts to the heart of the Columbia River Basin.

"The real problem in the Columbia Basin stems from repeated ... roadbuilding, logging, grazing, mining, introduction of exotic species, recreational use, and other human-caused impacts that have profoundly affected ecosystem processes and functions," wrote FSEEE field director Bob Dale, who in the 1990s is spearheading an alternative ecosystems approach to Forest Service planning that includes one hundred of the agency's own experts. The commentary appeared in the *Inner Voice,* the FSEEE's underground newspaper. Dale continued,

> The evidence [of degradation] is a precipitous decline in the quantity and quality of habitat for many species of fish, plants, and wildlife. The quickest and cheapest solution is to give the land a rest. Does this mean we need to put the whole interior Basin off-limits to roadbuilding, logging, grazing, and the like? I don't think so, but we do need to make some thoughtful choices about which lands are suitable for these activities and which lands are not. The hard truth is that many places cannot withstand further human-induced disturbance without an extended breather. Relatively undisturbed places, including roadless areas, deserve protection, too. They ought to be most valued for the important and irreplaceable role they play as fish and wildlife habitat and in maintaining watershed integrity.

More than one hundred thousand acres of primarily roadless national forest lands were put up for grabs first by the salvage logging rider and then by the guise of promoting forest health through intensive logging. Basically, the last best headwater spawning areas for salmon and trout in the Northwest are at stake. "The Clinton administration says, 'Trust us.' But I don't trust any federal agency with the kind of unlimited power granted by this salvage amendment," says Oregon's own Congressman Peter DeFazio, a Democrat and normally an ally of the president.

"The Forest Service has been captured by powerful corporate special interests, particularly the timber, grazing, and mining industries," DeBonis said in testimony before the U.S. House of Representatives Government Operations Subcommittee at the dawn of the Clinton administration, which at the urging of Forest Service Chief Jack Ward Thomas sanctioned the salvage measure to placate the timber industry. "The agency is comfortable with lying and misinforming the public about the environmental impacts of such industries. The attitude of the agency is typically one of 'we know best,'" DeBonis said. "When faced with mounting criticism of its prodevelopment programs, the agency relies on the crutch of needing public education. The fact is that as the public becomes more aware and educated, people become more outraged at what is happening on our national forests."

Forest supervisor Gloria Flora has her own take. "What concerns many of us in the Forest Service is the message being sent by Congress which the public perceives as an attempt to open up the gate to developers. I would like to be told that no matter what we do, we should do our best in adhering to the letter of the law. I would say that given the rancor of the existing Congress, I don't see natural resource law being mandated in that manner but used instead as a political chip. We should all sit up and pay attention because this is sending a message that I'm not sure how many people want to hear."

~

DeBonis says he wants the timber industry to know that he is not indifferent to the pain of blue-collar workers. He sympathizes with the family logger who was told there were enough trees out there to last forever—enough timber to pay wages, feed families, and send the kids off to college. At first, in the style of silviculture that made him want to work for the Family, the dream was possible. But nobody bothered to tell the loyal worker that as the end came into sight for the corporate timber barons who pushed yields to outrageous levels, the commitment to guarantee a job forever to the worker no longer existed. The move to modernize mills, which has eliminated more jobs than anti-timber-cutting appeals and spotted owls, showed that the logging companies' commitment is to satisfying corporate shareholders. After the biggest trees are cut, many of the larger companies don't give a damn about what happens to communities. Their sights are set on Russia, roadless Canada, and China—but first a detour through America's last pockets of forests that are ramparts for biological diversity.

When we envision the perfect sort of Forest Service dissenter, who better to pinpoint the flaws of clearcutting than the man drawing up the sales? Oddly enough, although DeBonis's timber beast colleagues saw him as a turncoat, his objectivity remained while he kept preparing the agency's timber offerings. However, DeBonis also attended gatherings sponsored by conservation groups on weekends. Though he did not discuss proprietary information pertaining to his office work, the mere association was deemed treacherous.

In an especially egregious timber sale, DeBonis was told to alter an environmental document by his superiors, which he did, but he also mailed a copy of the original to the Oregon Natural Resources

Council (ONRC). DeBonis was outraged when the Willamette moved forward with the sale even though it was clear that it jeopardized owl and fish habitat. "It was a mess," he says. "The short story is that ONRC used some of my data, appealed the sale, and won the challenge to stop it. One of my coworkers who was obviously pro-timber asked me how I could be a timber beast by day and do in timber beasts at night. I expected to be fired, but AFSEEE suddenly caught on so wildly and I became bulletproofed."

In a three-page notice, Willamette Forest Supervisor Michael A. Kerrick spelled out his concerns about DeBonis while at the same time acknowledging that the First Amendment is valuable to the function of the Forest Service. Kerrick had no choice. He knew the First Amendment is considered inviolate by his friends in the timber industry who frequently invoke it to attack government regulation. "Although this memorandum sets forth many of the potential pitfalls in the exercise of free speech rights arising from an employment context, I do not wish to discourage you from speaking on issues of concern to you," he wrote to DeBonis. "The Forest Service has no interests in silencing agency employees. The free exchange of ideas with the agency and, secondarily, outside the agency is important to sound policy decisions. My concern is that any free speech activities be exercised responsibly, in the context of your employment with the Forest Service."

The impressive element of DeBonis's dissidence is not that he broke rank like Martin Luther and posted a defiant challenge to authority but that he did it and survived. At least, he stayed as long as he wanted to. He succeeded because he informally recruited support from his fellow workers, the court of public opinion, and the media. He caught the establishment off guard, trumping his superiors by exercising his First Amendment right. The tactic made him virtually untouchable in retaliation, but he knows he was lucky. Few fare as well.

DeBonis was rumored to be a trust funder. His detractors claimed that independent wealth was the backbone of his outspokenness. They said this to illegitimize him, to lessen his impact. They said it so other Forest Service whistleblowers contemplating a similar path, yet dependent upon their monthly paycheck and trapped in the fear of losing their jobs, would be dissuaded from speaking out. They said it, perhaps out of envy, to crush any notion of DeBonis being an idealist. The rumors were incendiary, yes, but they were false. Utterly false.

DeBonis said one of his greatest fears was the finality of having no income and no pension to fall back upon.

Although DeBonis certainly is not the first agency employee to blow the whistle on mismanagement, others failed because they played by the rules the bureaucracy gave them, which was tantamount to asking permission to disagree. The lesson is a poignant one for future whistleblowers. By allowing an agency to control a grievance as an "internal personnel matter," the whistleblower seldom wins. Going public is certainly fraught with peril and thrusts the whistleblower past the point of no return professionally, but with solid documentation, corroborating witnesses, and stories appearing on the six o'clock news, it becomes far more difficult for an agency to stage a cover-up. Mary Dalton learned this from DeBonis's playbook.

DeBonis's saga began in cyberspace, found its way into the local newspapers, and eventually was featured on ABC's *Prime Time Live.* His impact was quickly felt. He set a goal of enlisting 10 percent, or three thousand, of the Forest Service's thirty thousand workers. Circulation of the *Inner Voice* climbed steadily until 100,000 copies of each issue were being distributed. The membership ranks during this decade have swelled to more than ten thousand, and the AFSEEE has become a model for similar organizations.

"A fair percentage of people in the agency said, 'Oh good, I'm glad we finally have this kind of outlet.' Then there were others who thought AFSEEE had gone overboard and biased in an opposite direction," says Gloria Flora. "I do know there were a lot of people, including myself, who read the *Inner Voice* and subscribed to it. It was another opinion that needed to emerge. I don't think anyone was surprised to hear about the Forest Service's dirty laundry. It was well known within the agency but not so well known outside of it."

Flora says she is more cognizant of the voice of dissent as an upper-level manager. "I like to hear different views and opinions. I don't think an agency experiencing the kind of change inundating us can survive by being myopic and plugging our ears. We need to change attitudes about what propels the government and its budget. It's not that what we're doing is all bad, but the processes could use some serious examination."

I asked both Flora and Iverson if it is possible to do what DeBonis did and still have a place in the agency. "Only if you're extremely lucky or extremely crafty," replies Iverson, a board member of

AFSEEE, which has since dropped the A and now is known by the acronym FSEEE (Forest Service Employees for Environmental Ethics). "The rules are simple. You must perform better than everybody else at your job and make yourself invaluable to them. You must let it be known to them in polite ways that you have a good knowledge base and you are prepared to take it with you if they threaten to drum you out. You must choose your values and venues for action carefully. Don't go around pissing people off gratuitously, and you'd better champion as many things as you are beating up on. I've never seen anybody become a whistleblower and thrive. Jeff could have stayed, but he left because everything he did after that would be placed under a microscope. The agency would have been waiting for a good reason to discredit him. Sure, it's a demoralizing reality. There are a whole lot of wonderful people in the Forest Service that are browbeaten by a bad system."

Recognizing that he would forever be castigated, DeBonis left the Forest Service and FSEEE and moved to Washington, D.C., to found Public Employees for Environmental Responsibility, which affords shelter to whistleblowers in all government land management agencies, not just the Forest Service. DeBonis is convinced that the Forest Service cannot fix itself.

The appointment of Forest Service Chief Jack Ward Thomas, succeeding Dale Robertson, who was fired by Bill Clinton, was initially greeted with high hopes. A prominent ecologist who had worked on the spotted owl controversy, Thomas was viewed as a person who would restore the agency's integrity, which has become moribund over the past two decades. In the end, Tom Kovalicky says, the bureaucracy and political machinery "ate him alive." During an interview with Thomas before he departed under fire from conservationists and Forest Service reformers who said he betrayed their trust, Thomas offered some observations on DeBonis. "When Jeff set up AFSEEE, the agency accommodated him and he was able to provide another avenue for debate within the Forest Service," Thomas tells me. "I think his impact has been considerably less than it could have been had he stayed in the Forest Service. The changes the agency has undergone in the last few years have been significant. Being on the outside lessened his effectiveness in shaping that change."

Thomas's changes, DeBonis says, were lip service only, and he responds to the former chief's assessment that he would have been more influential from "the inside" with disbelief. His departure was not an easy choice but the most difficult of his life. For Thomas to suggest that the agency "accommodated" him is to imply, he adds, that free speech is a privilege, not a right. On that premise alone, the climate inside the agency for the rank and file is still an obsequious one punctuated by a condescending attitude from managers. The reason he left was that he felt he was on a leash, that the Forest Service was waiting for the slightest slip to try to ruin him.

I ask Thomas what he perceives as the benefits and liabilities of DeBonis's crusading and the organizations he founded. "On the positive side, Jeff early on turned up the volume on a topic that all of the professionals in this agency are concerned about: professional ethics in resource management. On the down side, this increased volume was done in a manner that alienated a good chunk of the agency to the extent that his message was lost in the inflammatory rhetoric. Both PEER and FSEEE have a tendency to be more of a polarizing agent than one that would bring the people of the agency together."

I ask if he believes that as organizations FSEEE and PEER are too impatient. "No, I wouldn't say that," Thomas responds. "I for one feel that you can never be too impatient when it comes to pushing for ethical behavior. I will say, however, that they appear to be unaware or unwilling to recognize the changes that have occurred in all land management agencies. It is easy to pontificate about many things when you are held responsible for none."

DeBonis says it is also easy to stonewall. There's little doubt that Thomas knew better, and DeBonis the watchdog was there to remind him of a pledge he had made to his workers upon taking the helm. Thomas dispatched these ideas via an e-mail memo—just as DeBonis had done to launch his revolt. "Tell the truth," Thomas wrote to the rank and file. "Obey the law. And practice Ecosystem Management." As timber beasts winked, glasnost was short-lived, and it was only a matter of months before Thomas fled his agency with, as one colleague said, "his tail between his legs." Thomas, himself a scientist, was accused of betraying whistleblowers and kowtowing to the GOP Congress because it clenched his purse strings. He became a servant to the bureaucracy rather than a leader of it. DeBonis says Thomas blew a golden opportunity to win the hearts of those beneath him.

Agitation and front-line activism have made DeBonis a target not just of timber loyalists but of Wise Use groups in general. A large percentage of politicians in the American West, where the bulk of national forest land is located, has received generous campaign contributions from extraction groups with ties to the Center for the Defense of Free Enterprise. Founded by Ron Arnold and Alan Gottlieb to serve as a political lobbying vehicle for the timber, mining, off-road vehicle, ranching, and oil-drilling industries, the center and its cronies are smart enough to identify DeBonis as a formidable threat. The kind of institutional changes he endorses would break the industrialists' stranglehold on the federal bureaucracy.

Himself a rebel, Arnold has always claimed credibility through his former role as an activist for the Sierra Club. Despite this emphasis on his background, some Wise Users don't seem to appreciate an individual like DeBonis. At a rally of resource developers held in the Dirksen Senate Office Building in the shadow of the U.S. Capitol, DeBonis demonstrated his mettle as an agitator. He showed up to hear more about proposals being presented by Wise Use groups to the GOP-dominated Congress that would roll back environmental standards on 570 million acres of public land in the West. Although the meeting took place in a public building, Charles Cushman, a friend of Arnold and Gottlieb and a zealous attacker of government regulations, confronted DeBonis, calling him a "liar" and a "slimebag" while ordering him to leave the premises. The intimidating tactics were witnessed by a television reporter from San Francisco.

DeBonis did not back down, but he suggests that his experience is analogous to what hundreds of federal employees in natural resource professions face in the field every day from people like Cushman, executive director of the American Land Rights Association in Battle Ground, Washington. "Cushman ranks among the elite set of Wise Use leaders and is their recognized bad boy," wrote a reporter for *Western Horizons,* a publication of the Western States Center and the Montana chapter of the AFL-CIO. "Cushman relishes his 'rent-a-riot' nickname and calls himself a 'tank commander' for the Wise Use movement. In fact, he compares his tactics to those of World War II General Erwin Rommel. All this talk is not just metaphorical. Cushman earned the rent-a-riot label from the violence and threats of violence which have followed in the wake of his organizing campaigns around the country."

In his provocative and excellent book *The War Against the Greens,* David Helvarg described Cushman this way: "With little obvious control over his organizational, financial, or personal life, Chuck

Cushman has been forced to go for the adrenaline rush: fighting new battles while raising funds to pay off his old ones, eating on the run, worrying about his health and weight, catching flak from the media. Almost by default, he has taken on the role of the anti-enviro movement's smoke jumper, flying from place to place across America looking for local brushfires to break out so he can add fuel to them." Cushman's antipathy toward conservationists is shared by many foresters in Forest Service district offices.

In a press conference for the Nature Conservancy, of which he is a national board member, retired U.S. Army General "Stormin' Norman" Schwarzkopf said in so many words that blaming environmentalists and Forest Service reformers for timber woes in the Pacific Northwest was a misguided approach. "These Wise Use extremists claim that economically you're going to take their jobs away from them; they're all going to become poor; their children are going to starve; and it's all because you're a bunch of fuzzy-headed tree huggers," he said. "It's blatant lying in many cases in how they present things."

Although Cushman has denied any involvement in the attacks on public employees who continue to hold Wise Use constituents to strict environmental compliance, DeBonis says the type of irresponsible rhetoric used by the extreme right has resulted in the bombing of the federal building in Oklahoma City and Forest Service and BLM offices in Nevada as well as prolific threats of physical violence against federal employees and their families. Forest Service and BLM workers have been advised to always be in radio contact and to travel in pairs and in unmarked vehicles. Months after the Oklahoma City bombing, a Forest Service official predicted that there was a "50 percent chance of a Forest Service employee being murdered in either Idaho or Nevada." In Wyoming and Nevada, state legislators encouraged citizens to buy firearms in case they need to keep federal natural resource officials at bay. Right-wing radio talk-show host Rush Limbaugh said, "The second violent American revolution is just about—I got my fingers about a quarter of an inch apart—is just about that far away. Because these people are sick and tired of a bunch of bureaucrats in Washington driving into town and telling them what they can and can't do with their land." What Limbaugh failed to mention is that in the West private interests—loggers, miners, ranchers—erroneously view their use of federal land not as a privilege but as a right. And despite their reviling of government, they have no trouble pocketing hundreds of millions of dollars in federal resource subsidies.

"Hostile actions by members of the Wise Use movement and certain members of Congress are increasing, especially in the West," DeBonis suggests. "In the face of this intimidation, we are working to challenge the illegal actions of Wise Use activists and to protect public employees who are being harassed. PEER is monitoring incidents of gross abuse and preparing a strategy to counter the Wise Use movement's intimidation campaigns against public employees."

Not surprisingly, DeBonis has received death threats, but he continues to speak out. For his courage, the thirty-thousand-member California League of Conservation Voters, the nation's oldest and largest state political action committee on environmental matters, named DeBonis the recipient of its environmental leadership award. "Jeff DeBonis's tireless efforts and innovation have led to a new awareness of the problems faced by environmental managers across the country," the organization's executive director, Sam Schuchat, said. "Public Employees for Environmental Responsibility has provided a safe haven for conscientious environmental employees who want their stories heard." The plaque was added to the ONRC's award for government service and the Olaus and Margaret Murie Award given by the Wilderness Society.

∼

Before stepping down from the U.S. House of Representatives in 1994, the late Congressman Mike Synar of Oklahoma made a scathing indictment of the Forest Service and its perverse incentives. "In my opinion, the Forest Service is spinning sawdust into gold," he told his legislative colleagues, some of whom had close ties to the timber industry. "Instead of objective analysis and usable information, Congress and the taxpayers are getting reports and plans from the Forest Service that consistently overstate the financial benefits of the federal timber program and understate its costs in both fiscal and natural resources.

"The American taxpayer deserves full and accurate information about all of the consequences of the federal timber sale program, especially with regard to the expenditure of public funds and the wise-use of taxpayer assets. Instead the Forest Service tries to justify uneconomic timber sales by the jobs they support; and, to justify its management direction for the National Forest System by the number of the so-called special interests which disagree with its plans."

Synar encouraged Congress to give more credence to science, and he praised the work of DeBonis for offering whistleblowing scientists a medium for making their views known. "There is a fundamental difference between what information Congress and the taxpayers demand from the Forest Service and the information which the agency is providing," Synar said. "What we need is an objective analysis of the financial and resource consequences of the federal timber-sale program. But what we are getting is highly subjective and largely self-serving."

The same year Synar retired, the Wilderness Society heeded his words. Economists with the conservation organization prepared a little-known document titled "A Shareholders' Report of National Forests" that served the same purpose as a corporate report except that it was completed on behalf of U.S. taxpayers. "Americans have a right to know whether their tax dollars are being spent wisely by the Forest Service," the organization stated upon release of the document. "The Shareholders' Report lets them know that their money, and their investment in the future, are being squandered."

To put the findings in plain terms: If the Forest Service's timber program were a privately held corporation and we as citizens owned stock, the public would be fiscally foolish for continuing to invest. Over the course of a single year, American taxpayers lost nearly $1 billion investing in the management of our 155 forests and twenty grassland units under the care of the agency. Fully $614 million was lost in 1993 through the timber program alone—about eighty out of 123 national forests lost money by expediting the sale of public timber. A recent assessment showed that only two dozen forests made money on timber.

By far one of the biggest charades played out in forest lands is the way that taxpayers subsidize or credit to timber companies the construction of roads into the forest so that private outfits cutting trees or digging mines or exploring for oil or natural gas can make a profit. There are enough miles of roads in national forests—400,000 miles' worth—to cover the total length of our interstate highway system eight and a half times. With the new assault of logging targeting roadless areas, the total length of roads could reach half a million miles within twenty years at a potential loss of hundreds of millions of dollars.

These same roads, paid for by you and me to benefit giant corporations, are also the principal cause of water-quality contamination in streams; crashes in wild fish populations; displacement of rare animals such as grizzly bears; a higher incidence of wildlife poaching; and losses of opportunities for nonmotorized recreational visitors, hunters, and people who just enjoy unmarred solitude.

"It is a hidden subsidy to big timber for the taxpayer to pay the Forest Service for building roads into the best virgin forests," wrote conservationist David Brower in his book *Let the Mountains Talk, Let the Rivers Run.* "It is a hidden subsidy that these companies can come onto public land, clearcut the forests, and not even have to plant more. Or, if they plant more, to brag about the number of trees but forget to mention they are replacing an insignificant fraction of the volume they have removed. It will then be necessary for taxpayers, for generations to come, to cover the cost of replacing the excellence of say, a 500-year-old tree, and its surroundings. This is an enormous subsidy."

A subsidy that Congress has refused to curtail. Here is what the $1 billion frittered away by the Forest Service might have bought instead:

- The hiring of 23,116 police officers
- The employment of 22,785 new schoolteachers
- The cost of recovering eight imperiled species (the bald eagle, Florida scrub jay, Florida panther, West Indian manatee, American peregrine falcon, chinook salmon, red-cockaded woodpecker, and northern spotted owl, the last two of which were designated indicator species by the Forest Service to warn when management practices were having a harmful effect). Furthermore, the Congress of Newt Gingrich cut funding to the Forest Service's scientific research program so that field biologists would not have the money to identify plants and animals that are likely to suffer and save millions by prescribing foresighted measures to prevent declines of imperiled animals.

Even ex-Chief of the Forest Service Max Peterson, who cut more timber on his watch than any other chief, was quoted in 1989 as saying, "Anybody could have figured out on the back of an envelope that the rate of timber harvest cannot be sustained." How lopsided is the agency's focus? As of 1996, there were roughly twelve thousand logging-oriented foresters on the payroll compared to just one hundred scientists specializing in ecosystem management. It doesn't take a genius to figure out where the agency's priorities still lie if the perception is that there may be a whole lot more timber left to cut.

Only months after Peterson made his candid confession, U.S. District Court Judge William Dwyer ruled in a lawsuit filed by the National Audubon Society to save old-growth forests on behalf of the spotted owl that federal agencies had demonstrated persistent and deliberate violations of environmental laws designed to protect wildlife.

"Ecosystem management isn't about getting the science right; it's about getting the politics right. We just don't seem to get it," Iverson says. "By and large we are working against the public interest with appropriations riders that created salvage logging. Jack Ward Thomas as a scientist himself should have been blasting away condemning it every time he went on the Hill and defending the law. Instead, both he and Jim Lyons [the assistant chief of the Forest Service] were beating the bully pulpit of timber salvage and excluding people from the planning process, which is how responsible decisions are made."

Iverson says the environmental movement also shares in the blame by making tactical mistakes and spawning enough citizen anger to give rise to Gingrich's Contract with America. "The environmental community, while having done wonderful things over the years, got in bed with the left-wing limousine liberals in the Beltway. That unholy alliance got people into a lot of problems. All of a sudden, when the Republicans were able to gain some standing in Congress and apply pressure on the White House and the Forest Service, environmentalists found themselves shut out of the game, to the detriment of the environment and the millions of people the organizations represent."

"Real change in the Forest Service should not depend on its chief alone," wrote Melinda Pierce, a public lands lobbyist for the Sierra Club, in *Sierra Magazine*. "It will require sweeping structural reform, continued litigation [to keep the agency in compliance with its own laws], reduction of consumer demand for forest products, and as ever, constant pressure from an informed public."

American Forests, a citizens' conservation group founded in 1875, decided to commission a public opinion poll. One of its questions, presented to one thousand registered voters nationwide, was who was more trustworthy in presenting arguments that form the basis of public opinions. The results are as follows: 59 percent trusted scientists employed by universities and federal forest agencies, compared to 21 percent who had faith in scientists representing environmental groups and just 7 percent who thought scientists hired by the timber industry were persuasive. The only constituency not trusting Forest Service biologists is the Forest Service itself.

In congressional testimony, DeBonis said that incidents of quashing agency scientists were not isolated occurrences. "One of the most insidious aspects of the agency's mismanagement in recent years is the pressure and harassment applied against agency employees like wildlife biologists and other resource specialists.

"This pressure is an attempt to intimidate employees into approving or 'rubber-stamping' ecologically damaging projects and excessive timber cutting and grazing. When employees speak out against these practices internally, they are often ignored or told to get in line. If the employee insists on being heard, then additional pressure is applied by intimidating or ignoring the employee.

"Their reports may be changed or altered, and employees are often verbally abused and harassed into silence. Often employees are pressured to move or quit. FSEEE and PEER receive numerous calls each month from distressed employees who are seeking advice on how they can retain their integrity and ethics in job situations they cannot tolerate anymore.

"Many biologists receive so much pressure they refer to themselves as 'combat biologists.' The sad face of the matter is that the combat they are referring to is with their own supervisors, rangers, and forest management teams."

DeBonis went on to describe the case of Tom Lake, a wilderness ranger in the Modoc National Forest who was harassed after he attempted to inform his supervisors about misuse of wilderness management funds and illegal activities occurring within a wilderness area Lake managed. DeBonis also told of the case of Frances Mangels, a wildlife biologist who was pressured, harassed, and intimidated into altering reports to allow timber sales in sensitive wildlife habitat important to spotted owls and bald eagles. He offered a synopsis of the case of Buzz Williams, a former river ranger in the Sumpter

National Forest in the Southeast who was intimidated, harassed, and discharged for being outspoken about environmentally damaging timber sales within the corridor of the Chattooga River, a congressionally designated wild and scenic river. He also related how Tina Barnes, Williams's immediate supervisor, was intimidated, sexually harassed, demoted, and forced to resign when she supported Williams in his allegations.

One of the most blatant cases involved Karen Heiman, a botanist in a national forest in North Carolina who was fired because she refused to conduct endangered-plant surveys during the winter months when there was snow on the ground. She had allegedly been asked to do the survey at that time because her supervisor knew that if any plants were there, they could jeopardize a timber sale. There are hundreds of other such cases, DeBonis says. "These are not acceptable ways for bosses to be treating their employees, let alone bureaucrats who hold the fate of important government scientists in the palm of their hand. What does this say about our government?"

DeBonis's advice to young greenhorn foresters coming out of college: Stay professional at all costs. Don't let anyone above you demand that you do their dirty work. When you are assigned to complete an environmental assessment, don't change it to suit someone else's (including a conservation group's) agenda, and always keep an original copy and get your orders in writing.

"Too many young people allow themselves to be manipulated so that by the time they get ten years in they don't know right from wrong anymore, and if they do, they can't make waves for fear of being blackmailed. It takes guts to stay professional," says Dave Iverson. "Unfortunately, the quiet ones that perpetuate the lies get promoted, and that's the reason why it will take a major overhaul of the system, which Jeff DeBonis is trying to bring before the American public. The only way the Forest Service will survive is if it heals itself."

~

So now we have arrived near the end with a question: Should the U.S. Forest Service be destroyed and rebuilt with a new modern conscience in mind, or can internal reform overcome its behavioral and fiscal dysfunction?

"Jack Ward Thomas didn't put enough emphasis on cleaning out the old guard, and he didn't have enough people to whom he could offer his trust. He's a green-shirted field guy. He wasn't about to take on the agency in a radical way, but that is what's needed. The only way to make significant change is to go in and be brutal and clean house," DeBonis says.

"Now you have retrenchment in the Congress. The old guard is sitting back and lighting its cigars and loving it. Personally, I think the climate today is as bad as its ever been and will probably get worse. Every time the agency gets into a high cut mode, which is what started with the salvage logging rider, they cut more fragile, more delicate areas better left alone. They are getting in the last refuges for a number of species, wiping out the last bits that are just too important. The only way to stop it is to disband the Forest Service entirely like they did in New Zealand."

In an astute examination of the Forest Service, Steven L. Yaffee of the University of Michigan published an essay in the journal *Conservation Biology* titled "Why Environmental Policy Nightmares Recur." Specifically, Yaffee explored the evolution of the spotted owl controversy, but he noted that the mishandling of biological information has ramifications for numerous other policy issues:

Agency leaders knew the owl was threatened, old growth was the issue, and changing federal forest management was necessary, but they were unable to respond effectively. They avoided learning more about the owl and its management implications, refused to focus on the underlying issue of old-growth protection and management, tried to put the issue into standard operating procedures that were not intended to deal with such issues, and aggressively sought to put off choices into the future. No doubt powerful political forces opposed effective agency action, and the stakes involved in various outcomes were extraordinarily high, but the net effect of the nature of the choices made through the history of the owl dispute was to embroil local, regional, and national institutions in a controversy that was more costly than necessary.

Meaningful action is waylaid by stalling and more stalling to justify the stalling. The tendency for any bureaucracy is always to solve problems by expanding bureaucracy. Public participation is used as a subterfuge for pretending to make difficult decisions. How many times have we all witnessed government responding?

Observed Yaffee: "The most frightening aspect of the owl case is not that the [Forest Service] made some bad choices about not moving aggressively on owl protection in the early 1980s; rather, it is that a similar organization [I might add here, the Park Service, BLM, Fish and Wildlife Service, Bureau of Reclamation, or for that matter any federal or state resource agency] dealing with a comparable choice would have a good chance of making the same mistake again. Observing the Forest Service leaders in the late 1980s, one could sense that in their dreams they must see themselves walking down a path that never ends and that at times feels and looks exactly like their starting point."

Reformers in all of the agencies face a Sisyphean challenge. The debacle of the spotted owl still echoes loudly, and it suggests that true reinvention of government cannot succeed without some wholesale changes in the political process. The more science is held captive to the interpretations of Congress or political appointees, regardless of their party affiliation, the more the truth is fated to perpetual subjugation. Science will remain a market commodity, bought and sold, molded and manufactured to fit the needs of those who control political access. And given the spans of political careers, the caprice of leaders, and spasms in the economy, outcomes are never viewed over the long term. Studying the Forest Service, Yaffee identified what he called "five behavioral biases that lead to policy impasses and poor choices":

1. Short-term rationality out competes long-term rationality; a tendency to make decisions that are rational and effective in the short term, yet counterproductive and ineffective over the long term.
2. Competitive behavior drives out cooperative behavior; a tendency to promote competitive behaviors at the expense of cooperative actions, yet often cooperation is needed to find good solutions.
3. Fragmentation of interests and values; a proclivity to split the different elements of a society, avoiding the integration of interests and values necessary to craft an effective course of action.
4. Fragmentation of responsibilities and authorities: a tendency to divide those responsible for resource management, diminishing accountability, and ensuring that management strategies are often piece-meal solutions to crosscutting problems.

5. Fragmentation of information and knowledge: a proclivity to fragment what is known about a situation and its context so decision makers make bad choices because they are operating with inadequate information.

In 1997 the General Accounting Office published what many considered to be a landmark report to Congress titled "Forest Service Decisionmaking: A Framework for Improving Performance." A scathing overview of the report begins with the fiscal problems and moves into the realm of behavior, the kind to which DeBonis often alluded but to deaf ears. Not only do taxpayers need to demand massive reform in the Forest Service; we cannot afford not to. The report begins,

> The decision-making process used by the Department of Agriculture's Forest Service in carrying out its mission is costly and time-consuming, and the agency often fails to achieve its planned objectives. The agency has spent over 20 years and over $250 million developing multi-year plans for managing national forests. It also spends about $250 million a year for environmental studies to support individual projects. However, according to an internal Forest Service report, inefficiencies within this process cost up to $100 million a year at the project level alone. In addition, by the time the agency has completed its decision-making, it often finds that it is unable to achieve the plans' objectives or implement planned projects because of new information and events, as well as changes in funding and natural conditions.

A liability plaguing Forest Service leadership is its inability to plan for the long term and its myopic, almost isolationist methods of plotting its management course. "Issues that transcend the agency's administrative boundaries and jurisdiction also affect the efficiency and effectiveness of the agency's decision making. In particular," the report continues, "the Forest Service has had difficulty reconciling the administrative boundaries of the national forests with the boundaries of natural systems, such as watershed and vegetative and animal communities, both in planning and in assessing the effects of federal and nonfederal activities on the environment."

Besides its structural inability to fully grasp ecosystem management, the agency is a whirling dervish of procrastination, costing taxpayers money by its constant demand that Congress give it more funding for studies, the results of which are rarely implemented. For example, the report states, in 1991 Congress asked the Forest Service to develop a multiyear program to reduce the costs of its timber program by not less than 5 percent per year. "The Forest Service responded to those and other concerns by undertaking two major examinations of its timber program and is now preparing to undertake a third. However, with no incentive to act, the agency has not implemented any of the recommended improvements agency wide. In the interim, the costs associated with preparing and administering timber sales have continued to rise. As a result, for fiscal year 1998, the agency is requesting $12 million (six percent) more for timber sale management than was appropriated for fiscal year 1997 while proposing to offer 0.4 billion board feet (10 percent) less timber for sale."

Obviously, the answer is not to sell more timber. The problem of the Forest Service is symptomatic of the way government functions as a whole. So long as the incentives are to waste money and natural resources rather than conserving them, how realistically can we as a nation ever expect to achieve ecological balance in the nation's forests? This is the argument advanced by well-known forest economist Randal O'Toole of the Thoreau Institute in Oak Grove, Oregon. O'Toole has written brilliantly about the Forest Service in a number of forums, most notably his book *Reforming the Forest Service*. He believes that dismantling the agency, as proposed by DeBonis, won't work. "The danger is that if you kill it to save it, you end up with something a lot worse," O'Toole tells me. "Jeff DeBonis has a lot of great ideas, but he never figured out the role of incentives. They play an important role in shaping the goals of the agency."

In a newspaper column for the *Seattle Times* titled "Politicizing the Forest Service," O'Toole wrote, "The U.S.D.A. Forest Service will be one hundred years old in 2005—if it survives that long. There is a good chance it won't. Instead, the next Secretary of the Interior will probably propose to merge the Forest Service into the Department of the Interior. ... Similar proposals from Interior secretaries such as Harold Ickes in the 1930s or Cecil Andrus in the 1970s were met with stiff opposition. Environmentalists, timber companies, ranchers, and other national forest users all saw the 'independence' of the Forest Service as something worth protecting."

He noted that when Pinchot shaped the Forest Service in 1905 out of a cluster of forestland reserves, he intended the agency to be managed "by experts, not by politicians." Keeping it in the Department of Agriculture instead of Interior afforded it a degree of insulation from politics. Another sacred aspect of the agency was that its chief be picked from within the ranks, serve for life, and have a hand in picking a replacement. "Clinton changed that tradition when he replaced Dale Robertson with Jack Ward Thomas," O'Toole wrote. "Thomas was a lifetime Forest Service employee, but he lacked the rank and expertise of previous Forest Service chiefs. One result was that he was unable to prevent meddling by administration officials. Firing Robertson was the administration's first step down the proverbial slippery slope towards politicizing the agency. It has now taken the next step."

Indeed, the 1997 GAO report confirms O'Toole's assertions: "While the agency continues to reduce its emphasis on consumption and increase its emphasis on conservation, the Congress has never explicitly accepted this shift in emphasis or acknowledged its effects on the availability of other uses of national forests. If the Forest Service is to be held accountable for its performance, the agency will need to consult with the Congress on its strategic long-term goals, as the Government Performance and Results Act requires. This process may entail identifying legislative changes that are needed to clarify or modify the Congress's intent and expectation."

Until that happens, however, the Congress will continue to be influenced by resource-extraction zealots and a Forest Service bureaucracy that treats environmental protection as a blind spot. "During field visits, we found that timber production still often receives more emphasis than other uses and still plays a significant role in individual performance management, career development, and play and promotion," GAO investigators wrote. "As one district ranger said, 'of course, all targets are important, but everyone understands which one is considered by the agency to the most important—timber.'"

O'Toole asserts that current chief Mike Dombeck, who worked for both the Forest Service and Bureau of Land Management, is "little more than a yes-man to the Clinton administration." And here's the rub, that without addressing the conundrum of economic incentives in the Forest Service, any current or future chief will be doomed to fail in attempts at reform. Dombeck should not be dismissed yet.

Early in his tenure as chief, Dombeck won a couple of key show-downs with the Congressional delegations from timber states. Moderate Republicans parted company with their radical, right-wing colleagues in the West and joined Democrats in fighting a salvage logging proposal intended to aggressively topple more trees under the guise of promoting "Forest Health" and wild fire prevention. "It's not about forest health. It is about a waste of taxpayer money and a devastation of our national forests," proclaimed U.S. Representative George Miller, a California Democrat who was joined by fifty-one Republicans in voting down the salvage logging bill sponsored by U.S. Rep. Bob Smith, a Republican from Oregon who is chairman of the House Agriculture Committee.

Dombeck also received de-facto Congressional backing with the defeats of bills to prop up below-cost timber sales and taxpayer-subsidized road construction into virgin drainages. Despite insidious resistance from the old-guard timber bosses and a plethora of former agency engineers, including former engineer-chief R. Max Peterson, Dombeck is slowly but surely cultivating a groundswell among the Forest Service rank and file. The silent majority—the sleeping giant of agency esprit de corps—is walking up and saying enough is enough.

When Dombeck said he intended to initiate an "ethical era" in the Forest Service, where honest science and good conscience are openly rewarded and bad science and corrupt deeds openly punished, the silent majority believed that perhaps a deliverer had arrived. If Dombeck proves to be unsuccessful in reforming the agency and steering it on a new course, many say they will join him in going down with the ship, rather than fighting for its survival under corrupt regimes and partisan micromanagement. Even for devout subscribers of Forest Service tradition, killing a corrupt, environmentally destructive agency is preferred to watching public support wither. If they can't feel proud working for the agency, DeBonis says, then the agency has no reason to exist.

"The Clinton administration thought that more political chiefs would effectively counter political meddling by Congress. Yet Congress has far more power over the agency than the president because it has power over the budget, which effectively shapes the agency's incentives," O'Toole says. "Politicizing the Forest Service will be bad for national forests and all their users. The flaw in Pinchot's design was not that he insulated the Forest Service from the president but that he failed to insulate the national forests from Congress—in particular, from the appropriations committees. For the last fifty years, appropriators have funded the national forests mainly as pork."

O'Toole says that ethics, adherence to existing laws, and good science depend on incentives that reward individual forest supervisors and district rangers who focus on delivering them. DeBonis counters that decisionmakers shouldn't have to be bribed to have a green ethic and that cleaning the house of timber beasts may be faster than recalibrating the Forest Service appropriations process in Congress. O'Toole worries that if a new cabinet-level Department of Public Lands is created, many of the 120 existing Forest Service administration units would be sacrificed to timber interests or other forms of industry.

"In short, national forests operate under a Soviet-style system that rewards managers for losing money on timber and penalizes them for earning a profit or for emphasizing resources such as wildlife or recreation," O'Toole wrote. "But put the best people in a Soviet-style bureaucracy and they still end up acting like Soviet bureaucrats, making national forest management expensive, inefficient, and slow to respond to new ideas."

O'Toole and DeBonis agree that neither the Clinton administration nor Congress are likely to initiate change. Newt Gingrich's reformist Contract with America has been a sham, PEER executive director Jeff Ruch says. "The Republicans came into Congress promising open government, but the way the GOP has chosen to operate is more behind closed doors and at the beck and call of insider lobbyists," he said. "The recent Congresses will be remembered for creating an environment where federal workers trying to uphold the law were held in contempt. More than any other preceding it, the last Congress has legislated on bills that the public never have an opportunity to comment on. At least when the Democrats controlled Congress there were public hearings, but that has not happened with the Republicans. They refuse to hold public hearings."

The most stalwart of conservatives know this. John Baden, who founded the Foundation for Research on Economics and the Environment, a conservative think tank, astutely recognizes that the challenge is enormous. "Character alone cannot consistently produce good policy," Baden wrote in his organization's newsletter, which is received by most of the prominent Republicans and Democrats on Capitol Hill. "Over time, the incentives generated by institutions usually trump ethics. The Forest Service is a friendly environment for those who think science should be subservient to budgetary imperatives. Forest Service employees whose ethics lead them to think otherwise find that promotions are elusive. But the Forest Service is not unique."

The revolution that Jeff DeBonis started must come from within, and it must be a personal decision embraced by every rank-and-file worker on the public payroll. "Jeff DeBonis demonstrated that public agencies can be pushed off of their command-and-control model through the activism of their employees and by creating an organization that lets the public have access to the expertise of public employees," Ruch says. "Jeff wasn't forced out of the Forest Service, he decided to leave and found another organization. The whole premise of PEER is that with a little outside assistance you can help facilitate change inside the agency. Our goal is to keep people in agencies and avert the situation where people have to fall on their sword."

~

Postscript: Autumn again. It is some five years after I first met Jeff DeBonis in person. He is in jeans and a flannel shirt, wearing a tool belt around his waist, assessing structural integrity and reform not of the Forest Service but of his own home. Newly married, carried by a light spirit that had been lacking as the battle wore him down, he is trying his hand at carpentry in an old residence that he intends to restore to its former glory. Layer by layer, he removes outer sheetrock and paneling and linoleum and carpet that have covered original moldings and fixtures, high ceilings, and hardwood floors. The interior of this old home, a picture of magnificence, has been shrouded by the changing tastes of its previous inhabitants.

DeBonis left PEER when he felt the symptoms of burnout approaching. He may never work in government service or the public arena again. But he is content because he realizes there is more to life than conflict. As Dave Iverson says, one hundred years from now when the history of the Forest Service is written, there will be a chapter on DeBonis describing his crusading as a freedom fighter.

Ebullient, as the rays of afternoon sun fall through the stained glass into his home, DeBonis feels connected to the people who occupied this space before him.

A Grizzly Future

*Only those able to see the pageant of
evolution can be expected to value its
theater, the wilderness, or its outstanding achievement, the grizzly.*
                    —Aldo Leopold

THE CALLIGRAPHY OF impressions looks almost human. Wide
and flat, outlined by a sheen of sparkling, frozen water, the solitary
diagonal tracks emerge from a fog of steam rising off the creek bottom and detour up a barren mountain pitch. They cross a glacial
moraine, meander around a bramble of juniper, proceed steadily
through snowy talus, and dead-end, finally, in the exposed root-
tendrils of an ancient, warp-trunked whitebark pine tree.

With the afternoon high temperature in northwest Wyoming
hovering at five degrees below zero, it is late in the year for a grizzly bear to be taking a saunter. But food has been scarce. This mama,
a pregnant sow with twin cubs growing inside her belly, reaches her
den after striking out on a circumnavigation of territory. Hers is a
desperate, hyperphagic quest for calories. To the frosty high meadows for yampa root and camas; to the windblown ridgetops for a
failed crop of whitebark pine nuts; to the lowland thickets for serv-
iceberries; and through the dangerous riparian corridors of the national forest, where humans carrying loud sticks always leave behind
fresh elk and mule-deer meat. Occasionally they leave behind dead
bears, too.

Gorging herself instinctively, like an NFL lineman attempting to
keep his weight above 320 pounds, she has covered 250 miles in less
than a month before reaching the den for ninety days of slumber.
Coated in creamy, tawny fur, she will sleep, having no understanding that on this frigid December afternoon in 1993, an alarming
message affecting the future of her kind has resounded from a
human bureaucratic fiefdom hundreds of miles south in Lakewood,
Colorado.

At the annual year-end summit of the Interagency Grizzly Bear Committee, a consortium of state and federal wildlife managers from the northern Rockies, a remarkable decision has been announced. Offering no advance warning, committee members voted unanimously to appease antigrizzly forces in the Greater Yellowstone Ecosystem by resolving to delete *Ursus arctos horribilis* from the federal list of threatened species. The move, on many levels, represented a dramatic shift in how the federal government approaches protection of the most famous population of wild grizzlies in the world. It was only a decade earlier that representatives of many of the same agencies had pronounced, by signing off on a memo, that it appeared the grizzly was doomed to regional extinction in Yellowstone National Park and the surrounding twenty-five thousand square miles of public land.

The sudden reversal to "delisting" the great bear left environmentalists stunned. In layman's terms, what the decision means is that the bear's protected status could be downgraded not long after the next millennium begins so that oil and natural-gas developers, loggers, and livestock grazers can penetrate public lands previously off limits. It could result in a sport hunt of grizzlies in Wyoming, Montana, and Idaho; spawn approval for ranchers to shoot grizzlies on public lands if the predators harass their cows; and afford leniency to poachers now facing the possibility of large fines and time in prison if they put a bruin in their gun sights and pull the trigger. Most important, it gives a green light to continued habitat destruction.

"We were struck speechless and frankly outraged by the Bear Committee's cavalier support for delisting the grizzly," said an incredulous Brian Peck, who attended the meeting on behalf of the National Audubon Society and several other conservation groups. "The committee's own lead scientist, Chris Servheen, said publicly that because of doubts about the status of the bear, delisting wouldn't even be considered for another ten years at the earliest. But by the time he and the other good-old-boy bureaucrats were finished, it became very clear that this meeting had been a political setup from the start. It proves that the whole process of managing bears is built on subterfuge and mistrust. The Bear Committee acted quickly, and it arrogantly skirted public scrutiny because its members knew the science allegedly justifying their position doesn't hold up.

"Of course," Peck added, "they ignored their own best expert."

Conspicuously absent from the meeting was the man regarded as Yellowstone's premier grizzly bear biologist—a field scientist who had been pressured to leave his post studying bears only a few months earlier. For daring to say that bear habitat should be stalwartly protected from invasions by timber and oil companies, logging roads, mines, and human development on public and private lands surrounding Yellowstone National Park, David Mattson was cast into professional exile from the special government team assigned to monitor bears on the ground. His forecasts pertaining to the health of Yellowstone's bear population are far from the sanguine picture politicians and special interest groups resentful of the Endangered Species Act portray in the late 1990s.

Why is a decision announced by the Interagency Grizzly Bear Committee in 1993 important? Because scientists believe that it reveals what the bureaucrats in charge of bear survival are currently thinking, how much they're willing to gamble with the Yellowstone population, and the fact that many of them apparently believe the process of removing federal protection has already begun. To Mattson and his supporters, the gist is that bears are now more vulnerable than ever. At the center of the controversy is what Mattson describes as "the deeply flawed arithmetic" some government biologists employ to determine whether the population of Yellowstone grizzlies is growing or declining, in good shape or bad.

"I do admit that I have little patience with the smoke and illusion that constitutes the so-called science being used to justify the removal of grizzly bears from federal protection in the Yellowstone ecosystem," Mattson says. "If anything, we should be expanding the net of protection, not pulling it in and claiming victory. What victory will we achieve if we have grizzlies here in fifty years but doom them to extinction in one hundred by our unsubstantiated optimism today? If you ask me, that's a false victory."

Before his bizarre indoctrination in the politics of grizzly bear management, Mattson never thought of himself as one who would help lead a new movement in the nascent discipline of conservation biology. Nor did he expect that the differences between short-term preservation of large carnivores and long-term viability of such plans would leave him poignantly in the middle of a national philosophical debate. The outcome has practical scientific consequences as well as spiritual implications in the context of Native Americana. It was, after all, the aboriginal elders of this continent who said that whenever a decision is reached, its consequences should be considered over the span of seven generations. Figuring roughly twenty-five years per generation, the focus here extends to about the year 2175.

One night during a snowstorm in a western Idaho college town where he resides in exile, Mattson tells me he is collaborating with other prominent scientists, including Craig Pease, a wildlife demography guru at the University of Texas, to develop a new approach to studying—and essentially counting—bears based upon the government's own data. Mattson and Pease's initiative is exactly the kind of stuff that led the government to brand them a threat, though they are not alone in their criticism of current grizzly bear management. No fewer than two dozen other prominent independent scientists in the vanguard of conservation biology, including the modern godfather of conservation biology, Michael Soule, and his protégé Reed Noss, say the Interagency Grizzly Bear Committee is trying to cook numbers and cover up the truth. They not only charge that the government's plan to delist grizzlies is premature, they also assert that the recently completed Grizzly Bear Recovery Plan and its author, Chris Servheen, ignored vital information that Mattson had spent more than ten years publishing in scientific journals. Servheen, a biologist with the U.S. Fish and Wildlife Service and the man considered the government's "grizzly czar," is also said to have been instrumental in forcing Mattson out, an allegation he denies.

Just 150 years ago, perhaps 100,000 grizzlies roamed from central Mexico to the Arctic Ocean. Today the species in the lower forty-eight states occupies less than 2 percent of its former range and maybe one thousand individual animals are clustered primarily into two relic island populations: the Greater Yellowstone Ecosystem and the Northern Continental Divide Ecosystem anchored by Glacier National Park. The reason for the decline is that *Homo sapiens*, the bears' chief rival predator, hasn't done a very good job of coexisting with them. The call of alarm is not new to our generation, though it has grown more desperate as large carnivores disappear around the world in spasms of extinction. The question is, do we value grizzlies enough to modify our own destructive behavior?

"The grizzly needs protection at once, needs your active interest now. He is making his last stand and is surrounded by relentless foes," wrote naturalist Enos Mills in his 1919 book *The Grizzly— Our Greatest Wild Animal.* "Protection only will save him and enable him to perpetuate himself. Without the grizzly the wilds would be dull, the canyon and the crag would lose their eloquent appeal. This wild uncrowned king has won his place in nature which no other animal can fill. We need the grizzly bear."

In the government's Grizzly Bear Recovery Plan, Chris Servheen and his coauthors say that taxpayers will spend an estimated $26 million trying to restore or sustain bear numbers in the ecosystems mentioned above and four other areas of the West, including the Selway-Bitterroot Wilderness of central Idaho and the North Cascades ecosystem in Washington state. Critics say the government is squandering its financial resources on voodoo science.

~

Snow is falling in Moscow. The streets are nearly deserted. Nursing a glass of lager as the tape recorder rolls, Mattson sits with me in the dark corner of a hotel bar, lamenting the chain of events that led to his purge. It is easy, perhaps, to draw a Soviet-style analogy to our setting, given the circumstances, but Mattson and I have not rendezvoused in the Russian capital. We are twelve thousand miles to the west in a small Idaho farming community and college town of the same name. Mattson is in academic seclusion, and his supporters want him to return.

Mattson does not fit the profile of a trademark macho grizzly bear biologist. A docile, even-keeled family man with a wife and two kids, this fortysomething naturalist is lean, cerebral, and impressively thoughtful. Serious and pensive, he has a silver stud in his left earlobe, hiking boots on his feet, wire-rimmed glasses, short, thinning hair, and a penchant for reading poetry when he isn't out searching for bear spoor and rotting elk carcasses a day's march from the nearest sign of civilization. Mattson has covered thousands of miles on foot and written more scientific papers on the grizzly than any other person since the bear was placed on the Endangered Species List as a threatened animal two decades ago. He has bridged the art and folklore of the beast with its science. He is both a left- and a right-brained thinker.

Mattson has overt empathy for his subjects, and it stems from his own childhood on the Great Plains. Born in 1954, he grew up in the cow town of Rapid City, South Dakota, but spent considerable time hiking through the Black Hills. "I had in South Dakota about as close as anybody comes to experiencing a sacred place," he says of a family cabin in the wooded mountains. "Most of us have them, inviolate retreats that we hold in our minds and set off limits to certain kinds of development because it is incongruent with the values we hold in our hearts."

When Mattson left South Dakota for the University of Idaho at Moscow in 1972, nothing energized him more than field research, except perhaps a great work of literature. "I didn't realize that the profession of wildlife biologist even existed," he says, telling how he naturally fell into line with people involved in biology and wildlife at the university because they enjoyed the same things he did. It took him seven years to earn an undergraduate degree in forestry and botany because he kept taking jobs in field research, spending sixty days a summer in the bush, mostly in plant studies in the national forests of Idaho. Near the time of his graduation, he heard about a project sponsored by the Yellowstone Interagency Grizzly Bear Study Team that called for conducting radio telemetry work to track the movements of collared bears. His new boss, Richard Knight, was impressed by Mattson's crackerjack mind and agreed to supervise a proposed master's project on wetland vegetation relating to grizzly bear nutrition.

Knight knew immediately that Mattson was different from the other biologists whom he had hired. Mattson had no fetish for "controlling" bears. He wanted the animals to show him the answers. "Most people that go into wildlife biology are focused on the animal. They want to get their fingers on the fur. They want to be trappers. They want to be out trapping and drugging and handling the bears," Mattson says. "I had no interest in that at all. I wanted to come at grizzly bear research from another angle. Dick recognized that and gave me a lot of encouragement. I will always respect him for giving me my start." No one knew it then, but Knight would eventually turn on him in a traumatic encounter that both now regret.

Bert Harting met Mattson in the early 1980s while both were working toward master's degrees and conducting bear research for the Yellowstone Interagency Grizzly Bear Study Team headed by

Knight. "I recognized right off how exceptional an individual Dave was in a number of respects—in addition to being one of the finest botanists you've ever run across, Dave could identify anything." Harting says. "Hand him a weathered toothpick and he could decipher the kind of tree it came from. He didn't fit the usual mold of a wildlife biologist in that he had a gentle, zenful side to him instead of the hard-ass Daniel Boone persona that was generally favored by most large-carnivore biologists."

Harting says that after a few years Mattson was singled out for the task of trying to synthesize years' worth of disparate data that had accumulated since the grizzly bear study team was formed in 1973. "Dave's involvement in building an ecological profile of the Yellowstone grizzly was the first time that somebody took it upon themselves to congeal all of the information the study team had relating to habitat use, food sources, and locations of bear scat," Harting notes. "It was fascinating the level of insights that Dave had, things Dick Knight had never thought of trying. He possesses this incisive perception and ability to divine things from the data that I don't believe anyone else would have been able to do. Patterns emerged in bear behavior that just wouldn't have been revealed through any kind of dry statistical analysis, regardless of how sophisticated the person examining it was."

Mattson pursued several trains of thought that at first appeared somewhat convoluted to those around him, but as he refined his preliminary analysis, his associates took note. He discovered that two completely different types of bear populations exist—those along the front country (roadside areas), where people can see them, and backcountry wilderness bears that are elusive and difficult to track. He concluded that the bruins existing near civilization, in many cases, are younger animals who have been forced out of prime remote habitat by more dominant bears into areas where they are vulnerable. They represent the largest percentage of bruins that die because of run-ins with people. The backcountry bears, meanwhile, are those with the best chance for survival because they make a habit of distancing themselves from people, or at least travel stealthily near civilization.

Mattson meticulously documented what bears were eating, when and where, and how human activities affected their behavior. Charged many times by bears, he developed almost a sixth sense that allowed him to trek through their space without eliciting hostility. In assembling a complete view of grizzly ecology, he proved that roads and development, previously thought to be largely benign, were actually displacing grizzlies from critical food sources. These hypotheses were tested by tracking radio-collared animals.

"The really impressive thing about Dave is not just his science," says Harting, who wrote a comprehensive document, "The Grizzly Bear Compendium," while working for both the National Wildlife Federation and the Fish and Wildlife Service from 1985 to 1987. "While I can say from my perspective that he has been impeccably attentive to detail, I don't think he's one who clings to a hypothesis out of ego or a favored research agenda either," Harting adds. "Dave is flexible and not closed-minded. When the data runs counter to his hunches, he admits it and readjusts his thinking."

Which is a reputation markedly different from the government's. Some alumni of the Interagency Grizzly Bear Study Team believe that Mattson's acumen is a threat to Chris Servheen's ego.

∽

Grizzly bears have been on a noticeable nomadic prowl in recent years around Yellowstone, wandering into places where they hadn't been seen in decades, prompting locals to believe there are more bears on the prowl out there. Bruins have broken into cabins along the North Fork of the Shoshone River west of Cody, Wyoming. They have left tracks in the muddy river drainages around Jackson Hole and attacked cows in the Gros Ventre mountains. They have ambled within a few miles of urban Bozeman, Montana, and are reportedly colonizing the Crazy Mountains, the Gravelly Range on the west side of the Madison Valley, the Caribou Mountains, the Tobacco Roots, and the Bighorns and making inroads into northern sections of the Wind Rivers. Geographically, those areas are hundreds of miles apart. In the locales where bears are appearing, they are also getting shot. Since the early 1990s alone at least five dozen bears and a fairly high percentage of breeding-age females—the bedrock of the population—are known to have died.

Mattson believes the burgeoning number of grizzly sightings may be due not to a rapidly expanding and healthful population but possibly to a desperate and stressed one striking out in search of food, giving the false impression of ballooning numbers of bears. For him and his large group of supporters, it is a frightening paradox. Disaster may be imminent if the bear population, instead of growing into stability—as Servheen claims—is actually biologically static or losing ground. Such a miscalculation might not show up for several years, and by that time, when there is even more human population pressure squeezing the ecosystem's edges, there may not be opportunities for reviving the species—particularly when the best bear habitat is less than secure.

The best bear habitat in Greater Yellowstone, after all, is found not in the sixteen million acres of public land but on the two million acres of private land abutting it. All of the major lowland river valleys beyond Yellowstone's borders are dominated by human settlement and livestock ranching. Correspondingly, setting aside for a moment the high number of bears shot by hunters, the most significant black holes for bears—also known as population sink areas—are in developed enclaves that bears cannot avoid and usually cannot escape from without being killed. *Black holes* is a colloquial term for places where bears go but do not come out alive.

A bad omen is that the twenty counties comprising the Greater Yellowstone region are among the fastest growing in the West, with new subdivisions, sprawling dream homes, and recreational resorts being proposed on a weekly basis in areas into which bears are expanding their range. Plenty of estimates are being kicked around these days in the scientific community for how many grizzlies actually inhabit the Yellowstone ecosystem and whether or not the population has stabilized since its downward spiral toward extinction began in the early 1970s. Certainly one way to assess the health of grizzlies in the nation's oldest national park, long synonymous with Yogi and Booboo, is through the establishment of bear numbers. Some say there is a minimum of 229 bears, others insist on at least 270, and still others claim the number is closer to 300, 350, or 400. The problem is that no one knows for sure, yet plans by Servheen to delist the bear are being based on the most optimistic—and possibly frightening—projections.

Under Servheen's guidance, the Interagency Grizzly Bear Committee established the following criteria for a biologically "recovered" bear population: (1) at least 158 bears widely distributed across a core bear-protection zone; (2) human-caused bear deaths cannot exceed a prescribed limit over two consecutive years; (3) deaths of mature females of reproducing age can not exceed 30 percent of total annual mortality, or three breeding females a year; (4) female grizzlies must inhabit at least sixteen of the region's eighteen established "bear management units."

Mattson says these numbers are not only arbitrary and virtually meaningless but politically capricious. With these criteria, Servheen and other members of the Bear Committee say the goals are already being met. "In terms of numbers of grizzly bears, there are more grizzly bears in the Yellowstone ecosystem today than when John and Frank Craighead were researching in the area in the 1960s," Servheen wrote in a rebuttal to criticism. "The ... total population estimate made by the Craigheads for the late 1960s was 229. The minimum population estimate for the Yellowstone ecosystem as of 1993 is 229." In 1994, Servheen said the minimum estimate had risen to 270 bruins, and he now believes it is probably closer to four hundred.

"Okay," Mattson asks, "so what? Even if it were true, what does that mean? We don't know what that means for the population's long-term prospects because part of the problem with the recovery plan is the people who wrote it haven't made that connection either. There is no long-term strategy."

Mattson uses the analogy of a person driving cross-country from Seattle to Boston without a road map and trying to get there by hunch, relying on signs as they emerge on the highway. Another scientist who still works under Servheen offers a different metaphor: "The Bear Committee has boasted that it is doing chin-ups with bear recovery after lowering the bar down to the chest level." All the while that Fish and Wildlife Service officials speak optimistically of justification for delisting, bears continue to die in disturbing numbers.

Internationally renowned conservation biologist Mark Shaffer, who has written extensively on grizzly bear ecology and served as an adviser to the Fish and Wildlife Service as well as the Wilderness Society and the Nature Conservancy, says the government has egregiously underestimated the population size needed for viability. He believes that two thousand to three thousand grizzlies (equal to double and triple the number currently present in all of the lower forty-eight states, five to six times the current number in Yellowstone) may be required to ensure population stability and genetic health in the Yellowstone region. He also says that setting aside corridors of habitat to connect Yellowstone to other ecosystems is vital to ensure inward and outward migration of bears. However, Shaffer told me the Grizzly Bear Recovery Plan and Servheen's justification for it are "grossly inadequate" since neither the numbers nor the habitat question is substantively addressed.

"The simple truth is that in the case of the grizzly bear, merely attempting to stabilize existing populations is too little, too late," he wrote in a critique of the plan. "Such a strategy will leave an archipelago of isolated population remnants, none of which is sufficiently large to be viable in its own right." Furthermore, he accused the government of developing a "fortress grizzly strategy" that deflects valid criticism from established experts such as Mattson. Many of Shaffer's colleagues would agree that the government's approach is medieval. The key to maintaining a healthy population of bears, Shaffer asserts, is dependent not on numbers of individual animals per se but on setting aside enough habitat to support the numbers indefinitely. And the only way to protect habitat is to aggressively limit the types of harmful activities that have doomed grizzlies in the past and continue to limit any net gains.

In the Yellowstone ecosystem, grizzlies are managed according to zones fashioned like a round target holding a bull's-eye. In the center, represented by the borders of Yellowstone National Park and areas slightly beyond, bears are supposed to be given primacy over all human uses, even though several prime areas of habitat have been sacrificed to tourist campgrounds and developments. This is called Situation I Habitat. The next layer of the circle, called Situation II, is supposed to represent an area where bears are allowed to colonize as the population grows, but the Interagency Grizzly Bear Committee has routinely moved bears in recent years whenever they wander into this zone and come into contact, or prey upon, domestic livestock. It is a zero-sum strategy.

Yellowstone National Park alone, scientists agree, is insufficient to maintain the numbers of bears necessary for a healthy population, which means that affording bears a safe haven on lands outside the park is vital. Yet in the Grizzly Bear Recovery Plan, and in direct response to pressure exerted by politicians, the boundary lines of Situation II Habitat have not grown significantly outward in accordance with what Servheen and those pressing for delisting claim is an expanding population. Hence, any bear that shows good biological instincts in trying to establish new territories gets either shot, moved, or euthanized. A perfect example is a grazing allotment straddling Situation I and Situation II used by Jackson Hole cattle rancher Paul Walton. Walton's foreman has killed a couple of bears preying on cattle, which range across public grasslands in the Bridger-Teton National Forest that happen to be exceptional bear habitat. The range also lies in the middle of a major bear migration corridor between Yellowstone National Park and the Gros Ventre mountains. The interests of bears have been viewed as subservient to the interests of cattle.

The recovery plan is a failure because it sacrifices necessary grizzly habitat to traditional land uses, and furthermore it prescribes no limitations on the very human activities that have proven to be lethal for the bear, numerous biologist critics assert. There is also the prickly matter of biological trends inside Yellowstone, which makes Situation II Habitat outside the park all the more crucial. Recently Yellowstone officials discovered that someone had secretly introduced exotic lake trout, known in some parts of the country as "mackinaws," into Yellowstone Lake, one of the world's largest high-elevation tarns. Lake trout, being piscivorous, eat the cutthroat trout that are a primary staple for grizzly bears because in the spring they are available to bears in spawning streams. Fisheries experts predict that over the next few decades cutthroat trout could decline severely, and because lake trout are deep-water fish, the lost grizzly food source will not be replaced. This problem comes on the heels of some other incredible bad news: Researchers say that an epidemic arboreal disease called blister rust is attacking and killing whitebark pine trees. Whitebark nuts, found in cones, are a primary autumn staple for bears before they enter their winter dormancy. Biologists know that in years when there is poor production of nuts, grizzlies disperse over larger areas and wander into human developments in search of food. And that tendency, of course, gets them killed. If blister rust doesn't annihilate Yellowstone's whitebark pine population, global warming will. Whitebark pine grow in cold, hostile, high-elevation settings, and according to global-warming models, high-elevation areas are expected to warm so much that more aggressive lowland trees could overtake whitebark. Yellowstone bear biologist Dan Reinhart, a friend of Mattson, says that if the number of whitebark pine is severely reduced, he believes the grizzly population will not survive. Although fish and blister rust are beyond the reach of human control, habitat fragmentation is not, which makes the objectives of the recovery plan even more crucial and raises serious doubts about the basis for delisting.

~

In the behavioral realm of scientists, there exists a premise that humans take on some of the physical characteristics of the animals they study. If this notion is true, then Dick Knight, Mattson's mentor and recent supervisor, is an irascible silver-tip grizzly. Knight's personality is that of a gruff loner who once upon a time paid no attention to the political-science side of managing bears. Those who know him, though, say his hardened exterior is merely a cover for a man who is painfully shy and normally bighearted.

At meetings of grizzly bear experts, Knight often did not talk unless asked a question, and then he may have barked back a terse, politically incorrect response. Of more interest, perhaps, is the fact that throughout the 1980s, when many colleagues were trying to point a rosy picture of the grizzly's recovery, Knight was always one of the skeptics. Part of this skepticism was based on his own instincts and part on the field data that began pouring in. Mattson helped elaborate Knight's status. For years Knight had been the man in the sky, tracking radio-collared grizzly bears by airplane to pinpoint their location and movements across the Greater Yellowstone Ecosystem. Before his retirement in late 1997 (he still serves as a consultant), he was the first to recognize whether grizzly bears were experiencing a poor natural food year by the places he found bruins in the late summer and autumn as they gorged themselves with enough energy-rich foods to sustain them through winter. The years 1994 through 1997, on average, will go down in the books as abominable years for bear food and the number of bruins killed by run-ins with big-game hunters. The trend shows no indication of abating.

Who better to comprehend the precarious status of grizzlies in the Yellowstone Ecosystem than Knight? After all, he mentored Mattson in the reasons why one should remain skeptical about grizzly bear recovery when politicians and bureaucrats attempt to paint a sanguine picture.

In the early 1980s Knight realized that the government's age-old practice of removing "problem" bears from Yellowstone was wrong. Whenever a grizzly wandered into a conflict with humans, the management policy usually involved eliminating the bruin rather than trying to modify the human behavior that caused the encounter. So many bears were being "weeded out" that Knight identified this policy as causing a serious drain on the population. He attempted to alert agency managers, who gave him a tepid response.

"We were removing bears inside the park when they got into trouble, because we didn't know any better," he said in a recent interview published in the journal *Yellowstone Science*. "It wasn't until about 1980 that we had a suspicion that we didn't have as many bears as we'd thought. By 1982, I had the data to show it."

Confronted by government stonewalling, Knight took matters into his own hands and, it could be argued, set an example for his protégé Dave Mattson. Knight secretly contacted a Park Service biologist in the Washington, D.C., office named Ro Wauer and leaked the data findings to him. Promising not to blow Knight's cover, Wauer composed a now famous internal memorandum documenting the downward trend in grizzly bear numbers that forced the government to take action.

"I was talking to John Townsley [the Yellowstone superintendent from 1975 to 1982]; he'd been listening to me since 1980, but nobody else really was—it was just like the bear wasn't listed," Knight admitted after he retired. "We had enough data to show we had a declining population. And I went to Ro and said, 'Look, we're going downhill fast and we've got to do something.' And I gave him all the stuff, and he wrote that memo to the [Grizzly Bear] Steering Committee—the precursor to the Interagency Grizzly Bear Committee [IGBC]—and leaked it to the press, and got transferred to the Virgin Islands for it! ... The upshot was, they created the IGBC, and the land managers started taking grizzly bear management seriously, specifically by targeting adult female mortality, really all mortalities."

Knight's concern, however, did not end there, and one could argue that it was inherited by Dave Mattson, who was about to join Knight's team.

In 1985 Knight collaborated with wildlife population biologist Lee Eberhardt on an article that appeared in the journal *Ecology* and stated, to much attention, that the bear population was sinking. "Clearly the population will decline in the future if our estimates of certain essential parameters are correct," the authors wrote. "The simulations suggest that extirpation is not likely over a 30-year period, but there is, of course, no way to be sure that present conditions will persist for 30 years. Most likely they will not, in view of the virtual certainty of greatly increased human use of essential parts of the Yellowstone Ecosystem. Nor do we have any way to predict the impact of reduced population size on its viability." The paper was an admission that habitat conditions for bears were expected to keep deteriorating and that there was too much uncertainty to be optimistic. These points stand in marked contrast to the opinions Knight would express later.

"My sense of Dick Knight was always as somebody who held the welfare of the bear first," says Bob Ekey, formerly a reporter with the *Billings Gazette* and now the northern Rockies regional director of the Wilderness Society. "Dick either insulated himself from or ignored the political pressure that other people who deal with bears had succumbed to. I always felt I could go to him and get the truth. He was cautious, and even if there was a brief time when he was optimistic, he would say he was cautiously optimistic."

Ekey remembers when Knight, out of character, called him late one evening in 1989 and "was beside himself." An outbreak of bear deaths had occurred throughout the ecosystem that autumn. "He was very upset that grizzly bears were getting shot by hunters at the high rate they were," Ekey explains, suggesting that no one knew then that it would get worse. "He said something needed to be done. I was left with the impression that here is a man whose heart is really with the bear. I don't know what changed him."

Something did change in Knight between 1989 and 1993, and the change has direct relevance to how the federal government now justifies its support of delisting. For some reason, Knight began taking the path of least resistance, his workers say. In place of his stalwart caution, Knight suggested that the Yellowstone grizzly population suddenly was on an upward trajectory. During one recent year when fourteen grizzly bears were believed to have been killed in human-bear encounters—an inordinately high number of deaths, Knight no longer was emotional, and he began criticizing Mattson's passion for bear conservation. People who worked with him said Knight—the closer he came to retirement—took on a more political persona geared to preparing data that would reinforce Servheen's contention that the grizzly population was bouncing back.

Gary Brown, the former chief ranger in Yellowstone who worked with Knight in managing grizzlies, says if anything, conditions for bears have become more perilous. Brown, author of a popular book about bears of the world, says the Yellowstone Interagency Grizzly Bear Study Team needs informed dissenters like Mattson to keep Servheen and Knight honest.

"I think deep down Dick still genuinely cares about what happens to bears, but his priorities shifted to sustain himself in a good-paying job where he didn't have to work very hard and he can retreat from things that could jeopardize his comfortable situation," Mattson suggests. "Part of what made him turn on me was I put him in a position that he perceived as holding certain risks, and he felt that he had to protect himself by lashing out."

Over ten years Mattson emerged as the nation's leading authority on grizzly bear behavior in Yellowstone, writing fifty-three peer-reviewed journal articles and technical reports, including seventeen papers delivered to international scientific conferences. "I've talked with a lot of grizzly bear biologists. I've subpoenaed many and put them on a stand under oath in the courtroom over lawsuits. I've also reviewed a substantial amount of the body of scientific literature," says Doug Honnold, a senior attorney with the Sierra Club Legal Defense Fund (which has since taken a new name, EarthJustice Legal Defense Fund). "In my mind Dave Mattson stands head and shoulders above the others. He is admired for the way he attacks a problem and generates a scientific hypothesis, then questions how you can develop information to prove and disprove the hypothesis. Within the scientific community that specializes in grizzly bears, there's a real branch in the road between old-guard biologists and those in the groundbreaking field of conservation biology, which is a look at the processes that cause animals to go extinct. Mattson is a guy who has a solid foot in both of those camps."

Kate Kendall, an alumnus of the Yellowstone Interagency Grizzly Bear Study Team and now a top grizzly bear biologist in Glacier National Park (the only other major outpost of grizzlies in the lower forty-eight states), is well acquainted with the caliber of Mattson's work. "He's one of the best scientists I know," says Kendall, who works for the Biological Services Division of the U.S. Geological Survey and was the scientist who documented the outbreak of blister rust in whitebark pine trees. "The amount of work Dave does is staggering. He often has a really fresh approach to getting at a problem that other people have worked on but never got very far toward resolving. There is no doubt that he has made a big contribution to bear conservation. He puts other researchers to shame."

Mattson was nearing the point of synthesizing all the data and putting it into comprehensive papers that described the ecology of the grizzly and threats to its habitat. He called upon his old friend Bert Harting to independently review his conclusions as one veteran scientist to another. Harting had taken a temporary job with a conservation organization, the Greater Yellowstone Coalition, and when word leaked that Mattson had given Harting the paper, Forest Service officials in the region came unglued. Although Harting never shared the document with other environmentalists, Mattson was accused of consorting with the enemy because the Forest Service knew his findings did not support the agency's logging and road-building program in the six national forests that rim Yellowstone National Park. Constructing new roads to facilitate logging not only brings humans deeper into bear habitat and increases instances of poaching but displaces bears into less than optimal habitat. Thus, the end result is increased mortality.

Politicians were pressuring forest managers to keep cutting trees because trees equal jobs, and jobs bring votes for reelection. "In a meeting with some people from the Targhee National Forest, it came out that I had seen those papers," Harting says. "Unbeknownst to me, word got around in the Forest Service, to Dick Knight, and Chris Servheen, and they really began hammering on Dave. They were beside themselves because he had circulated a paper that was highly critical of how the agency did its business, and they didn't like the heat."

The known impact of logging roads on grizzlies is hardly new. In 1986, after years of extensive logging, the U.S. Congressional Research Service compiled a report for Congress on threats to the Greater Yellowstone region. Part of the report focused on grizzly bears, and the findings have relevance for logging operations. The report said that "substantial clearings and sustained human traffic (from roads) could permanently eliminate grizzlies from this habitat. ... Increased (human) access is harmful to grizzly bears, because most bears avoid human contact whenever possible. Since access is necessary for timber harvesting, timber cutting restricts bear habitat and can alter bear behavior."

The Targhee National Forest straddles eastern Idaho, western Wyoming and southwest Montana. Between 1981 and 1992 in the Targhee's Plateau Bear Management Unit alone (one of eighteen such units that the government uses as barometers for gauging the

health of the grizzly population in the Yellowstone region), a thirty-
five-thousand-acre area was stripped of 70 percent of its vegetation,
mostly through logging and, to a lesser extent, forest fires. In the past
twenty-five years the same area has been inundated with one thousand miles of new logging roads to the point that there are now six
miles of road per square mile in some areas of the forest, one of the
highest logging-road densities in the country and comparable to
some suburban grids. The Plateau Bear Management Unit in particular has one of the poorest records for bear production within the
core bear protection zone as specified by the Grizzly Bear Recovery
Plan, and, conveniently, the Forest Service wanted it exempted from
the requirement of having to sustain perpetual, year-round bear oc-
cupation. Servheen showed little public resistance.

Timber sales, the construction of logging roads, mining, and other
activities come under review as part of Section 7 of the Endangered
Species Act, which requires that the Fish and Wildlife Service rule
whether proposed activities such as logging in a certain area would
jeopardize the bear. But seldom has the agency rendered "jeopardy
decisions" precluding harmful land management practices. Wildlife
biologists allege that the government is playing a shell game in
which Servheen avoids his responsibility to vociferously protect bear
habitat from the Forest Service. The Forest Service then says the job
of enforcing environmental laws pertaining to habitat for threatened
species lies in the jurisdiction of the Fish and Wildlife Service. And
ultimately, both agencies refer back to the recovery plan as the arbiter, sidestepping responsibility for habitat destruction.

Bob Ekey of the Wilderness Society says it is morbidly laughable
that Servheen "seems bewildered that there are bear black holes in
the Targhee." To anyone standing in the blighted panorama of a
clearcut and mazes of roads, the explanation is self-evident. "When
you lose 70 percent of your cover, you lose the heart of the habitat,"
adds Ekey. "We know from a battery of studies, including the work
done by Dave Mattson, that bears avoid Forest Service roads, and
those that don't die." He says Servheen's lack of vigilance in protecting bear habitat shirks accountability by the Fish and Wildlife
Service and the Forest Service.

As a result, the Forest Service was sued by the Sierra Club Legal
Defense Fund on behalf of ten environmental groups for failing to
shut down harmful logging practices in the Targhee, where grizzlies

have virtually disappeared from the Plateau region and another bear management unit. On February 22, 1994, a settlement was reached in which three hundred miles of logging roads were to be closed to provide bear security. For the Targhee, modifying its timber-cutting practices and submitting to road closures was not voluntary but mandated as part of the court agreement. However, a few months later the Targhee's forest supervisor, Jerry Reese, unilaterally stated that he wouldn't close roads in deference to loggers and off-road-vehicle users. This announcement confirmed Reese's reputation as a shill for resource extractionists.

Chuck Lobdell, a Fish and Wildlife Service enforcement specialist in Idaho, who helped broker the agreement, was furious at Reese's obstinacy and vowed to prosecute Forest Service officials for egregiously violating the Endangered Species Act. The Fish and Wildlife Service did not support his vigilance. "The Targhee is the worst case of mismanagement I've ever seen in almost thirty years of wildlife protection. It is a national disgrace," Lobdell tells me. "It isn't just Reese but four out of five of his predecessors. They are violating their own organic statutes relating to grizzly bear habitat, they are being defiant about protecting an endangered species, and I'm going to win this battle for the bear even if it sends some of those people who are responsible for this to jail."

Now retired but a committed conservationist, Lobdell believes it is "ludicrous" that a citizen could be fined and sent to jail for illegally cutting a few trees on a national forest for firewood while agency supervisors and their foresters can orchestrate environmental destruction on a landscape level with no fear of the law. Just as white-collar criminals can be prosecuted on felony charges, he believes that forest supervisors and their staffs who break environmental laws should be held personally accountable. He also says the Grizzly Bear Recovery Plan should require the Forest Service to meet environmental performance standards, which it does not. "The real culprit is not solely Chris Servheen, as some conservationists claim, but rather our western senators and congressmen who are into resource exploitation and have no regard for conservation. They are the ones applying subtle intimidation. It's like the massacre of civilians by the U.S. military in Vietnam. Orders came down from the top, but I know that is no excuse," Lobdell says. "The recovery plan is the result of many compromises and may be inadequate to assure restoration of the grizzly bear on the Targhee. If we weren't forced to cut deals, nothing would ever be implemented because of defiance by the Forest Service and political interference." He says that compromise has rendered the recovery plan practically useless.

Lobdell came under intense fire for his outspokenness and was re-assigned to a desk job after raising concerns about grizzlies and de-clining bull-trout populations due to logging in Idaho. Warned about his aggressive commitment to uphold federal law, and hassled for it, he suffered a heart attack that his doctors blamed on stress. "I've rocked the boat, and some people who put making money be-fore everything else didn't like it. But the American people hired me to do a job. If you're going to fall on your sword for any issue, you'd better make sure it's worth dying for because if you make a big gaffe, you're done. You can't make one mistake, or the people who have the politicians on a string will try to get rid of you because you're dispensable."

Mattson, he says, fits that profile of the martyr to a cause and rep-resents a threat because he challenges the failed land management practices of the past. Worried that a controversy would erupt if bear managers suggested halting timber sales in order to save the grizzly, Servheen and Knight wanted to rein Mattson in. According to Mattson, this is when Servheen's "smoke-and-mirrors show" began.

To test his biological hypotheses about roads, Mattson started cor-responding with Craig Pease at the University of Texas in Austin. Pease was among a reputable group of independent scientists brought together to examine grizzly bear management issues be-cause conservationists were concerned that some agency science was being co-opted by empire-building bureaucrats and regulators who were captive to special interests. Although Knight gave Mattson per-mission to share information with Pease, he later became irate when he heard that Pease was preparing an independent analysis of the field data and a review of the recovery plan that probably would not be favorable. Until then, the Interagency Grizzly Bear Committee had carefully guarded all the information it generated, making out-side scrutiny of its effectiveness next to impossible and raising legit-imate questions about its accountability.

The beginning of the end for Dave Mattson's tenure with the Yel-lowstone Interagency Grizzly Bear Study Team had been brewing for months, but it crescendoed at a meeting in northern Montana where a group of government and independent scientists gathered to examine the relationships between logging roads and displacement of bears. At one point in a closed-door presentation by Servheen, Mattson pointedly asked a few questions about why the Fish and Wildlife Service planned to continue allowing logging roads to pierce grizzly habitat. Servheen appeared flustered and annoyed at being questioned by someone under his command. Mattson engaged Servheen on these points: Scientific evidence shows conclusively that the rate at which bears die parallels the density of roads that the Forest Service builds to accommodate logging and other industrial uses. The more access provided by roads into grizzly bear habitat, the higher the number of bear deaths. Secure bear populations, no matter the size, require large tracts of undisturbed terrain. So do elk and a number of other peripatetic species. And that means putting more land off limits to logging, mining, and general development.

That night, after the encounter, Servheen and Knight went away by themselves and talked. Mattson knew something was up, but what emerged was beyond his wildest expectations. Acting at Servheen's behest, Knight returned to Bozeman early and acted quickly to halt Mattson's dissent by raiding his office. He deleted data files and confiscated floppy discs from Mattson's computer, tore out pages of research from his notebook binders, and removed field data from office filing cabinets, including information that was critical to Mattson's ongoing job performance. He then put it all under lock and key, off limits to Mattson. Ten years' worth of accumulated data—the result of thousands of hours afield gaining an intimate view of bears—was taken away from the scientist most capable of interpreting it. Stunned, Mattson wrote a memo to Knight asking for an explanation. Storming out of his office, glaring at Mattson, Knight said, "Dave, it is time that I start acting like a real bastard." Knight does not deny this description of the sequence of events and in fact appears to delight in his reputation as a "hardass."

If there are any two people who understand the wrath of government and the move to purge Mattson to prevent him from using data that contradicts the "official position," it is the famous Craighead brothers, John and Frank, who were banished from Yellowstone in the early 1970s because they locked horns with park managers over policies affecting bear management.

Millions of Americans are familiar with the Craigheads' studies because the brothers wrote articles in *National Geographic* magazine and were featured in numerous television nature documentaries. "When people from the outside like Craig Pease or within the organization like Dave Mattson become more concerned with the truth and doing the right thing rather than following the bureaucratic program, they find themselves in trouble," says octogenarian John Craighead, founder of the Craighead Wildlife-Wildlands Institute, who, with his brother Frank, conducted twelve years of groundbreaking research on grizzlies in the Yellowstone ecosystem that began in 1959.

"Bureaucrats try to discredit anyone who challenges their narrow way of thinking," he adds. "I can tell you from personal experience that [the government] will try and destroy your reputation. You can't win because they have you outgunned and it takes all your time to fight those bastards."

Craighead, a pioneer in using satellite telemetry to map wildlife habitat, has documented the toll that intensified logging, mining, recreation, and road building have taken throughout the northern Rockies. It is a legacy of destructive public land management that government agencies are loath to admit. The Craigheads were kicked out of Yellowstone after they stated publicly that abruptly closing open-pit dumps in the park would result in the deaths of many bears who depended on the dumps for food. They didn't think closing the dumps was a bad idea; rather, they endorsed a plan of slowly weaning bears from unnatural human foods and returning the population to a diet based on natural foraging. They warned of dire consequences if bears were cut off too quickly from their dependency on the dumps.

Yellowstone wildlife manager Glen Cole and park superintendent Jack Anderson, however, pushed for abrupt closure. Cole and Anderson's option won out, and within two years a large percentage of the Yellowstone grizzly bear population died or was removed from the ecosystem because the bears' search for new food pushed them into encounters with people. When the Craigheads openly criticized the management tactics, they were censored by their employers—the National Park Service and the Bureau of Sport Fisheries and Wildlife—which demanded that anything they published on Yellowstone bears get prior editing and approval. The Park Service argued that scientists had no business commenting on management.

The Craigheads' contention was, and remains, that good science should be a guiding light to management decisions and the two are not mutually exclusive. If the public pays for science, it ought to be able to scrutinize it.

Today, John Craighead says the logic that forms the foundation of the new Grizzly Bear Recovery Plan is highly suspect in the way that it blindly supports the politically motivated calls for delisting the bear from the Endangered Species Act. "I think delisting is the worst thing they could possibly do," he says. "The Wyoming Game and Fish Department claims that because bears are moving back into their old historic habitat, there are more bears and the population is doing well, but that argument has no basis in fact.

"Bears are moving out of the national park into the national forests because they need secured and multiple sources of food," he adds. "Yellowstone Park is not big enough by itself to support a viable population. The only motivation to delist the bear is so it can be hunted and management of the public lands can go back to business as usual, which is why we came close to losing the bear in the first place."

Craighead says the grizzly is an indicator for dozens of other species. If bear habitat is eroded so much that grizzlies can't survive, he argues that other animals that need an undisturbed environment—such as wolverines, lynx, wolves, raptors, and fish—are not going to survive either.

"The American taxpayers have to decide where they are getting the best investment," Craighead insists. "Some of the agencies are looking at ten to twenty years down the line while those in the independent scientific community like Dave Mattson are looking at how we can have a healthy and self-sustaining bear population in perpetuity."

After the Craigheads involuntarily left Yellowstone in 1971, the scientist hand-picked by the National Park Service to repair any public relations damage and to head up the newly formed Yellowstone Interagency Grizzly Bear Study Team was none other than Dick Knight.

~

Now, let me offer an aside. As a reporter, I have interviewed Dave Mattson, Dick Knight, and Chris Servheen on dozens of occasions. I have no personal bone to pick, nor do I doubt their capabilities. But

politics makes strange bedfellows. I don't claim to have the answers
for what motivates people to act in ways that they normally would
not act, probably motivated by forces in their personal lives that we
cannot see. Apparently good people—among whom I count Dick
Knight and Chris Servheen—can under unusual circumstances be
driven to behave in ways they would not like to see in others.

This much I know from writing about Yellowstone grizzlies since
the mid-1980s: Unequivocally, information is power. Those who
control the dissemination of information are able to ration it to individuals who will confirm their own conclusions. This is not an example of good science. All along, it has been Mattson's contention
that because he is a public servant whose salary comes from taxpayers, any information he gathers should be shared with independent
scientists who potentially can make a contribution to helping the
bear.

After Mattson's office was raided, Knight and Servheen told him
that the data collected by government scientists were "proprietary
information" and should not be shared with anyone outside government agencies because they might be used to criticize grizzly
bear managers. Their added justification was that poachers might use
the information to kill wandering bruins, which Mattson says is absurd because he had no interest in publicly revealing the locations of
specific bears.

After the raid Knight implemented a system of "mail management" whereby all outgoing mail written by Mattson or incoming
mail addressed to him was screened. Knight said Mattson had forced
him to perform "damage control" because of growing public suspicion about government statistics. "I am concerned that your actions
have been part of a systematic effort to isolate, silence, and intimidate me because of efforts on my part to fulfill my job requirements
and facilitate implementation of research results," Mattson wrote to
Knight. "You have justified your actions as a means of 'bringing me
under control,' and that 'certain managers' [read Servheen] perceived
me as a threat. ... Your comments strongly suggest that you think
science should be quickly shucked if the indicated direction is uncomfortable to managers or not politically expedient."

Knight told Mattson that Servheen might have to "reconsider"
funding for his Yellowstone grizzly bear research projects if Mattson
continued to criticize the policy of bear managers. Servheen denies

that he ever threatened to withdraw funding, but Knight added in a written response to Mattson, "To set the record straight, Chris never said that he would cut off funding. I said that he could cut off funding. ... The 'raid on your office' was simply my retrieval of data that I am responsible for before it was used to further criticize the government."

Soon thereafter, Knight also slashed Mattson's travel budget so that it became difficult to confer with other biologists or attend conferences on conservation biology. Mattson found himself stripped of amenities that were necessary to do his job. When he asked Knight for the data that had been confiscated, he was rebuked. Finally, the way the information was returned to Mattson was, ironically, by Honnold at the EarthJustice Legal Defense Fund, which had to file a Freedom of Information Act request that was met coldly by the federal agencies.

"The case they wanted to make was that I was in bed with the environmentalists, which is false," Mattson says, noting that the government routinely uses this argument to neutralize its own biologists. "The only thing I did was provide information to those people who asked for it, and received it with Dick's blessing. It's funny, but I felt that people outside the agency were more sincerely interested in the actual science than those in the agency."

Ultimately it was conservationists, not Mattson's superiors, who gave him back his own data. "Chris Servheen told me, 'Dave, you've got a chip on your shoulder. We deal in political reality. We can't deal with emotion because we're scientists.' It is almost as if the government uses science as a shield to prevent its employees from having anything but a cold, purely analytical relationship with the resources they come in contact with. I think this is a tremendous mistake," Mattson notes. "What it's doing is not only making public servants treat the land with indifference but making them treat people that way too."

Mattson says if you can't become an emotional advocate for saving something as big and mysterious as a grizzly bear, what things in life should you get emotional about? "I think we all have emotions that we bring to bear on any situation, and it is important to recognize what those emotions are and the context in which they are brought into our lives. I know that I recognize that emotional context, and I don't think that it's good or bad. It's a fact of being human," he says. "What's not so good are the people who deny that they have feelings at all or are forced to suppress them. Chris [Servheen] is the man with whom the American public has entrusted the future of the grizzly bear in the lower forty-eight states, and I think people expect him to be an advocate for the bear, not for loggers or miners or ranchers. He is not getting paid to accommodate them."

To placate Mattson, who collected his paycheck through the National Park Service, then Yellowstone superintendent Bob Barbee and John Varley, chief of the Yellowstone Center for Research, offered him a transfer, ostensibly to keep him from causing a controversy. Varley told him the government would pay for his tuition in a Ph.D. program at the University of Idaho, and it was implied that Mattson should not make a fuss about departing from the bear study team. He was also given a position, in absentia, with the Biological Services Division of the U.S. Geological Survey. Critics say Varley, with Servheen's approval, tried to buy Mattson's silence. "Yes, I took the deal, but really, what were my options? They made it impossible for me to do research and they made it a professional liability to question anything they did. I took the offer as a way to salvage my career," Mattson says. "It didn't make sense that they would go through all this trouble unless they were trying to keep me quiet."

When I ask Varley whether this assessment is true, he replies forcefully, "Absolutely not. Dave had a choice, and I think we gave him a pretty good deal." I say that "choice" implies that Mattson had two options. Could he have remained on the study team? "No," Varley says. "We wanted to give Dave an acceptable way out."

Mattson's motives were not venal. He knew what had happened to the Craigheads. "My situation there became untenable, and they made it real clear there wasn't a place for me doing field research. The Park Service was very much invested in preserving Dick. He was doing for them what they needed, giving them a scientific rationale that the bear population was doing fine so they could wave it as a success of management, as a success of the ESA [Endangered Species Act] not being a deterrent to resource developers and tourism. They offered to pay for my Ph.D. program at the University of Idaho to get me out of the way. I realized that if I didn't take charge and try to cut the best deal I could, I would be destroyed. What's most telling is that despite the vindictiveness of Dick, absolutely nothing was done to discipline him. I think it proves that this is a system of very perverse incentives," Mattson tells me.

The case of Dave Mattson sends a chilling signal, says Louisa Willcox of the Sierra Club Grizzly Bear Ecosystems Project. Willcox herself is considered one of the most knowledgeable conservation leaders on grizzly bear issues in the United States. She is among a group that has asked Secretary of the Interior Bruce Babbitt to oust Chris Servheen. "What the treatment of Dave Mattson says is that the people who are our best hope for bringing strong science and good management and conservation to the fore are unlikely to succeed in the current system."

Servheen, meanwhile, asserts his own view. "Personalities had something to do with it, but it is a personnel matter," he says. "I don't feel very comfortable talking about it."

What kind of biologist was Mattson? I inquire.

"I think he's a good biologist," Servheen acknowledges, "but there is more to life than being a good biologist."

Michael Scott, program director of the Greater Yellowstone Coalition, a regional conservation group based in Bozeman, Montana, says Servheen appears to purposely discredit Mattson's gifts. "Mattson always comes up with fresh ways of looking at questions and problems relating to grizzly bear management that shed new light on innovative approaches," Scott says. "It makes him a very valuable resource within the scientific community, but it also makes him valuable to decisionmakers and policy people because he's able to take fairly arcane and difficult-to-understand science and make it relevant. With that, policymakers can outline their options and know what the real consequences of their actions are. That's a pretty special talent."

～

Whenever the subject of Dave Mattson's ouster is raised with a member of the Interagency Grizzly Bear Committee, the stock-in-trade rationale is that Mattson is an anomaly: he deserved the punishment he received, his concerns are not widely shared, his problems stemmed from a "personality conflict," and his muzzling was "an isolated incident."

If any of these comments were true, the tale of Mattson's treatment could be dismissed as anecdotal. We could consign him to purgatory under the label of "troublemaker," albeit a brilliant troublemaker. We could safely assume that the grizzly bear is in good hands; we could blithely accept the implied assurance that science has not been co-opted by political agendas and bureaucrats who appear compelled to skew the actual biological status of the grizzly in a blizzard of distortions.

If this is the answer you desire, then it is prudent to refrain from directing questions to field biologists involved with management of the Yellowstone grizzly. Ask them to provide a candid response, away from their superiors, and they convey the details of a very different picture. I spoke with no fewer than a dozen current or former members of the grizzly bear study team, biologists with the Forest Service, National Park Service, and Fish and Wildlife Service and retired bureaucrats. Is there a conspiracy to silence dissidents?

For several years in the 1990s, Fish and Wildlife Service biologist Jane Roybal was placed in charge of her agency's Section 7 ESA consultation practice; other federal land managers had to run their proposed actions by her for a biological opinion on whether those actions would affect the grizzly. Roybal was praised whenever she determined that a given action would not jeopardize the bears' survival, and she was excoriated for challenging actions—such as timber sales, oil and gas development, or road construction—that she thought might be a problem. A coincidence?

Roybal's first confrontation swirled around a famous location in the center of Yellowstone National Park known as Fishing Bridge, on the northwest corner of Yellowstone Lake. The location is surrounded by several streams whose hundreds of thousands of cutthroat trout spawn every spring and summer. The convergence of the fish attracts substantial numbers of grizzlies, but unfortunately a large campground and a wing of tourist motel rooms have been built right in the middle of prime grizzly bear habitat near the spawning streams. Tourists, no matter how fastidious they are in keeping a clean camp, inevitably dispose improperly of food, which leads to injured people, bears that are destroyed, or both. The development also displaces bears, preventing them from using this valuable food source.

Over the years several dozen bears in the vicinity of Fishing Bridge have been killed, relocated to other sections of the park, or sent to zoos because of continuous encounters with people. A logical action, since trout streams cannot be picked up and moved, would be to remove the worrisome campgrounds and not open the motel units until late in the summer, after the trout spawning season ends.

During the mid- to late 1980s, following exhaustive bear behavioral studies by Mattson, Reinhart, and others, Yellowstone announced that because of the area's irreplaceable importance to the ecosystem's core grizzly population, campgrounds needed to be closed and a later opening date for nearby motels needed to be considered. When details of the proposal reached U.S. Senators Alan Simpson, who hails from the park gateway community, and Malcolm Wallop, of Sheridan, the political response was swift and direct. Simpson told then park superintendent Robert Barbee that there was no way he would tolerate closure of camping spaces and delay of motel openings because the Cody business community deemed them essential to luring tourists through the park's east gate and thus through Cody along the North Fork of the Shoshone Highway. As a trade-off, Simpson said he would endorse closure of tent sites at Fishing Bridge if the Park Service agreed to build new camping facilities at a place called Bridge Bay, also along Yellowstone Lake and in grizzly habitat. Because a recreational vehicle (RV) campground would remain at Fishing Bridge, biologists informed Barbee that the deal might lead to even greater bear habitat disturbance and bear displacement. Eventually a review of the matter was bumped to the Fish and Wildlife Service in Cheyenne, Wyoming, where it fell into Roybal's lap. Senator Simpson let it be known that he intended to take a keen interest in Roybal's conclusion.

Despite a verbal message from the Fish and Wildlife Service's regional office in Denver that it would be in Roybal's best interest to be accommodating, Roybal wrote a biological opinion that concurred with the initial proposal to close the campground and not replace it. She founded her conclusion on the strong likelihood that keeping the campground open—and opening camping spaces at Bridge Bay—would amount to a "taking" of grizzlies either through bear fatalities or bear displacement.

The ESA, Section 7, is very specific in forcing land managers to justify eroding habitat for a protected species, especially in the center of America's mother national park and especially when Yellowstone's wildlife icon is involved. Nonetheless, before an official copy of Roybal's report could be completed and released to the public, Simpson and Wallop protested. Apparently someone had leaked them a copy (no such copy was made available to the environmental groups that also requested it). Roybal's supervisor, Chuck Davis, demanded that Roybal rewrite the document. She refused. It then was handed over to another Fish and Wildlife Service biologist with no direct knowledge of grizzly bears who delivered a finding representing the position that the senators wanted to hear.

Before he was transferred to a regional director post in Alaska, Superintendent Barbee acknowledged that the Wyoming congressional delegation had applied pressure to get him to change the park position on campground closure and delaying motel openings. At one meeting with park officials during which Barbee announced that Yellowstone managers would "be more flexible," Roybal indicated that she would not change her position. Afterward, she says, Barbee followed her to her car, glaring to demonstrate his disapproval. It was her introduction to the politics involving grizzly bears.

Roybal also wrote a biological opinion that oil and natural-gas development inside the Shoshone National Forest, east of Yellowstone, could jeopardize the grizzly's use of army moth hatching sites, which are an important source of bear nutrition. And she wrote an opinion critical of a proposed Shoshone National Forest timber sale actually inside the grizzly bear recovery zone, where grizzlies are supposed to be given priority over development. How did Roybal know about the high density of bears likely to be displaced by those resource extraction activities? Because a dozen of the bruins had been captured and equipped with radio collars and were being tracked by the Yellowstone Interagency Grizzly Bear Study Team (which was conspicuously mute on the issue). She also received confirmation from a Shoshone National Forest biologist, Carrie Hunt.

Before taking a job as a Forest Service regional grizzly bear specialist, Hunt had crafted an innovative model for ways to redefine the recovery-zone boundaries for grizzlies while working for the Wyoming Game and Fish Department. Her path crossed Roybal's on the Brent Creek timber sale when Hunt was supposed to draft an internal biological evaluation of the effects of logging on the bear population. She got a taste of her agency's antipathy toward honest science when she raised doubts about the sale and how it would degrade bear habitat.

"My district ranger read my report and wrote a message across it that said, 'This is shit!'" Hunt said. "Then the forest supervisor, Barry Davis, and the district ranger ordered me to rewrite it. When I said I wouldn't, they did, and then they ordered me to sign my name to it. I wouldn't do it. Any biologist associated with grizzlies was constantly being hammered on, and the abuse transcended agency affiliations. There are many of us who have our tales of mismanagement, illegal activities, and personal intimidation."

Hunt said if she ever expressed reservations about a proposed timber sale or oil and gas development, her supervisors would assemble twenty Forest Service staffers who supported development to gather around and, amid taunting, force her to tell them why she thought they were wrong for promoting use of the forest. She empathizes with Jane Roybal.

When Roybal warned in another biological opinion that increased development along the North Fork of the Shoshone River corridor (prime grizzly habitat) between Yellowstone and Cody would degrade more habitat, Chuck Davis intervened by again telling another biologist to write a watered-down review. To give an idea of the tone, it need only be said that the new version pleased Senator Simpson. Meanwhile, Roybal watched her career disintegrate.

"She was a rising star, a long-term employee and a good biologist who ran into the buzz saw of science meeting politics. At best it diminished her career, but I would argue her career has been ruined. She has been permanently tarnished by what they did," says Jackie Taylor, a Denver attorney representing Roybal who works for Public Employees for Environmental Responsibility (PEER). "When you set out to destroy a scientist's professional standing, the objective isn't only to destroy the individual. That is just a means to an end. The objective is that if you can ruin the scientist, you also ruin the science. When the science is gone you no longer have an obstacle."

Roybal's experience, she says, offers a textbook example of dissenters being purged. "First they told Jane to change her conclusions as a means of assuaging the politicians, and when she refused they decided to attack her," Taylor says. "They suddenly gave her bad performance reviews, took away professional responsibilities, gave her deadlines which were unmeetable, and subjected her to continual harassment in the workplace. When that didn't work in driving her out, they began badmouthing her in the scientific community and within management circles. It was designed to erode her credibility and damage her personally."

Roybal's case was brought before the federal Merit Systems Protection Board, which upon reviewing the merits of her complaint urged the Fish and Wildlife Service to agree to a settlement. Part of

the settlement called for her supervisor, Davis, to leave his post. Ironically, he received a promotion.

Roybal's attorney also pursued a parallel grievance with the Equal
Employment Opportunity Commission (EEOC), citing discrimination, harassment, and retaliation, relating to an assertion that Roybal
suffered abuse in part because she was a woman. As of the summer
of 1998, Roybal's EEOC case was still pending without resolution
in the Denver federal district court.

Conservationists say the Roybal matter, intentionally kept hidden
from public knowledge by Fish and Wildlife Service officials, is sym-
bolic of how the informed science purportedly guiding management of grizzlies has broken down. "Jane Roybal was forced to
tackle the most sacred of the sacred-cow issues in northwest Wyoming—tourism, logging, and development," Louisa Willcox of the
Sierra Club tells me. "You might consider what she confronted a test
of loyalty. Either way, she loses. She could play along with her supervisors and various user groups who wanted the biology swept
under the rug, or she could respond truthfully and professionally,
which is what she did. The travesty here is that many of her own
colleagues watched the abuse unfold and did nothing to intervene.
What does that say about the integrity of the Fish and Wildlife Service? Those of us in the conservation community did not even know
it was happening at the time because it all happened behind closed
doors."

Under Chris Servheen's direction, Willcox says, many decisions
pertaining to grizzly bear recovery in this country have been made,
deliberately it seems, without public involvement. "Based on that,
the public has good reason to be cynical," she says from her office
in Bozeman, Montana. "Chris Servheen has established a pattern of
sealing himself off from the real debate. By keeping the flow of information controlled internally, he knows that it is difficult to throw
Jane Roybal, Dave Mattson, Carrie Hunt, and other biologists a life-
line when they need help. We need to open this whole process up
to make it accountable. We have hope that Jamie Clark [the new director of the Fish and Wildlife Service] will seize the opportunity to
show the public that she does not condone or tolerate intimidation
inside her agency."

Transferred out of the Yellowstone region, Roybal says the Fish
and Wildlife Service, with no resistance from Servheen, has demonstrated that any advocates adhering to the letter of the ESA will be

punished. "The agencies try to segregate you and work you over one on one. What they fear most is gathering all of the biologists together in a public forum and letting them air their concerns about Chris Servheen and the direction of grizzly bear management without fear of being punished."

Roybal says the method of attacking strong-willed biologists weeds out those who want to make a difference. "The objective is to isolate you, to prevent you from achieving a forum where your concerns can be corroborated. A stigma is created so that you are a troublemaker. If anyone associates with you, they get attacked with the same label and are ostracized. It makes everyone paranoid about honestly doing their job.

"Everybody has that line they have to draw for themselves and say enough is enough. Unfortunately, the agencies who abuse their power know that for most of us, we need the job to put food on the table and pay the bills, send our kids to college, or get a recommendation if we want to move on. They hold these things over our heads. And as you compromise your personal integrity—the very thing that led you to work as a biologist—you start to doubt yourself and realize you are on your own. The hardest part is having your colleagues, who agree with you in private, be put on the spot to criticize you. You see it eating them alive because they are forced into a position of having to betray you and their work. They have to pay bills, put their kids through school. They can't take the risk of telling the truth."

Sara Johnson and Marynell Oechsner are also proof of a deliberate campaign to silence dissenters. Johnson worked six years in the Targhee and eight years in the adjacent Gallatin National Forest in Montana. "When I went to work on the Targhee, I had no idea what I was getting myself into," Johnson, a biologist, says. "If you disagreed with what they wanted to do, which was cut trees no matter what the ecological cost, they would attack you verbally and start wearing you down. They would take me out to look at a proposed sale, me being the one biologist and they with their twelve machismo foresters in cowboy boots. It would be constant harassment for the whole day. They would do this same routine sale after sale and berate me in a patronizing tone if I said anything about protecting wildlife. If I made any recommendation that interfered with their timber harvest, then the ranger would come in to speak with my supervisor and complain about how I wasn't a team player. The system is set up as a trap. You're either for the team, which means timber, or you're against the team, which means a poor job-performance review."

Like Hunt, when Johnson ascertained that a timber sale would harm grizzly bears in the Gallatin National Forest her bosses had her replaced with another biologist who told them what they wanted to hear. "It took me fourteen years before I finally gave up," says Johnson, who has been called as an expert witness in lawsuits filed against the Forest Service. "It was like the Stepford wives. It started to drive me crazy. While I worked for the Forest Service, I had a tremendous amount of respect for Dave Mattson on the Yellowstone Interagency Grizzly Bear Study Team. He was one of the best biologists I ever encountered. From my own experience, the Forest Service hates the grizzly bear. I think we can save it, but I'm not sure we will."

Johnson didn't go public about her harassment until the end of her tenure because superiors threatened to permanently assign her to a desk job. Oechsner, meanwhile, brought her case to Capitol Hill and testified before the House Government Operations Subcommittee on Environment, Energy and Natural Resources. After eleven years working as a government biologist, Oechsner took a field position with Montana's Kootenai National Forest in the Three Rivers Ranger District. "In the Forest Service, biologists and hydrologists and other scientists are called ologists," she told members of Congress. "At Three Rivers, ologists were second-class citizens. ... Resources other than timber were viewed as constraints. Ologists were browbeaten and intimidated to follow the leader, and their professional judgment was discredited and discarded when it did not meet with management's approval. For me, 'dissension,' in the form of speaking up for the resources, taking a stand for wildlife, precipitated a threat of removal, reassignment, or demotion."

Oechsner said the Forest Service routinely announced that logging would have no impact on grizzlies after she had explicitly informed the agency the bear would suffer. Only after she complained to an agency environmental officer was the sale against which she was protesting rescinded, though her complaint set her up for a series of confrontations. Although her opinions were reinforced by other biologists, one of her supervisors, who also oversaw timber management, began saying her work was deficient. Finally she was given relief only after filing a lawsuit that allowed her to transfer without fear of retribution. "I learned that at the Three Rivers District, the timber cut came first, and woe to anyone who gets in the way," Oechsner said. "Basically they just wanted to cut it all. Once they cut a road into an area, they went after every last stick of wood to the point that you didn't find wildlife there anymore."

Roybal says that Servheen was very vocal in characterizing biologists who criticized extractive industries as conspiring with "ecofreaks." "We are taught to heed the opinions of cattlemen and loggers and miners as holding validity, but the other side is regarded as if they are communists," Roybal says. "I used to think good science was made by objective minds hearing all sides and all opinions and brainstorming on those and coming up with foresighted solutions. But that's not what happens. That's not what the leaders of the agencies and the people in charge of protecting endangered species want."

The greatest tragedy, Roybal says, is that the public has been deceived. "I think the public perceives, and I naively perceived, that the U.S. Fish and Wildlife Service, the designated advocate of species like the grizzly bear, is following the law. I think the public assumes that we know the best course of management for the species, that we are the species experts, that we are guarding over them, and if we say it is okay to proclaim a victory, then it is. But that's a fallacy. A lot of us in this arena argue whether we are really doing a bigger disservice to the bear. In fighting these battles and having our careers ruined, with the animal coming out on the short side and losing a little more each time, the impact is almost imperceptible. We are a Band-Aid on a serious internal injury, and that gives the public false assurances. You feel bad about taking your salary, and you think, 'If the public only knew the real story.' There are many of us who think that maybe it isn't worth fighting; maybe we should let the atrocity occur on such a large scale that it cannot be ignored, that the aftermath will make the bad biology and the corrupt politics impossible to deny."

Of Chris Servheen, Roybal says, "I have witnessed situations where I felt Chris was selling the bear out. He plays political games, and a lot of biologists feel he's been the biggest problem. The fact is that Chris Servheen is just a manifestation of a bad system of administering science-based management. Chris Servheen isn't doing anything, no matter how dishonest, that his supervisors don't want to be done. I'm not sure if he's taken out it will change the management or its philosophies as long as Jamie Clark and her successors pretend there isn't a problem. The only way that change can happen is for the public to take notice and say this is BS."

As early as 1990, John Mumma, a regional Forest Service manager who today is director of Colorado's state wildlife agency, was transferred to a paper-pushing job outside the region after asserting that inflated timber targets were violating the ESA. He quit rather than capitulate.

Late in 1997 two organizations dedicated to representing whistleblowers, PEER and the Government Accountability Project (GAP), published a report titled "Grizzly Science—Grizzly Bear Biology in the Greater Yellowstone." According to both PEER and GAP—which circulated a questionnaire to field biologists in two national parks, seven national forests, three national wildlife refuges, and three state wildlife agencies—manipulation of science is rampant in the Greater Yellowstone area.

Among the examples documented in anonymous responses: The Fish and Wildlife Service issues favorable rulings on whether development will affect grizzly bears even before biological reviews—as mandated in Section 7 of the Endangered Species Act—have been completed. Biologists also said conclusions in environmental documents are routinely falsified, even over the protests of the original biologist, who is then asked to sign off on the doctored information, which allows development in bear habitat to proceed. One biologist who challenged Forest Service management over its cozy relationship with the timber industry was told to see a psychologist. Pressure to acquiesce is most severe at the Forest Service district level, where rural managers are almost always sympathetic to loggers, miners, ranchers, and hunters—rather than their own scientists—when conflicts with bears arise. When one wildlife specialist tried to ensure that logging complied with environmental laws, the employee was asked by the district ranger, "Are you going to yell about every little dickey bird the way the last biologist did?"

~

If there is any enduring symbol of what is wrong with grizzly bear management in the Yellowstone region, it is the Grizzly Bear Recovery Plan. Although it establishes easy-to-meet criteria for when the bear population should be removed from protection under the

Endangered Species Act, the plan does virtually nothing to stop the kinds of activities that have led to the bear's decline. Worse, it sets so-called recovery goals at levels that prompted federal protection of the bear in 1975. In effect, Mattson says, it dooms the bear and land management agencies to recurring modes of crises.

Servheen, the plan's principal author, defends the plan by suggesting that protection of grizzly bear habitat is required in all of the management plans for national forests surrounding Yellowstone Park. However, most forest plans since the mid-1970s have been driven by timber targets, with forest supervisors rated on their performance by how well they get out the cut. "The recovery plan is not a document designed to manage each national forest," Servheen says. "Each national forest around Yellowstone has its own management plan, which must comply with federal laws, including the Endangered Species Act. The recovery plan is a document that outlines threats and a cookbook of suggestions to make forestry compatible with bears."

Servheen admits that the previous bear recovery plan did nothing to diminish the extent of harmful clearcutting or road building, even though the revised version of the plan states, "Grizzly bear habitat management complements or is often analogous to sound forest management." "I'm not happy with what is happening on the Targhee," Servheen says. "The situation is one that is poor because of erosion of habitat security, and that needs to be rectified. We have informed the Targhee of that in no uncertain terms. Right now it's bad." Has he taken any action? No.

Conservationists say Servheen only made that admission because the extent of the cutting is under public scrutiny. The extent of deforestation is so extreme that satellite photographs are able to delineate the western boundary of Yellowstone because logging extends right up to the park border. Critics point to Servheen for failing to stop, or at least publicly condemn, logging that he knew was harming the bear.

"We're much better off today than in 1975," Servheen insists, "but the bear will only exist with high levels of management. We will never get to the point where we can walk away from the grizzly bear. The role of science is to continually seek the truth. Everything we do with the grizzly bear is to seek the truth. We have an interest in the future of the species, and we believe our decisions are right. Nobody that I know of in the biological community working on behalf of the grizzly bear is trying to hide something or put something over on the public or anybody else."

Given the local hostility toward grizzly bears in ranching and logging communities, Mattson and other scientists pleaded with Servheen to err on the side of caution when crafting the new Grizzly Bear Recovery Plan and pressed to give grizzlies more security cover. The best way to separate would-be poachers from bears, Mattson says, is to close logging roads. It is an ecological maxim that the amount of suitable habitat for a species like the grizzly, in particular contiguous suitable habitat, is a primary regulator of a population's size and likelihood of long-term persistence. For the grizzly, if you are dealing with shrinking habitat it is an absolute certainty that apparent growth in bear numbers will not sustain itself.

"The first thing the plan fails to do is protect habitat. Without habitat, you won't have any bears; it's that simple," says Bob Ekey of the Wilderness Society. Protecting habitat falls through the cracks of jurisdictions, he says. Despite the appearance of the first bear recovery plan in 1982, Targhee managers allowed loggers to continue to cut swaths of trees through bear range in what many say was a violation of the Endangered Species Act, the National Environmental Policy Act, and the National Forest Management Act. As a result, bears have fled the area, resulting in a net loss of habitat.

~

Conservation biologist Peter Brussard once compared the incremental erosion of grizzly bear habitat to "being nibbled to death by a duck." The impacts—a single logging clearcut here, a road there, a subdivision here, an oil and gas well there, a grazing allotment or ski resort—are subtle on a piecemeal basis but cumulatively so devastating that a population can slip into irrevocable decline before there is enough time to react. Or the scale can seem overwhelming. During the mid-1990s an area covering fifty square miles of national forest had been logged in the Yellowstone region, nine hundred new miles of logging roads proposed in addition to the ten thousand-plus already existing miles. Energy companies have sought permits to drill exploratory oil and natural-gas wells—and build necessary access roads—in some eighty thousand acres of national forests. Resorts are expanding across formerly productive bear foraging areas, and more people are living at the periphery of the ecosystem, ensuring that a net gain in bear habitat will not be achieved without intervention to create room for them to wander. Furthermore, large numbers of bears are dying each year in reported and unreported cases.

Researchers know that many bears are killed each year both by humans in accidental encounters and by poachers. At any one time there are an estimated twenty-five to fifty radio-collared grizzlies in the Yellowstone ecosystem enabling researchers to decipher their whereabouts. It is compelling but hardly surprising to note that of the bear deaths recorded by researchers, those wearing radio collars account for between two-thirds and three-fourths of the known mortality rate. Troubling to those who manage bears is the unknown quantity of anonymous, uncollared bruins that die and are never seen. These animals tend to be the ones Mattson classifies as the "backcountry bears."

Conservation biologist Lance Craighead, an adjunct professor of biology at Montana State University, research director of the Craighead Environmental Research Institute and the son of Frank Craighead, says it is the invisible bears, those not equipped with radio collars, that are important to long-term survival of the grizzly. "A large percentage of uncollared bears are three- to four-year-olds," observes Craighead, who has extensive field experience tracking grizzlies in the Rockies and Alaska. "When they leave their mothers and strike out on their own, their probability of survival is lowest of any time after their first year. If they die from natural factors or human poaching we often will never know, and their loss to the population will not be felt or noticed for as long as a decade."

Undercover law-enforcement officers assigned to antipoaching patrols maintain that a lucrative black-market pipeline exists for grizzly gallbladders that are illegally exported to Asian countries and sold as ingredients in herbal teas and as aphrodisiacs. One veteran law-enforcement agent with the U.S. Fish and Wildlife Service told me that for every bear known to have died in Yellowstone, there is probably at least one other bear that has been poached for profit or as an act of protest against the Endangered Species Act. Some grizzly bear researchers believe that they are able to account for only one-fourth of the overall bear losses. This information is important because it shows that it is difficult not only to track and count uncollared backcountry bears but to ascertain how many die, which is

vitally important to managing a few hundred individuals and correctly evaluating how many actually exist.

The old western saw of "shoot, shovel, and shut up" is alive and
well, fueled by politicians who have sent a message to ranchers and
resource extraction companies that the Endangered Species Act is
something that can be flouted. No example is more poignant than
the one set by Steve Symms, a former congressman and U.S. senator from Idaho. Now retired from politics, Symms, while he was still
a legislator on Capitol Hill, reportedly walked into the office of a
high-ranking U.S. wildlife official in Washington, D.C., placed a
spent 30.06 shell casing on the official's desk, and made this pronouncement about a grizzly that had been preying upon sheep in
the Two Top Meadows section of Idaho's Targhee National Forest
outside Yellowstone: "You needn't worry about that bear on Two Top
anymore because it's no longer a problem." Days later, a bruin was
found dead from a rifle shot, but no charges were ever brought. The
arrogance is illustrative of a pervasive attitude. When I asked Symms
about the remark, which he didn't deny making, he said there is tangible angst among livestock producers, who don't believe they
should have to move their cows or sheep from public land to
accommodate grizzlies—even if the livestock is in prime bear habitat. Symms believes there were good reasons for exterminating the
grizzly from areas frequented by humans in the West.

Just as most imperiled species do not tumble toward extinction
overnight, the recovery of the grizzly cannot be accomplished
quickly, certainly not within the five-year spans that are the scope of
the Grizzly Bear Recovery Plan. Those short intervals are meaningless in the minds of conservation biologists who try to plot out
whether an organism can make it over the long term. By *long term,*
they mean centuries or more.

Conservation biologists do not believe the Yellowstone grizzly
will disappear altogether within ten, twenty, or even fifty years. In
fact, a century might pass before adverse trends—based upon poor
management decisions today—begin to fully manifest themselves.
Dan Goodman, an internationally respected population demographer at Montana State University, has studied statistical probability
and risk in the natural environment for many years. Goodman, besides being a good scientist, is a numbers cruncher. Although he has
never studied grizzlies in the field, he knows enough about the sur-
vivability quotients for large peripatetic creatures like grizzlies to

suggest that if they become "islandized" and cut off from other populations of their kind, they vanish.

Goodman cites a study done by Mark Shaffer, formerly a senior scientist with the Fish and Wildlife Service, who collected available data on the Yellowstone grizzly population, ran a computer model, and tried to extrapolate trends that would hint at the bear's long-term fate. His research concluded that although the Yellowstone grizzly has a high chance of persisting for the next one hundred years, it has a high probability of going extinct not long after that. Several of Shaffer's colleagues say that in order to ensure survival, a minimum base population of two thousand bears, more than seven times the current estimates, would be needed.

"From a genetic and demographic point of view, I like to think of 'two thousand bears for two thousand years' as a starting point to maintain a viable population," says Lance Craighead, an authority on grizzly bear genetics who completed his Ph.D. on the subject. "I believe that we can accomplish that with interconnected core reserves and still accommodate the healthy, inevitable growth of human populations in the area. We can have a high quality of life for both grizzlies and people, but we need to begin right now before our options are precluded by continuing poor management decisions. We need to afford the grizzly larger spaces. The Grizzly Bear Recovery Plan should promote that objective."

Goodman has viewed the trends in other ecosystems. "I would guess that as development continues on the national forests and private land surrounding Yellowstone Park, what you do is essentially shrink the boundaries of bear habitat back until they match the park borders. Bears will get forced into a smaller and smaller box of habitat instead of a larger and larger box, which is what they need to establish population viability. Rather than having the perimeter areas of the ecosystem as a source of colonization for bears, they become a sink," Goodman says. "I don't think that any population demographer would tell you that bodes well for the bear over the long term."

In fact, in 1994 Knight, his researcher wife, Bonnie Blanchard, and Eberhardt wrote in the journal *Canadian Zoology* that "if the population is actually increasing, and continues to do so, the limited habitat available will ultimately result in cessation of population growth."

During the 1990s a promising bilateral initiative crafted by Canadian and American scientists has emerged as a model of conservation biology. Called Yukon to Yellowstone, the plan aims to connect

and protect available grizzly habitat stretching from northern
Canada to western Wyoming. Without such links to ensure an inward and outward flow of genes, biologists fear that island populations will suffer reproduction problems through inbreeding. More
importantly, the initiative identifies the wide-ranging grizzly as an
umbrella species that if progressively managed will provide benefits
for suites of species that have similar habitat requirements. Contrary
to the opinions of the Interagency Grizzly Bear Committee, the
proponents of Yukon to Yellowstone make no apologies for pushing
scientific advocacy.

In a report titled "Large Carnivores, Science and Conservation
from Yellowstone to Yukon," Stephen Herrero, professor emeritus of
environmental science at the University of Calgary and an international authority on grizzlies, laid out the principles:

> Science is fundamental to conservation in the Yellowstone to Yukon
> region. Scientifically-based knowledge is significantly objective and,
> at least in theory, replicable. The public holds scientists in high es-
> teem, and "scientific results" are more often trusted than political or
> bureaucratic assessments. Scientific data often provide the basis for
> policy and management decisions affecting large carnivores. Scien-
> tific standards and concepts are firmly embedded in scientific para-
> digms. A paradigm is a conceptual framework for understanding
> events. This is not a trivial matter; our interpretations of the world,
> the questions we ask, the levels of significance we ascribe and the
> levels of confidence we accept are all based on the paradigms we
> hold. The interrelationship of people's differing values, attitudes and
> actions toward nature can be defined as their paradigm regarding na-
> ture, and in the context of carnivore conservation, people generally
> hold one or the other of two very different paradigms. In one, a per-
> son believes nature exists only for human use and consumption; in
> the other a person believes human beings are a part of nature and
> that human use of resources should be carefully regulated not only
> to conserve the resources, but also because nature has inherent value.
> Scientists, like all human beings, orient themselves to the world and
> their work on the basis of their paradigms. In this case, science is not
> fully objective. Conservation biology can be viewed as an emerging
> paradigm. With its mission of encouraging science that helps to
> maintain biological diversity and natural processes, it places signifi-
> cant inherent value on wild nature. Many of the scientists working
> on Yellowstone to Yukon subscribe to such a view, and out of that

view are asking for longer-term, more protection-oriented planning, and for a conservation interpretation of scientific results so that we do not err and lose populations. This conservative approach, favoring the application of the "precautionary principle," is based both on values and science. With its commitment to maintaining biological diversity and natural systems, conservation biology focuses on different questions and accepts different levels of confidence than do traditional resource utilization oriented paradigms.

In other words, it is an approach to protection squarely at odds with what some might argue are the Pollyannaish, industry-driven objectives promoted by the Interagency Grizzly Bear Committee and the Grizzly Bear Recovery Plan for Yellowstone.

Detractors of Serwheen argue that conditions are desperate for the bear, that reasonable solutions were foreclosed on years ago when the Forest Service continued to log and build roads into bear habitat while ignoring compelling evidence that such activities were harmful. "I just don't think their optimism is warranted at all," Pease, a staunch conservation biologist, tells me from his lab at the University of Texas, where he is completing a demographic study of the Yellowstone bear population. "I think it's absurd that they would try to delist the population without having done an adequate analysis of their own data."

One month after the Interagency Grizzly Bear Committee gave its unanimous endorsement to delisting the Yellowstone grizzly, Pease and Mattson wrote a letter summarizing a three-year examination of the study team's data. "We are now far enough along in our analysis of the Yellowstone grizzly bear demography data to have identified some major problems with previous analyses," they stated, citing problems with the standards Serwheen used to tally bear numbers and deaths. They noted that the way the government measures bear fecundity (i.e., females with cubs and corresponding population estimates), counts male bears, and estimates bear mortality are, at best, suspect. "Moreover," they added, "the problems with the existing analyses of the available data are large enough that correcting them could easily lead to a major revision in our understanding of the status of this population."

Serwheen insists that the documents painting a positive-sum picture of the grizzly population have been peer reviewed, yet few of the papers have been offered for review to those who seriously question the government's conclusions. "I can say emphatically that their science has not been peer reviewed because I've never received one of their manuscripts, and I think that's pretty damning given how much I know about these populations," Pease says. "This is not the first time that something like this has happened. They provide access only to those who are willing to toe the party line."

Shortly before the recovery plan—designed to guide grizzly management into the next century—was finalized in 1994, it came under a scathing barrage of criticism from twenty independent scientists. Shaffer said, "This current draft plan remains so weak that it calls into question not just the future of the grizzly, but the meaning of recovery under the Endangered Species Act." Thirty-eight conservation groups, led by Honnold at the EarthJustice Legal Defense Fund, sued, arguing that the plan failed to address habitat loss, establish minimum population levels to assure viability, and provide a mechanism for upholding the ESA. In 1996 a federal district court judge ordered the Fish and Wildlife Service back to the drawing board, calling the plan "arbitrary and capricious." The plan is being rewritten. It was an unprecedented defeat and embarrassment that, according to one U.S. government attorney, "rocked Chris Servheen back on his feet." The judge wrote that the Fish and Wildlife Service had no proof that the plan, which ostensibly would provide the groundwork for delisting, would result even in short-term recovery of the bear.

"If you use the current delisting criteria as laid out in the recovery plan, you're telling the public that everything's okay, and it is obviously not," Honnold says. He adds that Servheen has become an apologist for the Forest Service and the timber industry. Another conservation group—the Great Bear Foundation—has asked for the abolition of the Interagency Grizzly Bear Committee and the appointment of a new independent scientific panel. Says one Great Bear Foundation board member, "While the Great Bear Foundation does not yet have a formal proposal to oust Chris Servheen, we have suggested very vehemently that it is time for the Interagency Grizzly Bear Committee to be dismantled. The problem is larger than Chris Servheen, but he is the icon on the committee."

All the talk of delisting the grizzly makes environmentalists nervous, but Servheen believes they are overreacting. "Delisting just transfers the management from the federal government to the states.

I can tell you the pressure will be on the states, and they will be held to scrutiny. I have confidence in them, but if they screw it up once the species has been delisted, we can move to have the bear relisted in fifteen days."

Such a rationale provides no solace to bear supporters because the bear under state management nearly became extinct. Many of the low-lying valleys where bears prowl and used to gather around streams are made up of old-style cattle ranches that are quickly being transformed into residential subdivisions. In addition, the West remains a bastion for conservative politicians who align themselves with the Wise Use movement—a movement whose proponents despise grizzly bears for anything but hunting and would vehemently oppose any attempt to relist them under the Endangered Species Act.

In a stunning confession before he retired, Knight admitted to John Varley, the Yellowstone National Park research chief involved with the Interagency Grizzly Bear Committee, that he has reservations about delisting the grizzly. "It's too bad that delisting removes all the protection of the Endangered Species Act," Knight told Varley, as reported in a recent *Yellowstone Science* article. "I can imagine people out there with chain saws and herds of sheep ready to move in when the bear population is delisted, and that scares me. Because I don't know how to protect habitat. We just don't know. You can write some laws, but hell, we couldn't protect the Targhee from widespread clearcutting and roadbuilding in grizzly habitat, even under the Endangered Species Act. You get an administrator who wants to get around a law, and he'll do it."

The failure of government to protect grizzly habitat, however, transcends partisan politics. No party has a monopoly on hypocrisy. Even one of Secretary of the Interior Bruce Babbitt's righthand men, and a former golden boy of the environmental movement, George Frampton, failed to intervene on Mattson's behalf. Prior to Bill Clinton's election in 1992, Frampton had been president of the Wilderness Society, an organization that was a harsh critic of the way previous Republican administrations had managed bears. Today he is again a practicing attorney, hired, among other things, to represent Vice President Al Gore in the investigation of Gore's campaign fund-raising practices. Yet when Babbitt tapped Frampton to become the Department of the Interior's assistant secretary for fish and wildlife and parks, his crusade to beef up the federal government's protection of bear habitat stopped, even though the same resource managers and deleterious policies still were in place.

In fact, once Mattson's allegations were made public, Frampton organized what he called a secret "mock court" in Washington, D.C., where Servheen and conservationists were asked to present their cases. Inexplicably, Mattson was not asked to defend himself, which begs the question: Is Dick Knight to blame for Mattson's ouster? Or is Chris Servheen, George Frampton, or even Mattson himself? Was his removal caused by sinister motives or a serious lack of communication? The more likely instigator is a system of managing public wildlife that is resistant to change and innovation. "With some good luck and intensive management, I think that a small population of grizzlies could possibly hang on indefinitely in the Greater Yellowstone Ecosystem, but the essence of those survivors would be gone," says Lance Craighead. "We can do better than that. We must do better than that. We need visionary thinkers. We have a chance to provide a more balanced lifescape in the northern Rockies. We can plan for a healthier situation than that of the last tigers in India, or the last brown bears in Spain, or the last pandas in China. We can provide a high quality of life—not just for humans but for native plants and animals. We can protect and maintain biodiversity, but we need to think big."

Politics still controls the purse strings of land management agencies, and few bureaucrats or scientists in their right minds are willing, as they say, to bite the hand that feeds them. It means that science is forever a hostage to politicized science and meddling. "The Interagency Grizzly Bear Study Committee needs to decide whether it is going to be a decisionmaking body or continue as it has as a group of bureaucrats that gets together twice a year to talk and compare notes," Scott of the Greater Yellowstone Coalition says. "Not much in the way of meaningful progress is made with the committee, which leads one to ask, then why does it exist? The way it's structured and the kinds of decisions it doesn't make, it's not productive use of the managers' time or the public's time and money. It either needs to be a real ecosystem coordinator of making hard decisions or it needs to disband and quit pretending to be something it is not."

With several Republicans who are outspoken critics of the Endangered Species Act now presiding over key committees in Congress, in the years ahead it will be even tougher for the people who hold the grizzly's fate in their hands to do the right thing.

Will those who wear the uniform of the Fish and Wildlife Service and the Park Service—which partially funds the Yellowstone Interagency Grizzly Bear Study Team—assume their mandated role as advocates for wild places? Or will the people in charge wither under their own desires to assure their paychecks through ineffectual management with one foot constantly in retreat?

Richard West Sellars, a historian with the Park Service, pinpointed the flaws of public land management in his remarkably candid 1997 exposé, "Preserving Nature in the National Parks: A History." His analysis is a prescription for grizzly managers.

> In this era of heightened environmental concern, it is essential that scientific knowledge form the foundation for any meaningful effort to preserve ecological resources. If the National Park Service is to fully shoulder this responsibility at last, it must conduct scientifically informed management that insists on ecological preservation as the highest of many worthy priorities. This priority must spring not merely from the concerns of specific individuals or groups within the Service but from an institutionalized ethic that is reflected in full-faith support of all environmental laws, in appropriate natural resource policies and practices, and in the organizational structures of parks and central offices. When—and only when—the National Park Service thoroughly attunes its own land management and organizational attitudes to ecological principles can it lay claim to leadership in "the preservation of the natural environment."

The survival of the grizzly is not a "bear problem" but a problem of managing people. Bears will show us which habitat is best for them, but we must be willing to heed their message. "Really, in the end, it's not going to be science that saves the grizzly but human values," Mattson says. "We already know what the preponderance of science says—that large, wide-ranging omnivores that are slow to reproduce and ill adjusted to human presence are doomed unless we make room for them. Society has to ask itself, 'Do we value grizzlies and the type of environment they represent?' I believe the public does want to see the bear survive, and they are willing to make adjustments." As Mattson points out, the challenges in saving wide-ranging carnivores is determining the proper place for residential development, mines, hiking trails, clearcuts, and cows.

Mattson has yet to take his final stroll through the thickets of Yellowstone grizzly country. "We know a lot about the side issues relating to bears, but we know very little about how to ask the important biological questions. Dave Mattson is a person who can answer them and help us ensure that we are not acting blindly. We face a habitat crisis that may mean the only place people see grizzlies are in zoos and stuffed in museums," says Honnold. "If a few years from now Mattson is not at the forefront of grizzly bear biology, the Yellowstone ecosystem will be a sorrier place."

Latter-Day Frogs

*The frog does not drink up the pond in
which it lives.*—Inca proverb

DURING THE MIDDLE OF the nineteenth century, pioneers crossing the Great Basin had a folksy method for assaying the potability
of fresh water. If there were snakes and frogs in the bubbling springs
and ephemeral pools along the Humboldt Trail, they figured it was
safe to scoop a drink. In the silent absence of such creatures, the
logic was to beware—something was wrong.

This tried-and-true technique never failed its practitioners. It
helped slake the thirst of thousands of eastern religious refugees converging upon the arid territory of Utah. By 1847 Brigham Young
and his plucky tribe of Mormons were establishing their diaspora in
permanent settlements near the southern shores of the Great Salt
Lake, and the location supplied physical sustenance that the spiritual
teachings of Joseph Smith, the founder of Church of Jesus Christ of
Latter-Day Saints, could not deliver. Water and, in a manner of speaking, frogs formed a prescription for survival.

Soon Young and his clan drifted southward along the towering
western wall of the Wasatch Mountains, crossing the Bear, Weber,
Jordan, Provo, and other smaller rivers in succession. The Provo
River alone was home to riparian cottonwood, and spanned more
than a half mile across in spots and was veined by half a dozen channels. Today, it has been reduced to a single channel. In the backs of
their minds, fluent with scriptural literacy, they were thinking of
Mesopotamia while studying the engineering practices of beaver.
Biblically speaking, it was not a wilderness of milk and honey before them, but the land had potential.

As tributaries stormed down from the high country, running fast
with snowmelt, water filtered through the ancient bed of Lake Bon-
neville, which once submerged the Salt Lake Valley. On the knolls
rising above their future capital, the immigrants discovered surprisingly fecund meadows and seasonal ponds that held tadpoles. In the
evenings egrets, herons, cranes, and other wading birds sailed into

113

the backwater sloughs, ornamented with the domes of beaver lodges, to feed upon, among other animals, frogs, toads, and salamanders. Lining the larger river channels were cottonwood galleries, and at the foot of the mountains more grassy marshes and dark, sheltering pools. At night amphibians ratcheted up their primordial symphony. In this desert containing frogs and clean water, Young must have known he had reached a promised land.

A century and a half later, his messianic dream of a prosperous religious colony has come to full fruition. Riding a tidal wave of corporate business relocations and aging émigrés spilling in primarily from California, Utah is experiencing an unprecedented development boom, filling the provincial coffers with budgetary windfalls. Although most states in the United States are struggling to keep their government treasuries out of the red during this final decade of the second millennium, Utah is basking in the fiscal equivalent of winning the lottery. According to economists, the indicators of capitalistic wealth are as boisterous as a bullfrog.

Between Salt Lake City and Provo, new construction is racing down the Wasatch Front in anticipation of the 2002 Winter Olympic Games at Park City. Around St. George and Cedar City, in the downstate counties of Washington and Garfield, landowners are clearing the sagebrush for retirement dream homes and shopping centers where once there was unbroken desert crawling with desert tortoises. In the resort community of Moab, the outdoor recreation mecca of the inland West, tourists are making cash registers pipe like a tabernacle choir throughout the surreal red slickrock canyons. And just beyond the borders of Zion National Park, developers are planning to dam the soporific Virgin River and channel the flows to golf courses and swimming pools.

Yes, one could argue that the happy days of materialistic providence have arrived, but the frogs that guided Young to the well of paradise are no longer singing. They are croaking at an unsettling rate, and the stage for their demise was set years ago. An irrigation network started by early settlers now delivers water to towns and farms along the Wasatch Front. The system is huge and extravagant; some 7,500 ditches and trenches have been spliced from the natural wetlands and creeks. And, with the multibillion-dollar Central Utah Project (CUP), based on the Jordanelle Dam, further extending the tentacles of development, amphibian habitat is disappearing fast. And today the scientists charting the declines of native frogs, reptiles, and fish are as endangered as the animals themselves.

In the early 1990s the state of Utah announced that it had achieved a $200 million surplus due to swelling tax revenues. Rather than celebrate, Governor Mike Leavitt and a powerful group of ranching cronies decided, rather abruptly, that a little fiscal belt-tightening was in order. The first place Leavitt started was the Native Wildlife Section of the Utah Division of Wildlife Resources (DWR). Almost overnight a plan was hatched in the conference rooms of the state Capitol to purge the division's entire staff of nongame biologists, including the agency's only full-time herpetologist—a sincere and soft-spoken young man named David Ross.

The timing was uncanny—even developers chuckled at its daring—for Leavitt's surprising austerity measures were initiated just weeks after Ross had begun a novel study to identify wetlands and general habitat essential to Utah's threatened anurans (frogs, toads, and salamanders). His work focused on species that happen to live inside, or next to, prime real estate owned by those who figure to gain much from Utah's fast-growing economy and out-of-control land speculation. Implemented with the tacit blessing of the Utah state legislature, the plan to downsize had the fingerprint of one special interest constituency all over it—the opprobrious Cowboy Caucus, soon to be renamed the Western States Coalition. "There wasn't any mystery to what happened. David Ross started asking poignant questions about frogs, and for that curiosity he got summarily hacked apart because it made the local politicos nervous," says Ken Rait, former public lands director for the Southern Utah Wilderness Alliance (SUWA), which watched the action unfold. "David was essentially made an example by the Leavitt administration and the Department of Natural Resources of what will happen to any biologists who try to practice science that does not jibe with the politics of the Cowboy Caucus. That's why Utah is now headed for an ecological crisis."

The study of herpetology encompasses both amphibians and reptiles, but in more specific biological parlance it pertains to frogs, toads, salamanders, lizards, snakes, turtles, and tortoises, of which Utah has a lion's share, given the incredible range of habitat diversity from snow-capped peaks more than two miles above sea level to broiling deserts that routinely reach 110 degrees Fahrenheit.

Like his subjects, Ross prefers to hang back in the weeds and would rather avoid public attention. He is bashful, husky, funny, and intense, a classic introvert averse to making waves. He tries to be objective in a decidedly subjective world. Even when divulging the circumstances that led to his startling termination as a nongame biologist, there is little inflection in his voice. He obviously doesn't enjoy naming names, but get him started on a discussion of amphibian behavior and he can tick off, in rapid succession, the status, Latin genus, and exact location of a dozen reclusive species in the family of ranids. Nearly all, he says, are now in trouble. "You need to understand," he explains one evening at a Mexican restaurant in Salt Lake City where we feast on enchiladas and drown them in Coronas, "that Utah is different from any other place in the country."

Where Ross comes from in Maryland, not far from the famous estuaries of Chesapeake Bay, field science was held out to him as a virtuous pursuit. Rachel Carson tracked the residues of DDT there, Aldo Leopold took great delight in watching the spectacular annual convergence of waterfowl, and countless naturalists owe their beginnings to the vast mosaic of water and land. Slogging through the reedy marshes of the Eastern Shore, netting frogs and turtles along the way, Ross learned from older, accomplished scientists that a career in biology could be exotic and meaningful. "I didn't go to school or become a biologist in order to be politically subversive," he says, making sure I don't mistake him for a radical. "But I didn't want to become a doctor or lawyer either. I wanted to make a contribution because I just can't see the utility of ignoring the fact that species are being eliminated from our world every day. Science for me is a way of helping to understand why."

Fresh out of West Virginia University, Ross embarked upon a master's degree at the University of Wisconsin in Stevens Point and completed his thesis on aquatic turtles. He had a knack for deriving insight from the tiniest of details, and his professors were impressed. He instinctively knew where to find his boggy subjects in all seasons of the year. In Wisconsin, where Leopold wrote *A Sand County Almanac* and ushered in a new age of ecology, a broader picture of amphibian ecology took hold in Ross's head.

When an advertisement appeared for a herpetology position at the Utah Division of Wildlife Resources in the early 1990s, Ross was elated. The job represented a perfect opportunity to depart from the chilly glacial lake country of the upper Midwest and explore a state renowned for its herpetofauna. Landing the job, he drove west feeling giddy as his route paralleled a portion of the Mormon Trail. Upon arrival, Ross quickly developed a reputation for thoroughness in his data collection, but, ironically, it was his enthusiasm for his work that caused his superiors to worry. They hadn't anticipated, and apparently didn't want, someone quite so eager.

~

Herpetologists generally are a hard-core, eccentric lot who look out for their brethren. I heard about the now infamous purge of Utah's nongame division from several apoplectic friends who slip on hip boots and chase frogs on weekends. The dispatch came in the form of an e-mail from a federal biologist: "Todd, you should look into this." News of Ross's ouster had circulated quickly through national herpetology circles, though it netted only a few days' notice in the Salt Lake newspapers and then evaporated from the public eye.

The modern tale of wildlife management in Utah is a saga of odd coincidences that begins with a group of maverick federal-government-hating officials called the Cowboy Caucus. Seldom before in America has there been a more cavalier attack on the people assigned to study endangered species. In many ways, Utah seems an ideological extreme unto itself, even in the "New West."

What *is* the caucus? I pose the naive question to a friend and Utah-born conservation biologist who lives on the edge of Salt Lake City. "How much power could it actually have?" I ask, incredulous. "It sounds like some John Wayne anachronism." Politics is pervasive. It has become the cultural filter through which truth flows, I say. My attention perks when she laughs, then turns serious and puts her hand on my arm, playfully mocking. "What you don't understand is that most rural politicians in this state believe it is still their duty to tame the frontier," she says. "The attitude of manifest destiny didn't die at the turn of the century. It is merely shifting from ranching to development, and woe to the environment caught between."

In a 1995 story about the West's hardening of rightwing zealotry, the generalist magazine *Newsweek* pointed to a mentality that is rife in the caucus and the Western States Coalition. The paradox is that those who loathe the federal government most are those who derive the greatest benefits from its relative benevolence. Count the ways that Uncle Sam shows them the money: Below-market-value live-stock grazing fees, subsidized water and flood insurance, subsidized logging, subsidized wild predator control, and sweetheart mining deals are under increasing scrutiny by fiscal conservatives trying to corral the national debt. Still, "the old West won't go quietly. Its stalwarts will fight, and fairly or not, one of their main targets is the federal government, blamed for regulating the old extractive industries to death," the *Newsweek* reporter wrote. The antiregulation, anti-federalist, antizoning fervor, besides being a catalyst for obvious attempts to gut the Clean Air, Clean Water, and Endangered Species Acts, has resulted in a systematic attack on science. Carrying the "ignorance is bliss" banner is the Cowboy Caucus, known by a variety of names depending on which Western state you're in.

A cultural throwback, the Cowboy Caucus in Utah comprises mostly powerful Mormon families involved in the livestock, land speculation, water development, and tourism industries. Unabashedly hostile to preservation (in fact, it fought the creation of Utah's wondrous national parks that today form the basis of the state's tourism economy, and it is opposed to setting aside 5.7 million acres of wilderness, a move most citizens in the state favor), it has strategically worked to elect its anointed anticonservation representatives to state and federal office, including such well-recognized names as U.S. Senators Orrin Hatch and Bob Bennett, Congressman James V. Hansen, and of course Governor Mike Leavitt.

In his best-selling treatise, *The End of Nature,* Bill McKibben took note of the man-shall-exploit-the-earth-dogma that begins with the Bible and ends with the backhoe. "To get a sense for [this] meaning requires only a trip to Utah," McKibben suggested, "where the state motto is 'Industry' and the Mormons have made a great project of subduing nature, erecting some towns in places so barren and dry and steep that only missionary zeal to conquer the wild could be a motivation."

Enter David Ross.

Ross didn't know it at the time of his initial frog field studies, but the bureaucrats who created his position hired him, more or less, to keep the U.S. Fish and Wildlife Service from aggressively listing species proposed for protection on the Endangered Species List because of the ramifications for developers. As the actions of the Leavitt administration and those of the governor's legislative cronies imply, the state apparently had no intention of documenting the declines of frog and toad populations, which, by the time of Ross's hiring, were already well known.

Ross innocently set out to investigate reports that certain species had vanished from areas where they had historically lived. One species in particular—*Rana pretiosa*, the pretty western spotted frog—caught his attention. A striking creature, *R. pretiosa* has unmistakable brilliant markings. The coloration of the ventral surface, though quite variable, is alluring; the tint can be the color of king salmon or pumpkin orange, a garish feature for predator evasion. When the frog moves, the flash of color alarms its pursuer and creates a dodging effect, like a firefly at night, except in the water. "These are remarkable animals," Ross says. "They deserve our attention."

By late 1992 the Fish and Wildlife Service, citing frightening trends, decided internally that the spotted frog warranted listing as endangered under the Endangered Species Act (ESA). Utah's congressional delegation, knowing that a listing might slow down development that was already causing fragmentation of frog habitat, applied pressure, and Secretary of the Interior Bruce Babbitt ruled that *R. pretiosa* would be "precluded" from the list because of other species in more dire straits. It was the beginning of a trend. This decision was just another engagement in a protracted conflict over the Endangered Species Act, but it caught both the frog and Ross in the crossfire. In 1993 Department of the Interior officials stated that they would not list the spotted frog if Utah demonstrated that it could craft an aggressive conservation strategy for saving the species on its own.

Environmentalists immediately saw this statement as a ruse for inaction, and one could argue that their suspicions have been confirmed. Herpetological experts from around the region suggest that *R. pretiosa* has become so rare along the Wasatch Front that it is nearing a point of no return. Confirmed sightings were already scarce when Ross took up his search. Launching several surveys into the frog's traditional range on both sides of the Wasatch, he found the accumulating evidence to be nothing short of alarming. Wildlife demographers say that the long-term viability of a species is threatened whenever the number of individuals drops below five hundred.

Where there had historically been continuous populations of frogs—and where frogs were assumed to exist—Ross was able to document only patchy islands of frog populations, disconnected from one another and all below the crucial numerical threshold. In a report presented to the Fish and Wildlife Service, which he coauthored with biologists Dennis Shirley, Patricia White, and Leo Lentsch, the species' shrinking distribution was verified. A second report, prepared by the same authors plus Mark Stanger and Kenneth McDonald, examined the abundance and distribution of spotted frogs in Utah's western desert. Together, the surveys alluded to several possible factors for frog declines and, in passing, mentioned a few land practices dear to the hearts and pocketbooks of the Cowboy Caucus—cattle grazing, pesticide use to control insects (which frogs eat), the introduction of hatchery-raised trout (which eat native frogs) for sport fishing, and draining of wetlands for development. Ross also completed a survey of boreal toads that turned up just three individuals in northern Utah. Nearly all of the historical populations of boreal toads across the West are gone. More may or may not exist in Utah, Ross told his superiors, but little could be deduced without a census.

Although Ross's midlevel supervisors praised his performance, a conspicuous hush was the response as the information rose higher through the bureaucracy. There were growing concerns regarding how the Fish and Wildlife Service might interpret the findings. Ross didn't know it yet, but his days were numbered, and it didn't take long for him to start feeling the heat. He heard the first rumblings in 1993 that "my job would be toast." In July he was called upstairs. Behind the scenes, landowners allied with the Cowboy Caucus had expressed disapproval of attempts to pinpoint the location of frogs. "When my boss dragged me up to the director's office, I had no idea what was going on," Ross says. "I was the first one in a whole line of people they wanted to get rid of."

In a memorandum, he was informed that his job and the entire nongame division were being eliminated through a "restructuring plan" that would save the taxpayers of Utah money. Ross asked Tim Provan, then acting director of the agency (before a man named Bob Valentine was hired) why he was being fired. He was told to take a position studying brine shrimp in northern Utah or leave the department altogether. Fifty other nongame scientists were forced out too, many of them with oversight responsibilities for assessing the status of vulnerable plant and animal species. When asked for an explanation, Provan said to Ross, "All I can tell you is it's political."

Leavitt and his head of the DWR, Ted Stewart, feigned innocence, with the governor claiming flatly that there was no collusion between his administration and developers.

The normally reticent Utah Association of Herpetologists saw it differently. Following Ross's ouster, scientific members of the association wrote in its newsletter, *Intermontanus,* "It is rumored that the [herpetology position] in regards to the management of the spotted frog [*Rana pretiosa*] and the desert tortoise, as well as a number of other herp species was a major factor in the decision to eliminate the herpetologist position. Apparently Dave Ross has been able to open a few eyes which were, politically, better left shut. So all in all the Utah Department of Wildlife Resources has decided to let the Wasatch populations of the spotted frog go extinct, and to ignore the rest of the state's herpetofauna."

One manager at the DWR, who still works in the agency but wishes to remain anonymous, suggests, "Ted Stewart and Bob Valentine couldn't understand why all this fuss was being made about frogs and toads. [Stewart] thought about the only value they had was being dipped in a fondue pot and put on the end of a hook and jiggled beneath a cane pole." This, I was told, has become the typical agency view of any species that cannot be shot, caught on a line, or bought or sold for profit.

Although the DWR is charged by law to oversee some 630 species of wildlife in the state, just seventy-one fall under the category of "consumptive use," though they account for an overwhelming percentage of the budget. Yet the number of people in Utah involved in nonconsumptive enjoyment of wildlife was 61 percent higher than the number of sport hunters and fishermen, according to Wayne Martinson, a lobbyist for the Audubon Council of Utah. The implication, Martinson says, is that Utahans and tourists coming into the state have an abiding appreciation for a full range of species, not just those that wind up on the dinner table—including spotted frogs. Wildlife diversity, he says, translates into better quality of life for humans. Still, there exists a great disparity that favors production of game species because they are a cash cow.

A disappointed Tim Provan left the agency in August 1995. He says "realignments" of wildlife departments are not unique to western states, "but none have been as extreme as what went down in Utah. There's a power struggle being waged between governors, legislatures, and fish and game departments that are perceived by development interests as having too much power. The legislatures want to rein them in."

Provan's successor, Bob Valentine, was a favorite of political strategists from the Western States Coalition. A former personnel manager at an aerospace firm, Valentine, who has since retired, had no biology experience when he helped dismantle part of his own bureaucracy. He became director only after the legislature changed a rule that had specified that the position be filled by a wildlife professional. As a duck hunter, Valentine met the new requirement that the director needed only to "have an interest in wildlife."

Valentine maintains that the shakedown among nongame biologists was merely a staff consolidation. "What we did was fold the nongame people into either the aquatic or wildlife section. I don't think it was an unprecedented thing. It's been done in other states. ... The reductions and consolidation were really based on a six-month review of the division by the Wildlife Management Institute out of Virginia. That was their recommendation. To suggest anything else is a blatant falsehood." As a point of fact, the Wildlife Management Institute's recommendations did indeed look at ways to "streamline and consolidate," but nowhere was there a suggestion to eliminate the nongame division.

Although Valentine claims there was little political influence exercised on his agency, Met Johnson, a downstate rancher, two-term legislator, and well-known provocateur with the Wise Use movement, is not nearly as equivocal. He openly and unabashedly boasts that it was the caucus that ordered the purge of the nongame division. Today he is director of the Western States Coalition, and he and his allies claim credit for pulling the strings that got Ross and other biologists ousted.

"The first year of the reduction in staff [1994]," Johnson notes, "we shut down the funds for the nongame division. Seventy employees got the ax. Whenever we spoke, they [Valentine and Division of Natural Resources head Ted Stewart] jumped because they knew we meant what we said. Just to list the damn frog and put all that land in jeopardy is wrong, and we won't have it. They [the department] were told in essence that they could go out and create new habitat for the frog if the frog was in trouble, but don't even think about being cooperative with the Fish and Wildlife Service [in protecting habitat] because if it presents a problem for private land owners, you're dead, which they knew meant they'd be out of funds."

Johnson says the Western States Coalition has transformed itself into a juggernaut. "Three years ago, us so-called members of the Cowboy Caucus got together with legislators in Utah and other states and started a coalition that now has four thousand members, most of them elected officials from the county commissioner level on up to legislators at the state level. We've had several members of Congress who say they support us, but they have their own caucus in Washington. We do work together, but not officially."

During the summer of 1997 the Western States Coalition sponsored a "fact-finding mission" that brought House Speaker Newt Gingrich and a handful of key senators and congressmen through the West. Among them were some of the most notorious Republican critics of the Endangered Species Act, including U.S. Rep. Helen Chenoweth (Idaho), U.S. Rep. Barbara Cubin (Wyoming), Utah's Hansen, Don Young (Alaska), Texas's Tom DeLay, and Montana's Rick Hill.

Johnson lays out the mission of the Western States Coalition: "We've dedicated ourselves to making a difference in failed public policy and to counteract the strategies of the extremist environmental movement that do more harm than good." He notes that the coalition has plotted a clear agenda on spotted frogs and any other imperiled species. "The Fish and Wildlife Service would be damn fools to not clean up their image by not cooperating with us," he says. "We have the potential to generate enough outcry that not only can we do away with two-thirds of the U.S. Fish and Wildlife Service but we'll have them crawling to us on their hands and knees. That's not a threat. They're making themselves enemies everywhere. Pretty soon there will be enough enemies and we'll derail the whole Endangered Species Act train. If they don't accommodate us, they are stupid."

The housecleaning that swept up Ross extended through the ranks and targeted anyone with a conservation ethic that might clash with the ideas of the Western States Coalition. Clair Jensen, a regional DWR supervisor, made the mistake of supporting a plan to protect some of Utah's prized rivers in the Dixie National Forest as wild and scenic. The action enraged Met Johnson, and as a result the popular Jensen was ordered to take a paper-pushing job in an

attempt to punish him. "You can bet most of the agency's employees are not working there for the money," wrote newspaper colum-
nist Ray Grass, condemning the ongoing purge in the *Deseret News*.
"They're there because they love, or loved their work and care about
their charges, be they deer or barn owls. [The Cowboy Caucus]
went after the DWR and it looks now like they won. They taught
the agency a lesson: Mess with us and you'll be sorry."

~

Blunt and disturbing, the philosophy isn't new, but the action had a
mammoth-sized iceberg lurking beneath it. Scientists have known
for half a century that Utah's approach to the environment was draconian. In 1948 noted ecologist Vasco M. Tanner (an acquaintance
and contemporary of Aldo Leopold) delivered a paper to the Utah
Academy of Sciences, Arts and Letters. The pioneering author of
Amphibians of Utah, published by the Academy of Sciences in 1931,
Tanner noted long before research confirmed his hunch that amphibians and reptiles have incredible value to humans and the environment. His comments on the politics of wildlife management in
Utah would also prove prophetic decades later when the purge of
threatened- and endangered-species biologists was well under way.

"Just as we have disregarded the native fish fauna in developing
game fishing in Utah, so have we ignored 69 species of amphibians
and reptiles in the state," he noted. "Without the help from toads,
frogs, lizards and snakes the agricultural interests would be greatly
changed."

In fact, the heavy-handed land use practices endorsed by the
Cowboy Caucus in recent years have doomed many species and led
to a need for more pesticides. "We know from actual study that the
toads and some frogs are worth [many dollars apiece] in biological
control on the cultivated land of this state. We must do more to
make this known and to protect their numbers. The rodents and
other small mammals found on the range and mountain lands are
food for many of our native snakes. In fact the snakes play a major
role in reducing small mammal populations. More attention should
be given to promoting the welfare of the serpent population of our
state," Tanner said.

Tanner foresaw the need for ecosystem management, and he recognized that political maneuvering by progenitors of the Cowboy
Caucus was, even then, resulting in the loss of nongame animals.

"This line of thinking leads to the conclusion that we must deal with all the species of plants and animals as well as the environment of this region in working out a conservation program," he went on. "We should have the best-trained personnel that the state can produce and provide them with the best equipment and facilities at our disposal. This personnel should not be tied to political apron-strings, but be free to carry out a program in keeping with the findings, and with our peculiar conditions. No group should be able to dictate a short-sighted program which deals with a few species at the expense of the whole. We need more science and biology in our management."

After Ross, Jensen, and dozens of other biologists were targeted for dismissal, the SUWA attempted to pull back the curtain on the back-room deals that have been de rigueur in the state for years. SUWA filed a Freedom of Information Act request that sent members of state government scrambling. What seemed on the surface to be the simple elimination of one herpetologist is actually a single strand leading into a much broader web of patronage.

State officials at the DWR, trying to throw up an economic roadblock to public disclosure of their activities, responded to SUWA's request by saying they would bill the organization $40,000 to copy documents in DWR files. Eventually the DWR backed down after SUWA members offered to go through the files themselves. SUWA's probe uncovered numerous examples of meddling by the Leavitt administration in the management of Utah's wildlife and science programs. The governor's own family, it turned out, had a sticky situation to fix. In the 1990s outbreaks of whirling disease have surfaced across the West in wild trout streams. The spread of the pathogenic protozoan *Myxobolus cerebralis*—potentially catastrophic to certain wild fish species such as rainbow trout because it deforms their skeletal systems—was traced to hatchery-raised fish, which are notorious vectors.

Although the state of Utah has a policy forbidding the release of hatchery-raised fish into wild streams unless they are proven to be disease free, in 1991 whirling disease was traced back to the Road Creek Ranch hatchery, owned in part by Governor Leavitt and two of his brothers. The Leavitt family initially denied responsibility. However, the investigating agency was none other than the Utah DWR. In a stunning confession, Stewart, who oversaw the DWR, intimated in personal correspondence that he had not acted as aggressively in investigating the Leavitts as if the situation had involved a normal citizen. "I have not been able to take some of the actions I would have liked out of fear that I would do your son, the Governor, more harm than good," he wrote in a letter to Leavitt's mother obtained by the SUWA.

Department investigators also revealed that there was little question about the source of disease, and they wrote a damning internal memo, "It must be pointed out that the inappropriate transfer of live fish from [Road Creek Ranch] facilities not having the necessary fish health approval resulted in the transfer of *Myxobolus cerebralis* to other facilities. The other private [fish] growers in the area were checked and found to be negative." No fewer than thirty violations of state aquaculture laws were documented and filed by the Utah attorney general's office. The Leavitt family pled no contest to eight of the violations.

The political ambitions of Governor Mike Leavitt are no secret. Many expect him to make a run for the U.S. Senate or possibly accept a nomination for Secretary of the Interior under a GOP administration. He has even been mentioned as a possible Republican presidential contender in either 2000 or 2004. Doubtless, one of his campaign planks would be a promise to spread Utah's development boom to the rest of the country.

Critics of the Leavitt administration see plausible connections between the fish-hatchery incident and the purge of nongame biologists. Hatchery-raised game fish such as the brown trout produced and sold by the Leavitts as a private business endeavor were also identified in Ross's reports as threats to amphibians. A spokesman for the governor dismissed the suggested connection as "conjecture and coincidence."

According to SUWA, coincidences were popping up all over the place. "Though it may be coincidence, during the 1994 legislative session, Utah's cowboy caucus introduced a bill to transfer control of private hatcheries from the Division of Wildlife Resources to the State Department of Agriculture," SUWA representatives wrote. "Supported by a minority of private fishing interests—the Leavitt family included—it seemed the legislation was a reprisal for the DWR's crackdown on whirling disease."

Yet another coincidence was the elimination of the state fisheries chief: Bruce Schmidt, who had a hand in the investigation of the governor's family business, found that his job had disappeared along with eighteen other mid- and upper-level management jobs in his department.

However, skirmishes over frogs and fish were only part of a much larger story, according to Bruce Johnson, who oversaw the state's habitat protection programs for all endangered species. Looming large was the Cowboy Caucus's fear of what protecting the habitat of threatened desert creatures might do to the exploding suburbanization of southwestern Utah. Prominent among these species were the desert tortoise and the Gila monster.

"I don't think there is any question as to why the nongame section was abolished," Johnson says. "It had to do, in part, with the hatchery controversy and the amphibians, but those were just tips of the iceberg. In my estimation one of the most compelling reasons was fear of what listing the desert tortoise [as an endangered species] might do to developers in southwestern Utah. The Cowboy Caucus, going back to the time that Utah prairie dogs were listed, had been positioning itself to subvert the process."

Listed as a threatened species under the Endangered Species Act, the Utah prairie dog *(Cynomys parvidens)* resides on public and private lands in southern Utah. During the 1980s, developers in Cedar City were up in arms over restrictions to save the last vestiges of habitat. Although guidelines allow private landowners to kill thousands of prairie dogs each year, the red tape left the Cowboy Caucus poised to beat back further application of the Endangered Species Act and sent its chief ally in Congress, James V. Hansen, to do its bidding.

"The anger that began with the Utah prairie dog carried over to the desert tortoise in Washington County," says Johnson, who says he was threatened by landowners who ordered him to not do his job of protecting tortoise habitat. "The best tortoise habitat happens to be on land where residential subdivisions and shopping centers are being built. When development in St. George started booming, landowners who saw that prairie dogs were allowed to be killed in certain situations wanted the same provisions for the tortoise. Our department took a lot of heat for upholding the law."

Met Johnson (no relation to Bruce) of the Western States Coalition appears to agree: "If you saw your neighbor's property taken away and rendered useless because of a desert tortoise, what would you do the next time you saw one of them tortoises on your property? I'll tell you this: You know them tortoises aren't going to last long. People are going to do the shoot, shovel, and shut-up routine."

Debunking the notion that federally protecting a species necessarily brings economic calamity, Stephen Meyer, director of the Environmental Politics and Policy Center at the Massachusetts Institute of Technology, took a long, hard look at what has become a widely held perception. After examining the impact of ESA listings on state economies, Meyer found that "endangered species listings have not depressed activity as measured by growth in construction employment and gross state product." He noted, "The assertion that the Endangered Species Act has harmed the American farmer, hobbled agricultural production, and decimated the forest industry is baseless."

Furthermore, it was reported in the *Sloan Management Review* that "of the 781 domestic species for which the Fish and Wildlife Service was responsible as of May 1993, the majority lived on private land." Yet, the writer noted, "no count has ever found that operation of the ESA has taken private property in violation of the Fifth Amendment."

When I ask Met Johnson to give me a few examples of his neighbors' property being seized by the government or rendered useless because of the desert tortoise, he can't come up with any, but he assures me that "there are a lot out there." Such assertions possess cachet to those for whom alleged land grabs are part of larger government conspiracy theories: Belgians flying black helicopters, one-world governments trying to subvert freedom in the United States through the designation of world heritage sites, and allegations that thousands of Nigerians are now poised on the border of Canada ready to invade our sweet land. Paranoia and antifederalism—the two go hand in hand.

~

In the American West today, there is a widely held perception that the latest backlash against federalism began when Bill Clinton wielded his executive power to create the new Grand Staircase–Escalante National Monument. But in southern Utah, the seeds of rebellion were actually sown months earlier as bulldozers owned by Garfield County tore through the fragile desert soils of Capitol Reef

National Park. For advocates of public land protection, the date, February 13, 1996, is considered a day that will live in infamy and a possible foreshadowing of what is yet to come. Not long after sunrise, the heavy-equipment operators entered Capitol Reef and defiantly widened the historic Burr Trail, a bucolic dirt roadway that runs through the park from the town of Boulder to the Bullfrog Marina on Lake Powell. Before shocked park rangers could halt the incursion, the fleet of county bulldozers, road graders, and dump trucks had penetrated a mile into the scenic preserve, cutting through hillsides, crushing vegetation, and realigning the roadbed.

Capitol Reef superintendent Charles Lundy, known for his otherwise calm demeanor, surveyed the damage, then issued a fiery press release. He likened the Garfield County trespass to the sneak attack by the Japanese at Pearl Harbor. Had the premeditated action been carried out by individual citizens, their vehicles would have been confiscated and they would have been immediately arrested, thrown in jail, and charged with felony vandalism for destroying public property. Instead, the defense used by Garfield County was that local officials (who went unpunished) were merely adhering to the letter of federal law. Those same local officials in Garfield County are an example of the dogma perpetrated by the Western States Coalition. Invoking an obscure and thinly worded code drafted a year after the Civil War ended, these hostile rural lawmakers have deployed Revised Statute 2477 as a battering ram to punch highways into wild areas previously off limits to modern encroachment. Calling it "the Right-of-Way Law," several counties blessed with the tacit support of U.S. senators and congressmen have asserted some seventeen thousand road claims in national parks and forests, wildlife refuges, and tracts administered by the Bureau of Land Management (BLM).

If strung together, the length of miles sought in the current RS 2477 land grab would reach the moon. Some 160,000 miles, enough to encircle the earth many times at the equator, have been staked out in Denali, Wrangell–St. Elias, and Glacier Bay National Parks in Alaska alone.

"This is a very real concern," says Capitol Reef's Lundy. "Albeit somewhat difficult to understand at first blush, it is not an abstract threat. Right here in the wake of bulldozers we have an example of lands, normally afforded the highest level of protection by citizens, being breached with RS 2477."

In a 1993 internal memorandum, the National Park Service (NPS) estimated that sixty-eight Park Service units nationwide, encompassing seventeen million acres, could be affected by RS 2477. Tens of millions of acres of Forest Service and federal BLM holdings are vulnerable too. "[The roads] could cross many miles of undisturbed fish and wildlife habitat, historical and archaeological resources, and sensitive wildlands," the memo stated. "[They] would undoubtedly derogate most unit values and seriously impact the ability of the NPS to manage the units for the purposes for which they were established."

Although boosters of RS 2477 say their intention is simply to gain access to vast stretches of the federal estate, especially in states where the majority of land in counties is federally controlled, Mark Peterson, Rocky Mountain regional director of the National Parks and Conservation Association (NPCA), sees it as a subterfuge for more ambitious goals. Not only are the congressional delegations of Utah and Alaska promoting RS 2477 interests on behalf of natural resource developers who contribute generously to their campaigns, but the law represents a powerful tool for mounting an ex post facto retaliation against Clinton for his creation of Grand Staircase–Escalante. It also can be summoned as an argument against protection of wilderness. In Utah, where citizens have demonstrated resounding support for setting aside 5.7 million acres of BLM land as wilderness, much of that land would be eliminated from consideration as a result of RS 2477 highways.

Descended from the same architects of manifest destiny who drafted the now archaic 1872 Mining Law—which elevates mineral development as the supreme use of federal lands—RS 2477 evolved from a clause embedded in the Mining Law of 1866. The original intent was to establish right-of-ways, vis-à-vis "highways," to provide access to natural resources across public lands. But conservationists note that it is essential to consider access in the context of nineteenth-century travel. Again, consider, say, the wagon train of Mormon émigrés traveling westward.

"The definition of *highway* then, from now, is arguably different," says Destry Jarvis, a National Park Service resource specialist in Washington, D.C. "We don't think that cow paths, sled-dog routes, jeep tracks through riverbottoms, hiking trails, traplines, and abandoned carriage routes translate into justification for modern highways that can accommodate eighteen-wheelers. Further, the intent was to provide access across federal lands, not simply to spawn a bunch of dead-ends, which is what most of these claims do. They lead to nowhere." And they can cause environmental havoc.

Apparently, the U.S. Congress and President Gerald R. Ford agreed with that assessment twenty years ago, for in 1976 enactment of the Federal Land Policy Management Act (FLPMA) essentially repealed RS 2477, honoring only valid existing claims.

However, in 1988 the specter of RS 2477 rose from the grave. As a parting gift from the Reagan administration to its Sagebrush Rebellion allies in the West, Secretary of the Interior Donald Hodel abruptly announced that all claims existing prior to 1976—no matter how nebulous—could be reasserted. The action flung open the door for states and counties to map out highway right-of-ways based even on previously ephemeral travel lanes long overtaken by sagebrush. A new land rush sprang to life overnight. (The term *Sagebrush Rebellion* refers to the movement of resource extractionists to have the federal government sell off public lands to the highest private bidders.)

During the past decade, the NPCA and other groups have banded together to expose the insidious implications of the law, though most park visitors remain oblivious to its existence. Peterson says the worst part of RS 2477 is that local government entities are trying to circumvent public review. Constructing the right-of-ways, road crews could skirt compliance with environmental regulations that shield endangered species, air, water, and archaeological artifacts. The loophole, watchdog groups warn, is big enough to drive a semi through and wide enough to transform backcountry trailheads into off-road-vehicle (ORV) express lanes. On the tender tundra of the Arctic National Wildlife Refuge, RS 2477 is regarded by oil industry planners as a perfect excuse to run a pipeline across virgin habitat for caribou, bear, and birds. In Utah, it is a wrecking ball aimed at habitat for imperiled amphibians and reptiles.

"With the exception of the Burr Trail," the Park Service's Jarvis says, "I know of no examples crossing the national parks where there is an RS 2477 claim that meets the definition of the RS 2477 statute, but, of course, it all depends on your perspective. Are you re-siding in the nineteenth century, when wildness was a thing to be conquered, or is your home in this one, when it is something to be cherished?"

NPCA's Alaska regional director, Chip Dennerlein, an expert on the nuances of RS 2477, argues that the kind of access promoted by special interests could destroy the very elements synonymous with the state and invite ecological havoc. Five years ago an analysis by the Congressional Research Service found that a strict process of gauging the validity of claims was badly needed. Shortly thereafter, Secretary of the Interior Babbitt attempted to do just that administratively, to undo the damage started by Hodel, but counties fearing that he would steal their thunder filed a lawsuit. "In our national parks, we've managed to save a few remarkable examples of God's creation for our children," Babbitt said. "Do the American people really want them covered with asphalt?"

Angered, the Western States Coalition, an umbrella group representing mining, logging, grazing, and real estate interests, demanded Babbitt's resignation. This controversy set the stage for lawmakers from Utah and Alaska to draft giveaway right-of-way legislation.

Yet in a demonstration of political gamesmanship nonpareil, Senators Frank Murkowski and Ted Stevens of Alaska joined Orrin Hatch and Bob Bennett of Utah in slyly expediting RS 2477 claims by attaching a rider to the bill intended to provide disaster relief for North Dakota flood victims in the summer of 1997. The "Pave the Parks" rider that refers management of claims to the states was exposed by Senator Dale Bumpers of Arkansas but still squeaked by. In addition, U.S. Representative James Hansen, another Utah Republican, authored a bill even more egregious, a county-drafted plan that put the onus of reviewing claims on the federal government and stipulated that any that could not be invalidated would be considered legitimate. Responding to the ramrod tactic, the *Salt Lake Tribune* wrote in a critical editorial, "The Hansen proposal is just another reactionary strike in the Republicans' reverse war on the West."

Conservationists today find themselves facing a conundrum. Although groups such as NPCA have spearheaded efforts to remove parks from RS 2477 claims, the SUWA fears that any exemption would focus intense pressure on BLM and Forest Service lands, which are the heart of proposed new federal wilderness areas and habitat for threatened species. Such angst may be moot. A spokesman for Hansen said the congressman has no intention of excluding parks and in fact believes that the Burr Trail episode in Capitol Reef had validity as Utah seeks to implement its alleged five thousand right-of-way claims. Department of the Interior solicitor John Leshy, who prepared a process for sorting out RS 2477 claims, testified that what the Alaska and Utah delegations have in mind goes "beyond the mischievous to the truly staggering."

Managers from several parks in the West said they were hesitant to speak candidly of their apprehension about RS 2477 because they fear retaliation. But Denny Huffman, who recently retired as superintendent of Dinosaur National Monument and held the same position in Colorado National Monument, bluntly describes RS 2477 as a "spaghetti Western." "They don't deny it," Huffman, a thirty-four-year veteran of the Park Service, says. "The strongest backers of this movement admit they wouldn't mind making the backcountry of the West and Alaska look like a plate of spaghetti, which I believe most Americans would find wholly unappetizing."

Huffman suggests that the western county commissioners who take issue with Babbitt's attempt to examine the validity of RS 2477 claims are suffering from a contradiction in logic. "They had no problem when Interior Secretary Hodel asserted his own standard of what qualifies as a road, but now they are denying the same authority to Interior Secretary Babbitt," he explains. What is rarely mentioned, he says, are the subtle environmental impacts and the fragmentation of solitude. "In remote areas of Dinosaur National Monument, we have peregrine falcon aeries where the wisest management decision to ensure falcon reproduction is to protect those nest sites from intrusion," Huffman says. "If someone asserts they have a right to go in there under RS 2477, where does that leave recovery of the peregrine? Every park in the West has similar problems."

The confrontation in Capitol Reef, a park where 99 percent of the rugged terrain is managed for primitive qualities, is a striking example of what happens when counties take matters into their own hands. The Burr Trail is one of the seminal scenic drives in the West; it ascends through switchbacks and affords spectacular views of the Henry Mountains and the signature Waterpocket Fold geologic feature. Despite objections from park officials, Garfield County road crews have continued to widen the Burr Trail—almost doubling its girth over the past decade—in the name of RS 2477. At present the Boulder-to-Bullfrog stretch averages just twenty-seven cars a day, but if the county succeeds in getting the dirt road blacktopped, vehicle numbers are expected to climb into the hundreds.

None of the RS 2477 critics dispute that the Burr Trail qualifies under the right-of-way provisions because it has received continuous use. The objection is that Garfield County has never been willing to scrutinize the appropriateness of marshaling bulldozers in a national park. "Garfield County's outrageous actions along the Burr Trail only highlight the damage to our national parks possible by this outdated law," NPCA's Peterson says. "Straightening and widening the road as the county would like to do fundamentally compromises the primitive attributes of the park. Rather than having the feeling of traveling through the 'Old West,' visitors will feel no different than if they were driving to their local Burger King."

Even though county officials grumble about never having enough money to maintain their other roads, they are headstrong about upgrading the Burr Trail because RS 2477 allows them to trump the federal government on its own turf. Capitol Reef isn't alone. Other counties have used RS 2477 as a preemptive maneuver to deliberately degrade the character of the landscape. When Kane County commissioners received word that the Department of the Interior was examining BLM lands near Canyonlands National Park for inclusion in federal wilderness, bulldozers were dispatched to the scene. San Juan County followed suit. Defying a federal cease-and-desist order, heavy-equipment operators in both counties plowed a swath of earth disturbance into the middle of the desert and then turned around.

An indication of the Utah delegation's apparent willingness to assert the supremacy of RS 2477 over the national interests of park protection and fiscal conservatism is revealed in a press release issued by Senator Bennett. He took the controversial stand after some of his constituents cried foul over the abuses at Capitol Reef, where "standard road maintenance" resulted in the razing of hillsides. "In the interest of public safety, the county performed road work in the park boundaries. They removed some earth within the right-of-way," Bennett stated, chastising the Park Service for bringing suit. "This administration is grasping at ways to reverse 130 years of legal precedent and limit essential access of many rural communities. We cannot allow this to happen."

Barbara Hjelle, an attorney who has represented Utah counties in a number of RS 2477 cases and is a chief ally of the Western States Coalition, went so far as to suggest in testimony before Congress that her clients, not federal land managers, should have final control over the distribution of access. Her message to Babbitt: Butt out and leave the bulldozing to us.

"[Babbitt's] policies have resulted in excessive intermeddling by federal agents in the day-to-day management of public rights-of-way in the rural West," she said. "These public rights-of-way should be managed by the state and local governments that have traditionally exercised jurisdiction over them."

What neither Bennett nor Hjelle mentions is that U.S. taxpayers are the ones who will get stuck holding the bag. A congressional study suggested that investigating the thousands of RS 2477 claims could cost the U.S. treasury up to $5 million each. In Utah, with its five thousand right-of-way claims, taxpayers would shell out between $5 million and $25 million to process the claims.

At Capitol Reef there is also a troubling irony. Thanks to the disbursement of federal highway funds to local counties, part of the destruction in the park was subsidized with U.S. tax dollars. Adding insult to injury, citizens had to pay twice when federal lawyers were called in to prevent further resource damage.

"When people read this story, their first reaction might be, 'What a shame. Too bad for Capitol Reef,' and in so doing conclude that the Burr Trail is an isolated incident. But it's not," Lundy says. "The conflict here is only the beginning. Pick a favorite public land. There are hundreds, if not thousands, of other Burr Trails waiting to happen."

～

Of all that can be loathed or admired about the political machinery of the Western States Coalition, former law-enforcement specialist Bruce Johnson, a practicing Mormon, says that what must be most admired—and reckoned with—is its irrefutable base of power. Members of this fraternity, many of whom also hold prominent positions in the Church of Jesus Christ of Latter-Day Saints, are connected at multiple levels.

Johnson says he and his staff eventually got tired of coping with constant interference and obstruction in doing their job. They vowed they would undertake enforcement actions on behalf of imperiled species regardless of what the landowners affiliated with the Western States Coalition said. He should have known better. Johnson had twenty-three years of distinguished service with the DWR when the political powers eliminated his job and then pressured him into early retirement. Today he teaches wildlife enforcement classes at Brigham Young University.

"We said anybody who drives over a tortoise with a bulldozer is going to be prosecuted," Johnson says. "No one ever told me directly to stay out of the area, per se, but I received word second- or third-hand many times that the Cowboy Caucus would retaliate. And it did. The governor let it be known that his director of Natural Resources, Ted Stewart, was pretty upset with our stand and that we were supposed to be kinder and gentler and turn the other cheek. They [the governor at the behest of the caucus] started to pull our funding away, but a few of us kept doing enforcement work anyway. At the same time I notified the Fish and Wildlife Service that there was trouble. Less than a year later I and others were forbidden to do any more enforcement [protection of habitat] on endangered species."

Funding for enforcement shrank, and it got more difficult for Johnson's staff to do its job. "We were already short of funding, although there was a surplus [of as much as $200 million in the state treasury] available at the time, and things got worse. We had truck-mileage restrictions and boat-mileage restrictions. As a way of keeping us from doing our job, it was very effective."

Johnson says the austerity plan that targeted Ross and gutted the nongame program also eliminated the law-enforcement section of the agency, which at the time had eighty-five people and a $5 million budget. The branch was later reorganized to handle only hunting and game management issues. Johnson, as a top-level manager, was privy to budgetary matters. "It was never a money issue as they claimed in eliminating my position or Clair Jensen's or David Ross's or the game management chief Dwight Bunnell. That was all a lie," he says. "We know for a fact that the executive director of Natural Resources and the interim director of Wildlife Resources were offered the money to cover whatever shortfalls were allegedly imagined, but they [Leavitt, Stewart, and new DWR director Bob Valentine] turned it down. They didn't want the money. They had another agenda. I'm a firm believer that there are places in any organization where you can cut, but to eliminate an entire division? We spent hundreds of hours trying to make it work by spreading around the cuts, but they threw it out the window and eliminated everyone who was perceived as a thorn in their side. The only people who were spared were fence-sitting older managers who had never done a damn thing for wildlife and knew very little about threatened and endangered species."

A year to the day after the purge was completed, the number of DWR staff members miraculously returned to previous levels, but the positions were filled with game biologists told to refrain from identifying endangered species. "Friends who escaped the layoffs tell me morale is in the gutter," Johnson says. "No one is willing to stand up and do what is right. They do what they're told, which is to not rock the boat. Gutting science is the name of the game. A lot of the pressure came down not just from the Cowboy Caucus, but we had a feeling it came from the highest levels of state government because of particular families' involvement in businesses from insurance to fish farms."

Bob Williams, the former Utah state director for the U.S. Fish and Wildlife Service, says the mechanism for tracking the status of amphibian and reptile populations has been dealt a serious blow. Implementation of a conservation plan for the spotted frog, which the Leavitt administration promised to deliver to stave off federal listing, continues to stall, and the frog is vanishing. Development in the Heber Valley at the base of the Park City ski slopes, where the 2002 Winter Olympics are scheduled to be held, continues to destroy crucial remaining habitat. "We relied so much on DWR nongame biologists to give us on-the-ground decisions on herp animals, and without that resource it will be more difficult to make good decisions. It would appear they [the state] don't have much concern for snakes or frogs or other herps that don't bring in the money."

Still, the SUWA believes the Clinton administration has soft-pedaled listing the spotted frog so as not to further alienate Utahans, already enraged over the creation of Grand Staircase–Escalante. Yet the still amorphous conservation agreement and de facto listing moratorium appear to violate both the Endangered Species Act and the National Environmental Policy Act, which require public comment.

"The Fish and Wildlife Service gave the spotted frog the highest possible priority without listing years ago. It did the same for other species less threatened but animals that were listed," says Jasper Carlton, executive director of the Biodiversity Legal Foundation in Boulder, Colorado, a clearinghouse for information on declining amphibian and reptile populations in the West.

The stalling tactic has links to completion of the massive Central Utah Project, anchored by the controversial Jordanelle Dam on the Provo River, a pet project of former U.S. Senator Jake Garn, a Utah

Republican. Garn is best known as the senator who went into orbit on the space shuttle, less known as a yes-man to the Cowboy Caucus. Getting the Jordanelle Dam built represented one of Garn's crowning achievements before he retired from Congress in 1992 after serving eighteen years. During an interview with Judy Fahys of the *Salt Lake Tribune,* Garn candidly claimed that the intent of the Endangered Species Act was to protect popular high-profile fauna such as grizzly bears and eagles, not frogs and other "minor species" such as the imperiled Kanab ambersnail. "Well, who cares?" the senator said. "I've got enough snails in my back yard. ... I guess some people would be trying to save the dinosaurs."

The prospect of listing the spotted frog gave Garn a bad case of heartburn because it represented a major obstacle to the completion of the Jordanelle Dam near Heber City. Garn knew that if the frog fell under the banner of the ESA and the public realized that his pork-barrel baby was partially responsible for pushing the species toward oblivion, a sensitive Congress would be less inclined to cough up the estimated $1 billion needed to finish construction. An irony, of course, is that for a state so adverse to federal government intervention, right-wing elements had no problem using U.S. taxpayer money to build a water project the state likely didn't need. "If the people who are pushing this [spotted frog listing] think they can stop the CUP, then I'll stop the whole Senate," a congressional aide reportedly heard Garn say, warning other senators that if they supported the listing he would block funding of key public works projects in their states. As a member of the Senate subcommittee that held jurisdiction over the Department of the Interior budget, and thus the Fish and Wildlife Service, Garn also threatened to derail funding for implementation of the ESA. Garn's successors in Utah have amplified the threats.

"It is economically irresponsible to create an endangered species protection program and then starve it of needed resources," wrote Andrew Hoffman, Max Bazerman, and Steven Yaffee in an article titled "Balancing Business Interests and Endangered Species Protection" in the *Sloan Management Review.* Hoffman, a professor at Boston University, Bazerman, a professor at Northwestern University, and Yaffee, a professor at the University of Michigan, assert that underfunding endangered species recovery actually hurts business interests instead of helping them. "An impoverished program is

likely to lead to delays, uncertainties, and impasses, which create uncertainty for business, which, in turn, causes more delays and cost
overruns. Complete, credible data, coupled with more stakeholder
interaction, require personnel who are trained and skilled in nego-
tiation, communications, and development processes."

A biologist who suffered Garn's wrath was James Miller of the
Fish and Wildlife Service, who completed a report on the spotted
frog's status and then was ordered to rewrite it. Miller says the government hired an independent biologist from Canada's prestigious
McGill University, David Green, to perform genetic testing on frogs,
and the research showed that based on differences in genetics and
morphology, the Wasatch Front frog population was a distinct subspecies like no other in the world. As such, it was given the name
Rana luteiventris. Despite assertions from Garn and the Utah delegation that the Fish and Wildlife Service had manipulated the data,
Miller says such claims are absurd because the agency had no rational self-interest in arriving at information that justified listing.
"The Utah delegation made my life hell. They tried to discredit me
and ruin my name as a professional," says Miller, one of the few
African American biologists in federal wildlife management. "I've
been a combat biologist, I've been wounded, and now I want my
Purple Heart."

Under the guidelines of the ESA, the government is required to
try to save imminently threatened subspecies. The conclusions of
Miller's data were clear: that without intervention to vigorously preserve remaining habitat and restore other tracts that had been destroyed, the frog was doomed. But listing would also make it illegal
for Congress to earmark money for a project that would involve
taking over habitat.

Garn hastily scheduled a meeting with then Fish and Wildlife
Service national director John Turner, and according to documents
ferreted out by Fahys through the Freedom of Information Act, the
senator attempted to intimidate both the Fish and Wildlife Service
director and Miller. "All hell had broken loose and some documents
got shredded, but I kept as many as I could to protect myself," says
Miller, who later was accused of incompetence and was taken off the
project and assigned to a desk job. Thomas Devine, a staff attorney
with the Government Accountability Project in Washington, D.C.,
says this is a classic tactic used by repressive agencies to take puni-

tive action against scientists. "The first thing an agency will do is transfer the whistleblower to a bureaucratic Siberia, both to make an example of the dissenter and to block the employee's access to damaging information," Devine says. "The most popular reprisal technique has been to reassign employees from active environmental monitoring projects in the field to headquarters desk jobs where they don't receive any substantive assignments and are monitored by bureaucratic babysitters. Then they place the employee on a pedestal of cards. The strategy is to give the whistleblower an assignment but make it impossible to complete it on time or in a professional manner. This technique involves telling the dissenter to solve the problem but ensuring that completion is impossible through a wide range of things, including making sure adequate funding is never available. The finale is to fire the employee for being incompetent when the problem is not solved." Although pressure was applied by Garn to muzzle Miller—pressure that Garn did not deny applying—Turner stood by his biologist. He told Garn's staff, "We don't spank our biologists for being too aggressive." Yet in the end, with Miller suffering a variety of physical ailments from the stress and with his reputation damaged, Garn got the money pushed through Congress and the foundation of CUP was laid. It resulted in the Fish and Wildlife Service granting permission to the U.S. Bureau of Reclamation to destroy marshes and sloughs, which were home to the largest known colonies of spotted frogs in the Wasatch.

Fish and Wildlife officials denied that Garn held up the listing. Galen Buterbaugh, the outgoing director of the Rocky Mountain regional office, attributed the delay to fiscal cuts that have left his agency chronically understaffed and underfunded and hence unable to address all the species that need attention. "Until Congress funds it [reauthorization of the Endangered Species Act and its mission] adequately and the administration supports it, we will have this problem," Buterbaugh told Fahys. "That's the fact of the matter, not all this intrigue. Jake Garn didn't jerk the chain out from under us." Miller says Buerbaugh covered up the truth.

Garn may have gone away, but the controversy has not, and Garn's ideological offspring, Orrin Hatch, Bob Bennett, and James Hansen, have kept up the antienvironmental drumbeat. Half a decade later the frog is still not listed, and its numbers have dipped lower still. Among the vocal proponents of Utah developing its own "habitat conservation plan" (HCP) for spotted frogs to prevent the federal government from intervening was the Cowboy Caucus. Under Section 10 of the Endangered Species Act, states and private landowners can sidestep listing by crafting their own HCPs. If the Fish and Wildlife Service approves the plan, it then can issue permits allowing "incidental take" (read: killing) of species during development activity as long as the violator agrees to promote species conservation. Although this clause was intended to provide flexibility in safeguarding animals in a downward spiral, HCPs have been roundly criticized by some of the country's leading landscape ecologists as licenses to perpetuate destructive land use. Ross says the fact that the state of Utah and the Cowboy Caucus endorse the implementation of an HCP for the spotted frog confirms the suspicion that the Leavitt administration has no intention of vigorously pulling the frog back from the ledge leading to extinction. "The Wasatch frog subspecies should have been listed ten years ago, if you want to know the truth," the Fish and Wildlife Service's Miller says. "They're just hoping it will go extinct; then they won't have to deal with it anymore."

Among the swelling list of critics who doubt the honesty of state officials and condemn the Fish and Wildlife Service as having been snookered is nationally respected geneticist Jack W. Sites Jr., professor of zoology at Brigham Young University. "The Utah Department of Wildlife Resources does not have a single bona fide amphibian ecologist on the recovery team," Sites observes. "Several ecologists (Steve Corn and Dave Ross among them) sent detailed comments to the Fish and Wildlife Service offices in Salt Lake City, urging the agency not to sign off on the plan. I submitted detailed comments on the conservation genetics and came to the same conclusion."

Increasingly, Sites said, the DWR has controlled the number of species collection permits granted to outside researchers as a means of limiting scientific evaluations that could expose the agency's ineptitude.

In Utah, Bruce Johnson says, the state is willing to allow development of any patch of ground or river and believes it can accomplish its objective with impunity from intervention by the federal government. "If they think they can build eight or ten new homes, they will sell out the species that occupies the ground," he adds. "I don't know if it will take five or ten or fifteen years, but desert tortoises in Washington County will be down the tubes because the locals don't value them and there's nobody there encouraging them to follow the law." The same fate awaits fish species in the Virgin and Colorado Rivers, which are being drained by water developers, he says. "[Conservationists] may be able to stop development of the dam on the Virgin River because of fish, but [developers] are going to dry that river up." Among the long list of imperiled fishes are the woundfin, Virgin River chub, Colorado squawfish, humpback chub, bonytail chub, and razorback sucker.

～

Botanist Jayne Belnap is a native Utahan and proud of it. A nationally recognized expert on desert soils, she is painfully aware of the hostility that federal and state biologists such as David Ross confront in Utah, particularly those dealing with creatures that can't be hunted or commercially sold. Belnap has attracted flak herself for documenting declines in rare endemic plants that survive in the sensual slickrock country of southern Utah around Canyonlands and Arches National Parks. At a recent public meeting in Moab that Belnap attended, she was excoriated for supporting careful management of Utah's sensitive desert wildlands, which are being threatened by cattle grazing and ORV use. In front of a large audience, the president of the Moab Chamber of Commerce stood up and lambasted her for having the gall to suggest that humans are causing species extinction. At the time Belnap was conducting biological profiles for the National Park Service and today works for the Biological Services Division of the U.S. Geological Survey. "The speaker didn't mention me by name, but the crowd turned around and looked at me because it was obvious who he was talking about," Belnap says. "The audience nodded their heads and asked that the park superintendent shut me up. Today, when I walk down the streets of Moab, people still glare at me. They really hate me here because they think I'm trying to stop them from doing what is their supposed God-given right to drive a four-wheeler. They justify their decision by turning to the Bible and saying the earth was put here for us to use, which they interpret as exploiting without consequence.

"By attacking me," she adds, "they forget that I, like them, grew up in Utah, and I have the same sort of reaction to outsiders. It pisses the hell out of me when the government tells me what to do. It pisses me off when the Park Service or BLM tells me where I can go, but this is just my gut reaction, which is visceral and not very rational. I realize the knee-jerk hostility perpetuated by factions like the Cowboy Caucus makes no sense. I am not going to tell other people how to live, but there's another valid perspective out there, and it is to accept limits so that my own greed doesn't encroach upon and destroy our quality of life. The only way we, as resource advocates, are ever going to win the biodiversity argument is not to try and scare people by telling them we'll die if a plant goes extinct. Instead, we're going to die if we run out of oxygen."

A devoted and well-respected combat biologist, Belnap says environmental groups have lost credibility by forecasting disasters that never materialize. "That's not to say the wolf isn't going to show up, because I believe it will. The biggest problem I have with environmentalists is they talk about doomsday and it doesn't come. They create an atmosphere for right-wing politicians, who don't want to hear the truth about the destruction of the biosphere, to thrive. The conservation community has cried wolf so many times, and the wolf has never showed up. But I don't see why certain people think they need to exaggerate the problems in order to get the attention of the public. Things are bad enough that the reality should speak for itself."

With current trends allowing for more development and less protection of wild ecosystems, the prospects are dim. Belnap sees the breakdown of nature occurring not in one giant episodic collapse but as a whimper following the continued erosion of essential life-support systems. "When you dismantle the desert piece by piece, species by species, frog by frog, or plant by plant, eventually you have a system that cannot be put back together again because you've lost all the critical elements," she explains. "What we are doing everywhere with the environment is creating systems that are just super-simplified and less complex. As we strip them down, we may need to 'fess up to the fact that there might not be a place for us in the future. Nature will definitely go on, but whether we survive as a species is an issue that hasn't quite been resolved yet."

Eons from now, humans may be sharing the land with cockroaches, rats, slime molds, and mosquitoes because those are some of the only creatures that thrive in an altered landscape. "The politicians just don't get it," she says. "Obviously, they can't see into the future. I would just appreciate it if once in a while they considered what was here biologically so at least they would take note of what it is they are wrecking."

~

David Ross views his troubles in Utah as part of a much larger puzzle. It's hardly a secret, he says, that the disappearance and decline of amphibian populations is a worldwide phenomenon. "The state seems to have zero interest in why the frog populations are crashing and what effect that is going to have on bird life and the rest of the food chain. Recently, scientists discovered that skin extracts from certain frogs are effective in fighting cancer, but that's not the reason we should care," Ross says. "Frogs are the ultimate indicator species. If a marsh suddenly is vacant of frogs, and it's caused by siltation from construction or livestock grazing or water diversion, that should be a strong warning that maybe we should think about how it is affecting the quality of our drinking water. The state just doesn't want to see the connection."

Frogs are indicators of environmental change on a macrocosmic and a microcosmic level, he says. They exist where there is clean water, as the Mormon pioneers astutely recognized. They also occupy an important niche in the food chain between fish and reptiles. As voracious eaters of insects, they are predators; in turn, as sustenance for birds, reptiles, and small mammals, they are prey. Their persistence, or lack thereof, suggests that something may be seriously wrong ecologically, considering that amphibians are vanishing from pristine wilderness areas as well as from disturbed habitats in the middle of civilization.

Amphibians have been on earth for at least 350 million years and are unique for spending portions of their life cycles on land and in water. Roughly two hundred million years ago, smack-dab in the middle of the Triassic period, frogs emerged as distinct entities. Despite wild climate changes, floods, diseases, and a long parade of predators, including humans, they are still with us, having outlasted the dinosaur and the dodo. They are adaptive, yes; resilient, yes; numerous and widespread, obviously, for there may be as many as 3,800 varieties of their kind dispersed across the northern and southern hemispheres. Some even have utilitarian uses, besides frog legs.

Before he was harassed, Ross looked into the scientific literature and completed his own regional summary on "species of special concern" in Utah (i.e., amphibians and reptiles deemed vulnerable to habitat alteration). Here's what he found in addition to the precarious status of *R. luteiventris:* A relict subspecies of the leopard frog, the Utah frog *(R. onca),* is already extinct from the Virgin River in Washington County and from almost all of Utah and Nevada; the lowland leopard frog *(R. yavapaiensis)* is rapidly declining; and the southwestern toad *(Bufo microscaphus)* is in trouble along the Virgin River. Furthermore, the western toad *(B. boreas)*, the northern leopard frog *(R. pipiens)*, and the Pacific chorus frog *(Pseudacris regilla)* are either significantly declining or occupying a limited and withering range. Utah's only population of Gila monsters *(Heloderma suspectum)* also happens to be found in southern Washington County and is declining due to illegal collectors and habitat fragmentation, and the future of the chuckwalla *(Sauromalus obesus)* is questionable at best.

To get a taste of what herpetologists are encountering on a wider scale, consider a scientific experiment you can run yourself. The next time you're at your favorite pond, lake, or stream, count the number of native frogs or tadpoles at the water's edge. Listen for them twanging at night. Record your findings in a little notebook, then compare the tally against the number your memory tells you were there a decade ago, and then against your census next year. Chances are the population next year will be smaller. That is, if you're counting native frog species and not nonnative competitors.

I can speak from personal experience. When I was a child exploring the farm country of central Minnesota and running an autumn trapline for muskrats, I remember encountering throngs of leopard frogs at the lake behind our house. They were so abundant that I would collect pailfuls of the hopping creatures. Now, when I return home as an adult with my own son, the frogs are seldom seen in their old haunts, though on the surface the habitat is, for the most part, unchanged. For a couple of years I casually attributed the decline to cyclical fluctuations in their numbers, such as one might see in grouse, lynx, and snowshoe hares. But late in 1997 the Associated Press reported that an outbreak of frog deformities in Minnesota lakes and streams—frogs born with extra limbs, shrunken eyes, and small sex organs—was due to tainted water. Researchers from the National Institute of Environmental Health Sciences said the specific contaminant is unknown. In some areas of the state, people were told to not drink tap water. The absence of healthy frogs tipped off health officials.

A larger connection registered after I went to the university library in the Montana town where I now live and read a short story titled "Where Have All the Froggies Gone?" in the March 1990 issue of the journal *Science*. From Brazil to Colorado's Rocky Mountain National Park, from Death Valley to the glaciers, frogs, toads, and salamanders are disappearing in the New World as well as around the globe. This realization prompted David Wake, director of the Museum of Vertebrate Zoology at the University of California at Berkeley, to have his colleagues at the National Research Council look into the matter in the late 1980s and early 1990s. Even skeptics realized something was up when the findings accumulated. "The data are anecdotal," declared Duke University ecologist Henry Wilbur in *Science,* "but it's so well repeated they certainly are believable."

Added distinguished ecologist James MacMahon, of the faculty of Utah State University, not far from where Ross lives, "Amphibian species are going extinct, but so is everything else." MacMahon was also quoted in *Science* as noting that although long-term studies are essential, so is immediate action based upon available facts. "We don't have much time to do this. By the time we can get enough data, the problem may be past us and unsolvable."

Native frog populations, the preponderance of evidence shows, are plummeting. No one knows exactly why, but herpetologists say the culprits appear to be intuitively obvious: Destruction of wetlands and degradation of habitat is one catalyst; contamination of water supplies by biocides, pollutants, and acid rain is another. A third is the introduction of nonnative predators such as voracious game fish from hatcheries as well as bullfrogs and crawfish that eat the eggs of native frogs. A fourth is natural population variations. The fifth factor is a fungus-caused disease called saprolegnia; the affliction has been fairly common in hatchery fish runways, but only recently has it spread to the wild and wreaked havoc. All of these factors, beyond the natural swings in population numbers, represent conceivable explanations for why some amphibian populations have declined by as much as 50 percent and others have gone extinct in certain locales.

But the sixth reason—depletion of the ozone layer—is at this moment both an obscure and a frightening proposition. Think for a moment: If epidemiologists warn that sunbathing in the southern hemisphere has caused an onslaught of skin cancer, what are the effects upon a creature like a frog dwelling in a delicate, thin layer of water and suited in gas-permeable skin?

Are the frog declines in Utah, which are outpacing most other areas, due to a melting of the ozone? Are they a foreshadowing of a system collapse? Are they really aquatic versions of the canary in the coal mine? Currently there are more than 130 species of amphibians and reptiles listed as threatened or endangered worldwide, and ten of those are frogs and salamanders in the United States. Twenty-six different species are classified as endemic to areas west of the Mississippi River, and twenty-five species reside in the east. Since 1980 the number of endemic amphibian species suffering from serious declines more than doubled, and there are dozens of frog subpopulations that conservationists say warrant listing.

"Substantial scientific evidence exists to indicate that many species of amphibians are declining in Utah and the western states as well as in other areas of North America," wrote Jasper Carlton, director of the Biodiversity Legal Foundation, who is suing the state of Utah and the Fish and Wildlife Service over the spotted frog. "Leopard frogs, boreal toads, spotted frogs and tiger salamanders are experiencing serious declines. What is particularly alarming is that many amphibians occupying pristine habitats are also disappearing at a previously unseen rate. These declines appear to be widespread and have been particularly serious for twenty years."

Consider some of the other troubling hotspots, possibly in your own back yard:

- Numerous salamander and frog populations in the southeastern United States have been negatively affected, some severely, because of degradation of stream habitats. Another cause of declines is the conversion of natural pinewood and hardwood forests and associated wetlands to plantation forestry, agriculture, and urban development. Among the victims is *Rana capito*, better known as the gopher frog, and the hellbender *(Cryptobranchus alleganiensis)*.
- Leopard frogs *(Rana spp.)*, which are commonly used in teaching and research institutions, were once prolific in most of the United States. Populations of this diverse group have declined, sometimes significantly, in portions of midwestern, Rocky Mountain, and southwestern states, including Utah, to the point that they are candidates for listing.
- Several species of amphibians are fading from small forest streams in the Pacific Northwest. Frogs, it appears, can't tolerate clearcuts because the toppling of trees removes shade from their spawning areas and exposes eggs to sunlight. Because timber is harvested without adequate streamside protection, many populations of the tailed frog *(Ascaphus truei)* and torrent salamanders *(Rhyacotriton spp.)* have been severely affected; some populations soon will warrant consideration for listing.

In the late 1980s Carlton made a pilgrimage to southern Arizona to see the last live specimen in the United States of the Tarahumara frog, which was in captivity at a museum in Tucson. "A few weeks after I left, it died. The last of its kind in the U.S., and it disappeared from human negligence and apathy more than anything else," Carlton says. "I vowed that I would never let anything like this occur again."

Carlton is no lightweight in determining when species have been pushed to the brink. He takes pride in having sued every secretary of the interior since James Watt to spur the government to list more species and bring heightened awareness. By his own count, he personally has had a hand in litigation for over one hundred of the nearly 950 species currently on the Endangered Species List. He has a ratio of winning ten cases for every one he loses. Nothing has troubled him more than the dubious status of amphibians and certain reptiles. His hunches are backed up by the former National Biological Service and the National Academy of Sciences, which gathered irrefutable evidence that prodevelopment groups would rather the public doesn't hear.

Biologist Michael C. Long, an administrator for the Los Angeles County Nature Centers, a division of the Department of Parks and Recreation, has also tracked the status of amphibians in the mountains rising above greater Los Angeles for a quarter century. To hear him describe the trend of *Rana muscosa* is eerily familiar: "I remember, like it was yesterday, seeing yellow-legged frogs jumping off rocks in the creeks on my hikes in the San Gabriel Mountains," Long says. "I saw them disappear during twenty years but, like so many others, didn't realize it. It is a really frightening feeling to know something is nearly gone and will not be back. It becomes personal."

Southern California yellow-legged frogs are a unique offshoot of the more common yellow-legged frogs *(R. sierrae)* found in the Sierra Nevada range. Prior to 1970, *R. muscosa* was the most abundant frog in the majority of mountain streams that rushed out of the San Gabriel, San Jacinto, and San Bernardino Mountains, but in the 1990s it has practically evaporated from 99 percent of those areas and now numbers less than one hundred adults that cling tenuously to half a dozen drainages in the San Gabriels and San Jacintos.

If the species is not listed under the federal Endangered Species Act and strict measures for habitat protection not enforced, both Long and herpetologist Bonnie M. Dombrowski, who has completed amphibian surveys for the U.S. Forest Service, believe *R. muscosa* may become a statistic of extinction by the end of the century. Even though *R. muscosa* is more imperiled than the arroyo toad *(B. microscaphus)*, which was declared legally endangered, the movement to save this fascinating creature has stalled. Under pressure from the Republican-controlled Congress to curb the number of species added to federal protection, the Fish and Wildlife Service probably will not act in time.

Another troubling fact is that even if a species navigates the political maze and nets protection, it must survive continuing damaging management practices on public land. It's clear that federal and state agencies are indifferent to the plight of frogs. Nancy Sandburg, a counterpart of David Ross employed by the Los Padres National Forest in California, was threatened with a two-week suspension for calling attention to the agency's illegal bulldozing of a creekbed that contained a fresh population of baby arroyo toads, a legally protected species. The road-maintenance project killed hundreds of the young amphibians, which, like *R. muscosa,* are said to be in trouble biologically.

Without the required permits from the U.S. Army Corps of Engineers, the Forest Service ordered the bulldozing in one of the last havens for toads in an island of habitat that stretches from central and coastal California to Mexico. One biologist said 80 percent of the toad population was wiped out in the creek, which is also home to the western pond turtle *(Clemmys marmorata)* and the California red-legged frog *(Rana aurora draytonii),* which was protected under the ESA in 1997.

A short time later the Forest Service also sanctioned the pouring of concrete into two streams, an act that allegedly killed thousands of toad tadpoles. "We have a serious problem here," Sandburg said in an interview with the Santa Barbara *News-Press.* "We're losing all the threatened species habitats in this forest through negligence, bit by bit."

After alerting a biologist at the University of California at Santa Barbara about the damage, which Forest Service officials do not deny, Sandburg was told abruptly that she would be disciplined for alleged "neglect of duty" for not supervising a crew that defied her orders and caused the havoc with concrete in the creek.

Attorney Sarah Levitt of the Government Accountability Project represented Sandburg and filed a complaint with the U.S. Office of

Special Counsel (OSC), which was designed to protect whistle-blowers. The OSC intervened only after Sandburg was forced to serve a two-week suspension. With that action, the Forest Service sent a signal of intimidation down the ranks.

"All too often the OSC does too little too late. Sandburg is a classic case of an employee who tries to get her agency to follow the law—then suffers retaliation," Levitt says. Sandburg eventually won a subsequent grievance with the Merit Systems Protection Board, but the losers, she says, are the toads. Scientists say the conflicts in Utah and in the Los Padres are indicative of needless habitat destruction taking place on public lands coast to coast.

"All the data in Utah show consistent declines relating to water diversion and disruption to ecosystems, but the Fish and Wildlife Service and Bruce Babbitt are not going to proceed with listing species that might affect the management of those facilities. Why?" asks Carlton of the Biodiversity Legal Foundation. "Because they're scared shitless of the Utah congressional delegation and the Cowboy Caucus. It shows you that bureaucratic gestures mean nothing. What really frightens me is what if Congress would have its way in diluting the Endangered Species Act, turning federal land over to the state and banishing law enforcement? Many of these species will not be recovered, ever. In Utah, we're witnessing a prelude to politically sanctioned extinctions."

One could argue, as has been suggested by Utah's U.S. Representative James Hansen and other enemies of the Endangered Species Act, that species on earth have always come and gone and that threats to survival have always existed. (Hansen, it should be noted, is the same enlightened congressman who drafted a bill that would obliterate our national parks system and open up those lands to mining and oil drilling and as a sandlot playground for ORVs).

Yet, during the brief time humans have been around, it has been a rare event indeed when declines have occurred so universally across a whole suite of species, such as the anurans, herpetologists say. The trouble with destruction of the ozone layer, a concept that is now irrefutable, is that no one knows for sure what it means because in the span of our own species' existence, it is an unprecedented event.

Frogs have always dealt with loss of habitat due to natural events and competition from other species. But to beset them with chemical contamination, susceptibility to disease in a stressed environment, widespread loss of habitat from avoidable human causes, introduction of predatory hatchery fish and bullfrogs, *and* the effects of harmful ultraviolet light seeping through a tear in the atmosphere may be more than they can cope with. Ultraviolet light especially, because studies have shown that these unseen rays of sunlight weaken immune systems and make frogs prone to diseases such as redleg, which has been rampant of late in many localized frog colonies. Scientists may not concur in the exact cause of the declines, but they do pretty much agree that human manipulation of habitat should be kept to a minimum. And having more data certainly can't hurt.

"Because of their functional importance in most ecosystems, declines of amphibians are of considerable conservation interest," wrote R. Bruce Bury, P. Stephen Corn, C. Kenneth Dodd Jr., Roy W. Mc-Diarmid, and Norman J. Scott Jr. on behalf of the National Biological Service's landmark 1995 report to Congress titled "Our Living Resources." "If these declines are real, the number of listed or candidate species at federal, state and local levels could increase significantly."

When I interview Steve Corn at his office at the Aldo Leopold Center—funded by several government agencies—in Missoula, Montana, he says the paucity of conclusive information—a direct result of scarce research dollars—is crippling scientists' ability to provide answers. "Whether the enormity of amphibian declines is predominantly caused by local human-related activities or a larger global phenomenon, we don't know," he says. "But at the same time one cannot make the leap of logic that because we don't know the answer, there is nothing wrong.

"In fact, I think we can say with a great deal of confidence that where amphibian populations have undergone declines, the most common reason is habitat destruction. The spotted frog is a good example and obviously declined simply because of development, water projects, and land subdivision."

Corn says the fate of the Wasatch spotted frog population, which could perish independent of any development impacts under a scenario of global warming, points to broad philosophical questions. Is there a human obligation to prevent the frog, or any imperiled species, from going extinct regardless of the cause?

Ethical and ecological considerations aside, the genetic makeup—the uniqueness of the Wasatch population versus other variations—may have utilitarian values not yet realized. The Houston toad, for example, produces alkaloids that are being tested by pharmaceutical companies because they may prevent heart attacks or function as anesthetics more powerful than morphine. "Yet," as the National Wildlife Federation declared recently in expressing concern about amphibians, "it is on the very brink of extinction, another member of the Endangered Species List."

~

Almost singlehandedly, Peter Hovingh, a biochemist by trade and a well-respected naturalist, was the one who gathered the data for initially listing the spotted frog under the Endangered Species Act and delivered it to the Utah Nature Studies Society, which filed the petition. "Utah is basically a theocracy, and if these species aren't important to leaders of the theocracy—if they can't benefit financially from them—they won't be of importance to the people down below," Hovingh explains. "It doesn't matter how much you wreck the environment on earth because everything will be rosy in heaven. Maybe a frog will be up there too; maybe all of them will be because they're not long for here, that's for sure."

Hovingh says there is far more public interest in biological diversity than the politicians assume. "There are people who like these animals," he tells me one afternoon. "I know a farmer who found spotted frogs and his wife told him that she liked having them around, so he made sure they remained by protecting the habitat."

Hovingh became interested in the coagulant qualities of amphibian systems and their potential application to humans. But then he, like David Ross, became a passionate advocate for their protection. As a result, Hovingh spearheaded a literature search to pinpoint the historical locations of amphibians in Utah. He visited many desert springs cited in the literature and found no native frogs but lots of exotic bullfrogs.

Hovingh and Ross agree that the situation is not a lost cause—yet. In the counties along the Wasatch Front where spotted frogs used to occur, there are over 7,500 water diversions, ranging from trenches one can easily step over to swift-flowing ditches running in straight lines and depleting either streams or seasonal ponds. "I am amazed at the number of diversions," Ross says. "Any semblance of a natural system is gone. The frog populations along the Wasatch Front are extremely fragmented. Basically, almost every farmer in the bottoms of these valleys has either drained off the wetlands or channeled off the flows. The mass conversion of frog habitat into marginal agricultural cropland just doesn't work, and it's not too late to repair the damage, but it's getting awful close. We still have a chance."

Hovingh is less optimistic. "Unless something is done fast along the Wasatch Front, these species are going to be lost. I don't see any hope, especially with the explosion of development in anticipation of the Winter Olympics and the general growth between Salt Lake City and Provo," he says. " Slowly people are waking up, but I can't save the spotted frog by myself; neither can David Ross, nor can federal laws without funding or cooperation from the state. Maybe extinctions will wake people up enough so that they come around on other species and we don't lose them all. I wouldn't count on it, though."

Republican politicians and right-wing activists such as Met Johnson assert that society can offset losses to prime habitat through mitigation, that is, creating alternative wetlands to the ones being destroyed. Years ago, when the Jordanelle Dam was first proposed for the Provo River southeast of Salt Lake, a lush and extremely rare cottonwood riparian forest was sacrificed. The plan called for creating banks of vegetation on a newly formed reservoir and complementing it with a series of artificial ponds. Seasonal wetlands were purchased and set aside as part of the Environmental Protection Agency's demand for mitigation—a regulation viewed as intrusive anathema by local politicians. Similar projects are proposed as mitigation for damming the Virgin River. Will it work and become a safe haven for frogs? Will the species take to the new surroundings?

"Unfortunately, one can only judge the success of a mitigation program fifty years later, and then it may be too late," Hovingh says. "Whenever they've mitigated wetland losses they've always come up short of expectations. They [the water developers] always say it will be good frog habitat, but they aren't replacing the same kind of habitat they're destroying. When you step into frog habitat, you step up to your knees in muck. All these ponds have hard clay basins. After millions of years of evolution, you can't tell a frog to stay there and be happy. It means a lot of money is being spent, and for what?"

⌣

One could suppose the same kind of replacement-habitat logic was used with David Ross. In exchange for eliminating his job, he was simply moved to another part of the bureaucracy where he couldn't do any harm. Tom Devine, a national authority on whistleblowing cases, says it is common for an agency to lay off dissenters even as it is hiring new staff and then offer the fired employee an inane job in place of his or her original job.

Once Ross was out of the picture as a full-time herpetologist, the agency posted a notice for a "nongame biologist" specializing in wetland-associated species and invited him to apply. He interviewed for the position after being told he had a lock on the job given his performance ratings and excellent background in aquatic ecology. He told his employers that he looked forward to continuing his frog work under the new assignment.

Despite a clause against nepotism, the job coincidentally went to the son-in-law of one of the regional supervisors, whose field experience involved sage grouse and deer but no background in water creatures. When Ross asked why he didn't get the job, he was told that his credentials as a scientist were excellent but he needed to bone up on his interviewing skills. "Getting hired is not based on what you know but who you know," he says, adding that more recent examples of nepotism relating to nongame species in the department raise questions about agency ethics and professionalism.

To keep Ross quiet, the state dangled another job in front of him. He had a choice to make: either resign or take a reassignment in Ogden studying brine shrimp in northern Utah, an area that also happened to have the lowest diversity level of amphibians and reptiles in the state. The outpost would become his gulag. "Yes, I am gainfully employed. Yes, I would like to get out of here because it's damned frustrating. I don't feel like I'm doing anything for the resource," he tells me months after he took the job out of financial necessity. Never losing his sense of humor, he adds, "But really, how much controversy is there in studying the behavior of brine shrimp?"

When Ken Rait was with the SUWA (he now works for the Oregon Natural Resources Council), he compared the iron-fisted influence of the Cowboy Caucus to rule by Stalinism and said there will be lingering impacts of "the slaughter" of Utah's nongame division for decades to come. He would like to see the citizens of Utah launch a revolt of their own. Not long ago a public opinion poll showed that in direct contrast to what Republican politicians such as Hatch and Hansen were claiming, the majority of Utah citizens support protecting the state's remaining public wildlands as wilderness as well as protecting the species that depend on them for survival. Rait says many of the elected leaders are out of touch and living in the past.

"What needs to be done is the equivalent of traveling into the twentieth century from the Dark Ages," he says. "Before science regains a meaningful place here, there has to be a complete separation of politics and biology. Over the last decade there has been a concerted campaign of misinformation waged by the Cowboy Caucus, and there needs to be a whole lot more truth-squadding to expose the cozy relationships, corrupt deals, and good-old-boy gamesmanship. An environment needs to be created where people like David Ross and the frogs he has a passion for can survive."

In the spring of 1998, the Department of Interior finally announced the finalization of a conservation agreement with the state of Utah to stave off listing of the spotted frog. Critics, including a slate of numerous independent and government scientists, panned the agreement as overt political capitulation by the Clinton Administration. The agreement requires the state to complete and implement a Habitat Conservation Plan. Here are two interpretations of the agreement, the first from an Associated Press (AP) story that appeared in western newspapers and the second from a prominent government biologist.

The headline to the AP story declares "Babbitt signs pact to protect Western spotted frog" and then the text begins:

Heber City, Utah (AP)—Donning waders and a parka, Interior Secretary Bruce Babbitt waded into a marsh in search of the Western spotted frog moments after signing a novel conservation agreement to protect the amphibian.

Babbitt said the agreement represents a model of cooperation between federal, state and Indian governments in an attempt to avoid expensive and contentious legal confrontations over endangered wildlife.

"This is an attempt to say we can have it both ways," Babbitt said Thursday. "We can develop and we can protect God's creation. What we have here is a remarkable example of that."

Babbitt spoke in the shadow of the Jordanelle Dam, which had been threatened in 1992 when it was discovered that altering the course of the Provo River was destroying the frogs' habitat.

According to the new agreement, the dam will now be used only for flood control, meaning the river below it can be restored to its natural frog-friendly state, commission executive director Michael Weland said.

In turn, the U.S. Fish and Wildlife Service will recall its petition seeking endangered species status for the frog, which has been pending since 1993.

Sloshing into a manmade marsh just below the 300-foot dam, Babbitt searched the mud and sawgrass in vain for one of the 6-inch reptiles that had once pitted environmentalists against businessmen.

Babbitt didn't find one, and no wonder. Fish and Wildlife Service biologist Janet Mizzi said the frogs were still hibernating. "We won't expect to see them for a couple of weeks," she said.

Later, a staffer gave Babbitt a plastic frog after he had jokingly wondered why the wildlife agency hadn't planted a few live ones for his trip.

Contrast that account with an interpretation of the agreement from a renowned government herpetologist who dispatched this assessment over the Internet but asked to remain anonymous because he fears retaliation from Babbitt. He feels he could lose his job for voicing dissent. The scientist wrote:

The Department of Interior just signed a Conservation Agreement with Utah for the spotted frog. This agreement was written by the Utah Division of Wildlife Resources and put out for review this winter by the Fish and Wildlife Service. Every knowledgeable biologist who reviewed it thought it was a load of crap, and everyone was taken by surprise by the quick acceptance of the agreement by the department (there was almost no advance warning of Babbitt's visit). No one has seen a revised version (if it exists) to judge whether the criticisms were addressed.

This isn't about the merits of the frog as a candidate species ... but it's about the current politics of the Endangered Species Act. The pressure to come up with solutions that make everything possible, e.g., "We can develop and we can protect God's creation. What we have here is a remarkable example of that"—leads to questionable management backed up by bad science.

As for Ross, he never thought he would become an expert on brine shrimp, though thanks to Governor Mike Leavitt, his job description shrank significantly, so much so that he felt himself being squeezed out. From his office in Ogden he would stare over the expanse of the Great Salt Lake on clear afternoons, with the smog of Salt Lake City in the distance, and imagine what the first Mormon settlers encountered and the frogs that led them to quench their thirst.

"I think in some cases Utah will easily end up being a biological black hole, especially in those limited habitats where there is already solid evidence of species declines. I hate to paint a pessimistic picture, but I don't know how I can paint an optimistic one."

Ross finally left the state not long ago to pursue a Ph.D. at Idaho State University in Pocatello, just up the road. This isn't what he had in mind for a career in biology. "Conservation is a cuss word in Utah. What I've learned is, if you care for organisms that don't have antlers or quack, don't take a job down there. I'm dismayed and kind of in a state of disbelief about how state government works. I never imagined it would be so primitive as it is here. If you want to protect the diversity of amphibians and reptiles that the desert Southwest is famous for, don't go to Utah. They don't want you, and they certainly don't want those animals. It's one of the saddest places I've ever seen in my life."

Before he departed for academia again, Ross put his hip boots back on and strolled through relic-spotted frog wetlands in the Heber Valley, where the world's finest winter athletes will converge in 2002. Remember this as you turn on the television for the downhill or luge or cross-country skiing events. Remember David Ross when the camera makes a wide pan to show a backdrop of pretty scenery, remember what the view of extinction looks like. Remember there were once pretty spotted frogs in the dell. Remember *R. luteiventris*, whose existence has been sacrificed to the Olympic gods of progress.

Fear and Loathing the EPA in Las Vegas

Government is actually the worst failure
of civilized man. There has never been a
really good one, and even those that are
most tolerable are arbitrary, cruel, grasping,
and unintelligent.—H. L. Mencken

LEANING INTO THE MICROPHONE at a radio studio in Las Vegas, Jeffrey van Ee began the evening interview by recounting how the federal government made a mess of his life. Wracked by stress, weighted with insomnia, he stared blankly over puffy, purplish bags of dread that had parked themselves beneath hazel eyes. For an instant the nerdy engineer bore an uncanny resemblance to Bill Gates, albeit a slimmer and more haggard Bill Gates who had not slept in a week.

In hindsight, van Ee (pronounced *van-aye*) admits that he possessed little understanding of what awaited him on the radio that night. He was, after all, reaching out to an audience that normally spends its daylight hours becoming indoctrinated in the holy gospel of right-wing capitalism according to Rush Limbaugh and G. Gordon Liddy. No sooner had he finished delivering his woeful account of Big Brother's harassment than the lights on the AM station's switchboard lit up with callers across the Great Basin. Van Ee had struck a nerve, but what kind he wasn't sure. With a spontaneous outpouring of solidarity, ranchers, hard-rock miners, dirt-bike enthusiasts, tax protesters, and general antigovernment zealots responded to his soliloquy by informing him that they *identified with his struggle.* "I'm telling you, Jeff," one sympathizer said in a cocksure tone, "the time has come when the masses ought to rise up and ..."

Before the caller completed the sentence, van Ee realized that in this declaration he had mistakenly wandered into something radically abstruse. He had actually found a common thread with the

158

enemy. *Rise up and do what?* he wondered. His worst fears were confirmed when another riled listener chimed in with the notion of overthrowing the government as a means of giving Washington, D.C., back to the people.

"They seemed to be identifying with *me*," van Ee explained later in a quizzical voice as we drove down the Las Vegas Strip buzzed on caffeine and bombarded by neon at two in the morning. "They mistook took me for a Sagebrush Rebel railing against the Endangered Species Act when all I was trying to do was relate the hazards of being a good citizen. I had no idea I could get into this kind of trouble for moonlighting as an environmentalist." In fact, being an environmentalist represents only half of van Ee's woes. Apparently unknown to the radio listeners who found succor in his words was the slightly relevant detail that in his day job he happens to be one of their most loathed figures—a civil servant in the employ of the federal government. Van Ee resides in a state where it isn't wise to admit, publicly at least, that you work for Uncle Sam. This kind of confession can be hazardous to one's health. Long before domestic terrorism awakened the nation at Oklahoma City, Nevada had established itself as a niche for militant demonstration and social unrest.

On March 31, 1995, someone bombed the office of retired U.S. Forest Service ranger Guy Pence in Carson City, and five months later explosives were planted beneath the Pence family vehicle parked in the driveway of his home. Through blind luck, no one, including Pence's kids who were playing nearby, was harmed. Still, the statement was sent as an implicit warning that somebody disapproved of the methods Pence had used to manage cows on the open range.

A year prior to those near misses, Bureau of Land Management (BLM) offices in Reno were blown up too. With alarming regularity, federal workers employed by land management agencies such as the Forest Service, BLM, and National Park Service have received death threats; watched as their kids have been tormented by bullies in school; and had to endure, in disbelief, their spouses being shunned in grocery stores and community churches.

Only reluctantly did Jeff van Ee, a pollution specialist with the U.S. Environmental Protection Agency (EPA), agree to appear on talk radio, and his decision came in the wake of a CBS television news broadcast that detailed his problems relating to the Endangered Species Act. Dating back to the days of the Bush administration, van

Ee has endured threats of criminal prosecution from the U.S. Justice Department, attempts to terminate his job, the possibility of jail time, fines, and personal humiliation for being what one of his attackers described as an "unwanted agitator." Given the seriousness of the allegations, one might suppose that his persecution stems from espousing allegiance to say, the Islamic hezbola, or perhaps the radical militia movement. But his crime is being a card-carrying member of the Sierra Club and defending wildlife habitat in his time off from the office.

What he's fighting for now by suing the EPA and the Office of Government Ethics is to recover free speech that's been taken away by a gag order preventing him from working for the EPA Monday through Friday and being a conservationist on weekends. It is his goal, he says, to strike a blow against "environmental McCarthyism." "When I became a government employee, nobody told me I had to surrender my rights as a citizen, but that is precisely what the EPA insists on telling me. The irony is that even during an administration that is supposed to be friendly to the environment and promoting of open government, my own agency continues to punish me for being a conservationist. Protecting the environment is not a nine-to-five job. There must be free speech and debate if we are to discern the true threats to our environment and reconcile our differences."

Today, if he is successful in his current legal crusade on behalf of his First Amendment rights—and indeed, he intends to take his case, with the help of the American Civil Liberties Union and other whistleblower groups, all the way to the U.S. Supreme Court if necessary—his act of protest could prove as powerful as a truckload of fuel oil and fertilizer. "I don't think it's any mystery that some people at EPA and inside the federal government have a problem with Jeff van Ee, and that's putting it mildly. Far worse, unprintable things have been said," notes John Flyger, van Ee's lead counsel from the respected Washington, D.C., law firm of Steptoe and Johnson. "Obviously anytime you end up in litigation with your employer, whether it's the government or not, things get heated and ugly. I suspect they thought he would roll over and surrender when this nightmare first started. They certainly don't like the fact that Jeff is smart. They like it even less that he is disagreeing with them. And they like it least that he is persistent and winning ground by raising valid questions that resonate with a lot of other federal workers."

Point blank, Van Ee was told he could not be a federal employee and be active in conservation organizations. He has spent a good portion of his savings defending himself against government attorneys who want to silence him. His decade-old struggle has potential ramifications for hundreds of thousands of federal workers whose behavior is presently dictated by a slate of broadly interpreted ethics regulations limiting what they can say and do after they leave work. Flyger says the federal ethics codes being tested could theoretically restrict a government worker from challenging the practices of a federally run day care center, or fighting a proposed highway project through a residential neighborhood, or doing something as inane as reserving a conference room in a federal building in order to hold a community meeting.

Although van Ee doesn't agree with the incendiary reaction to what many Nevadans label as government tyranny, his radio appearance confirmed that he is inexplicably hard-wired to the angst rural Americans feel toward the feds. There is, of course, an important distinction that must be drawn between him and members of the radical militia movement who subscribe to government conspiracy theories. Van Ee may labor for the perceived oppressor, but he knows through personal experience that the real enemy to the U.S. Constitution lurks within the very bureaucratic structure formed to protect it.

What did van Ee do to cause such a stir? "Living in Nevada," he says, "it's hard to avoid encountering public land since 86 percent of the state is administered by the federal government. You can't go anywhere without encountering the jurisdiction of a federal agency, be it an interstate highway, waterway, or mountain top."

As we pass the casinos and family resort hotels amid the general artifice engulfing the desert, he relates the circumstances that led to his involvement with the conservation movement and his trouble at work. Van Ee joined the Sierra Club in 1971 and got involved seriously in the organization's public lands agenda shortly after moving to Las Vegas in 1973 to take a job at the EPA's National Exposure Research Laboratory. An avid birder and amateur naturalist, he said the Sierra Club was a logical avenue for him and his wife, Nancy, to meet other people sharing the same interests. They were not alone. Dozens of public employees in the Las Vegas area are active in the Sierra Club and its affiliated organization called the Southern Nevada

Group, including, it should be noted, three of van Ee's former direct supervisors at the EPA.

Invigorated by the weekend hikes, van Ee wanted to make more than a monetary contribution, so he began volunteering with various wildlife and land protection projects the conservation group was involved in. When he wasn't active in the Sierra Club, he offered his spare time to the Nevada Wildlife Federation, AquaVision (a group focused on responsible use of scarce water), and the Nevada Outdoor Recreation Association. At night and on weekends he wrote letters and attended meetings on a variety of management issues affecting public lands, though he carefully made sure that his involvement had nothing to do with matters involving the EPA. Others in the conservation groups found his enthusiasm admirable, which led them to nominate van Ee for various elected positions in the Sierra Club. Eventually he was enlisted to answer questions from the press on a variety of subjects, from opposing the dumping of nuclear waste in the Great Basin to protecting endangered species, monitoring livestock grazing and residential subdivision growth, promoting conservation of water, and stopping plans for positioning MX missiles in Nevada. For the latter project, he received the coveted Nevada Wildlife Federation's Governor's Conservationist of the Year Award. His knowledge of issues affecting Nevadans was always thorough, and it brought praise even from members of the Nevada congressional delegation. A couple of times he even testified on Capitol Hill. In 1987 his résumé attracted a prestigious Legis Fellowship that allowed him to take a sabbatical and work for nine months in the office of U.S. Senator Harry Reid and with the Senate Environment and Public Works Committee. The fellowship is offered to federal employees who show great promise as future executive material.

Van Ee was a known entity to most of the federal land management agencies in Nevada because his comments were prolific. Although he chuckles at the label, some people describe van Ee as "the environmental conscience of southern Nevada." But then, in January 1990, his activism suddenly was deemed inappropriate and a professional liability. Holding a personal interest in the fate of the desert tortoise, which then was categorized as endangered and was subsequently downgraded to threatened under the Endangered Species Act, van Ee adhered to a procedure he had used many times before. He arranged with his supervisors to take an afternoon off—

on earned vacation time—to attend a meeting at McCarran International Airport between the federal government (the U.S. Department of the Interior, the BLM, and the U.S. Fish and Wildlife Service), attorneys for energy giant Kerr-McGee, and representatives of the Sierra Club Legal Defense Fund (recently renamed EarthJustice Legal Defense Fund). At the meeting van Ee signed the guest log simply using his name and made no mention of his connection with either the Sierra Club or the EPA.

For months he had tracked negotiations between the BLM and Kerr-McGee. The issue began to unfold following a massive explosion in 1988 at a facility owned by Pacific Engineering and Production Company where ammonium perchlorate (a key component of solid rocket fuel) was produced. The factory had been located inside the Las Vegas suburb of Henderson, and when the blast occurred it was so powerful that it shattered windows miles away. Several people were killed, and Kerr-McGee, owning the only other rocket-fuel plant in the country, also located in Henderson, decided it was time to move its operation away from populated areas. Everyone agreed it was in the public interest to relocate the plant, and the logical place was on twenty thousand acres of desert land held by the BLM. The selected site, however, happened to be habitat deemed critical for desert tortoises. Biologists concluded that construction would lead to the displacement of the threatened reptiles.

Consummating the deal required a congressionally approved transfer of land from the BLM to Clark County, Nevada, which in turn was prepared to make it available to Kerr-McGee. Van Ee and other conservationists had no objections to siting the plant in tortoise habitat so long as the company agreed to some measures of mitigation. Initially, in an environmental review prepared on the project, Kerr-McGee offered to set aside $10,000 as a "goodwill gesture" for creation of a mobile exhibit on tortoises for public education purposes and to erect tortoise-proof fencing to keep other wild tortoises out of their plant property. What van Ee and other environmentalists strongly objected to was a plan, hatched by the Fish and Wildlife Service without any public review, to spend the money on a research effort radio-collaring eleven desert tortoises to monitor their movement. The expenditure was foolish, they said, considering the animal's glacial speed and small home ranges. Backed by the opinions of independent biologists, they argued that such a study wouldn't yield any information scientists didn't already have. Instead, the Sierra Club Legal Defense Fund told the government it would sue based on a procedural violation of the Endangered Species Act.

Later government officials said that $400,000 would be used to fund a study of tortoises in the area. This news attracted van Ee's attention; he was quite familiar with the proposed relocation of the rocket-propellant plant and the problems posed to the desert tortoise by development, but he knew nothing about the reported study. Both he and officials of the Sierra Club Legal Defense Fund independently noted that money was desperately needed for habitat acquisition rather than a $400,000 study to track the movement of eleven tortoises, as the government had planned. Eventually, $225,000 was given to the Nature Conservancy for habitat acquisition.

"There was a larger issue," van Ee says. "The tortoise study was proposed at a time when people were arguing very strenuously in the community that the tortoise shouldn't even be listed as an endangered species. They were saying that there are plenty of tortoises out there. The problem is that we still don't know exactly how many tortoises we have on our public lands, and even on our private lands. We don't know where they are, and we don't know as well as we should how viable the population is. I thought rather than spend $400,000 to study a handful of tortoises, we could use that money to study the entire population and secure additional habitat that was being lost almost daily to development in southern Nevada."

Van Ee again says there was never a question about the wisdom of moving the Kerr-McGee facility, but it was his objective to make it a "win-win" situation for the company and the tortoise. "We have a tortoise on the Endangered Species List. How are you going to get the tortoise off the list if you continue to destroy its habitat?" he reasons.

Although these assertions seem to be common sense, government attorneys attending the meeting at the behest of Secretary of the Interior Manuel Lujan were nonplussed, including the researcher who had planned to make the tortoise radio-collaring his pet project. They didn't like the idea that van Ee could come in and interfere with an agreement that apparently had been a done deal, a deal that appeared to have been struck months earlier between Lujan's representatives and the company without public involvement as required by the National Environmental Policy Act. Someone at the meeting, who later would be identified as Department of Justice attorney Michele Kurac, decided that Jeff van Ee was guilty of an ethics violation and should receive a punishment he would never forget to teach the hotshot a valuable lesson, to tame his self-righteousness. Behind the scenes, without van Ee's knowledge, she contacted the EPA's national headquarters in Washington, D.C., to bring the hammer down.

A couple of months after the meeting at the airport, the telephone in van Ee's office rang. An agent from the inspector general's office in San Francisco was in town and summarily informed van Ee that he was in trouble. Big trouble. "I was shocked and felt sick to my stomach after a colleague tipped me off that [the investigator] had been asking questions about me," van Ee says. "I had no idea why, and certainly I never suspected that it had anything to do with my activism in the Sierra Club because I'd been outspoken for years but very careful about how and when I presented myself. Not long after I got the call, it was conveyed to me that this was a serious matter and that I might lose my job."

The government investigator, in fact, had already started a file on van Ee's involvement with the conservation movement. He had already determined van Ee was guilty. And he had already sought criminal prosecution before he even spoke to van Ee, though the request was later rejected by the U.S. attorney's office in favor of "internal administrative disciplinary action." When van Ee asked him who had lodged the complaint, the investigator refused to say. During a two-and-a-half-hour interrogation, van Ee was told he could be represented by an attorney but that since it was being handled as an "administrative matter," failure to answer the questions immediately would reflect on him negatively. Van Ee assumed it was just a little misunderstanding that could be cleared up, but the matter was presented to him thus: If he decided to plead innocent, which meant denying the charges against him, he faced possible suspension without pay, possible firing, a $10,000 fine, and six months in jail. And if he chose to plead guilty, he faced the same punishment.

"I was staggered," van Ee tells me. "I can honestly say I never saw it coming. I had been involved in conservation issues for twenty years—ones certainly far more controversial than the tortoise—and never had a problem. Why now?" His crime, in so many words, was giving "the appearance" of being a legal representative of the Sierra

Club (though he's not an attorney), fraternizing with representatives of the Sierra Club Legal Defense Fund, and allegedly violating federal law, Title 18, U.S. Code Section 205. That, at least, was the official version.

The unofficial story, later intimated to van Ee and revealed in documents obtained through the Freedom of Information Act, showed that he had enraged certain federal employees who held the power to make an example out of him for meddling in a deal where his presence wasn't appreciated. However, it was Title 18, USC Section 205, which he now is challenging in court, that was invoked to ruin his career. In the words of the investigator who bullied van Ee at the behest of Kurac, who initiated the action against him, "Title 18, USC Section 205, makes it a violation for ... an employee of the United States ... other than in the discharge of official duties [to] act as an agent ... for anyone before any Department ... in connection with any ... controversy."

The language, just as it appears, is obscure enough that it can be interpreted and applied with whatever whimsical malice one chooses. In broad terms, the code was intended to prevent conflict-of-interest situations, but as it was being interpreted by van Ee's own agency and those who wanted to punish him, he was told that he had no business participating in a federal meeting as a private citizen, even though he made no pretense that he was there on EPA time, as an EPA representative, or as a spokesman for the Sierra Club or the Sierra Club Legal Defense Fund. Most importantly, he had no personal financial stake in the outcome. In fact, the beneficiary was the public, which got a better deal than if he had decided not to get involved.

∿

On the morning that I finally talked to van Ee for the first time, he had received electronic mail from EPA employees across the country. They encouraged him to keep pressing forward with his court battle because he is perceived as an agent of change. Although few citizens outside the EPA and Nevada have heard of him, van Ee has a conspicuous but uneasy presence inside the federal system.

Flyger paints his client as loyal to the EPA but determined to stand up for his constitutional rights, and by implication for the constitutional rights of all other federal employees. What is most troubling, Flyger says, is that EPA has punished van Ee for actions that have not involved any conflict with his work at the EPA. "The loyalty that EPA has demanded of Jeff van Ee is not simply that he refrain from disagreeing with EPA and 'take the company position' on issues that are before EPA, but that he refrain from objecting to the policies of any other agency of the federal government, whether it be the Interior Department, BLM, or Air Force," Flyger explains. "In its essence, EPA's position is that Jeff and other federal employees owe undivided and complete loyalty to every branch of the federal government, with respect to every one of thousands or tens of thousands of issues that involve the federal government, even if those issues have nothing to do with their own agencies or their own work. This position rests on the mistaken view that a federal employee leaves his constitutional rights behind when he goes to work for the federal government. That view repeatedly has been held unconstitutional by the Supreme Court, including within the past few years."

When citizens are denied access to a group in their community or prevented from expressing an opinion, be it in the political majority or minority, they lose something intangible, he adds, suggesting that working for the federal government shouldn't require a Faustian bargain that involves wagering one's principles. Van Ee's tribulations, he says, speak to bureaucratic intransigence. "Because millions of Americans are federal employees, the importance of protecting their constitutional rights cannot be overstated," Flyger says. "Jeff has sacrificed a great deal professionally, not just on his own behalf but on their behalf. There's no question that EPA has punished Jeff for his refusal to accept their dictates. He rocked the boat by refusing to surrender his constitutional right to continue his work as an environmental activist on issues that do not involve his work at EPA. Had he simply acquiesced to EPA's demands and given up both his constitutional rights and his environmental conscience, life at EPA would have been easier for Jeff. His convictions are mostly what has sustained him at EPA, along with his determination to help make sure that this does not happen to other federal employees in a similar position."

~

What Title 18, USC Section 205 says is that if you're a federal worker, you cannot represent or appear to represent another entity when the federal government is also a party. "A strict reading of the law would say that if you're a federal employee, you cannot appear to represent anyone in a controversy involving the federal government," van Ee says. "But of course a controversy is what the EPA wants it to be."

He uses as a hypothetical example a federal employee who also happens to be the head of a local homeowner's association who has become active in trying to stop a federal Department of Transportation highway through the back yards of his neighbors. "Because you're a federal employee," van Ee notes, "you cannot even write a letter as a representative of that homeowner's association to the Department of Transportation protesting the highway. I don't think the framers of the Constitution had this in mind when they drafted the First Amendment. The law has tremendous implications for federal workers as well as for the public at large."

As soon as van Ee informed the EPA he was being initially represented by an attorney, Richard Condit of the Government Accountability Project (GAP) in Washington, the immediate threats of dismissal and prison time evaporated for the time being. However, a letter of reprimand was placed in his personnel file. The agency gave the strong hint that holding any leadership post in the local Sierra Club constituted grounds for dismissal. He was told he couldn't even reserve a Forest Service campground to hold a Sierra Club barbecue. If he gave even the vague *appearance* of possible conflict, his EPA bosses harped, he would lose his job.

Another consequence, van Ee found out subsequently, was that the letter of reprimand almost certainly would affect his chance for future promotion. Even though "with good behavior" the letter would be removed in two years, the professional stigma would remain indefinitely. Upon hearing of what had happened to him, his friends in the conservation movement stopped inviting him to attend important meetings because they didn't want him to get fired. Now he was alienated at work and in his private life. EPA officials refused to acknowledge that they were wrong and continued to warn him that if he chose to become active in the Sierra Club again, he would face regrettable consequences. He believes he was given little choice. Either he could give in and accept a black mark on his job performance for activities that had nothing to do with the quality of his work and relegate himself to passive involvement in conservation, or he could fight to clear his name. A decade and a $100,000 legal bill later, little is resolved.

The first thing van Ee and GAP did was appeal the action against him to the Office of Special Counsel (OSC), which exists to be an independent arbiter of internal agency disputes. Rather than exploring the questionable merits of the case against him and the potential waste of $400,000 in an inane and potentially illegal study of tortoises, the OSC chose to investigate van Ee and his ties to the Sierra Club.

The OSC ruled in the favor of van Ee's superiors, so he appealed the decision to the Merit Systems Protection Board (MSPB) for relief under the Whistleblower Protection Act. After the EPA asked the MSPB to deny van Ee's request to remove the letter of reprimand from his file, an administrative law judge with the MSPB in Denver sided with the EPA. These rulings suggested that somewhere strings were being pulled to ensure that his days as an activist were over.

The EPA again refused to tell van Ee who had initiated the action against him, ironically saying it was a *whistleblower* who had turned him in. Government officials refused to answer how long the investigation into his involvement with the Sierra Club had been going on, whom the investigators were speaking to, and why he was being singled out when millions of other federal workers similarly get involved with civic causes in their community. Only after Condit filed a Freedom of Information Act request that legally forced the agency to surrender key documents did he learn that the investigation apparently was motivated by officials who rose into key power positions during the Reagan and Bush years and didn't like van Ee's involvement with a group that questioned their decisions.

Van Ee says he feels like a character in a bad 1950s-era propaganda film about life behind the Iron Curtain. "People in the government can bring charges against you," he says, "but the government doesn't have to tell you who made the allegations. I suppose there's little mystery why the militia types saw my case as validating their paranoid beliefs in shadow governments. The irony is that I've spent my entire adult life working as a conservation activist on my time off, fighting Wise Use groups to protect public land. If I had been volunteering my time to promote logging or mining or destruction of tortoise habitat, that probably would have been okay."

$\sim$

Van Ee confesses that he isn't a saint. At times he knows that he comes across as a brainy, unrelenting egghead, which is why his friends and colleagues in the conservation movement routinely tapped his ability to strategize. Reared in Arlington Heights, Illinois, a middle-class commuter's suburb of Chicago, van Ee enjoyed a peaceful 1960s childhood generally insulated from the problems of the world. There was, even back then, a rebellious streak emerging, which was recognized by his mother. "I played hooky from Sunday school, which was not something good, well-behaved boys are supposed to do," he says. "I didn't like the indoctrination or the pressure to necessarily do what everyone else was doing. The people at EPA who tried to get me fired try to bring this up as a defect in my character. They believe I'm constantly trying to explore the bounds of appropriate behavior and that they have to contain me. That isn't true."

Van Ee wasn't always an augur. He almost bought into the conservative suburban ambitions of his folks. Almost. Good grades got him into Northwestern University. The political turmoil of the late 1960s forced him to reexamine his direction. "During the Vietnam War era, even in the Midwest at a school that was relatively conservative like Northwestern, people were questioning the government's actions," he says. "The liberal arts graduates tended to look at people like me in the Technological Institute as being part of the military-industrial complex. We were the nerds who were shortsighted and programmed. They said we had to wake up."

Van Ee's awakening was sparked in 1970 at a celebration of the first worldwide commemoration of Earth Day. Folk singer Tom Paxton was joined by Barry Commoner and Paul Ehrlich in the Technological Institute auditorium. "They were questioning not only what the government was doing but what we as a society were doing to our planet and ourselves. That woke me up, and I thought to myself, 'I want to make a difference. I want to do what I can to improve people's environment and their lives.'"

By the time he graduated in 1971, the job market for electrical engineers had softened, and van Ee toyed with joining a large aerospace firm or one of the companies involved in manufacturing computers or weapons. He had options to make a lot of money. But then he got wind of a new agency being formed in Washington. Motivated in part by the enthusiasm of Earth Day, President Nixon and Congress announced that they would launch an unprecedented stem of government called the Environmental Protection Agency. Van Ee made an application and entered nearly on the ground floor of research with the EPA's laboratory in Triangle Park, North Carolina.

In 1973 he was assigned to the EPA lab in Las Vegas. The facility exists to assess the health risks posed by contaminants in the air, water, and soil. His responsibility even now is to provide technical expertise as a laboratory scientist, not to make public policy. Van Ee's performance over the years earned him awards and high praise. As his responsibilities and position increased, he rose steadily through the ranks until he attained the level of GS-13, the equivalent of upper management in the private sector. Subsequently, he was responsible for managing a $1 million research budget for monitoring underground leaking fuel tanks, typically found at gasoline stations. The net effect of this program is that municipal water supplies and thousands of streams across the country are better protected from pollution. Not once was van Ee's integrity questioned. In recent years he has helped the EPA develop computer software to streamline the investigation of hazardous-waste sites. He wants to see taxpayers' money and the money from normal workaday folks spent efficiently in cleaning up pollution at the same time that people's lives and environment are being safeguarded. But in government service, as in the hedonism of America's gambling capital, all is not what it appears.

Although he's never aspired to be a gadfly, van Ee does admit to rejecting the sort of forced conformity that has made government service appear to be a fraternity for upwardly mobile white males. "I think we must explore the bounds of thought and look at the way we are conducting ourselves, whether on a personal level or in what we are doing collectively as a government," he says, pausing near the pyramidal edifice of the Luxor Hotel and Casino. "We need to ask ourselves if the old ways of doing business work. If the answer is no, then I think we should try to change in a constructive manner. There has been a lot of talk about the public not trusting government bureaucrats. In my mind, the worst thing we can do as civil servants is to perpetuate the myth that when the going gets tough, we should retrench to defend our fortress even if we're wrong. This approach has turned into a bunker mentality where you shoot the messenger in order to ensure the message is never delivered. It's a hard-headed scheme to defend programs at all costs, which is what happened with the tortoise. It is this refusal to streamline and admit mistakes that has given bureaucrats a bad image. They appear stubborn and irresponsible. They seem out of touch."

~

"Fabulous Las Vegas," the tourist slogan since the 1950s, could be described as either a monument to human ingenuity or, on the other side of the spectrum, a testament to grand excesses foreshadowing the end of civilization as expressed in the movie *Blade Runner*. It is now early in the morning, about three A.M., though you wouldn't know it from the hordes of gamblers in the streets. The throngs move between towers of paneled glass and streaking incandescent bulbs. Las Vegas is the country's fastest-growing metropolitan area. Besides its garish display of lights, this city of one million residents can also lay claim to an opulent rate of water consumption. "We are one of the biggest water wasters in the United States," James Deacon, a professor of environmental studies at the University of Nevada–Las Vegas told the *New York Times*. "The main reason is because we've tried to put an Eastern landscape in the middle of the desert."

According to the National Weather Service, Las Vegas receives about four inches of rain per year, which is typical for a desert. Yet at last count, the average person in Las Vegas was consuming three hundred gallons of water every single day, which is almost twice the national average and far greater than the hoggish per capita use of nearby Los Angeles and Phoenix.

Although developers insist that most of the water use can be attributed to the twenty-two million people who arrive to gamble in the casinos and vacation with their families, observers say that scenario just isn't the case. Every week about one thousand new émigrés move in with visions of filling swimming pools in their back yards and landscaping their estates into botanical splendor. There are also the fake waterfalls and tinted fountains and hundreds of golf fairways that shimmer emerald in August when the natural landscape is beige and brittle. Here, *mirage* is more than the name of a hotel.

At the end of World War II the panorama here was of a sweltering oven for six months of the year. Van Ee says he took up the cause as a conservation activist because so much is at stake. In 1992, with the election of President Bill Clinton and Vice President Al Gore, who committed themselves to a new era of "open government," he thought the cavalry would arrive and rectify his professional travails, but so far that hasn't happened. The charges brought against him were serious ones, and in the name of objective journalism I wanted to hear the EPA's version of what had happened. Van Ee warned me that I would get nowhere. The first telephone call I made was to the

EPA's National Exposure Research Laboratory in Las Vegas, where he works. The administrators there had no answers "on the record." They referred me to one of the EPA's regional offices, which referred me to the national office in Washington, D.C.

Because EPA administrator Carol Browner, a Clinton appointee, had stated publicly that she would ensure that an atmosphere of "openness" prevailed in her agency, I phoned her office with hopeful expectations of receiving a sensible reply. Browner fancies herself as a crusader. On April 20, 1995, she addressed the National Press Club on the topic of threats to science and questioned the ethics of the Republican-controlled Congress in rolling back vanguard environmental laws. Her comments coincided with the twenty-fifth anniversary of Earth Day.

"We have seen lawyers and lobbyists for polluters invited into the back rooms of Congress, where behind closed doors, without public debate, they have written for themselves special exemptions from the environmental responsibilities that all businesses have been expected to live up to," she declared. "We have seen a bill, passed by a House committee, that would increase the amount of sewage and industrial waste pouring into our rivers and streams. A bill that would allow the loss of over half of the nation's wetlands. A bill that systematically undermines each and every one of the tools we have used to clean up our water over the past two decades." And we saw the government try to cut a secret deal with private industry over tortoises.

You would think that, based upon Browner's stated concerns, she would applaud the after-hours work of EPA employees who altruistically invest themselves in environmental protection. After all, Browner has urged citizens more than once to get involved with their communities and to create a better world for their children.

And you might think that Browner, based upon her image, would be sympathetic to community activists such as van Ee and decry the kind of discipline "behind closed doors, without public debate" that led to his silencing by her own agency. Although her aides say she is familiar with van Ee's case, Browner has done nothing either to intervene on van Ee's behalf or to provide a public accounting of why her agency chooses to continue the harassment that began under her Republican predecessors. She has left him hanging.

Almost a decade after his persecution started, van Ee could lose his job if he represents the Sierra Club on any public land issue unrelated to the EPA. I wanted to ask Browner about the EPA's ethics in bringing ethics charges against van Ee for doing the very thing she says is helpful to the mission of her agency. When my telephone calls went unreturned after several people told me they would "investigate the matter and get back to me," I wrote a letter; when that drew no response, I wrote another. And I sent a fax. Twice.

During a visit to Washington I stopped by Browner's office and asked for an interview, hoping to hear her own opinion on whether van Ee, and others like him, should be restricted from being active in environmental organizations. The last thing I wanted to do in these pages was to cite the EPA as having "no comment." On seventeen different occasions I sought an official response from Browner on the matter of Jeff van Ee, and each time the word was mum. No comment.

So I redirected my search to the EPA's own ethics officer, Donnell Nantkes, the man who initially suggested that van Ee had violated serious conflict-of-interest codes and should be punished. In an internal memo obtained through the Freedom of Information Act (and one Nantkes probably never thought would reach public scrutiny), it was he who endorsed the inspector general's investigation into van Ee—despite the fact that Nantkes's primary responsibility is to help employees avoid apparent conflicts of interest.

Getting a straight answer from him was akin to deciphering a cryptic Chinese riddle. The following is the content of a telephone conversation with him (my comments are not in quotation marks).

What is the status of Mr. van Ee's case? I inquired.

"I can't tell you that," Nantkes replied.

Why is that?

"Because it's an internal matter."

Weren't you the person at EPA to suggest that van Ee had broken the law?

"Well, yes, but I can't answer any questions because it's a personnel matter and is being handled as such internally."

Who, then, can I contact within the EPA about details of the case because it is Mr. van Ee who wants the information made public?

"Well, it doesn't matter what Mr. van Ee wants. I don't think there is anyone here who can answer your questions. I don't think anyone is willing to talk about it."

Why is that?

No response.

But what convinced you that van Ee should be disciplined?

"It's a personnel matter, and I'm not going to discuss it with you," Nantkes said.

Wasn't it your opinion that Mr. van Ee had given the appearance of a conflict of interest even though the meeting he attended had nothing to do with his work at EPA? Even though Mr. van Ee had taken vacation days to attend the meeting? And even though he signed the meeting log as a private citizen? Are you suggesting that the EPA can dictate to its employees what they can and cannot do on their time off if it's not job related?

"Look, Mr. van Ee's case is a personnel matter, and we'd like to keep it that way."

I thought the point of personnel matters was to protect the employee. Mr. van Ee would like to have a public airing of the complaint against him and the reason for his reprimand. If tax dollars were spent investigating him, doesn't the public have a right to know what happened and why he was told if he becomes active with a conservation organization he might be fired?

"Look, several times a week I give advice to people that might involve personnel problems," Nantkes said. "Conflict of interest comes up in the course of discussing outside employment with lots and lots of people. Nothing that I know makes this case unique."

I asked Mr. Nantkes if Mr. van Ee's voluntary attendance at a meeting involving the Sierra Club Legal Defense Fund represented, in his mind, "outside employment"?

There was no response.

Was he serving as an attorney for the Defense Fund?

No response.

Did you discuss Mr. van Ee's alleged conflict of interest with him before you suggested that he be prosecuted?

"Well, no," Nantkes said.

Did you tell him that he was being investigated based upon your recommendation?

No response.

Did you give him any advance warning that his involvement with the Sierra Club constituted a conflict of interest, and have you informed all of the other EPA employees who are active in community organizations that they could be terminated for conflict of interest?

"No I have not, but his case is different."

Mr. Nantkes, isn't it true that van Ee's association with the Sierra Club Legal Defense Fund was purely as an observer with nothing to do with his job or expertise at EPA?

"That may or may not be true. I can't, and I will not, talk about this case," he replied.

Mr. Nantkes, I've telephoned the lab where he works in Las Vegas and made several requests to Ms. Browner's office for an explanation. If you can't discuss his case and explain EPA's position, then who can?

"You're talking about an internal matter here, and we will not talk to the press about that."

Mr. van Ee believes that you are using the "personnel issue" as an excuse to cover up the reasons you took action against him. I'm curious about why he had to file a Freedom of Information Act request to receive documents on an investigation in which he was the primary focus?

"I will not talk about the reasons he was disciplined."

Finally, I asked Nantkes how he would react if, hypothetically, he were confronted with the following circumstances. If he were facing conflict-of-interest charges, wouldn't he want to know why he was threatened with possible termination, prison time, and a fine? Wouldn't he want to know why a letter of reprimand was placed in his personnel file and that it likely would affect any possibility of future promotion? Wouldn't he like to know why attorneys for the government had begun an investigation of him and were raising serious doubts about his personal integrity and his ethics among fellow employees long before he was able to answer the charges?

"I don't know how I would react," Nantkes said. "I do not have to, and I will not, discuss details of his case with you, and I certainly don't need to justify to you why I made the decision the way I did."

There's a troubling irony here. Near the end of his term in the White House, George Bush issued a proclamation encouraging all federal employees to get involved in their community, to become part of the president's "thousand points of light."

So far van Ee has spent nearly $100,000 in attorney's fees, money taken out of his retirement fund to fight the government, which has martyred him for getting involved, while the government itself expends tens of thousands of tax dollars that we, and van Ee himself, pay each year as citizens to fight him. Van Ee has exhausted a large chunk of his retirement in the battle, but what happens to those citizens who are brought up on questionable charges and cannot afford to stand up to the government? They lose.

Van Ee is not the only EPA employee who was charged with ethics violations or harassed during the Reagan and Bush years, nor was he the only worker to find little sympathy waiting for him when Clinton and Gore were elected. "If it were truly a goal of President Bush, and now the Clinton administration, to encourage federal employees to become active in their communities, then the EPA has not heeded the call," van Ee says. "If it is the ambition of federal employees to do the best job that they can, then their work continues to go unrewarded. The message I continue to receive is to be conservative and not take chances—don't get involved in controversial issues outside the office, especially when another part of the federal government is involved, which is next to impossible to do when you live as a conservationist in a place like Nevada."

In his 1996 State of the Union Address, four years after he was elected, Bill Clinton applauded federal workers, calling them "hardworking Americans who are now working harder and working smarter than ever before to make sure the quality of our services does not decline."

The president added, "We have to go forward to the era of working together as a community, as a team, as one America, with all of us reaching across these lines that divide us—the division, the discrimination, the rancor—we have to reach across it to find common ground. We have to work together if we want America to work."

Fine words, but not once has the government reached a hand out to van Ee and admitted that its harassment of him was misdirected and politically motivated by supervisors who wanted to teach him a lesson.

Yes, there are reasons why van Ee's court case may resonate with the militia movement because it reaffirms their worst fears. Michael McCloskey, the national chairman of the Sierra Club, said the EPA's persecution of van Ee was gratuitous at best and insidious at worst, particularly with its warning that anything van Ee did on matters of environmental concern might constitute the "appearance of a conflict."

"Appearances *are* a major concern, as well as taking unfair advantage of one's employment association," McCloskey says. "The answer here is clearly to avoid any mention of one's employer, and indeed to issue a disclaimer if that is what the employer wants (though that really may be counterproductive). Since most people are employed by someone, the same problem of misrepresentation exists with respect to all employed people. Are they all to forfeit their First Amendment rights simply because an employer fears that someone will jump to conclusions? Are these rights to be available only to the unemployed or to those whose employers are a secret? Are you to lose your free-speech rights once your reputation grows and people know who you work for?"

Van Ee says his role in questioning government spending qualified him as a federal whistleblower and should have precluded retaliation. Congressman James Bilbray, a Democrat from Nevada, agrees, calling van Ee "a remarkable young man" who has not only dedicated his life to government service but has devoted his leisure time to protecting the public interest. The most frightening aspect of his case is that as a private citizen, van Ee risked his own liberty by reporting waste and trying to save the taxpayers' money, Bilbray said before introducing a special amendment in the House—named after van Ee—that would exclude federal whistleblowers from criminal prosecution.

Bilbray's gesture, while well intended, resulted in little solace because the government has refused to acknowledge van Ee's status as a whistleblower. The harassment of employees who don't agree with the bullying tactics of their superiors continues, as was borne out by a report from the General Accounting Office (GAO). "Overall, our work has shown that despite the intent of the federal Whistleblower Protection Act to strengthen and improve whistleblower protection, employees are still having difficulty proving their cases," said GAO representative Nancy Kingsbury.

That's why the outcome of van Ee's case in challenging the constitutionality of Title 18, USC Section 205 has potential benchmark ramifications. Until change happens, the message transmitted to van Ee and thousands of others is this: If you work for the government, you are precluded from being active in your community or challenging government decisions with which you disagree.

"I feel my constitutional rights, even as limited as they may be for federal employees, have been minimized," van Ee says. "I feel I can no longer say what I want, in the way I want, in association with the people I feel comfortable with, without a fear of losing my job." In essence, the EPA has succeeded in muzzling one prominent voice in the "environmental conscience of southern Nevada."

McCloskey sees a larger trend that transcends political boundaries. There are countless examples of agency employees not only feeling inhibited off the job but being muzzled on the job and not allowed to do professional work or present scientific information. At the national level, he saw an incident under the Bush administration in which James T. Hansen, a prominent climatologist at the Goddard Institute for Space Studies, was forced by the Office of Management and Budget to change his scientific testimony about what computer models showed regarding global warming trends. Hansen has since been vindicated, and his data now form the basis for the Clinton administration's policy on trying to address global warming, but it took a decade of harassment, marshaled primarily by the oil and coal industries, which tried to discredit him.

Not long ago a regional official of the Fish and Wildlife Service was fired when he refused to change the findings of a scientific report showing that oil drilling off the California coast would cause environmental damage. He was also the subject of intense political pressure to not have the spotted owl listed as an endangered species. In the end his data provided the impetus for a temporary ban on oil drilling.

The findings of the Department of the Interior report on the environmental effects of drilling for oil in the Arctic National Wildlife Refuge were also changed to fit the political views of the department, McCloskey notes, as were the findings of a government study conducted by the U.S. Geological Survey on the threat of geothermal drilling to Yellowstone's geysers and hot springs.

When Republicans took control of both the Senate and House of Representatives in 1994, one of the first gestures they made was to reorganize key committees and do away with hearings normally called on behalf of federal whistleblowers. However, a few months prior to the Republican takeover, U.S. Representative Tom Lantos of California held a hearing and asked McCloskey to testify.

"You have spoken of chilling effects," Lantos asked. "How widespread do you think this chilling effect is across government agencies that deal with the environment?"

"I have had a number of people who work for federal agencies tell me that they have been harassed, for instance, for being members of the Sierra Club, often in subtle ways, but it was suggested to them that this was trouble to have such an association," McCloskey answered. "And as I have said, there are instances with the other agencies, such as the Fish and Wildlife Service and the National Park Service, where their employees have tried to honestly present scientific information and have been told in no uncertain terms not to do it."

He said the Clinton administration has not stood by its pledge to create a friendlier working environment for land managers and government employees trying to uphold environmental laws based upon sound ethics and science. "I have seen or heard nothing that gives environmentalists confidence that the Clinton administration has been willing to go to the mat for science," McCloskey mentioned. "The EPA has been making some limited accommodations, but by and large Carol Browner has been resisting fairly vigorously being led down the primrose path of defending committed servants like van Ee. She is anything but 100 percent stalwart to the cause of reform, which is why Jeff has been left out in the cold."

Limiting what employees can say when they punch out on the time clock is not consistent with a free and open democracy, constitutional guru Flyger says. "If you condone the type of behavior used by the EPA, it results in selective, thoroughly arbitrary enforcement. It is impractical for the federal government to regulate every communication made by every federal employee to every federal agency on behalf of a group. As a result, 18 USC Section 205 is observed mostly in the breach and will only be enforced selectively against employees who are perceived to be causing a problem. Such selective enforcement enables an administration to punish civil service employees essentially on political grounds, which contravenes the spirit of our civil service laws, if not their letter. It also transforms an ethics law into an instrument for punishing opposition and dissent within the ranks of federal employees, which is a transformation repugnant to our Constitution. This is, after all, the United States of America."

~

Postscript: van Ee's court battle continues, and recently when he asked his bosses which activities outside the office were "allowable," they replied that he could comment in a vague general sense on environmental issues but could not comment on "specific matters." In other words, he could argue that a stream in the West might be polluted, but he cannot name which one or which company is destroying it because it might give "the appearance of a conflict of interest."

In 1996 the National Wildlife Federation, the largest citizen conservation group in the country, honored van Ee for perseverance under fire and his selfless dedication to protecting America's wildlife. He was the only worker from the EPA on whom such recognition was bestowed. However, before he could receive the award at a special presentation in Florida, he was required to check with the EPA to see if it was ethical *and legal* for him to be provided with transportation to the ceremony and to receive a trophy with his name on it. In a strange twist, the request went before Donnell Nantkes, the same agency ethics official who sought to have him fired and whose harassment, ironically, brought van Ee public recognition. Reluctantly, Nantkes agreed to allow van Ee to attend the ceremony.

"For me, it's sad to have given twenty-five years of my life to the EPA and to see it has all come down to this," van Ee says as we drive in front of the Mirage Hotel and Casino, a brightly lit structure rising from the desert. The building is made of reflective glass that, like the EPA, allows those on the inside to see out but prevents those on the outside from looking in.

"When I began my career many years ago, I was told that I would be proud working for the EPA because it represented the best principles in protecting human health and the purity of the environment," he says. "I still want to keep believing it's true, but if it means surrendering my right to free speech the moment I walk out the door, it takes away something from working for the premier environmental agency in the world. The government can own my dedication, but it can't take my soul."

The Combat Biologist

Science is the knowledge of consequences, and
dependence of one fact upon another.
　　　　　　—Thomas Hobbes, *The Leviathan*

LAST NIGHT I MADE my camp along a river the Nez Perce call Kooskooskee. Stoking the coals of a fire hearthed with smooth-worn glacial cobblestones, soaking my sore feet in the frigid, muddied whirl, I cast a fishing line into the mellifluous current and it floated two hundred years into history.

Let me acknowledge before we proceed much farther on this little trek that I don't speak to the following point as an absolute authority because I wasn't with Meriwether Lewis and William Clark in mid-September 1805 as they passed near here and pushed deeper into the Clearwater National Forest of central Idaho. But I am willing to venture that neither Lewis nor Clark was very enthusiastic about the fine art of fly-fishing.

Poring over their journals, slogging miles in their wake, searching for the charred remains of long-extinguished embers, I believe we can surmise a plausible hypothesis: Had these first American Odysseuses been adept at slinging tiny artificial bugs to prodigious rising salmonids, they might well have judged the Clearwater country—a region still virtually synonymous with wild speckled trout—to be a vestige of heaven instead of primeval hell.

Although we are reminded ad infinitum of how eminently resourceful Lewis and Clark were, once they crossed the Continental Divide westward toward the Pacific Ocean, they entered topography that proved to be the most ruggedly formidable of any the Corps of Discovery would encounter. Tracing a Nez Perce footpath known as the Lolo Trail, which connected traditional buffalo hunting grounds on the Great Plains with the Cascade Range, they descended the ominous, snaggle-toothed inclines of the Bitterroot Mountains. After wading in moccasins and buckskin through a maze of translucent creeks, they stood humbly before the roaring draw of Kooskooskee. And here, resorting to behavior that until now has gone unreported, tough guys Lewis and Clark began to whine like eastern greenhorns out of their element.

Kooskooskee today is identified on maps as the Lochsa, and under either name it is the sum of myriad rivulets plunging down from the high batholithic crests of the Idaho panhandle. With channels gouged clean in ancient times by the gravity of receding Pleistocene ice, these innumerable pine-canopied watercourses swell violently in spring and summer with thundering volumes of snowmelt and rain.

The setting then, as now, was shadowy and harsh, with hale fish to match. In fact, some of the last significant spans of roadless terrain and *wild* fish habitat in the lower forty-eight states still persist in this stretch of the federal estate. I say *still,* but probably not for long. The fish are doomed, and the mucky omen is stuck to Al Espinosa's flippers. But before you try to stomp off through the forest to find the bearded frogman—who at present is haunting the Clearwater's isolated, ribbonlike pools—Espinosa would like you to imagine the arresting panorama that Lewis and Clark saw in the last week of summer two centuries ago.

Early snows had dusted the peaks of the northern Rockies. Rutting elk were bugling in the canyons below treeline. Waterfowl were on the move southward. Indians of the Northwest were heading home from the interior prairies with fresh buffalo meat loaded on their travois. Ablaze in vibrant ochre and chartreuse, the riparian corridors were abstractions of aspen and cottonwood. The broad-leafed trees glittered brightly against a green coniferous patina broken only by open-meadowed pockets where wildfire had swept through. Everywhere, in various stages of decay, the trunks of giant, moss-covered deadfalls lay at the feet of senescent spruce, cedar, and fir. Skulking in the humid shadows were grizzly bears, mountain lions, wolves, wolverines, and lynx. Flitting between the damp branches were new species of neotropical passerines as well as raptors ready to be cataloged for posterity. Among the feathered assembly was a bantering member of the crow clan, a camp robber we have since come to know as the Clark's nutcracker, *Nucifraga columbiana.*

"We ... continued our route over high, rough knobs and several drains and springs, and along a ridge of country separating the waters of two small rivers," William Clark, after whom the bird was named, wrote on Thursday, September 17, 1805, following a stop at

the bank of Kooskooskee. "The [trail] was still difficult, as several of
the horses fell and injured themselves very much so that were unable
to advance more than ten miles to a small stream on which we
camped. We had killed a few pheasants [grouse], but these being insufficient for our subsistence, we killed another of the colts. This want
of provisions and the extreme fatigue to which we were subjected,
and the dreary prospects before us, began to dispirit the men."

Famished, exhausted, swallowed up by the very essence of what
we call wilderness, I say again that Lewis and Clark might well have
responded differently to their surroundings had they clutched rods
and reels in their hands. Had they been anglers, their bellies could
have passed full through some of the finest, most fecund runs of bull
trout, westslope cutthroat trout, fluvial arctic grayling, steelhead, and
inland salmon in North America. But right now, as you read this
sentence, the last great repository of wild fish in the lower forty-
eight states and the very sheltering forests that towered over Lewis
and Clark are being erased by corporate timber titans with the tacit
approval of the U.S. government. Should you desire any proof, go
ask Espinosa, who wears a baseball cap with the words *combat biologist* printed above the brim. He is fighting a protracted ground war
that has raged outside the public notice for three decades, and his
war has little to do with dams.

"Al Espinosa is the original combat biologist," Cheri Brooks, a
former spokeswoman of Forest Service Employees for Environmental Ethics (FSEEE) tells me one afternoon before Espinosa's
dissidence led him into premature retirement from his job as a civil
servant. "Al's been blowing the whistle on the Clearwater's timber
program, and for that the Forest Service has exacted a high personal
and professional price. He's been ostracized, had his credibility attacked, and was offered as a sacrifice to the timber industry because
he dares to question the arrogance of what was going on around
him." An organization that represents hundreds of whistleblowers
who risk their careers speaking out against natural resource abuses,
FSEEE was founded by Forest Service timber manager Jeff DeBonis
(see the chapter "Confessions of the Timber Beast"). "He isn't the
first combat biologist, but the term was created with him in mind,"
Brooks adds. "As a result of Al Espinosa, there are a lot of government employees in federal and state natural resource agencies who
wear the title *combat biologist* as a red badge of courage."

When the former federal fisheries guru isn't snorkeling through rivers such as the Lochsa or the North or Middle Fork of the Clearwater River, the frogman-turned-scientific-agitator is searching for answers to explain dramatic piscatorial spirals, sometimes with a fly-line in one hand and water-sampling equipment in the other. In rippling pools that should teem with fish, Espinosa is alarmed by what he finds. Countless fishing holes are turning up vacant, reflecting the aftermath of a public logging policy gone awry.

Twenty years ago Espinosa experienced what amounted to a premonition. Breathing through his snorkel tube, surveying the cobbles and gravel beds of several Clearwater trout streams where fish deposit their eggs, he found the tips of his fingernails clotted in silt. The normally unblurred flows ran turbid, the tint of a cafe latte, the same hue as the mélange of logging roads in the area. Espinosa predicted then the eventual collapse of half a dozen fish populations currently proposed for protective listing under the Endangered Species Act. Harboring no delight in the accuracy of his prophecy, he has spent his entire career hoping to prove himself wrong.

Consider the prognosis for salmon alone, described in a 1997 scientific analysis written by Espinosa, Jon J. Rhodes, and Dale A. McCullough that appeared in the *Journal of Environmental Management*. The paper, titled "The Failure of Existing Plans to Protect Salmon Habitat in the Clearwater National Forest in Idaho," caught the attention of the Clinton administration and Congress. It begins,

Over the past 50 years, salmon populations have declined precipitously through the Columbia River Basin, historically one of the greatest salmon producing rivers in the world. The spring and summer chinook salmon runs in 1994 and 1995 have been the lowest on record in the past 35 years. Upriver summer chinook runs have dropped from about 125,000 fish in 1960 to less than 18,000 in 1994. Upriver spring chinook have declined from about 275,000 in 1973 to about 21,000 in 1994. It has been estimated that the annual salmon and steelhead runs numbered ten to sixteen million fish historically. Existing forecasts indicate that continued declines are likely for these salmon in the near future. All races (fall, spring, summer) of chinook salmon in the Snake River Basin were listed by the National Marine Fisheries Service under the Endangered Species Act in 1992; their status was upgraded to "endangered" in 1994. Recent salmonids are also declining through much of the Columbia River

Basin. The U.S. Fish and Wildlife Service has determined that bull
trout populations are warranted for listing under the Endangered
Species Act.

The late Mollie Beattie, the first woman to oversee the Fish and
Wildlife Service, which determines whether a species should be
listed, acknowledged to me during an interview in Jackson Hole,
Wyoming, a year before her tragic death from brain cancer that the
cause of fish declines is no mystery. "The reason that there are so
many [species in trouble] is because our waters are not in very good
condition and some are getting worse. They [several varieties of wild
fish] are going toward extinction because of overuse of water, but
particularly because of water pollution from a variety of sources, including siltation caused by logging and the building of Forest Service roads. The correlation is undeniable, and we're fooling ourselves
if we think that saving those species isn't in our best long-term
interest."

Beattie was continually frustrated by the politics of her government job, and she resented the tactics of forced political compromise
when the biological prognosis appeared so bleak. What upset her
even more than individual fish losses was the pace at which they are
collectively occurring. Whenever her agency issued a ruling that listing a species under the Endangered Species Act was "warranted but
precluded"—a common practice in the 1990s—she saw it as a
stalling tactic, a denial of the inevitable, a maneuver that undermined
the very mission of her agency. "Warranted but precluded" means
that the animal is already on the path to extinction, but another
species is farther along the trail to oblivion and gets attention first.

According to Beattie, the same political and industrial forces that
criticize the Fish and Wildlife Service for not being effective in its
charge of recovering species are compromising the agency's ability
to do just that by staving off new listings until deep conflict and economic hardship cannot be avoided. Beattie's boss, Secretary of the
Interior Bruce Babbitt, has labeled the debacle over old-growth
forests in the western Pacific states an "environmental train wreck,"
which implies that the harm is fixable—but it may not be, Beattie
acknowledged. Today the country's leading landscape ecologists say
that if the Forest Service allows loggers to reach the virgin drainages
remaining in public forests such as the Clearwater, that decision

could start a domino effect on inland trout and salmon leading toward an unraveling of aquatic ecosystems that has no precedent in human history.

~

"I feel bad for the timber industry, I really do," Espinosa says during a meeting at a coffee shop in northern Idaho following a snorkeling mission. "Only four decades ago they had 90 percent of the old-growth forests in the West at their fingertips ready to provide logs and jobs forever, but they allowed their own greed to squander the opportunity. Now the fish are paying the price, and the corporate logging operations are coming back to finish off what's left with the endorsement of a crooked Congress. Bruce Babbitt talks about environmental train wrecks with the spotted owl, but he ain't seen nothing yet. If we lose all of our aboriginal fish which are pressed to the brink, it is going to make the spotted owl controversy look like a fender-bender."

In a casual, restrained setting, Fernando Alexander Espinosa Jr.'s appearance reveals little of the steely reputation he's gained by going into battle with Forest Service managers whom he unaffectionately calls "timber beasts." If there is a single signature to his personality, it is a sardonic edginess that carries the polish of a stand-up comic. Often Espinosa resorts to levity as a means of coping with the gravity of the new timber wars. Despite the mounds of empirical data that fill his filing cabinets at home, he has a knack of explaining, in layman's terms, the dry minutiae of statistics with examples from the field. Consider his take on the Forest Service's latest commitment to promote "ecosystem health," a slogan that he dismisses as a shibboleth: "I'd sooner believe the mafia's going to sell Girl Scout cookies for charity tomorrow than the Forest Service is going to practice ecosystem management as it claims. For half a century the Forest Service has been coming up with new buzzwords, which are really just nice-sounding window-dressing for business as usual. Its latest justification for clearcutting—salvage logging, which is based on the argument of toppling the forest in order to save it—is sheer lunacy."

Echoing Espinosa's sentiments, independent biologists hold that it is no mere coincidence that the fleeting strongholds of native fish stocks in the West are all found in remote mountain drainages that have so far been spared penetration by logging trucks and chainsaws.

The lines of confrontation once drawn over Douglas fir, spruce, cedar, marbled murrelets, salmon, and spotted owls in coastal areas of the Pacific Northwest have shifted inland, hurdling over the Cascades and etching themselves into the upper Columbia River Basin of Idaho, western Montana, eastern Oregon, and Washington. Ground zero is the pockets of old growth in the Clearwater National Forest.

In the nearly two centuries since Lewis and Clark visited the Clearwater, modernity has profoundly impressed its presence upon the landscape. The old Nez Perce trail has been replaced by Lolo Highway 12. Portions of this paved, two-lane drive between Missoula, Montana, and Lowell, Idaho, rival the scenery of any motorway in the country. The route follows the Lochsa River into the heart of fish refugia. To understand what brought Espinosa into the fold of combat biology, stray off the main highway and travel up a few of the side draws that are embroidered with miles of gumbo-surfaced switchbacks. Many of these dirt lanes, built at taxpayer expense to ensure that private timber companies can record a profit for their stockholders, have cost more to engineer than the value of the felled trees. From the air the Clearwater's "developed" forest sections look like a golf green might if the sod had been endlessly and haphazardly cookie-cuttered to expose the raw earth. The plan is to apply a similar technique of tree removal to montane inclines where motorized engines have never been.

At the head of a few steep stream drainages, you come upon proposed timber-sale areas where logging-company bulldozers are poised to invade. What seemed impassable to nineteenth-century explorers is merely a tactical challenge for Forest Service engineers. Designing logging roads across aspects suitable for alpine skiing, they have targeted tree trunks with five hundred rings encircling their core. The arboreal giants, which tower over trout spawning areas, were half as thick when Lewis and Clark passed beneath them.

"There would not be much to argue over if it had not been for Al Espinosa. These areas of the Clearwater and the wild fish nurseries left inside of them would have been cut years ago," says Charles Pezeshki, a professor of mechanical engineering at Washington State University who moonlights as executive director of the Clearwater Biodiversity Project. In 1998 Pezeshki penned a blistering broadside against the Forest Service in his book titled *Wild to the Last—Environmental Conflict in the Clearwater Country*. "Metaphorically, Al has put down his body in front of the Forest Service wrecking crew, and he is an example of David fighting Goliath," he tells me. "It is no exaggeration to say that wild fish persist only because he would not give away the last pockets of habitat. But I need to add that one man cannot hold out forever if he is taking on an entire corrupt system like the Forest Service."

Espinosa says two species in particular are imminently imperiled: the bull trout *(Salvelinus confluentus)* and the westslope cutthroat trout *(Onychorhynchus clarki lewisi)* named after Lewis and Clark, who first encountered the beautiful fish near Great Falls, Montana. Both species should have received federal protection a decade ago, but because of resistance from politicians connected with the timber industry each was placed in the limbo of "warranted but precluded" by the Fish and Wildlife Service. In 1997 a court victory won by conservationists affiliated with the Alliance for the Wild Rockies and the Friends of the Wild Swan forced the agency to list bull trout, and a similar course of action for westslope cutthroat may not be far behind. However, the Fish and Wildlife Service hesitated to list the bull trout as endangered or threatened throughout its entire range in the Pacific Northwest, protecting only two distinct populations in the Columbia River Basin (as threatened) and in the Klamath River Basin (as endangered). "This is a great legal victory for the bull trout," Mike Bader, executive director of the Missoula-based Alliance for the Wild Rockies, said at the time. "But from a biological standpoint, the trout continues to lose because Fish and Wildlife continues to deny it legal protection. The more delay they create, the more ground the bull trout loses."

Espinosa's forte as a biological clocksmith is assembling the pieces of what makes a healthy stream tick. Relics from the Ice Age, bull trout once thrived across hinterland fluvial systems of the Pacific Northwest but have been reduced to a fraction of their former range. Burly, secretive, and voracious in their piscivorous (fish-eating) diets, bulls are capable of reaching fourteen pounds and thirty inches in length. Their size gives them their own mystique. "Bull trout and cutthroat trout are very sensitive to habitat disturbance," Espinosa notes one morning before setting off on a trek into roadless Clearwater areas. "They require extremely cold and clean water. That means they require shade to keep the water from heating up and vegetation to hold the soils in place. They're the best indicators of healthy ecosystem watersheds we have in terms of measuring erosion. When you strip away the trees from a mountainside, there is no longer any cover. The water temperature rises and the fish are more susceptible to predation. When you cut all the trees on the slopes above the stream, the water also gets inundated by a flood of soil washing in, which prevents them from producing a successful redd [nest]. For a fish population, those things are a deadly combination. That's why the bull trout is disappearing."

Flowing through the Clearwater are several almost mythical trout streams—the Selway, the Lochsa, the North Fork of the Clearwater—rivers that are known worldwide to anglers for native stocks of salmon, steelhead, westslope cutthroat, and, of course, wild bulls. Back in the hidden hamlets of destruction carefully crafted by Clearwater foresters to be beyond the view of citizens traveling the main highways, you come face to face with one of the reasons why so many of the wild fishery stocks in the American West are going extinct.

Not so long ago, while hiking the perimeter of a proposed cut at Espinosa's advice, I met a logger and asked him what he thought about cutting trees that ultimately could mean the end of the bull trout. He lumbered forth with a husky, big-bellied swagger, spoke in a low octave from smoking too many cigarettes, and answered my questions with an air of incredulity. The stare that emerged after I told him I was writing a book about a local whistleblower who criticized the Clearwater timber program left me uneasy. "You know, I don't understand why those damned preservationists are up in arms over this, and I don't see the connection between trees and trout," he said. "I've never seen a fish grow on a tree, have you?"

If he had posed the question to Espinosa, the retort would have been: In a way, yes, trout do grow on trees. For years the Clearwater has identified bull trout as a species of special concern. Native fish stocks represent the fittest of the fit in nature. Their ancestors became genetically imprinted on specific streams, even specific stream sections. Within larger regional populations there can be a complicated nexus of subpopulations whose ability to survive is tied narrowly to a particular drainage. Indigenous fish are hardier than hatchery stocks and more resistant to diseases and have adapted to the harsh conditions in which explorers such as Lewis and Clark found them. Most important, though tangential, they have their own right and reason to exist.

Despite their rugged image bull trout are, in fact, vulnerable to disturbance. Like arctic grayling, these endemic fish probably originated in glacial arteries of the Columbia River Basin as a distinct offshoot of their close anadromous (fish that spawn in rivers but spend part of their life in the sea) relatives the Dolly Varden *(Salvelinus malma).* Requiring frigid, shaded water that is low in sedimentation, they prefer to stack up in tight, deep channels, especially during spawning season as they search for a place to make their redds and chomp on other fish. Native American tribes obviously knew of bull trout because there are stretches of streams throughout the Northwest named after the species. Even Montana governor Marc Racicot, who fished in wilderness streams just across the Continental Divide from the Clearwater as a boy, counted bull trout as among his favorite species to catch, but in his state, at the easternmost edge of its range, this game fish has vanished from at least 60 percent of its ancestral reaches.

Do trout grow on trees? The message derived from Espinosa's research, which won him several awards from the Forest Service and independent scientific organizations, is unequivocally yes, they do. In the 1970s bull trout already were starting to disappear entirely from many drainages in the Clearwater, and Espinosa knew why. "My first year in Idaho definitely opened my eyes to the industrial capabilities of the Forest Service. Here I had been thinking of my agency as being kind of a garden pruner that weeds out trees in order to keep the whole forest healthy. I didn't realize that my supervisors were actually condoning a policy of killing all the crops in the garden. After a few months had passed, it became clear that the Forest Service was one of the greatest road-building bureaucracies in the world."

Tens of millions of tax dollars have been spent designing and building a network of roads in the Clearwater long enough to stretch from the Atlantic to the Pacific—4,580 miles—but a scanty amount of money has been earmarked for doing restoration work once the earthmoving is completed. For example, at a section of the Clearwater known as Lunch Creek, where vast sweeps of trees were toppled with little attention given to buffer strips, even foresters grimace when they look at the aftermath. Espinosa says the Forest Service overbuilt the road system, aligning it adjacent to streams, then watched shamelessly as slopes were rendered barren without any erosion control.

"The only thing they did was sprinkle some grass seed and fertilizer out upon the steep disturbed slopes," Espinosa says. "We knew it was only a matter of time. After two years of spring snowmelt and summer rains with nothing done to stabilize the soil, the hillside in Lunch Creek slid and the fish runs were heavily impacted. No, let's call them nuked."

When I ask Espinosa to give me a tally of streams suffering a similar fate, in two minutes he is able to rattle off nearly fifty different drainages where the Forest Service failed to meet its own standards, standards he helped write which were adopted by his superiors. Some of the worst cases of fish habitat destruction caused by logging in the United States can be found in drainages with names such as China, Osier, Skull, Parachute, Quartz, Eldorado, Pete King, Canyon, and Lolo Creeks—all tributaries to the Clearwater and Lochsa Rivers.

Before his premature retirement Espinosa completed a comprehensive survey of Clearwater streams. At least 71 percent of the drainages on developed (i.e., logged, mined, and "roaded") sections of the forest failed to meet the agency's standards for water quality. Many are so "trashed," Espinosa says, that they still violate legal standards laid out under the federal Clean Water Act and the National Environmental Policy Act (NEPA). There may even be violations of the Endangered Species Act for spoiling habitat and killing fish that are important to grizzly bears.

During the mid-1990s a series of flood events devastated Clearwater watersheds as hundreds of landslides from logging roads wreaked havoc on stream channels and fish habitat. Roaded and logged drainages were damaged far more than natural unroaded watersheds adjacent to them. A Forest Service report, completed over the objections of local Clearwater Forest officials, found that well over half of some 905 landslides recorded in a single year were caused by road building.

Silt in the rivers decimates fish in insidious ways. "Let's say you're a chinook salmon. During the winter juvenile chinook hover within the cobbles and small boulders on the streambed to dodge the ice," Espinosa says. "If sediment fills up those spaces, either the fish must run a gauntlet of predators to find additional habitat or they get pushed up to shallow water, where they are pummeled by ice. In the summer and autumn during the spawn, fish spend time in the deep pools. But silt fills them in. It buries the winter cover and entombs the eggs after the spawn. All salmonid species—salmon and trout—face this threat."

Now, with "forest health" bills from Congress spawning hundreds of proposed new timber sales, alarms are resounding, repeating what has already occurred in the national forests on the west side of the Cascades and coastal ranges in Oregon and Washington. In addition, the stated purpose of salvage logging is to rake the forest floor of dead trees and haul them off to mills, while toppling live trees under the premise that if they aren't felled they will burn and be rendered "useless."

Espinosa warns that much of the Clearwater's remaining timber base outside wilderness meets the general criteria for being an "extreme situation" (high risk for burying streams in sediments), which means it is not appropriate to allow logging and road construction as the Forest Service plans on doing. The reason is found in the steep batholithic slopes that anchor the trees and punctuate the forest's rugged isolation. Geologists say batholithic rock, made of soft, crumbling granite, is susceptible to easy decomposition and weathering. When it crumbles, it breaks down into coarse sediments and turns so unstable that it will not hold a roadbed. Remove the vegetation that affixes the thin soil and you create an environment ripe for landslides and severe infusion of loose dirt—silt— into the streams below.

As Espinosa says, "It's not necessarily taking the trees that dooms the bull trout but how they are removed and how the Forest Service has never learned from its past mistakes." As he did throughout the '70s and '80s, Espinosa still goes snorkeling in the creeks of drainages that have been stripped threadbare and compares them to others that have been protected. Upon reaching a pool, he scans it with a few casts to see if there are bull trout poised in the hidden pockets. He rarely gets a bull-trout fin to swirl anymore.

Espinosa's work as an independent consultant has turned him into an expert witness in court battles to get bull trout and westslope cutthroat protected before they are exterminated. Normally hesitant to endorse the listing of species for federal protection, Espinosa says *S. confluentus* and *O. clarki lewisi* need the shield of the Endangered Species Act to keep the Forest Service, let alone the timber industry, at bay. Unless their last few bastions are saved in the Clearwater and every other forest across the Northwest, there is a good chance the species will not exist to mark the two hundredth anniversary of Lewis and Clark's trek.

Forest Service Chief Mike Dombeck as a Band-Aid measure in 1998 called for an eighteen-month moratorium on new road building as a "time out" to assess the wreckage of Forest Service watersheds. "The benefits of forest roads are many," he said in an address to agency employees signaling that he was prepared for a donnybrook with members of Congress who threatened to bring Dombeck to his knees by slashing agency funding and bringing the Forest Service to a standstill, much like the disastrous national parks shutdown that backfired on Republicans. Yes, Forest Service roads have benefits, but then there are "the ecological impacts on watersheds. There are few more irreparable marks we can leave on the land than to build a road. Improperly located, designed, or maintained roads contribute to erosion, wildlife and fish habitat fragmentation, degradation of water quality and exotic species. So long as road management is unaddressed, public support for needed forest management will disappear."

It is a strangely retrograde echo of conditions in the Clearwater National Forest.

~

Al Espinosa traveled a long way to get to the Clearwater and emerge as an authority on Forest Service lawlessness. The son of working-class Latino parents, he was born June 13, 1939, in Fresno, California. His mother's roots stem from Texas, and his father became a naturalized citizen after immigrating from Mexico to pursue the American dream. He won respect in the community first as a formidable prizefighter and later as a police officer. Civil service imposed itself as a duty. That mixture of street-smart scrappiness and fidelity to the law rubbed off on Fernando Espinosa's son.

Fresno rests at the center of the San Joaquin Valley, the heart of California's fruit and vegetable industry. Nature had a powerful influence on Espinosa's life when he was a boy. He remembers being assigned to write a high school paper about the emerging American conservation ethic but became disheartened when he learned that the grizzly bear, whose profile still appears on the California state flag, had been rendered extinct in the nearby Sierra Nevada range. During the 1940s and '50s, Espinosa looked every day out his window toward the east and admired the high Sierra peaks. "On Saturdays as I got older we would go fishing in the mountain streams, and during the week I would daydream about the water," Espinosa recalls. "Later when Fresno began experiencing exponential growth, the clear days became rare and the mountains disappeared behind a curtain of brown haze. It made me want to see the clean streams all the more."

Espinosa knew education represented his ticket to liberation from an uncertain future, so he pursued a career studying trout and salmon. He left for the campus of Humboldt State, a university considered a proving ground for fisheries professionals, and took a degree in aquatic biology. But fate handed him an abrupt two-year detour within months of his graduation. Possessing no influential connections to secure a deferment, he was drafted into the army. "Had I been sent to a war, I would have gone without any hesitation to serve my country," he says. "When I got hired by the Forest Service, I thought I would be a patriot there instead."

Upon completing his army hitch, Espinosa went afield as a seasonal fisheries biologist in Oregon doing research on steelhead trout on the coast and kokanee salmon in the Cascades for the Oregon Game Commission. His boss at the time recognized his talent and encouraged him to pursue a graduate education and earn his master's degree at the University of Nevada–Las Vegas. Five years after finishing his thesis, Espinosa was hired by the U.S. Forest Service's Northern Region as the lead fish biologist in the Clearwater and Nez Perce National Forests in north-central Idaho.

In 1973 there were already minor tremors being felt in Congress foreshadowing the crises that have erupted over forest management in the Pacific Northwest. That year the first incarnation of the Endangered Species Act was passed. It had been preceded in 1970 by the landmark National Environmental Policy Act, which forced federal agencies to consider the consequences of public land development on other resources. "NEPA was not meant to be a quiet addition to the United States Code," noted Patrick A. Parenteau, writing in *Audubon Magazine*. "It was meant to shake things up, to challenge conventional thinking, even to make people uncomfortable, most of all the bureaucrats concealed within the thick gray walls of the federal establishment in Washington."

A rookie, Espinosa had no idea that one day he would be the foot soldier holding the Forest Service brass to the letter of the law and shaking up Washington with objective science. Until NEPA was passed, the conventional thinking had been to allow forest supervisors to make autocratic decisions as to how much timber would be cut, usually on the advice of local mills. It resulted in a relationship a deux between the timber industry and public foresters. For years elected officials, especially in the West, where there is a shrinking sea of federal timber reserves, have become beholden to logging companies because they make generous contributions to political campaign war chests. In turn, congressmen like to keep Forest Service employees under their thumbs because a high output of public timber means the logging companies create jobs, and jobs translate into votes. That isn't earth-shattering news, but the way the Forest Service decided to flout the law is.

Above all else NEPA was a gauge to keep political meddling in its proper place. The law demanded that the public be involved in shaping the direction of resource development on federal land and determined at what level environmental review should be undertaken. If a proposed action were deemed significant, for example, it could trigger an environmental impact statement (EIS) to weigh the benefits against the ecological liabilities. But built into NEPA is a provision whereby a savvy forest supervisor can circumvent an EIS. The loophole is called an environmental assessment, or EA. An EA allows a forest supervisor to administratively approve or disapprove of a timber sale without having to conduct a lengthy EIS. Since the 1970s, most forest supervisors who have close ties to the timber industry have simply rubber-stamped one timber sale after another using the EA process. Environmentalists have succeeded in slowing the harvest of trees through appeals, though such appeals did not evolve into a truly effective tool until the 1980s.

An eternal truth among federal land management bureaucracies is that decisionmakers have a disdain for public scrutiny. With a grin and a wink, Espinosa was told by his superiors on the Clearwater to protect the streams, but at the same time they suggested, slapping the young Hispanic kid on the back, "Now, we don't need to let the law get in the way of cutting a few trees, do we, Al?"

"It didn't take a rocket scientist to figure out the Forest Service had no intention of taking a serious look at how timber management was affecting fish and wildlife that live along stream corridors. The monetary commitment to developing a serious fisheries program wasn't there, the equipment wasn't there, and the data to make informed decisions wasn't there. I basically had to start from scratch," Espinosa says. "To me, it all smacked of extreme tokenism. They hired me merely to provide lip service for all of the logging that was going on and to help them find a way to circumvent compliance with environmental laws. In the beginning, and only for a brief period, it was important to me to be a team player. I went along with it because I wanted to belong to what I naively thought was a conservation agency."

During his first six months on the job Espinosa helped his colleagues design plans for building roads to remove millions of board feet of trees. The Forest Service's preferred method of toppling the trees was clearcutting. For the public that lives in America's heartland and has never seen a clearcut, I should explain that it is an indiscriminate way of harvesting trees based solely upon efficiency. Exploring a clearcut on foot has the same aesthetic feeling as witnessing the aftermath of a fatal automobile accident. The trauma is visible; beauty has left the scene.

Espinosa warned that it was merely a matter of time before environmentalists learned that the Clearwater was ignoring its scientific data. Overdeveloped watersheds were laced with too many roads, and the gravel beds and cobbled rock that offered sanctuary to fish were being filled with silt and mud, one drainage after another, to say nothing of mammal and bird losses on the slopes.

"I told the timber guys that if they didn't want environmentalists filing lawsuits and breathing down our backs they'd better listen up, because if the chinook salmon and bull trout are listed, their timber program could be over. They told me to mind my own business, and I told them that's exactly what I was doing."

He was given his first test of loyalty in 1974, and he failed. His timber bosses proposed a large sale of publicly owned trees in the Lochsa's Crooked Fork drainage not far from where Lewis and Clark had passed 170 years earlier. Essentially, the sale would allow a timber company to denude a mountain face all the way down to the river's edge. To help loggers reach the clearcuts with their heavy machinery, the Clearwater's resident engineers proposed bulldozing miles of roadway across steep slopes and highly erosive soils.

Espinosa stared at the incline and shook his head. He wasn't the only Clearwater staffer who had problems with the sale. Several of his peers noted to him privately that the slopes, if cleared of trees, were doomed to submerge the river under tons of damaging sediment. "Every day in Forest Service offices across the country, there are a lot of individuals who want to do the right thing on behalf of the resource, but they are afraid to meet issues head on. There are a lot of people in the Forest Service who claim to be supporting you, but they look the other way or refuse to make a commitment when their jobs are on the line. Instead they either remain silent or encourage other people to take the risks. It has created an environment of complete dysfunction."

When the Crooked Fork sale was offered, Espinosa, the young greenhorn biologist, was prodded by his coworkers to voice dissent, and after he did he was quickly castigated by his superiors. "It became a gut check for me because when my supervisor looked across the table and asked the rest of the scientific staff if there was anyone who agreed with my argument, the room fell silent. I realized that I was a minority of one. I went up against everybody, and the gutless wonders who were supposed to be doing their job never said one word. They hung me out to dry."

Timber managers who had anticipated no opposition looked at him belligerently and with suspicion. To question the direction of the timber program, they told him, was tantamount to treason. They demanded that he "rethink" his position, a euphemism for giving them everything they wanted, that is, fabricating documents to support their program.

Part of the charge of a fisheries biologist is being knowledgeable about environmental statutes. In 1976 Congress passed the National Forest Management Act (NFMA), which states that the cost of harvesting timber must be weighed against the loss of wildlife habitat. The act set in motion the idea of the Forest Plan, a long-term management blueprint that each national forest in the U.S. must prepare and review every five years. Each plan lays out annual timber targets that the Forest Service now admits were inflated over the past three decades due to political pressure from members of Congress in the West. A year after NFMA was passed, Congress amended another law, the Clean Water Act. It required that the Forest Service hold timber companies to a series of voluntary criteria known as best management practices (BMPs).

BMPs are designed specifically to reduce the degradation of water quality in streams. One objective was to leave "buffer strips" of trees along streams to help impede soil erosion. Under this law, the Forest Service is supposed to give preference to logging companies that abide by this standard. At Crooked Fork, as in dozens of sales offered in the Clearwater, those provisions were waived to get out the cut. "Through the mid-1990s I would take the silviculturists and foresters out to the drainages and say, 'Look at it, it's completely hammered. Let's put some money into restoring it before taking out any more timber.' They would reply, 'No, we've got to do another timber sale and we'll mitigate it by giving you some bucks to try and fix it later,'" Espinosa says. "In the jargon of the Forest Service, *mitigate* means to plant a few trees, not reforest. *Later* means not in this generation, or never. It's the agency's way of rationalizing additional damage in an area where you shouldn't even be thinking about cutting trees. It is the rationale used by an agency still in denial and one that is pressing ahead with a logging program in the upper Columbia watershed that has no sound basis in science."

Studies show that salmon and char survival in Idaho is between ten and fifty-five times higher in streams that have not been subjected to logging, grazing, and mining. Espinosa says the unavoidable listing of the bull trout, despite desperate last-minute attempts by the state of Idaho to stave off listing by developing a habitat conservation plan, is going to have as much or greater impact on people as on the bull trout simply because its range includes waters beyond the Columbia Basin into the headwaters of Hudson Bay. That's got a lot of people in the timber industry scared. And it's why the Forest Service attempted to destroy Espinosa's career with a vengeance.

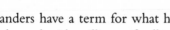

Icelanders have a term for what happens when the nose of a glacier, charged with millions of gallons of water, suddenly breaks loose and careens through a valley, destroying everything in its path. It's called a *jokolhaup,* and Chuck Pezeshki says that mini *jokolhaup*-like phenomena are occurring all over the Clearwater. "We used to have landslides in the larger rivers at lower elevations, but as logging and road building have moved higher into the mountains, the blowouts have begun decimating smaller tributary streams to the point that we are seeing debris torrents moving through whole watersheds." Pezeshki says not only has the Forest Service refused to pull back and reassess its timber program in the Clearwater in the aftermath of hundreds of landslides but foresters have cleverly figured out how to outflank environmentalists by gerrymandering the boundaries of proposed logging areas. "They gerrymander around pristine areas so they don't have to consider cumulative effects. Technically, they can tell the public they are not going into an area considered sacred to recreationists, but the real damage comes later after the habitat has been fragmented and the hills start to slide."

For nearly a decade environmental organizations and independent biologists have pushed for placing the bull trout on the Endangered Species List, but their efforts have been fought by legislators from timber states. Because of politics, the U.S. Fish and Wildlife Service has continued to drag its feet on listing, but there is growing dissent among agency biologists, fueled by mounting evidence.

"Poor land use practices threaten the long-term survival of bull trout," proclaimed the Pacific Rivers Council in a briefing book titled *Northern Rockies Forests and Endangered Native Fish* released in February 1995. "Forest Service–sponsored research has established that there is no safe level of sedimentation that does not affect bull trout spawning."

Bull trout are vanishing on both sides of the Bitterroots. In 1992 fisheries consultant Ginger Thomas prepared a document titled "Status Report: Bull Trout in Montana" for the Montana Department of Fish, Wildlife and Parks. "Data from the Flathead and Bitterroot National Forests are indicating a clear connection between logging activity, sediment levels, and bull trout production," she wrote. "The genetic information available makes it clear that in order to preserve genetic diversity in bull trout, *every population* needs to be protected. Changes in land use and fisheries management may be needed to protect this fish in its remaining habitat." Half a decade later, conditions have worsened.

"It's a real nightmare," Rick Swanson, fisheries biologist with the Bitterroot National Forest in Montana, was quoted as telling Greg Lakes, a reporter for the *Missoulian* on April 13, 1992. "The only way to maintain [bull trout] viability is to save every one of these populations."

By hook or by crook, the timber companies want in. After the epic forest fires that swept across the West in 1994, former Forest Service Chief Jack Ward Thomas endorsed a new "forest health" initiative that is as oxymoronic as the agency's new "ecosystem management" slogan. Calling it "preventative medicine," the agency proposed allowing extensive logging in some forests to prevent "potential" fires. The plan enabled forest supervisors to sell "salvage timber" in burned areas and skirt environmental review and challenges. Critics say it is merely a disguise to appease timber companies that have refused to accept responsibility for overcutting.

Under the government's salvage logging program, the public was stripped of its right to halt logging that threatens water quality and destroys the landscape. Even former Forest Service Chief Jack Ward Thomas admitted, in so many words, that salvage logging was wrong and was a violation of his agency's own environmental standards, yet he allowed it to proceed for political considerations that contradict the preponderance of scientific research. Nor did he rush to Espinosa's defense or seek his advice when the grim truth of the Clearwater emerged. Dombeck may not be so callous.

Espinosa says foresters on the Clearwater are not one bit squeamish about boldly suggesting they will "roll over" any scientific recommendation that does not jibe with their own goals. It is a free-for-all, he says, adding that there is no way traditional logging can occur without causing massive ecological devastation.

After Espinosa completed his seminal survey showing that at least 71 percent of the Clearwater streams in developed sections did not meet the agency's own standards for water quality, his superiors wanted the document quashed. Internally, the Forest Service countered that siltation is a *natural* phenomenon—that streams naturally become choked with soil—an argument with which Espinosa agrees, to a point. Over thousands of years fish and wildlife have adapted to tolerate periodic forest fires, flash floods, and loading of soil in a few streams. What sensitive species like bull trout and salmon cannot endure is the magnitude of logging-related siltation swept into drainages year after year with no relief. The theory of metapopulation states that in a healthy watershed, when catastrophe strikes one stream's populations, nearby healthy watersheds provide new fish to move back in as the watershed heals. Those refuges no longer exist.

Although fires themselves can be traumatic in the short term for fish populations that already are stressed, they are an essential ingredient to true forest health because they inject a massive recycling of nutrients in the soil that cannot be replicated through logging. Dead trees, even fire-scorched ones, have profound ecological importance as homes for cavity-nesting birds, boreal mammals, and bugs that birds eat; as fertilizer for plants; and for nutrients that get flushed into rivers from decaying matter. Espinosa says that sending in the logging trucks to extract blackened trees is akin to "mugging a critical-care patient in the hospital burn ward."

Steve Petro is a Clearwater forester with a quarter century of experience orchestrating clearcuts across the Northwest. He says

Espinosa's downfall came about because he got too passionate about fish and didn't uphold the mission of his employer. Petro, however, has a notorious reputation as a "timber beast," which is not something he's ashamed of, and he remembers almost nostalgically the number of times that he went head to head with Espinosa over proposed logging that tore across mountainsides. "I have to be honest, I'm very pro–forest management, and I believe in cutting trees," he tells me. "It's something we need to do. We have people who depend upon the forest for their livelihoods. With salvage logging, I feel like finally the timber planning is working the way it should. We're focused and we're in control."

Petro admits that he and the Clearwater managers have their eyes on roadless areas that environmentalists consider to be sacred ground. "Yeah, we realize that logistically some of these are going to be difficult sales to get completed in the years ahead, and it's going to bring heat from the environmental community down upon us, but we're ready," he says. "One of the things that really irks me is the characterization of this salvage program as being 'logging without laws.' All it means is that environmentalists can no longer appeal the sales administratively. They can still sue us, and we're going to follow laws like we always have."

Chuck Pezeshki says that's a major part of the problem, and armed with Espinosa's data, he intends to make forest mismanagement of the Clearwater a national issue in time for the bicentennial of Lewis and Clark's journey. "The timber guys are lying. They lie all the time, shamelessly," Pezeshki says. "If you look at how the funding is set up, it's disproportionately tiered to timber and engineering."

In 1996, following Clinton's signing of the salvage logging program that allowed the forest to skirt public scrutiny of some timber sales, the amount of timber being offered to local mills was seventy-six million board feet, almost four times what was sold the year before.

"The mistake reformers make is they assume that their adversaries have the same moral and ethical standards as they do," Pezeshki says. "Guys like Petro can't change, and won't change voluntarily, for two reasons. One is money, the other is culture. People on the outside think it's all about money, but it's not. Petro is a dinosaur. He has no desire to be retrained. He loves the *Apocalypse Now* approach to silviculture. Even though the streams are blowing out, even when the ecological world around them is coming to an end, the timber beasts can't admit their mistakes. It would be like the Nazis admitting during the Holocaust that Jews were human. They won't stop because they don't know how, so it's up to us to fire them."

I ask Petro this: Why not allow a forest to continue its process of natural succession, a concept taught at forestry school, which includes allowing trees to die? What's wrong with leaving a forest alone or pursuing only light, sustainable logging, given that such an approach has huge benefits for wildlife? Isn't that a form of management? "I don't agree with that because this is a national forest," he says. "I believe it is our job to manage these ecosystems [with logging]. If we don't do anything, we'll be fighting fire here, just like in Yellowstone, whose goal is landscape preservation." When I remind him that the forest fires in Yellowstone have actually been a boon for the ecology, he turns the subject to jobs, reciting the names of logging companies such as Potlatch, Bennetts, Konkolville, Three Rivers, CFI, and Plum Creek that have come to depend upon a steady flow of trees that critics say is not sustainable and is ecologically destructive. The Forest Service has pledged to mandate that logging companies leave three-hundred-foot buffer strips of trees around stream channels that still have fish and tree patches 150 feet wide around perennial streams that don't have fish. Agency foresters knew in the mid-1980s that such buffers should be required, but they did nothing to impose this practice.

"It's going to look like a real spaghetti pattern up there," Petro confesses. "We are altering the way we cut more out of social concerns than environmental concerns. I wish when I was preparing timber sales in the 1970s we had the same tools we have now. I do have a few regrets about how we did things in the past, but I'm not ashamed of any of it. People say that we should stop harvesting trees. If we do that, we stop working, myself included. I have a hell of a lot of incentive to keep going. There is a balance that can be achieved with salvage logging and timber management. I believe we can have it all, wood to keep the mills running and fish in the streams."

That, coupled with recalcitrance in addressing mining and livestock grazing, is precisely the belief that Espinosa says is dooming the bull trout and half a dozen other fish species. Those who suggest that salvage logging to allegedly achieve "forest health" is a viable method of replicating the conditions of forest fires and, in some cases, preventing fires, have missed the point because the scales in time and space are not comparable. "Mother nature also creates hurricanes that rip through Florida," Espinosa rebuts. "Does it make any sense to have man mimic that and run hurricane after hurricane across the forest?" He says the agency's sudden enlightenment is nothing more than cosmetic. The Forest Service's own scientists admit that salvage logging, in many cases, is the absolute antithesis of what is best for the fish, birds, and large mammals that already have been stressed by habitat loss and rely upon riparian habitat that is secure and undisturbed. Petro, however, says it makes no sense to stop logging now because the bull trout's prognosis is dubious. "The bull trout in this country would decline here whether or not we continue to log," he claims. "What they lived on were the thousands of anadromous fish, and the anadromous fish runs are so far down from the dams that it doesn't matter."

For decades dams built upon the Snake and Columbia Rivers have been blamed as the primary causes of fish population declines, but a recent review completed by the National Research Council at the request of Congress suggests that in the 1990s dams represent only a small part of the problem. If fish have no habitat in which to hide to spawn, they simply will not exist. Even if anadromous fish such as salmon miraculously make it back to their headwater birthplaces, they often find that their nurseries have been destroyed by logging, mining, and livestock grazing. The disappearances of bull trout, redband trout, and westslope cutthroat trout were not caused by dams.

The Forest Service's own data confirm what Espinosa had been telling his colleagues all along. "Recent surveys by scientists at the Pacific Northwest Research Station [of the Forest Service] have documented the continuing decline in fish habitat in selected Columbia basin rivers since the 1930s," stated a briefing paper from the Oregon Rivers Council, a conservation group headquartered in Portland that won a court battle to have bull trout listed in Oregon. "They found a habitat loss of 60 percent on the average, mostly associated with timber harvest, road building, grazing and related factors. These losses could be extrapolated region wide." Agency biologists also pointed out that habitat alteration was the cause of declines in over two hundred anadromous fish subpopulations on the West Coast, adding that "logging and road building practices in particular may be the major contributor to the decline of these stocks." Other scientists concur. "The most risk-free and effective approach to habitat improvement is to fully protect *all* watersheds from continued land disturbance and undertake only low-risk restoration activities, such as road obliteration, until monitoring indicates that substantial improvement has occurred consistently in the majority of the damaged watersheds," wrote Dale A. McCullough and Jonathan Rhodes, consultants for the Columbia River Intertribal Fish Commission, in a draft report on remedial action needed to rescue salmonid stocks. "Deviation from this conservative approach increases the risks of further habitat damage and failing to achieve habitat improvement ... in systems where habitat standards are not attainable, it is critical that conditions not be exacerbated by land use activities."

In 1992, the Alliance for the Wild Rockies and two other groups sued the Interior Department, namely the Fish and Wildlife Service, seeking to list the bull trout as an endangered species in six western states. Four other national groups—Trout Unlimited, the National Wildlife Federation, Defenders of Wildlife, and the Biodiversity Legal Foundation—were also rattling their sabers. "All the biological information gathered to date shows clearly that bull trout are headed quickly for extinction," says Mike Bader of the Alliance for the Wild Rockies. "This is more testament to the fact that the western United States has been heavily overcut."

I mention the following figures only because they are compelling and, when put together, damning of the Forest Service for continuing to cut trees in areas where it is cognizant of the damage it is exacting. A survey completed by the Forest Service and other fisheries biologists identified 438 bull trout populations in the Pacific Northwest, and at least 75 percent of them are in decline. At the same time that the survey results were published, the Fish and Wildlife Service commenced the process of determining whether the fish should be listed at the request of environmentalists. Director Beattie revealed to me in 1995 that listing was long overdue. More than ten years earlier, on September 21, 1983, the Fish and Wildlife Service had published a system for prioritizing species listings. Although the bull trout rated high in need of protection even then, the agency said other species warranted more immediate attention. At the time, it was contemplating rulings on nearly 500 species. Nonetheless, bull trout were elevated from a category 2 to a higher-priority category 1 candidate species, the highest ranking before official listing, after several environmental groups threatened to sue.

"Most river systems now contain only isolated, remnant populations of resident fish restricted to the headwater areas of a few remaining suitable tributaries," the Fish and Wildlife Service admitted in its decision notice published in the spring of 1994. "These remnant populations have lost their migratory life-history forms, exist in isolation, and are likely to be at extreme risk of extinction."

Pressured by the timber lobby not to list the bull trout, the Fish and Wildlife Service's regional office in Portland gave Beattie this contradictory recommendation: "Sufficient information on the biological vulnerability and threats to the species is available to support a warranted finding to list the bull trout within the conterminous United States." Yet when Secretary of the Interior Bruce Babbitt's office ordered that the trout be listed, the Fish and Wildlife Service balked, and a standoff with the timber industry was averted when the agency announced that listing would not occur because other species rated a higher priority.

However, agency officials made a chilling confession in writing: "Federal and state laws designed to conserve fish reserves or maintain water quality have not been sufficient to prevent past and ongoing habitat degradation and population fragmentation. ... Even without additional habitat losses, most isolated populations are not likely to persist. Even the few remaining 'healthy' bull trout populations are at risk as habitat fragmentation and degradation continues." Mentioning the Clearwater specifically, based largely on information gathered by Espinosa, the authors of the Fish and Wildlife Service decision added, "A large number of national forests in Idaho and Montana do not meet existing Forest Plan standards ... correlated with bull trout persistence. Timber sales likely to adversely impact bull trout populations are still being planned on several national forests. ... Even under recent court-ordered restrictions on timber harvest in the Clearwater National Forest, timber harvest is likely to continue in the remaining unmanaged [read pristine, roadless, and last remaining] drainages supporting bull trout. ... Watershed restoration activities on national forests are not expected to restore ecosystem functions for several decades to a century."

Those words highlight a troubling paradox regarding America's threatened and endangered species. The Fish and Wildlife Service could intervene to save bull trout habitat simply by rendering a "jeopardy" decision to stop logging and mining under the Endangered Species Act, but to do that the fish needed to be federally listed, and the agency confessed it didn't have the time, money, or political might to intervene. So the fish essentially falls through the cracks into oblivion. That leaves Espinosa disheartened and angry, to the point that now, as a civilian scientist, he refuses to leave the trenches of combat biology and go quietly into the night of retirement.

By the time all the trees have been removed and the Forest Service is ready to consider healing the harm it has caused, the fish and eons' worth of evolutionary knowledge that enabled it to survive in the region will be gone forever.

The travesty, Espinosa says, is that trees could still be harvested to meet the commercial demand for wood and bull trout could still be saved if the Forest Service sincerely dedicated itself to implementing a plan of lower output and selective cutting, preventing Alaskan timber from being exported cheaply to Japan, creating government incentives for recycling paper products, and putting out-of-work loggers back into the field to help restore the lands they destroyed. But in a major power struggle in Washington, D.C., Congresswoman Helen Chenoweth and Senator Larry Craig, both of Idaho, have threatened to slash agency funding as a punishment if the agency closes off roadless areas to logging and reduces the cut to comply with environmental laws. Critics say they are holding the agency of every honest Forest Service worker hostage, forcing such workers to be associated with an employer—the federal government—that must knowingly break the law.

~

From his earliest childhood memories, which meld into the years when he was a Cub Scout, Pete Geddes dreamed of becoming a district forest ranger, sharing a bunkbed with Smokey the Bear and wielding a Pulaski. Geddes, an inveterate outdoorsman, eventually went to work as a wilderness survival instructor for the National Outdoor Leadership School (NOLS). However, he never surrendered his ambition, and he was recruited into a Forest Service internship in 1994 to work with federal wilderness managers in the Northern Regional Office in Missoula, Montana—the office that oversees the Clearwater. It was his exposure to the War Room that left him changed. The War Room, a name created by Forest Service personnel, is an element of the decisionmaking process the public doesn't know exists, and Geddes now suggests that it reveals the agency's continuing bunker mentality. Assigned to be a member of the regional appeals team, Geddes and a group of specialists from timber, wildlife, hydrology, recreation, and minerals divisions (including secretarial staff with no professional expertise) would assess the merits of challenges brought against timber sales by environmentalists. "We operated behind closed doors, and we were sworn to secrecy," Geddes says. "What I remember most was the dry-erase blackboard with buttons that allowed leaders of the team to make sure any writing about strategy for approaching appeals was eliminated. They didn't want to have a written record. They thought that if the information ever got into the hands of the public, it could be damaging and expose the Forest Service's dirty laundry."

The procedure worked this way: Say the review team received an appeal of the XYZ timber sale in the Clearwater Forest; its job was to look at administrative compliance with NEPA, not to assess what the sale proposed to do or whether its effects would be good or bad. "NEPA is a law without a conscience that the Forest Service readily exploits," Geddes says. "It doesn't tell you what to do; it tells you how to do it. If you have any hope of reforming the Forest Service through NEPA, you're barking up the wrong tree."

It was no secret that the Clearwater chalked up the worst record of environmental compliance of any forest in the region. Some timber beasts even seemed to relish their outlaw image. "The Clearwater was notorious," Geddes notes. "Science doesn't matter, ecological values don't matter, aesthetic values don't matter. What matters is turning away the environmentalists' appeals. All the things you read about and all the horror stories you've heard about the Forest Service are true. One reason is that although the Forest Service has deliberately tried to decentralize its decisionmaking process so that shots are called at the local level, it only reinforces bad behavior. It was my first view of the belly of the beast. All bad decisions originate at the district level."

District rangers drink in the same bars as loggers in places such as Orofino, Powell, and Lewiston. They wear virtually the same uniforms: big belt buckles, polyester pants or blue jeans, cowboy boots or shit-kickers, flannel shirts, and crewcut coifs, and they share an affinity for military service. Most agency personnel hold bachelor's degrees; many drive big pickup trucks and use Forest Service roads for access to big-game hunts. There is a mutual interest in self-preservation, which means they hate "greenies" and progressive biologists who threaten to rock their apple cart. "Like an alcoholic, the first step to recovery is to admit you have a problem," Geddes says. "The Forest Service refuses to admit they have made major mistakes. It's a cultural mindset that is shaped by the district forester."

Chuck Pezeshki, who moonlights as leader of the Clearwater Biodiversity Project, mentions a conversation he had with Art Partridge, an expert on forest pathology at the Idaho College of Forestry. Partridge, whose nickname is "Doc," is as close as anyone can come to being a doctor in judging ecosystem health. He says that congressionally driven pressure to "thin" trees as a means of preventing forest fires ignores both the beneficial role fire plays *and* the ecological value of downed trees whose decomposition leads to the recycling of nutrients and ultimately rebirth of a healthy new forest. Such rebirth does not occur when biomass is removed through clearcutting and trees are replanted on bare slopes. What Congress has in mind will kill the forest by making it nutritionally anemic, not save it.

Partridge points to the Forest Service—to foresters such as Steve Petro, to district managers, to regional supervisors, to the chief—as publicly perpetuating a myth based on bad science. "There are two layers to the Forest Service—the honest part, and then there's the administration," Partridge told Pezeshki in the latter's fine book *Wild to the Last.* "People in the Forest Service are taught to lie. The official line is that problems are internal problems. Let's keep them in the family. Hell, that was true when I worked for the Forest Service back in 1956, in Columbia, Missouri, at the beginning of my career. It's still true today."

~

The first unwritten rule for snuffing out dissenters is to shame them by convincing them that they are ruining "the Family" and esprit de corps. If that doesn't work, you demote them, transfer them, or make their job so miserable that they quit. Or you can even utter racial epithets, a tactic that is not uncommon in north-central Idaho, home to various white-supremacist movements. Espinosa saw it happen to other friends and professional colleagues first. Al Isaacson had an experience that foreshadowed his.

"The beginning of the end of my career came in 1982," explains Al Isaacson, who spent a quarter century as a hydrologist on the Idaho Panhandle National Forest just north of the Clearwater. Isaacson was asked to testify before the House Government Operations

Subcommittee on Environment, Energy and Natural Resources. "The things that I have predicted, such as the devastation of watersheds because of overcutting, [came] true," he says, noting that the flouting of environmental laws began with the arrival of the Reagan administration in 1980 and continued through the Bush and Clinton administrations, even on Chief Jack Ward Thomas's watch. Will Dombeck tolerate more and, like his predecessors, turn the other way?

Isaacson too was asked to sign off on several poorly planned timber sales, but one in particular stood out. "I worked on the hydrology for this proposal and could not go along with the planned activity. This was our Waterloo. The ranger was a very strong individual with strong political ties to the Idaho congressional delegation. He was going to sell this no matter what. We did not cave in to the pressure exerted by the ranger."

The ranger went ballistic. He had made promises to his logger friends, and Isaacson claims that the ranger ordered him to doctor his report. Although he refused and ultimately stopped the timber sale from proceeding, his dissension prompted his superiors to give him an ultimatum: Either accept a forced transfer to Atlanta, Georgia, or quit. He chose to resign rather than suffer the humiliation of being shipped off to a place regarded as an agency gulag.

"The Coeur d'Alene River, like the Clearwater, has been devastated," Isaacson says. "This river once contained some of the best fisheries in the state; now the fish are gone. I predicted that if timber sales did not cease, or were not reduced as to the amount of the timber to be cut, then such a catastrophic event would occur. Unfortunately, today this unnecessary evil has occurred for the simple fact that specialists' warnings, advice, and knowledge were ignored."

The king of political bullying and chief antagonist of field scientists (before Chenoweth and Craig) were longtime U.S. Senators Steve Symms and James McClure, an Idaho Republican who retired in 1990 and now works as a lawyer representing clients from the timber and mining industries on endangered-species issues. McClure was not shy about throwing around his political weight. Given any hint that a biologist was challenging the timber mindset and slowing the volume of trees coming off a forest, McClure would order the chief of the Forest Service in Washington, D.C., to have the employee either fired or transferred. He allowed his staffers to throw their weight around, intimidating Forest Service field workers at will. It was an abuse of power reminiscent of mafia "enforcers," Espinosa says.

The same year Isaacson was axed, Espinosa noticed that the Forest Service timber specialists seemed emboldened with Ronald Reagan in office, and the arrogance has carried through both succeeding administrations. They were so cocky that they set off a public relations firestorm in the Clearwater when they announced a plan to log between twenty and forty million board feet of timber from Toboggan Creek, which drains into Cayuse Creek, a crown-jewel wild cutthroat trout fishery. "Our jaws dropped," Espinosa remembers. "We told them that if they messed with the Kelly Creek system they'd have the worst fight they'd ever had. They looked us straight in the eyes and said, 'To hell with you; we're going for it.' They implied that they were macho with Reagan in power, and their attitude was 'We don't give a shit.' And you know what, they really didn't." Many of the catalysts of that attitude remain in upper management of most forests. This atmosphere has driven hundreds of ethical biologists, hydrologists, and foresters from the agency.

Despite internal protests from Espinosa and a few others, the timber planners spent $150,000 finalizing the Toboggan Creek sale and setting out survey stakes that would guide the bulldozers. They did it even before approval for the logging had been granted—their environmental assessment was handwritten. Fishermen went ballistic when they found the survey stakes next to their favorite pools. Anglers began pulling up the markers and discarding them (which, ironically, is a federal offense). Some even vowed that they would lay their bodies in front of the heavy machinery. These were not just members of EarthFirst! but doctors, lawyers, and other professionals, many of them card-carrying Republicans, galvanized by a love of wild fish.

A scientist who sympathized with them was Bert Bowler, then the regional fisheries specialist with the Idaho Department of Fish and Game in Lewiston. Although Espinosa was forbidden to publicly decry his own agency, Bowler used data and slides that Espinosa gave him to launch a national campaign to save the river. A groundswell of opposition initiated by Trout Unlimited prompted U.S. Representatives John Seiberling of Ohio and George Miller of California, both members of the House Natural Resources Committee, to come out and make an inspection. They were aghast, and made an end run around the Idaho congressional delegation. Reacting to the

public opposition, the Clearwater's timber bosses reluctantly withdrew the drainage from logging for a period of ten years, but they
have begun eyeing such drainages again as the 1990s draw to a close.

"I think we put the fear of God in the forest supervisor," Bowler
says. "He got very upset at the public reaction because they never
wanted scrutiny to see the light of day. The Forest Service knew that
the economics didn't justify the action. The value of the trees was
far outweighed by the cost of building the roads to access them." In
this case, it was shown that trout really do grow on trees.

The victory elevated Espinosa to something of a cult hero. "It's
amazing he survived as long as he did, but he had [a racial] minority
status that protected him from getting the ax in addition to the fact
that his data was rock solid," Bowler suggests. "I believe it was an unwritten rule within the Forest Service to run him off because he
wouldn't let science get corrupted by political science."

Espinosa's initial dialogue with Clearwater managers consisted of
his polite requests that his data be considered in the decisionmaking
process, but when he was continually rebuffed and ignored, he began
incorporating his findings into the environmental reviews he was
assigned to prepare, knowing they would be removed. He wanted
his dissent to be part of the record. Although his opposition might
stop the same sale two, three, or four times over a short span, he discovered that his bosses kept resurrecting the projects under different
names or in reconfigured shapes that pressed the limits of their
creativity.

After he cited evidence of declining fisheries to convince foresters
not to permit logging in Laundry and China Creeks, his superiors
exposed their culpability by drafting a memo saying they would stay
out of the drainage. But the next year they were back again. "They
couldn't stay away. They were like addicts. I called them on it and
beat them back, but the waves of confrontation wear you down.
Eventually they managed to sneak a proposal by me, and they logged
the drainage. This happened all the time. It was real frustrating."

Espinosa, who became accustomed to snorkeling in muddy drainages, went to the mat so often with his own staff to protest clearcuts
that eventually he began wearing a camouflage-colored baseball cap
with the words *combat biologist*. His superiors accused him of not
being a team player and of undermining the work of his forestry
compatriots. Who cares about a fish? they said—but he replied that

fish do have a worth that far transcends biological value. Their loss is a symbol of governmental destruction and abandonment of ethics.

In 1987 Senator McClure's own zealousness—some would argue ecological ignorance—brought calamity as the Clearwater was read-justing its annual timber goals in accordance with its Forest Plan. Without any scientific justification, McClure dispatched a letter to the regional forester, John Mumma, instructing him to arbitrarily raise the annual timber cut in the Clearwater from the range of 140 million board feet to 173 million, an astounding increase. While timber beasts salivated in anticipation, Espinosa dug deeper, realizing that he might be turned into a martyr.

The annual timber output did climb, reaching as high as 149 million board feet before it started to collapse and came to a standstill five years later as environmentalists won challenges based upon numerous violations of environmental laws and the forest's own standards. Streams that once lived up to the name of the forest ran brown. Espinosa's forecasts were coming true.

And as millions of dollars' worth of environmental degradation continued to accumulate, no one was held personally accountable—the telling comparison being that if a private citizen felled a tree for firewood, operated heavy machinery off a Forest Service Road and through a stream, or caused the death of a single game animal—let alone a species—he would face prosecution. But landscape-level destruction is not only tolerated but promoted by politicians and rewarded by Forest Service managers operating under perverse incentives. The message is that if you want to break the law or have a bone to pick with the federal government over environmental protection, the best strategy is not to fight the Forest Service but to join it.

Under the new assault of logging, Toboggan Creek has emerged again on the Forest Service's radar screen despite pledges that it has been set aside for now. "We won that skirmish in the 1980s, but the battle is not over. There are still a lot of timber beasts in the Forest Service who are salivating over drainages like Toboggan Creek," Espinosa says. "They might try to log there again, given the current antienvironmental sentiments in Congress."

The Pacific Rivers Council commissioned a report on the economic value of fisheries to Idaho, Washington, Oregon, and northern California. Economist Hans Radkte and Carl Batten of the firm ECO Northwest estimated that salmonid species were responsible for more than $1 billion in personal income and the creation of sixty thousand jobs. When Espinosa raised this point, he was branded an "obstructionist" and "reactionary" by his peers and again heard racial epithets mumbled behind his back. Those who were called upon to prepare environmental reviews ignored his concerns that the Clearwater was breaking the law. In the mid-1980s the regional director of the fish and wildlife program for thirteen national forests had a message delivered to Espinosa's office. A few minutes before 4 P.M. on a Friday, word came that the Clearwater was eliminating his position, out of the blue. His superiors decided to replace him with an elk biologist. As it did with Isaacson, in what had become a cruel joke, the Forest Service offered Espinosa what he calls "a Jimmy Hoffa retirement plan"—a stint shuffling papers in Atlanta or somewhere else, like Guam.

But the news spread throughout fisheries circles in Idaho, and within a matter of days the regional director's office in Missoula was backed off by calls of support from scientists in other agencies. They threatened to blow the lid off the Clearwater's intimidation tactics and its attempt to keep the poor water-quality issue a secret. Two days later Espinosa was called into the Clearwater supervisor's office and informed that the agency had changed its mind.

"I told them our first priority should be to recover the watersheds and get them functional again instead of heaping on further abuse. They wanted more trees. Their approach was akin to taking someone who had just been involved in a bad car wreck and then running over them again before taking them to the emergency room. I have watched river systems on the Clearwater for twenty years, and although the cutting and the road building had been reduced in some drainages for more than a decade, some streams have shown no sign of recovering," he explains. "To resuscitate a stream can take from ten years to hundreds of years, and in some systems it won't *ever* recover because of the physical impacts. When you plow a road through a stream and change its course, it will never be the same. The Forest Service has done business this way because it is the easiest and cheapest way to punch in a road, even though it is the costliest ecologically. Now the environmental bill is coming due, and they want to ignore it."

If anything validated Espinosa's skepticism, it was his survey that documented the fact that three out of every four streams were polluted by elevated levels of silt eroding from roads and clearcut slopes.

The conclusion of the survey was staggeringly bleak and reverberated all the way to Capitol Hill. Politicians in collusion with the timber industry struggled to come up with excuses. Espinosa didn't realize it then, but he actually had a sympathetic, silent ally in Win Green, the Clearwater's forest supervisor brought in from Alaska's Tongass National Forest—a juggernaut for clearcutting—at the behest of regional forester Mumma.

Mumma, who began his career as a wildlife biologist, took over as manager of the Clearwater and twelve other national forests in 1987. In hindsight, Mumma believes the region could have generated a sustainable yield but gave it up to greed. "McClure threatened my very livelihood. So did other politicians in the region," Mumma says. "McClure once called me and other forest supervisors out to his office in Washington, D.C., and in front of other politicians yelled at us for ninety minutes telling us to get out the cut with no excuses. He was a tyrant."

When McClure retired, Larry Craig, another Idaho Republican, joined up with Montana's former Republican Congressman Ron Marlenee, his successor, Rick Hill, Chenoweth, and Montana freshman Republican Senator Conrad Burns in picking up where McClure had left off. In the summer of 1991 Craig sent out a flippant letter saying the agency had a dismal record of keeping the timber cut up. "He told me to work around the law," Mumma says. "I refused. He ordered me to make an accounting to him every month. I sat down and told him that was ridiculous, so he went to Secretary of Agriculture Ed Madigan and told him to start cleaning house."

To say a flicker of conscience doesn't exist at upper-management levels would be to unfairly paint agency executives as a group of timber troglodytes. The gathering crisis has indeed ignited a quiet, unpublicized flame of revolt. In a now legendary meeting known as the Sunbird gathering, named after the location in Tucson, Arizona, where it took place, sixty-three of 120 National Forest supervisors signed a historic petition. It was an overt expression of protest that members of Congress from Wyoming, Montana, Idaho, Washington, Oregon, California, and Alaska have been slow to heed.

"Public values and personal values of Forest Service employees are changing," the breakaway supervisors wrote. "Many members of the public with many of our employees no longer view us as leaders in environmental conservation. There is a growing concern that we have become an agency out of control."

Consider John Mumma, whose days were numbered after he expressed incredulity over congressionally mandated timber quotas. He
also received criticism from Republicans for trying to promote ecosystem management in the Yellowstone region, and he supported the
reintroduction of gray wolves to Yellowstone and central Idaho.
Those were black strikes that Republican members of Congress
could not forgive. Within months, Mumma was ordered transferred
to a desk job in Washington, D.C. Rather than face professional humiliation at the end of a thirty-year career, he resigned. "It hurt like
a death in the family," he says, even though he had helped orchestrate miles of damaging clearcuts. "Just to have a job isn't worth the
destruction of the land, and that is why I made my stand. The consequences were that either you can [break the law] and keep your
mouth shut or do something else. I chose not to prostitute myself. I
couldn't have lived with myself to have gone back and tucked my
head in the sand."

Few people were surprised when the Forest Service chief brought
in Dave Jolly as Mumma's replacement. Jolly, who worked in the Forest Service's regional office in Denver, had completed a tour of duty
in which he successfully watered down guidelines for protecting
northern goshawks and Mexican spotted owls, which posed threats
to meeting the unsustainable timber cut in New Mexico and Arizona. His reputation was that of a timber beast and political yes-man.

The architects of Green's arrival in the Clearwater arranged his
posting with the intention that he would do everything he could to
meet the proposed output demanded by McClure and Craig, as he
had done in the Tongass in Alaska. It didn't take Green long, however, to realize he had inherited a disaster in the making. As a result
of overcutting in the past, the forest was beset by a barrage of legal
challenges from environmentalists, which reduced the timber harvest
to a third of its projected output—about 27 million board feet—for
the year. By that time political pressure had reached the boiling point
because the declining yield of timber was costing jobs in the local
communities—jobs based on inflated quotas and ecologically un-
sound forest management.

After conferring with Espinosa and other biologists, it became apparent to Green that the Clearwater could not ever meet the quotas demanded by the timber industry without violating federal laws.
"As far as Al was concerned, there were some really heavy-duty

problems. He faced a lot of internal fighting and backstabbing," Green says. "I have to say that it was perpetrated by the dominance of the timber interests. Because of that dominance, the people who were trying to bring information to light that didn't support the high levels of timber outputs were pushed into the background and not allowed to have their day in the sun."

Green wouldn't bow to the pressure either and found himself a target of harassment by Craig and Jolly. "I found out later that certain politicians meeting with Dale Robertson, chief of the Forest Service in Washington, were doing all they could to get me transferred or fired, and you can guess who they were," Green says today. "I'm not a dyed-in-the-wool tree hugger. But you don't have to be an environmentalist to care about fish and wildlife. I'm a firm believer in sound natural resource management that is sustainable in the long term, and the Clearwater is well beyond that point. They wanted me to break the law, and I wouldn't."

Robertson denied there was any meddling, but the truth struck home during an overflight of the forest with Senator Craig, Green says. Observing the marred, washed-out remains of landslides, silted rivers, and broken pockets of wildlife habitat, Craig nodded as if he understood that the thresholds of logging had been surpassed. "I tried to bring honesty and truth and accurate facts to his attention," Green says. The next day Craig went on the air on the local radio station and totally ignored what he had seen with his own eyes. He lambasted Green, Espinosa, and other biologists working for the Forest Service.

Green attracted surprising support from then Idaho governor and former U.S. secretary of the interior Cecil Andrus, who had logged on the Clearwater as a young man. Andrus angrily told a gathering of Forest Service rangers that timber companies and politicians had pressured the Forest Service into inflating the volume of timber to unreasonable levels and condemning fish populations to biological annihilation. "But that was not good enough for Potlatch and some of those other greedy suckers who believe they have a God-given right to cut every tree that ever grew," Andrus said of one of the main private timber companies in the Clearwater area, adding that he was appalled at how science had been co-opted. "We [public land managers] do have an image problem, and we brought a lot of it on ourselves in our hell-for-leather rush from one coast to another."

Still, there was little Andrus could do to rescue Green or Espinosa. "It was like the politicians and the timber beasts were holding a gun to Win Green's head and telling him to tap-dance. You live in a democratic society, you get hired to do something, and once you start to do it they come down on you because the system doesn't want to hear it or allow it," Espinosa told Forest Service Employees for Environmental Ethics in its newsletter, *Inner Voice*. "My belief is that if the Forest Service is going to abuse resource specialists, then it shouldn't even have them, shouldn't even hire them. I think what they ought to do—if they want Stepford wives and lobotomized specialists—they ought to contract their fish, wildlife and hydrology work to independent companies and just use the information as they see fit. But don't hire scientists and then try to beat them up for the next 20 years, because they're just trying to do their job."

Green was eventually transferred into a meaningless job as a liaison between the Forest Service and the state of Idaho to try to bring forests into compliance with the Idaho Forest Practices Act. "Rather than kill the messenger the regional office had the option of supporting Supervisor Win Green or not supporting him," wrote John Osborne, a physician and coordinator of the Inland Empire Public Lands Council. "The historic record on the Clearwater reveals that the timber targets under the Forest Plan are based on political pressure and not based on science and scholarship. Sadly, the immense gap between these politically-driven timber targets and the Clearwater's realities is at the heart of the problem on this national forest. People who know the Clearwater country know that the trees in the timber targets are the phantom trees of politics."

It was too late for Green. He retired after thirty-two years with the agency. Perhaps an epitaph to his career can be found in the words of his predecessor, Fred Trevey: "The watershed and wildlife habitat conditions have been pushed to the limit by past activities. The same is true for the visual resource. Without what I believe to be substantial investments in major rehabilitative efforts in the very near future, I fear we will be facing significant timber shortfalls. ... Why analyze for timber output and create an expectation we cannot deliver?"

That hasn't stopped Idaho's congressional delegation from promising more trees to the mills from now until the next millennium. Shortly after Espinosa's damning stream survey was released, winning wide praise from independent scientists, Espinosa realized he was standing on a precipice. Bittersweetly, he had come full circle. "When I arrived on the forest, there was little data, and so ostensibly they hired me to collect data and offer a professional's interpretation. But then I gathered the data and would tell them that streams were being ruined, and they would ask me how I knew this. After twenty years, I didn't need a lot of data anymore. It's obvious that the streams are screwed up. It's like a doctor giving a diagnosis to a patient who is dying and telling him he is sick."

He literally could feel the heat burning in his stomach, and he began having bouts of insomnia coupled with symptoms of an ulcer. The Forest Service had severely stressed him, and now, with a new wife, he didn't want to sacrifice his family and health again. "It's like a cop on a beat. You get exposed to so much violence that after a while it doesn't affect you like it did before. For me, that's an indication that maybe it was time to get out."

In one last hurrah, the *Spokane Spokesman-Review* digested Espinosa's stream-survey findings and published them in a series titled "Our Failing Forests." Clearwater officials were incensed. Espinosa believes they reacted so angrily because, finally, their cover was blown. But in a rather odd attempt at damage control, they reacted by spending thousands of taxpayer dollars on a full-page advertisement in the paper refuting the evidence of their own scientists: "Logging alone generally puts very little dirt into streams, unless sales are poorly designed. Most erosion comes from roads built to haul logs away from the harvest sites. And most soil movement on roads occurs the first two years after construction—unless the roads are carved out of hillsides better left alone. ... Unfortunately, while the level of active sediment finding its way into streams has slowed to a relative trickle, dirt leftover from past errors is not going away in many streams. Part of the problem with forest planning models is that specialists expected recovery to happen just a little—well, maybe a lot—faster. ... Obviously, water quality—one price of the controversial land management puzzle—is a complex issue."

Espinosa chuckled when he saw the ad. Within months, dozens of logging and road-related landslides rumbled down forest slopes. "Who do they take the public for? Being idiots? I thought it was pretty lame given the fact that they were indicting themselves," he says. "The logging was poorly designed and roads *were* built into hillsides better left alone. They knew well in advance that this would happen because I told them it would, and now not only are they trying to play spin control with the facts but throughout the rest of this century they intend to hammer the remaining roadless drainages and repeat the same mistakes."

Officials with the Clearwater National Forest can deny the findings all they want, Espinosa says, because when it comes time to decide who is telling the truth, they can turn to the ultimate authority: the fish. You see, fish don't lie. They are barometers that the Forest Service itself has employed to determine whether an ecosystem is healthy. And so far, with fish stocks disappearing in drainages that have been severely cut, it means the agency is failing its own test. Just ask the bull trout—if you can find any.

After nineteen years and four months with the Forest Service, Espinosa did something he had never done before: He quit. Gone were Isaacson, Mumma, Green, and a cast of others who were worn down. Espinosa's departure brought a sigh of relief from the timber industry. His resignation and retirement came ten years before he thought they would, but he felt that the working atmosphere inside the Forest Service was deteriorating as quickly as the streams he surveyed. All he asked was that the agency come clean. "There wasn't any multiple use. It was bullshit, a banner, a flag, in name only," he says. "Go to the Clearwater today and see what they are doing with logging, then tell me what other uses they are managing for. How many fishermen or hikers or motorbike riders do you find excited about going out and exploring the majesty of slopes that have been ruined?"

Espinosa had joined the Forest Service as a young man believing in Gifford Pinchot's multiple-use maxims, but he learned those ideas were only a mirage. "As a taxpayer, I do not want to subsidize the destruction of our public lands. Knowing what I know, I would just as soon have the loggers not have a job and give them a paycheck every week for unemployment. At least you're not losing wildlife and watersheds."

The main problem, he adds, is the agency's approach to incentives. Employees are rewarded with bonuses and promotions for more trees being cut, but they are given nothing to produce the highest quality of water or grizzly bear or bull trout habitat, which, in turn, is the best habitat for all of the other native species.

When he finally bade farewell and punched out from the government's time clock for the last time, it was hardly as a man disgraced. No; the Forest Service itself, including a few of his professional adversaries, conceded his contributions by awarding him one of the agency's highest honors for meritorious service. Recognition and praise came from the scientific community as well. On behalf of his biologist colleagues, among whom he is revered for persevering under fire, he received an honor from the American Fisheries Society and was asked to give a talk about his tour of duty. The society cited his benchmark twenty-year river surveys that withstood pounding from the timber beasts.

Espinosa was worn down, shell-shocked, and more than a bit discouraged, but the enemy did not own him. He had a clear conscience, and still does.

Today he is a private fisheries consultant in Moscow, Idaho, who still haunts the Clearwater as a frogman searching for the last pockets of bull trout before they are gone forever. However, the Clearwater National Forest, now led by new supervisor James Caswell, who helped orchestrate some of the largest inland clearcuts along the border of Yellowstone National Park, is carrying out an ambitious plan to reach virgin drainages and take more timber out of degraded drainages through salvage logging.

"The politicians try to punish you for caring about the resource, but that is why I became a biologist. I don't understand how a fish or wildlife biologist can sell out the things he or she loves. When that happens, they become court jesters for management, trained lapdogs doing tricks, biostitutes," he says. "If you decide to sell out, don't call yourself a biologist any longer. Saving what we have left requires that scientists become advocates for the resource. If we had more people who stood up and were counted, we'd be in one hell of a lot better shape. There would still be bull trout in the pools."

As Mollie Beattie of the U.S. Fish and Wildlife Service said, "If we think for a minute that it's not of interest to human beings and that saving those species isn't a way of saving ourselves, we're not thinking very clearly."

Bull trout, westslope cutthroats, salmon, and other game fish are barely hanging on as the Clearwater timber machine roars, but they still have a defender in Al Espinosa. Lately, as he's submerged himself beneath the riffles, sucking air through his snorkel mask, he thinks about the Clearwater when Lewis and Clark came trekking through. To see it then. What a rewarding journey it might have been if only they had carried fly-rods.

~

Postscript: How does one ever know the personal impact one has in shaping the larger picture of, say, a single forest, or a cluster of forests, or the 155 forests and grasslands encompassed by the U.S. national forest system? In turn, what effect can the ripple of one combat biologist's actions have on a moribund agency that is the troubled caretaker of our wild heritage?

The deeds of Al Espinosa appear to have created a forum for the Forest Service's most conspicuous whistleblower in the agency's century-old history: its chief, Mike Dombeck. A trained fisheries biologist who knows the survival of the institution, as well as his own legacy, will rise or fall on watershed management questions, Dombeck threw down a gauntlet in 1998 as a challenge to timber-corrupted politicians and foresters in his own agency in a speech that was beamed via satellite to thirty thousand Forest Service workers nationwide. Dombeck, observers say, is boldly establishing a new course reminiscent of Mikhail Gorbachev's reforms in the former Soviet Union. Even if Dombeck becomes a casualty of politics, his legacy will be his attempt to face down the big timber interests that have dominated the Forest Service since World War II.

"Ours are not easy jobs. We often find ourselves caught in the midst of social changes, shifting priorities, and political crosscurrents," he told the rank and file in announcing the agency's resource agenda for the next century. "We can sit back on our heels and react to the newest litigation, the latest court order, or the most recent legislative proposal. This would ensure that we continue to be buffeted by social, political, and budgetary changes. Or we can lead by example."

Making an oblique reference to Espinosa's work and other biologists who have fought an internal war against industrial logging, Dombeck noted, "We can lead by using the best available scientific information based on principles of ecosystem management that the Forest Service pioneered. And we can use the laws that guide our management to advance a new agenda, an agenda with a most basic and essential focus—caring for the land and serving people."

It might appear to be a minor tweaking of bureaucratic lingo, but by placing "caring for the land" first and "serving people" second, Dombeck intends to push a paradigm shift—as dramatic as when the Forest Service was first founded in 1905—to restore emphasis on ecological function and deemphasize the "multiple use" interpretation of the agency's mission that elevated tree felling and propping up of a bloated timber industry as the paramount goals of forest management.

"Watershed maintenance and restoration are the oldest and highest callings of the Forest Service," Dombeck said, reemphasizing his decision to impose a moratorium on road building into roadless areas. "The agency is, and always will be, bound to them by tradition, law, and science."

Such a pronouncement placed Dombeck on a collision course with politicians in the Northwest who are wedded to influence peddling on behalf of the timber industry. Whether Dombeck succeeds, whether as a whistleblower he can withstand attempts to depose him, depends on whether the Clinton administration casts him in the role of sacrificial martyr (as happened to Al Espinosa) or backs up his crusade to prevent the Forest Service from self-destructing. At least nine hundred watersheds originating in national forests are sources of clean drinking water for millions of people. Watersheds dissipate floods, nurture wetlands that serve as natural filtration systems, and are the lifeblood of wild fish.

Now, at the end of a millennium, the real question is whether the natural systems can withstand the political assault. Will Dombeck, as the ultimate agency whistleblower and the ultimate arbiter of progressive dissent, leave his field personnel exposed? Will he create an environment for near mythical figures such as Al Espinosa to thrive, or will he fall prey to the manipulators of legitimate science?

"Jack Ward Thomas went down in flames because although he had the right ideas and wanted to do the right thing, he didn't have enough help from within and outside the administration," a Clinton administration insider said. "Dombeck has both, for now."

Whatever happens, Dombeck has moved his agency into a position from which it can never go back. A tide has turned. The Forest Service must return to its roots—there is no other way out.

Caveman Poet

*One can either curse the darkness
or light a candle to find the way
out.*—Adlai Stevenson

IN 1959, WHEN Ronal Carrel Kerbo reached his fifteenth birth-
day, the societal status of the adolescent from Lovington, New Mexico, was already precarious in the eyes of his community. A redneck
destined to become a hippie, he let his auburn hair drape long as an
act of protest against *Leave-It-to-Beaver* conformity. He stopped playing organized sports. He listened to black jazz rather than provincial
country-western. Losing interest in the regimen of school, he holed
up in the local public library reading comic books, beatnik poetry,
and the essays of two nineteenth-century rabble-rousers, Henry
David Thoreau and Ralph Waldo Emerson. Moreover, the farm kid
and former Cub Scout adopted other aberrant habits that unnerved
his manly colleagues at Lovington High. The sensitive teen not only
composed his own free verse, he also seemed to be spending an in-
ordinate number of hours going underground. Literally.

A guidance counselor who doubled as an athletic coach pulled
Kerbo aside and asked if he might be having girl problems. After he
quit school his senior year—and became a truant caver—teachers
informed him that if he continued in his current direction he was
bound for a lengthy stay in the state penitentiary.

Kerbo didn't doubt their proclivity for predicting moral turpi-
tude, but he had other things on his mind. While conversing with
older kids along Main Street one evening, he heard a story about
water-submerged passageways and a mysterious realm in the New
Mexican desert known as the Bottomless Lakes. Keepers of the
gothic fable declared solemnly to their impressionable listener that
no person had ever found the nadirous limits, and to try, even with
an air tank and diving mask, would be tantamount to suicide. Of
course, Kerbo couldn't resist the temptation, and the teasing borrowed heavily from the medieval notion of chance: Choose the right

passage, so it went, and one could end up ninety miles away in Carlsbad Caverns National Park, encountering secret subterranean chambers filled with fang-shaped stalactites and stalagmites, ornate crystal chandeliers, Roman-pillar columns, and pools glowing turquoise and jade. Select the wrong route and it was *highly probable* that an intrepid cave argonaut would come face to face with the dreaded Worm That Ate the World. Like Sasquatch and the Loch Ness monster, the Worm That Ate the World dwelled in the recesses of Lovington's collective unconscious. It also provided fodder for an aspiring poet.

That night Kerbo remembered what Emerson had written, that "a foolish consistency is the hobgoblin of little minds." And encouraging his imagination further was the example of his hero, author Richard Halliburton, who had dropped out of Princeton to travel around the world on a quest to find himself. Halliburton had taunted the gods by standing atop Mount Olympus during a fierce thunderstorm and was last seen alive sailing a crude junk into the South China Sea during a typhoon in 1936.

Reckoning that his call for personal adventure had arrived, Kerbo strapped on his wetsuit and drove into the desert. Within a couple of hours he was descending alone into a narrow crawlspace of earth (all of it completely underwater) with a cheap metal flashlight (which he thought was waterproof) to direct his search for the bottom of the Bottomless Lakes, the monster be damned.

Though he had scuba dived into other freshwater sinkholes, the ensuing blackness left him disoriented as he probed deeper. He did not anticipate problems, but at sixty feet, in the chilly murk, his flashlight went dead. Ropeless, he panicked in a fit of claustrophobia. Unable to distinguish up from down, he could not discern whether he was breaching the continuum to Carlsbad or had reached the verge of being sucked into the gullet of the worm, à la Jonah. "I assumed right then and there that I would die. And I berated myself for going in unprepared," he says. "I couldn't move; I couldn't think; it was like having a dream where you can't run."

When at last he managed to overcome the urge to rip off his air mask and scream for help, worry miraculously vacated his thoughts. A warm peace surged through his limbs and soothed his brain. He thought maybe he had perished and gone to heaven; then he remembered the flashlight clenched in his hand and tapped it gently against the walls pressed closely around him. He knew his air supply was running short and that without a beacon to light his way, he was doomed.

What was only seconds felt like minutes. He tapped the flashlight again.

A brief flicker.

He screwed the casing around the bulb tighter. More tapping.

The incandescent flame seemed to ignite before it went out.

Then he prayed to Halliburton's gods for mercy.

A column of white clarity shot out from his hand like a Jedi's laser beam. Empowered again, he contemplated going deeper to tempt his fortune, but his inner compass followed the direction of rising water bubbles. Resigning himself to reality, he opted to surface, denied in his heroic quest.

Kerbo didn't locate the mythological passage to Carlsbad that day, but in plumbing the tenebrous abyss he acquired a fearlessness and a commitment to preparedness that still remains. Today he enters Carlsbad and hundreds of other public caves officially, through the front door rather than the back. As the federal government's most outspoken cave guru, Kerbo is the only high school dropout in modern times to attain one of civil service's top natural resource positions—chief of cave protection for the National Park Service. No single individual, with the possible exception of Texas batman Merlin Tuttle, has done more to elevate the emerging value of subterranean wilderness into the consciousness of ordinary Americans.

During the 1990s, in the throes of a groundswell of cave protection, Kerbo has reflected often upon his potential rendezvous with the worm. It informs a private meditation on the purpose of laboring for his agency. The words are not his own but Adlai Stevenson's: "One can either curse the darkness or light a candle to find the way out." In Kerbo's mind, Stevenson's utterance perfectly describes the need for enlightened public perception to spare caves from the repercussions of political disinformation.

~

The date is nearly forty years after 1959, and Kerbo's backpack is loaded with metaphorical candles. He has just ascended into a place, paradoxically hundreds of feet below the ground, called the Spirit World. Around the time of the last summer solstice, he bade his wife adieu, filled his battered stuff sack with necessary provisions, looped a climbing rope across his shoulder, reverently removed his hiking boots to avoid making scuff marks, and climbed toward the dank cranny in Carlsbad Caverns to assess his professional options.

Politicians in Washington, D.C., were breathing down his neck. Roughnecks in the New Mexican desert wanted to skin his hide. It was unclear whether Kerbo's bosses in the Department of the Interior would leave him twisting in the wind or rally to his aid. Feeling exposed after delivering an "over my dead body" comment to reporters about proposed oil and gas development near the greatest cave complex on the planet, he sought out solitude, ruminating in a cave where the absence of light swallowed his apprehension. Hours passed while he listened to the maw breathe.

When Kerbo finally rappelled down a coarse headwall and returned to sunshine at the surface of the labyrinth, he resolved to pursue an ambitious idea that he had first pondered as a much younger man. What he has in mind at present could have broad implications for a natural resource—cave ecosystems—that 99 percent of the world's population has never seen but from which a large percentage derives benefits every day. Hidden beneath the ground in caves are vast vaults of biological diversity and insurance policies for clean water.

Every time people flush their toilets, pour motor oil down the drainpipe, or give their kids a drink of water from the faucet, Kerbo wants them to think of caves. "I want people to see and taste the symbiotic connection," he says. "Our dependence on caves is as genuine as our dependence on the sun."

Akin to the filters used for brewing our morning coffee, caves and the "karstic systems" that create them represent the earth's great, delicate water purification systems. Three-fifths of America's underground fresh-water supply—45 percent of all the groundwater in the country east of Tulsa, Oklahoma—is cycled through karstic systems.

Kerbo wants readers of this book to associate raindrops that fell at the time of Christ with the presence of artesian wells. He wants people to equate recent cancer treatments gleaned from the remote belly of Carlsbad with cave protection, and he wants to shine a spotlight on politicians who would sacrifice caves to an oil company's drill bit.

By the turn of the century, Kerbo and a growing group of cave explorers hope to create a special kind of federal wilderness that will grow beneath America's feet. Never mind that some of the keystone caves they aim to protect have yet to be discovered; most in the inventory are already charted, sieving the Earth's subcrust like pathways of a night crawler. Ancient, primordial, ubiquitous, these caverns represent the final frontier of terra firma, and they may hold answers to human survival.

If he and the National Speleological Society are successful, caves would formally receive the same kind of public respect now afforded pristine forests and mountains through the Wilderness Act of 1964. But because he is a civil servant, this is where Kerbo's life gets complicated. His detractors malign cave preservation as the hatching of a communist plot to rob red-blooded Americans of their God-given right to pursue industrial development. In fact, right now energy wildcatters are aspiring to probe the outer viscera of the country's most complex and wondrous cave, Lechuguilla, like mosquitoes swarming over a patch of unprotected skin.

Part of Kerbo's mission is to debunk negative cave mythology. "I understand that elk are easily seen and highly visible in many national parks. Wolves are animals that people become very emotional about, and they have a certain beauty as humans perceive beauty. Buffalo and grasslands and tall, shining mountains and birdsongs under blue skies and thunderclouds skittering overhead. I understand those magical pieces of the national park system because I enjoy them too, *above* the ground," he tells me one afternoon in Albuquerque, New Mexico, where federal land managers, academic speleologists (scientists who study caves), and amateur cavers representing two dozen grottoes (cave organizations) are meeting to discuss the campaign for cave wilderness.

"But my professional responsibility," he adds, "is to deal with places that are dark and wet and slippery and have loose rock that slides off into pits and pale, blind, strange-looking creatures that don't have warm, shining eyes, that don't provide a food base for people, that are not charismatic in the traditional sense; places where the temperature hardly changes, the humidity hardly changes, the bats by myth and legend are unclean and are purported to suck your blood."

Kerbo looks down at a map of Carlsbad Caverns that shows the extent of mapped caves and a vast area of unknown territory. "It's my job to tell the American people the Worm That Ate the World doesn't live in caves, the bats down there do not drink your blood, and you will not be yanked into some mysterious vortex and spat out ninety miles away. Which is not to say that caves are not dangerous or magical or symbols of something beyond our own ken. My point is, the only people who are irrationally afraid of caves, or have no respect for them, are the unfortunate souls who have never been in one, and I'm sorry to say it probably applies to a large percentage of the current Congress. We are destroying the last frontier on this planet through pure ignorance." The most frightening maze of passageways he's ever explored, Kerbo says, is the one on Capitol Hill.

~

For American cavers, a journey to Carlsbad is roughly the same as a Christian trekking to the Holy Land. Although other cave systems in the East have a longer history of interaction with settlers of European ancestry, the Carlsbad region, in U.S. terms, is the mother of all karsts and a proving ground for speleologists who want to pursue a career in cave management. Despite its dusty cow-town ambience, Carlsbad also attracts an eclectic mix of recreational cave bums, just as Aspen summons those on skis.

The mouths of Carlsbad are gateways to a mind-boggling array of continuous and disjointed passages that snake for miles through the escarpment of the Guadalupe Mountains foothills, crisscrossing federal tracts administered by the Park Service, U.S. Forest Service, and Bureau of Land Management (BLM) as well as some private land. Rising as a backdrop, the Guadalupes form an impressive profile. From Fort Stanton near Roswell to the lowland plains of the Pecos Valley at the foot of the mountains, the underground secrets of the earth cannot be detected by an untrained eye, but this desolate yucca-studded panorama is an inviting entrance to a complex of caverns scattered over thousands of square miles. Millions of years ago, when a great inland sea covered the Southwest, a reef called the Capitan was built up as waves crashed upon the shore and accumulated sediments. Beneath the beachhead, the genesis of what would become one of the greatest karstic systems in the world started to germinate.

As surface water percolates downward, it mixes with the rock and turns corrosively acidic, eating away at the sedimentary mantle beneath it, drop by drop. The process continues today. Both the Capitan limestone, laid down in the Permian Age, and the seabed of gypsum spread across southeastern New Mexico are highly conducive to the production of caves because the rock can be easily dissolved by phreatic and vadose waters. Between the Park Service holdings (which include Carlsbad Caverns National Park and nearby Guadalupe Mountains National Park), Lincoln National Forest, and the Roswell Resource Area of the BLM, there are more than three hundred caves out there, but without question the most fantastic of all is the honeycomb giant Lechuguilla, essentially a newborn sister to all of the known passageways in Carlsbad Caverns.

The existence of Lechuguilla Cave has been known, technically speaking, since around the time it was first mined for guano in 1914. However, it was believed to be of limited extent until a series of exploratory missions launched in May 1986 led to the discovery of a tiny passage that opened unbelievably into a series of virgin vaults, one after the other. Extending more than 1,600 feet vertically, it is the deepest limestone cave in this country, and with at least ninety miles of documented passageway, it is one of the world's longest. The glory of Lechuguilla is its trove of fantastic geokarstic formations and soup of endemic microbes that could rival the level of biodiversity in the tropics.

∿

Kerbo's trial by fire involves a never-ending fight to save Carlsbad from exploitation. I am angling south across the mesquite desert of New Mexico in the direction of El Paso late in the evening. Actually, it's well past midnight, and my plans are to walk the perimeter of Carlsbad Caverns National Park to survey the sites of proposed oil and natural-gas wells. Kerbo and his professional cronies are still in Albuquerque, but I left to see for myself the Stygian topography that is today an ideological war zone. At Roswell, the town made famous by an alleged government cover-up of an alien spaceship crash in 1947, I hear radio talk-show host Art Bell interviewing someone who allegedly saw the feds cart off the bodies of extraterrestrials. "You don't have to be a conspiracy theorist to believe that a cover-up went on," Bell says.

My windows are rolled down, an alternative to the air conditioner, and I cruise through the darkness toward Carlsbad trying to gain a sense of place. Besides the cows grazing on the sea of federal BLM lands flanking the highway—their eyes glowing in my headlights—I can discern the region's political climate just by taking a whiff of the air. A breeze carries the pungent bite of sulfur that is separated from crude oil and natural gas at the local refinery. Next to cows, oil and gas rules these parts. When I check in at a Carlsbad motel, the clerks, like Kerbo, have an undeniable Texas twang. Texas is just down the road, but Texas oil producers treat this part of New Mexico like a resource colony, and resource engineers have been generous with their help. There is a subtle antagonism between conservation-minded Park Service employees and resource specialists at the BLM.

The next morning, before the heat of the day turns the desert into a roaster, I drive out to the national park. Southward, the exposed, treeless horizon rolls in continuous whale humps, stretching farther away the closer one gets to the park boundary. Carlsbad Caverns is to public caves what Niagara Falls is to waterfalls, a spectacular natural wonder that would be far more enticing if it weren't for the throngs of people that swarm through it during peak months of tourism. That said, the Park Service has devised a clever management approach that has spared many passageways from being trampled by the masses. Natural resource professionals consciously decided to sacrifice portions of the caves to tourism by building an intrusive infrastructure replete with electricity, elevators, a cafeteria, and lighted asphalt pathways. As part of the trade-off, the rest of the Carlsbad system—including Lechuguilla—is closed to all but the most experienced cavers and scientific researchers knowledgeable in how to be light on the land. That part of the park also shakes beneath terrain that the BLM has more or less turned into a sacrificial area for oil and gas developers.

According to a study completed by the Lechuguilla Cave Project in 1988, 95 percent of the cave still may be undiscovered, making it, for science and exploration's sake, one of the most important on the planet. In the March 1991 issue of *National Geographic* magazine, writer Tim Cahill observed in what was Lechuguilla's formal coming-out to the public that few are aware of the cave's discovery even today. "It's not just the immense size of the rooms that is so amazing but also their lavish decorations—glittering white gypsum chandeliers 20 feet long; walls encrusted with aragonite 'bushes'; rippling strands of indescribably delicate 'angel hair' crystals, some 30 feet long but so fragile that a puff of air can break them. The cave's shimmering lakes, like liquid sapphires, have lain untainted for millennia."

Cahill added of the strange creatures inhabiting Lechuguilla's nooks and crannies, "[The cave] is a microbiological forest ... the air flowing deep in the cave transports tiny organisms that consume rock. There are bacteria ... that are chemosynthetic, able to feed off sulfur, manganese, and iron in the limestone. In turn, there are fungi that live on the bacteria. We're talking about bacteria and fungi directly influencing the growth of crystal decorations."

In 1997, the list of accolades included a possible cure for breast cancer. A microbe harvested from an undisturbed pool in the Carlsbad-Lechuguilla network proved effective in diminishing the size of tumors. The operative sequence here is harvested from an undisturbed pool.

~

A stout bulldog of a man who reads prolifically, often from the minutes of previous congressional debates over the creation of national parks, Kerbo notes that industrialists in the early 1870s condemned "crazy preservationists" who advanced the outlandish proposal to set aside Yellowstone as the world's first national park. Was that a mistake? he asks, noting that nothing worthy or visionary has ever sprouted from recalcitrant lawmakers whose sole vested interest is in maintaining the status quo. Caves are to the end of the twentieth century what Yellowstone represented at the end of the nineteenth.

Critics of Kerbo's style say he is impetuous, irreverent of the ways of politics, a loose cannon. That's why normal folk love him. When developers or members of Congress have proposed actions that would result in exploitation and potential damage to caves, Kerbo has gone on the *Today Show* or written guest editorials to counteract shady politics. In his three decades with the agency, he has served under a dozen different secretaries of the interior and Park Service directors, the bulk of them members of presidential administrations that cast a kind eye on natural resource development and viewed caves as expendable. Against a remarkable record of career advancement one can juxtapose a gun-flint reputation of defending caves against any perceived threat. He is an unflappable booster, for example, of establishing a national cave wilderness system. For his tenacious advocacy, he has had his life threatened and received unsubtle warnings to back off. His legend has burgeoned from those encounters, and the ongoing controversy over whether oil and natural gas interests should be permitted by the government to drill wells near Lechuguilla.

Consider the policy briefing in Washington, D.C., when he was called into the office of powerful U.S. Senator Pete Domenici, a New Mexico Republican. Accompanied by an aide to New Mexico's other U.S. senator, Jeff Bingamon, a Democrat, Kerbo endured fulmination from one of Domenici's staffers over his "preservationist" beliefs. The implication was that Kerbo's efforts were making the senator's constituents—ergo, campaign contributors from the oil and gas industry—nervous.

"You need to clean up your act," the staffer said, glaring.

"What is that supposed to mean?" Kerbo asked.

"We hear that you are just being too vocal about these matters," Domenici's adviser replied.

Kerbo turned to walk out of Domenici's paneled office. His escort, Senator Bingamon's aide, whispered, "I don't think we should leave."

Biting his lip, Kerbo first responded, "I don't think we should have come in here." But then, as in the Bottomless Lakes, the paralyzing fear vacated his senses, and he retorted politely, as the jaw of Domenici's staffer hit the floor, "I think if you don't believe in the conservation of this planet, then maybe you ought to go to another one."

Admittedly, Kerbo has staked out the edge of progressive thinking, and that has made him a target. "Ron Kerbo is an enigma. His significance is that he has flourished at a time when politicizing public land management agencies is rampant," observes Duncan Morrow, the former deputy chief of public affairs for the Park Service and now a spokesman for the U.S. Geological Survey. Morrow has witnessed the political pressure exerted to ruin Kerbo's career. "There's no question the only way someone like him can survive the whims of politics is to present himself as being so knowledgeable and confident that the political leadership becomes reluctant to take him on for fear it might cost them dearly in the public eye. Ron has done that, and continues to do it. His brilliance makes him almost untouchable."

Domenici, who was unaccustomed to encountering defiance from a feisty civil servant, was reportedly incensed by Kerbo's lack of submission. He complained first to National Park Service director James

Ridenour and recommended that Kerbo be fired or transferred to a
job where his crusading could be minimized. Ridenour, like his successors, say he is too valuable to dismiss. Privately, Park Service officials chuckle at Kerbo's savoir faire. He may be the most audacious
ecologist ever to wear a ranger's uniform.

"How can you do anything but marvel at seeing him in action?"
Morrow asks. "He risks everything and is honestly prepared to lose
it all, which is why he succeeds. It becomes apparent to those trying to stare him down or intimidate him that he will suffer the consequences but he will not suffer the role of fool. Other people in the
agencies may attempt to do what he does, but inevitably they fold
at a time of weakness. Ron isn't in the game to bluff.

"He figures, 'What's the worst that can happen to me? Losing my
job? Losing my paycheck? My pension? My home? My ability to
help pay for my grandchildren's college education?' He's isn't concerned about those things because what he fears most is losing his
self-respect. And his wife supports him. He continually reminds
himself why he's there, and it is to serve the *public* interest. He sees
no point in wavering on the principles that created the National
Park System or the hundreds of caves sprinkled across sixty different parks. Kerbo has the luxury of knowing there are millions of
people out there who agree with him."

To Kerbo's amusement, the Domenici staffer who attempted to
dress him down was working a few months later for none other than
the National Park Service.

~

Ron Kerbo has been called the Horatio Alger of the Park Service
because of where his humble roots as a speleologist began. Late in
his teens, when his tenure at Lovington High was voluntarily cut
short, Kerbo went underground as an outlaw caver. Befriending
other explorers who had descended upon Carlsbad from around the
world, he stole into passageways the Park Service had placed off limits. His out-of-bounds escapades won him the reverence of fellow
cave bums and those who viewed defiance of government regulations as a cat-and-mouse game with rangers.

In the 1960s caving was still a passion for eccentrics. The Park
Service, focusing its efforts on guided tours in Carlsbad's main cave
complex, ignored caverns sprinkled throughout the backcountry.
Because of a limited staff of rangers and liability concerns, the park

managed those cave entrances simply by locking them under iron doors, which posed no obstacle to the clandestine group of spelunkers who entered the portals at will. All the while that tens of thousands of park visitors were plying the lighted, heavily trodden paths flaring out from the sanitized Carlsbad Lunchroom (which actually houses an underground cafeteria), Kerbo's band of merry outlaws was mapping new routes, albeit illegally and without the knowledge of the Park Service.

Soon enough, word got back to park managers, who told the interlopers they were breaking the law. At the same time, they were curious. They wanted to know what kinds of things Kerbo and his friends had found. When some of the outlaws offered to share the cartographic data they had assiduously collected in journals, park officials were awestruck that the so-called bad guys and gals knew more about the park than Carlsbad's own rangers. Kerbo's expertise had a cachet he hadn't expected. Park officials wanted him on their side.

"I knew the cave specialist there, and when he left to further his career as a ranger elsewhere, another acquaintance suggested that I put in for the job," Kerbo says. "I had no idea what it entailed. The truth is, I had only a foggy notion that the National Park Service was part of the federal government. The only thing I knew for sure was that they were the people who tried to keep me out of caves, but I recognized that here was an opportunity to look for more caves and get paid to do it. I thought I had finally found utopia."

Initially, his thin résumé was met with incredulity, but as he volunteered to assist with rescues, upper-level managers became impressed with his self-taught prowess. His articulate command of language defied his skimpy credentials on paper. Eventually he was hired, and helped turn Carlsbad's corps of rangers into a source of speleological knowledge recognized nationwide. Within a few years he was assisting the superintendent in greeting visiting dignitaries. For any park ranger interested in practicing speleology, serving under Kerbo at Carlsbad became a mandatory tour of duty. When Kerbo started, he was one of the first full-time cave specialists among all federal agencies in the nation. In 1997, at a federal cave management symposium, the number had grown to sixteen, a rise owed in large measure to his relentless persistence in promoting caves as legitimate crown jewels of the park system. "I can't tell you how much pride I felt in looking down that table and seeing those faces," he tells me. "I remember clearly when I sat at the table alone. Now we have a cadre of people who can work on everything from how to light developed caves to exploring virgin passages and everything between."

Kerbo's résumé still stands in contrast to the curricula vitae of most top-level federal managers, to say nothing of the credentials of his fellow speleologists and lawyer politicians, who often come decorated with honors from the finest universities in the land. Although he dropped out of Lovington High School (he received his general equivalency diploma five years later) and never graduated from college, he was offered a position as a visiting lecturer at Western Kentucky University, which offers one of America's premier programs in cave science. Kerbo has also been asked to deliver scholarly (and inspirational) lectures at dozens of other universities, and he has received numerous commendations for cave rescues as well as the Freeman Tilden Award for excellence in interpretation and the life membership award, the highest honor bestowed by the eleven-thousand-member National Speleological Society. He was even asked to be the featured speaker before the Lovington Rotary Club as a symbol of success, addressing, among other people, classmates and former teachers who thought he would end up in the state penitentiary.

Not long ago, Kerbo was standing before a classroom of grade school students, and he asked them a question: "How many of you know where your pancreas is?" Only a few hands poked into the air. He grinned, then commenced a gentle narrative about adventures rappelling over cliffs and crawling miles on his hands and knees. After he finished, he asked his mesmerized audience another question: "How many of you would like to become a speleologist?" The affirmative response was unanimous.

"I guess I shouldn't be surprised that children and most grown adults don't know anything about caves when they don't know the location of something like the pancreas that they carry around every day and is vital to their life. My sole objective is to get people thinking not only about their own bodies but about the body—the life system—of the earth."

Despite a flurry of important discoveries being made in caves, Kerbo says it is misleading and presumptuous to justify preservation purely on the premise that a medicine exists somewhere in the slippery bowels of Gaia. No, he suggests, caves relate to more immediate necessities. "Why do we need to protect the rain forests? Because there's a cancer cure which has yet to be discovered? No, we need to protect our forests so that we can have oxygen and breath. I use the same argument with caves. We need to protect them so we can have some drinking water, which is another of life's little fundamentals. Without those things, all the cancer cures in the world won't save our species. Thoreau said that in wildness is the preservation of the world. He could just as well have been talking about caves."

Kerbo says he has been thinking about caves since he was twelve years old. After reading a chapter about cave diving in Jacques Cousteau's classic *The Silent World,* his interest led him to the Bottomless Lakes. Humans have always had a close association with caves. We have used them as places of worship, as sanctuary against enemies and the cold, as places to raise children, as tableaus for art, and as places for burial. The great painted caves in Europe and Africa bear this statement out. But modern civilization has abandoned its roots and its memory.

"Americans are so far removed from the food chain," Kerbo says. "We moved out of caves, we boxed ourselves in, and we turned to them and said, 'What are those?' We allowed our Puritan ancestors to associate caves with demons and evil."

～

A decade into his tenure, Kerbo was assigned to be a roving goodwill ambassador for caves; to assist with day-to-day management at Carlsbad; and to serve as a liaison with the private caving community, which is divided into local groups, or grottoes.

Like other Thoreaus of caving, who liken their activity to a transcendental experience, Kerbo has contemplated the philosophical implications of cave wilderness since the 1970s, but these ideas gathered substance in the late 1980s. A couple of years after the marvels of Lechuguilla surfaced, Carlsbad superintendent Rick Smith called Kerbo into his office and told him to shut the door. Lechuguilla would thrust both of them into the forefront of controversy.

Although the general public was overwhelmingly in favor of protection, tourism officials in Carlsbad saw Lechuguilla as a pot of gold. In order to make cave protection palatable to the general public, the government decided it needed to show pictures of Lechuguilla to the world, and Kerbo eagerly provided them. The images were exquisite, showing hair-thin gypsum strands twenty feet long hanging down from the ceiling; a chandeliered ballroom with massive claw-like sprays of crystal gypsum, areas of exquisite calcite flowstone, stalactites and stalagmites and columns, pools of cobalt and green.

Citizens in Carlsbad were giddy over the prospect of flooding portions of Lechuguilla with lights and carving new pathways and strips of asphalt to serve thousands of new visitors. "Our publicity program backfired somewhat because local people began to think that if it's that beautiful, then how come we're not throwing the doors open?" Kerbo says. "They didn't see that the stampede of people and the costly infrastructure to accommodate them would assuredly destroy the goose that laid the golden egg."

Smith suggested it was his dream that Lechuguilla become America's first official underground wilderness. Kerbo felt as though his mind were being read. "I thought, 'What a deal!' Here's a park superintendent who would go into battle for wilderness. It was absolutely the greatest thing I ever heard."

Acting on Kerbo's enthusiasm, Smith wrote a letter to the *National Speleological Society News* broaching the concept. Since humans still have not come even close to discovering the extent of Lechuguilla, he proposed an "expanding wilderness" designation that would offer immediate protection to new sections as they are mapped. Hundreds of cavers nationwide expressed their adamant support. The oil and gas industry reacted to the concept as if it were confronting a dangerous contagious virus.

In 1986 a trial balloon of sorts had been launched for cave wilderness. The Lincoln National Forest proposed formal wilderness designation for caves in the Guadalupe Ranger District, for which the forest's cave specialist, Jerry Trout, was lambasted by Wise Use groups, namely ranchers and resource extractionists. Trout supported the plan because he said it was the only way the caves could be safeguarded. Kerbo was flummoxed by the outcry that surfaced at a public meeting. Critics falsely claimed that the proposal was part of a scheme to usurp private property rights and shoot down resource extraction on public land. "I couldn't believe the ignorance permeating the room," Kerbo recalls. "I couldn't believe the stupidity, and I couldn't believe the way in which they were railing against concepts they didn't understand."

Kerbo was undeterred. Three years later he drafted a cave wilderness proposal that made its way all the way to the U.S. Senate. Pandora, however, was out of the box, and she touched off a political firestorm. The expanding wilderness idea again caused the energy and livestock industries to come unglued. "It jolted people off center," Kerbo admits. "Wise Use groups such as People for the West couldn't believe the Park Service would actually write a proposal that suggested wilderness *can continue to grow.* They thought it would lead to government-imposed restrictions on both private and public land. Once again, avarice and greed came into play. Odd in my mind was that the idea also drew flak from environmentalists who insisted it would undermine the strength of the Wilderness Act of 1964."

According to Kerbo, some environmentalists argued that legislated wilderness stretches from the core of the earth to the core of the sun. But in practice, legislative protection applies only to the planet's surface. He believes the idea is flawed and needs updating, especially when placed in the context of a cave. "Think about it, the language of the Wilderness Act says poetically that 'a wilderness, in contrast with those areas where man and his own works dominate the landscape, is an area where the earth and its community of life are untrammeled by man, where man himself is a visitor who does not remain.' Yet there are few wilderness areas above ground in the lower forty-eight states where you can escape planes flying over your head or smog or some trapping of civilization. Caves are what wilderness is all about in its purest form. It can't be photographed from a satellite in space or have a horse ridden over it. When you enter a cave, you have no idea where to go until you ferret out a way. In caves, you meet the environment on its own terms. This is wilderness."

During a cave management seminar hosted by the American Cave Conservation Association, Kerbo was asked who was behind the antiwilderness forces in the area. "It was people who had condominiums on their brains, the smell of dead beef on their breaths, and the reek of saddle leather between their thighs," he said. Told by the new Carlsbad superintendent—who was under pressure to not make waves—that the remark was inflammatory, he said, "If you don't want me to answer questions, then people shouldn't ask me any."

While he was still a natural resource specialist with the National Parks and Conservation Association, Destry Jarvis (now the assistant director of external affairs for the Park Service) agreed that it was time to think about cave wilderness as its own entity. But the concept, it turned out, was ahead of its time, for it was rejected out of hand by Senator Domenici.

Quietly working a grassroots angle, Kerbo has built a constituency, mobilizing hundreds of grottoes and thousands of citizens to show that there is compelling national support for protecting caves. Today, a fulcrum for cave wilderness is the federal Cave Resources Protection Act, which mandates that federal agencies compile an inventory of known passageways. It was a benchmark achievement passed in 1992, but it contained flaws. During the period when it was drafted, a copy passed through the Forest Service, and agency officials changed the wording from the objective of protecting caves to protecting *significant* caves. The difference allows the Forest Service to subjectively determine which caves are significant and which can assume a higher risk from development. "The act looks only at the large open space of a cave, not the systems that created the space or drive the ecosystem," Kerbo says, suggesting that the open manifestation of a cave is actually a "shadow" of the karstic process of creation, which is what needs protection. "It just looks at the hollows of the cave. A similarity would be to protect the trunk of a tree rather than its branches and roots. The wording represents a loophole which the Forest Service can interject to open the door to oil and gas drilling." Of course, it can be argued that few politicians want the inventory to be completed because of the hurdles it would represent to industry.

"The most idiotic argument against cave wilderness is that it will deny people access. The Wilderness Act of 1964, which would provide the framework for this, does not deny anybody. When you enter wilderness, you may have to come face to face with your own limitations, but the forest or the cave or the wild river should not be altered to accommodate everybody because once you do that you lose the resource."

~

The Spirit World is notched under the west parking lot at the Carlsbad Park visitor center. It was first reached with a technique designed by Kerbo in which balloons were inflated and floated up inside a parachute, lifting him and his gear to the portal without leaving behind traces of physical impact. The mouth of the subcave leads into 750 feet of passage. Once you get around a dome, you can't see any lights or the public, but you can fall two hundred feet and die unnoticed. After a recent battle for cave wilderness, Kerbo decided to come here to remind himself what he was fighting for. "It's exactly what the fathers of the wilderness act envisioned,"

Kerbo says, noting that the Spirit World is one of the areas proposed for wilderness status. "It's just you and the natural world and nothing else, even though you're within two hundred feet of a trail and nine hundred light fixtures. When you're here, you're in as remote a position as you might be on the dark side of the moon; it's just that simple."

He argues passionately that gathering knowledge through exploration is the only tool that can be used to inform public land managers about the risks of harmful surface development on Lechuguilla, which he says is the quintessence of cave wilderness. "The cave already goes onto surrounding Bureau of Land Management land. Lechuguilla knows where it goes. We're the ones who are ignorant. In this case we need to speed along exploration in order to know where it's going because that's the only way we can protect the entire cave ecosystem."

Although some conservationists would like to see every square inch of Lechuguilla mapped to prevent accidental drilling into it, Kerbo speaks to caution and, in some instances, holds back from allowing expeditions to propagate. Leaving something for subsequent generations to explore is the greatest gift to cavers of the next century. "To consciously deny yourself an opportunity is a hard thing to do, no matter what it is, whether exploring a virgin cave or drilling a gas well into geological formations that you don't fully understand."

The last thing Kerbo wants is to be accused of practicing elitism. He doesn't believe the government should be in the business of locking the public out of special places and throwing away the key. He agrees with former Carlsbad superintendent Smith (who went on to become the associate director of natural resources management in the Park Service's Southwest Region), who noted that it is important for the agency, through policy decisions, to refrain from turning ambitious cavers into bandits such as Kerbo was forty years ago. "To open a cave and then to close it without just cause breeds a lot of enmity from the caving community, which, in reality, are the most forceful allies of conservation," Kerbo says. "If you allow access and give them a peek of the great beyond only to turn them away, you force them to consider trying to circumvent authority. That's what happened to me at Carlsbad, and it's something that is well known within the mountaineering community. What we need to do is creatively tap the expertise of skilled cavers who in some cases know more about the resource than we do. But it has to be regulated and monitored and tiered to the caver who understands both the responsibility and the privilege of entering a place where pristinity is sacred."

And yet, if people can't commit themselves to exploring sensitive cave environments with a "leave-no-trace" ethic, a phrase coined by the National Outdoor Leadership School, then they shouldn't be allowed to enter places they could easily destroy. Uncompromising in his view, Kerbo walks a narrow line. He must, in one instance, try to please the hard-core caving community, which espouses the notion that the less that is known about cave resources the better, and the general public, which desperately needs to be educated.

A founding father of the American Cave Conservation Association, Kerbo comprehends the apparent contradiction because of his own introduction to Carlsbad Caverns. "The caving community is very polarized about these considerations," he says. "I myself have said I've never seen a 'Keep Out' sign. I equate exploration with using your imagination to gain knowledge. Personally, I believe that exploration is fundamental to our being. It is ludicrous to talk about exploration for the sake of exploration as being unacceptable. What an asinine statement that is. If that is the case, why did we send those guys to the moon? We didn't send them there for the altruistic reasons we now want to talk about. We sent them there because we cannot suppress that urge within our species to go beyond, as Lord Dunsany said, 'the fields that we know.' In reality, we are always searching for ways to journey beyond the fields we know, whether it is a retrospective search for manifest destiny or to find power, glory, and the hammer of the gods. The only people who do not believe in exploration are those who are small in spirit."

That yen has led Kerbo, at the invitation of other nations, to scrabble through caves in South Africa, China, the Azores of Europe, Ukraine (including the Crimean Peninsula), Russia, Hungary, Australia, Mexico, Canada, Puerto Rico, Hawaii, and the majority of mainland states. Despite having crawled and strolled hundreds of miles through caves on five continents, Kerbo has threaded his campaign for cave wilderness with the concept of restraint of the human ego. He has intentionally held himself back from exploring parts of Lechuguilla to prevent the appearance of being a hypocrite.

Cave ecosystems are among the most fragile on Earth. In caves that periodically flood, minuscule amounts of human hair, sloughed-off skin, and lint from clothing may be inconsequential if they get flushed out. The path of the footprints you make will smooth over, and there will be no trace of you—unlike the desert, where footprints or tire tracks can last forever. But not all caves are karstic or parts of river systems. Some of the desert caves in New Mexico, Arizona, and Nevada are places where minor changes in carbon dioxide levels can inhibit the way speleothems (mineralized structures) are deposited and organisms inside the caves survive. Lint and hair and shed skin can accumulate microscopically on the walls and invite invading organisms that kill endemic organisms by outcompeting them.

"Low-impact caving means pulling off your Vibram-soled boots so as not to make carbon-black scuff marks all over the flow stone and wearing some sort of booties. It means bagging your own feces, hauling out the garbage, and urinating into plastic bottles. It means making sure you don't drool food or level out a place to sleep at night. It means a conscious effort to conform to the cave. Otherwise, Lechuguilla and other wilderness caves will wither," he tells me.

Evidence of human disregard for caves is ubiquitous. The damage that has been done to them is a powerful reminder that the nineteenth-century method of waste disposal—merely digging a hole in the ground and burying toxic substances—does not make problems go away. In Florida antiquated septic tanks have leaked into caves, destroying the unique complement of life and contaminating the groundwater. At caves near the Potomac River, not far from Washington, corroding cans of Raid and other insecticides have sterilized underground pools. In Missouri hundreds of trilobite-like brine shrimp and blind crayfish were annihilated by the spill of corrosive chemicals from a truck miles away from the cave site. At Mammoth Cave in Kentucky explorers discovered a new underground river littered with dead cave brine shrimp. The source of death and polluted water was a leaking underground gasoline tank located twenty miles away. In Maryland health officials noted that one gallon of gasoline can contaminate one million gallons of water. Kerbo asserts that caves, with their vast array of sensitive endemic organisms, serve as indicators for measuring water pollution.

"What we do above ground can have irrefutable consequences to things we value below ground," Kerbo says. "I bet few residents in Florida know that most of the state draws its fresh water from karstic systems. Every time a resident sets down a questionable septic system they are running the risk of allowing their human waste to reach someone else's faucet. The same pollution that killed those brine shrimp in Mammoth Cave could someday poison you or your grandchildren."

~

The pools that collect in underground labyrinths and become the habitat for blind crayfish are often the products of antiquity. Contemplating the percolation process as he sat alone in the Spirit World of Carlsbad with a headlamp, Kerbo the bard scribbled the following free-verse poem. At my prodding, he recited it aloud.

> I imagined a length of time that water takes;
> scientifically proven—hundreds of years
> to move through the cave, through the rock,
> perhaps thousands of years;
> the water is still migrating.
> And then pooled in some cave
> which has no interest in the surface
> is the water that once upon a time
> held the reflection of Christ
> lying in the darkness of the Earth.

He shares the poem, one of hundreds he's written, bends his head in contemplation, and evinces a serious glance. Whenever Kerbo approaches a virgin pool, he peers into the reflection hoping that perhaps when his headlamp light is cast upon still water for the first time, it will mirror the faces of those who came in contact with the water above ground. A mystic's ritual? No; it is just Kerbo's method of paying homage to the constructs of spiritual subterranea.

Finally he breaks the silence with a thought that obviously has occupied his mind for years. "To me, the idea is incredible, that a molecule of water could rain down from the sky and in the sunshine reflect His reflection or that of any other spiritual figure throughout human history. Yet right here, as its own record of time, the droplet resides in a cave, having served as an epic sculptural force, and now, after all these years, someone enters. Against the ancient blackness flashes a new light to help us find our way."

Years ago Kerbo was asked to introduce an old hand of the Park Service and Forest Service, the late writer Edward Abbey, at a forum on caves sponsored by the Park Service. During that meeting Abbey gave Kerbo a signed copy of *Desert Solitaire* that he carries with him to this day. On the résumé that Abbey handed Kerbo, he scribbled three words in the section where he described his present job: "saving the earth."

"There are many of us who feel that way," Kerbo says. "It doesn't mean that we are martyrs, but we understand that we have to keep talking. We have to keep discussions open, to allow the people who have the passion in their souls to flourish." Prior to his death, Abbey was a stalwart supporter of protecting Lechuguilla and became a magnet for suspicion. His book *The Monkeywrench Gang* featured the protagonist Hayduke, who aspired to blow up the Glen Canyon Dam as an act of ecosabotage. In real life, the person after whom Hayduke's character was modeled, Doug Peacock, helped inspire the formation of EarthFirst! and was a close friend of Abbey. During the 1980s several seasonal Park Service workers, inspired by Abbey's prose, used their bare bellies to brandish messages of protest against Secretary of the Interior James Watt as Watt toured various parks. He didn't take kindly to the theater.

Someone alerted Watt that Kerbo had once introduced Abbey at a meeting of cavers. "Later, it was part of my duties to be in the entourage with Interior Secretary Watt as he toured Carlsbad Caverns," Kerbo says. "I was taken into a room and questioned about my environmental affiliations. They read from a file folder they produced and asked if I was a member of EarthFirst! And was it true I knew Edward Abbey? And would I do anything harmful or embarrassing to the secretary? I denied being a member of EarthFirst! because I wasn't. Yes, I knew Edward Abbey, and yes, I was with him for three days, but with the blessing of the Park Service.

"Any relationship with him was my own business; any memberships were my own business as long as they didn't interfere with my work," he adds. "And as far as doing anything to embarrass the secretary, I told them he was quite capable of doing that himself."

Watt was forced to resign his secretary of the interior post after he made a series of controversial gaffes.

~

The Lechuguilla Cave Protection Act was not Ron Kerbo's idea, but he gets blamed for it. Even he thought it was a brash move. It came from the pen of Congressman Bruce Vento, a Democrat from Minnesota who has been an outspoken advocate of environmental protection. Prior to the Republican takeover of Congress in 1994, Vento presided over several House subcommittees that looked after the welfare of national parks. Upon reading about Lechuguilla in *National Geographic,* Vento traveled to New Mexico on a fact-finding mission. Kerbo, who recently had been promoted to the nascent position of national cave coordinator, headquartered in Denver, was dispatched to offer Vento a tour. He spent several hours with Vento and briefed him on an emerging threat from oil companies that wanted to punch down natural-gas wells on the edge of Carlsbad Caverns National Park into the same structure of rock that produced Lechuguilla. Yates Energy Corporation hoped to sink several exploratory wells for oil and natural gas on tracts of land administered by the BLM at a site called Dark Canyon. If the wells struck paydirt, it could have led to full-field development, and if not, the bore holes could have posed serious harm to the cave ecology because no one knows precisely where Lechuguilla ends.

Even pinpricks such as bore holes can cause changes in air flows, which in turn change the concentration of carbon dioxide. Drill holes can also expose caves to the danger of deadly "sour" natural gas. Speleothems are dependent upon the release of carbon dioxide from the droplets of water percolating throughout the porous bedding plains and from the deposition of minerals. Change the composition and the thermal balance, and you could create a dead cave. Cave-adapted species cannot tolerate change or disruption to their environment. Caves on public lands provide natural laboratories for the exciting new science of cave ecology. Caves and their ecosystems are inextricably bound to the surface.

"The character of the surface determines the infiltration rate of water and nutrients to the cave system. If the infiltration rate is diverted by surface disturbance, previously active cave formations may begin to dry up and crumble. Disturbing the inflow of nutrients could affect the entire biology of the cave," wrote Jerry Ballad, outdoor recreation planner with the BLM's Roswell Resource Area, which was reviewing the proposal.

Weeks after Vento's visit, on the same day that Kerbo convened a blue-ribbon panel of internationally renowned cave scientists to examine the actual threat to the cave, Vento delivered a present. He drafted the Lechuguilla Cave Protection Act and, without notifying the Park Service or conservationists, dropped it in the hopper. It was

instantly supported by Rick Bridges, then president of the Lechuguilla Cave Project, and thousands of cavers across the country. It
was instantly condemned by U.S. Representative Joe Skeen, one of
the chief proponents of energy development and exploitation of
Lechuguilla, whose congressional district encompasses the caves.

Simultaneously and in language later attached to the bill, Kerbo's
blue-ribbon panel recommended that a cave protection zone in
which energy development would be prohibited be extended around
the periphery of Lechuguilla onto BLM land. The overwhelming
consensus was that any drilling posed a serious risk to the cave because of dangers from leaking gas or destruction of the sensitive
karstic environment. Kerbo and Doug Pharis, then with the Park
Service legislative affairs division, drew up the boundaries.

As designed, the Lechuguilla Cave Protection Act represented a
milestone because it recognized the sensitive ecology of caves and
formally identified external threats on the perimeter of Carlsbad
Caverns National Park. Discussion of the bill polarized the town of
Carlsbad into three camps: those who thought that all protected
lands are bad and an attempt by the Park Service to acquire more
land; those who think the cave ought to be developed for its full potential and opened to tourism; and those who think the cave ought
to be left alone.

Branded a heretic by industry lobbyists, Kerbo had already become an enemy earlier in his tenure for seeking tighter restrictions
on tourist activities in Carlsbad Caverns after cave specialists documented over eighteen thousand broken speleological formations.
The campaign for cave wilderness made him a target for stewing an-
imosity. Based on his record of vociferous advocacy, Kerbo and his
wife were ostracized in the community. Walking down Main Street,
he would hear people curse his name under their breaths. After he
asked the park concessionaire to stop selling oranges in Carlsbad's
famed underground Lunchroom because the fruit was being tossed
against stalactites and was finding its way into sensitive pools, his
wife's job with the concessionaire was suddenly terminated. In a
restaurant one evening, a state senator seated near the Kerbos spoke
just loudly enough to be overheard: "Before this is over, we're going
to teach him a thing or two."

The situation in Carlsbad was already tense and getting worse.
Carlsbad mayor Bob Forest, who favored developing Lechuguilla,
convened a special citizen's advisory board to make recommendations

on the future direction of the cave. Knowing that Kerbo's presence as an official park representative would expose him to hostility, the agency told him he could attend the meetings only as a private citizen. Each year tourism to Carlsbad Caverns generates at least $50 million for the local economy. A disaster in Lechuguilla from a potential natural-gas leak could be disastrous for the resource and for public relations, park officials warned. Had it been the Old West, Kerbo might simply have been dragged off into the desert and lynched, but instead he found himself one evening in front of the modern equivalent of a community mob—a public hearing on Lechuguilla in the heart of Wise Use country.

As the future management of the caves was debated, Kerbo and other park staff were subjected to continual haranguing. A minister rose to his feet and quoted a verse from the Bible to criticize the federal position on cave protection and wilderness. With an aide to Skeen in the audience treating the public hearing as a pep rally for the Wise Use movement, Kerbo and other park officials felt as if they had been ambushed.

Kerbo thought it absurd that some community members were using the meeting as a forum to level paranoid and untrue accusations against the government. Shaking his head and grinning, he locked eyes with the minister. "If I was going to be one of the meek that the Bible says will inherit the earth," he said, "I'd be really pissed off at what you did to my part of it."

Someone in the audience taped the statement and told Kerbo that unless he backed down it would be used to publicly embarrass him. Kerbo responded that it was ludicrous for a man of the cloth to be invoking religion as an excuse for plundering one of God's greatest gifts to humankind. "I've never tried to be obnoxious. There are, after all, guidelines of ethical conduct for government workers, and I've never been accused of presenting myself in an unethical manner. Vitriolic, yes, I can accept that criticism, but unethical, no. Taxpayers pay me to get excited about caves," Kerbo says. "If you don't want to hear about caves, then don't talk to me. There were people in Carlsbad who would rather that I had gone away, permanently."

The test of Kerbo's courage escalated to its ugliest moment. An angry rancher who opposed protecting Lechuguilla and cave wilderness approached him and, in front of another witness, said the thought had crossed his mind of "just getting my rifle, filing down the firing pin, coming down to the [Park Service] offices, and just opening up on you bastards."

Kerbo wouldn't admit it, but for the first time he was afraid. He had been suffering from a growing physical pain in his chest, and one evening after the rancher's threat he assumed he was having a heart attack. He checked himself into the hospital, and doctors told him that he was fortunate in that he didn't have cardiac problems but that the worry and strain had led to increased production of acid in his belly, and it had begun burning his esophagus. He underwent surgery with strict medical orders to slow down and some friendly advice that "nothing other than your family is worth dying for."

Kerbo wasn't convinced, but he did change his strategy.

~

Call it a tangent, but there is an uncanny parallel that can be drawn between the wonders of Carlsbad and the constellation of geothermal phenomena occurring in the nation's flagship national park, Yellowstone. At the same time that conservationists in New Mexico were pushing for passage of the Lechuguilla Cave Protection Act, their counterparts in the Rockies, with the help of U.S. Representative Pat Williams of Montana, were trying to get a similar measure—the Old Faithful Geothermal Protection Act—moved through the same politically charged congressional committees. What the geysers, hot springs, and mud volcanoes of Yellowstone share with Lechuguilla is this: Besides their priceless aesthetic values, they are unique biological storehouses. Each contains its own complement of bacteria, algae, and other microbes that potentially hold astounding importance to society down the road. In Yellowstone the prospecting for microbes by biotechnical companies has given birth to a multibillion-dollar industry and resulted in such scientific breakthroughs as DNA fingerprinting, better natural preservatives for food, and de-icers for airplanes and cars.

Organisms that live in hot environments are called thermophiles, Latin for "temperature loving." According to park officials, the upper temperature limit for vascular plants is around 113 degrees Fahrenheit (45 degrees Celsius); for algae it is about 140 degrees F (60 degrees C). From the sky the hot springs of Yellowstone are a rainbow of pigments. What yields the colors? They are produced by single-celled bacteria called cyanobacteria, and the colors are those of various cell pigments, including chlorophyll, the pigment essential for photosynthesis.

The upper temperature limit for the photosynthetic process is 161 degrees F (72 degrees C). The first life found growing above the photosynthetic temperature limit was discovered in Yellowstone's Lower Geyser Basin in 1967. Thomas Brock, working under a Yellowstone research permit, placed a clean microscope slide into the 176 degree F (80 degree C) waters of Mushroom Pool. After a few days he viewed the slide under the microscope and found that it was covered with cells, which he grew in his laboratory. He named the organism *Thermus aquaticus*.

For hundreds of years humans have known of and used bioprocesses to better their lives. Yellowstone's geothermal ecosystem contains thousands of thermal features teeming with unusual life forms that have evolved to a point where they can withstand radical extremes of temperatures and pH levels. Scientists realized that organisms living in 176 degree F water contained enzymes that were stable in these steamy vats. They began to search for other life growing above the photosynthetic limit; dozens of novel species were discovered. The first industrial use of heat-stable enzymes from Yellowstone thermophiles was in laundry detergent additives. However, with the knowledge that DNA is the informational code that directs the manufacturing of a cell's enzymes and structures—as well as recent advances in molecular biology and genetic engineering—a new use was discovered for Yellowstone's array of enzymes.

In the late 1980s, DNA polymerase (the enzyme that catalyzes the replication of a cell's DNA) from Brock's *Thermus aquaticus* was employed in a laboratory process called polymerase chain reaction. This technique allowed copying and amplification of "target" DNA in a test tube and thus created "DNA fingerprinting." The 1993 Nobel Prize for chemistry was awarded to Kary Mullis, the man who perfected this process, and the patent has yielded billions of dollars' worth of dividends to the biotech industry.

The success of that application alone has led to a dramatic increase in research activity in Yellowstone's geothermal springs. More than fifty microbiology research projects are currently permitted in the park for the collection of samples. Yellowstone and Carlsbad have become beachheads for a new era of "bioprospecting" on America's public lands.

"So often the opponents of preservation portray it as a lock-up of real estate or an attempt to close down opportunities," says John Varley, Yellowstone's chief of research. "But here in the country's oldest national park we have been preserving Yellowstone's thermal features since 1872, and only now are we beginning to fully appreciate their value."

For years numerous international bioprospecting firms have focused their attention largely on tropical rainforests while temperate regions in the United States have been overlooked. Now experts believe that the estimated ten thousand geysers, hot springs, and steam vents of Yellowstone may hold as much biological diversity—and natural capital to draw upon—as the richest stretch of jungle in Brazil or Costa Rica. "National parks by their nature are repositories of diversity which makes them outstanding laboratories for the biotech industry," Varley says. "Often the preservation arguments get into all of this fuzzy-faced altruism—that we should aggressively protect these resources because it is the right thing to do. But here is bona fide proof that not only can we reap economic rewards, yet through the guidance of prudent science we can extract organisms which benefit humankind."

To put the richness in perspective, about five thousand thermal microbes have been cataloged to date worldwide. In a typical tablespoon of water lifted out of a Yellowstone hot spring, there are between ten thousand and fourteen thousand novel organisms never before seen. Furthermore, less than 1 percent of all the microbial species thought to inhabit park waters have been identified.

"For its biological diversity and potential discoveries, we're talking about orders of magnitude greater than what we've found elsewhere," says Terrance Bruggeman, chairman and chief executive officer of Diversa Corp., a San Diego–based biotech firm prospecting in Yellowstone. "Within ten feet of each other you can find geothermal features where the water temperature, pH, and variety of microorganisms are distinctly different."

Varley says the park's boiling pools may hold answers to deeper philosophical questions, such as the origin of life on earth. He considers it a quest to find Eve.

"There is a group of scientists worldwide who believe life originated in a hot spring," Varley explains. "They make a persuasive case for this primordial soup having all the building blocks of life but lacking a spark. We know that electricity comes out of the sky, and that may be all it took."

Other microbiologists currently are preparing instrumentation for the next Mars lander, which will gather samples of the Martian soil for evidence of extraterrestrial life. These experts are working with living and fossilized microbes collected in Yellowstone to help ground their instrumentation in the event that organisms are identified.

At Carlsbad researchers have recently isolated endemic microbes in caves that show promise as potential new antibiotics in an age of increasingly drug-resistant strains of disease. Larry Mallory, a bio-chemist from the University of Massachusetts, recently received a $350,000 grant to hunt for bacteria that might be effective in killing cancer cells. And more money is being poured into the effort.

To preserve the natural systems that created these organisms means protecting the processes that drive them. And in the case of both Yellowstone and Lechuguilla, it means recognizing that the underground natural plumbing systems are indelibly connected across subterranean miles that stretch even outside national park boundaries. As Kerbo has pointed out time and again, oil and gas drilling, if done haphazardly, poses unacceptable risks to the caves in and around Carlsbad because it holds the potential to affect how air and water move through the underground fissures. A similar argument was made around Yellowstone, where a New Age religious sect called the Church Universal and Triumphant announced plans to develop a hot-water well a few miles north of the park that potentially had links to features inside the park.

Yellowstone's famous resources, like Carlsbad's have survived unscathed, experts say, only because they have been beyond the reach of energy developers. Everywhere else in the world, wherever humans have tampered with geothermal systems by trying to develop them, harm has inevitably been wrought. As a result of increasing controversy and concern from environmentalists, Congress authorized a study by the U.S. Geological Survey (USGS) with consultation from the National Park Service to assess the risks posed by the Church Universal and Triumphant pulling water from its well. From the start, however, it was clear that Secretary of the Interior Manuel Lujan had an agenda that supported development in spite of fears that such landmarks as Old Faithful could be jeopardized. When the USGS delivered its report, it concluded that there appeared to be no discernible underground connection, essentially supporting Lujan, who argued that denying the church its right to develop would constitute a taking of private property.

However, there were growing voices of dissent not only within the Park Service but from one of the USGS's own distinguished senior scientists. Irving Friedman, a veteran geologist stationed with the USGS in Denver, has studied geothermal phenomena around the world. Having viewed the destruction of other geysers and springs firsthand in Europe, Iceland, and Russia, he is unconvinced by the findings of his own agency.

"For me, the central issue is risk," he tells me. "The USGS says there appears to be no connection, but it cannot prove there is not a connection. Therefore, the decision that must be made is whether the government is willing to gamble on the suspicion that there may, or may not, be consequences for the phenomena in the park. If development moves ahead, what happens if they are wrong? It is my contention that where the geysers and hot springs and fabulous travertine terraces of our first national park are concerned, no risk, no matter how small, is worth taking."

As expected, it did not take long before Lujan, Congressman Ron Marlenee, and Senator Conrad Burns—the latter two Montana Republicans and both in favor of development—let it be known that they did not appreciate Friedman's comments. Friedman received verbal reprimands for putting his concern about Yellowstone before loyalty to his agency, which appeared to endorse development. Furthermore, park officials in Yellowstone were warned that they might lose their jobs if they publicly disagreed with the USGS findings. In a show of solidarity, Friedman, Yellowstone resource chief John Varley, and then park superintendent Bob Barbee refused to comply with the gag order. They submitted comments to Congress on behalf of the Old Faithful Geothermal Protection Act that would prevent geothermal development on the periphery of the park. The bill, however, became stalled by politics and was never passed. The geothermal phenomena in Yellowstone remain at potential risk.

Around the world, nine of the largest geyser fields have been destroyed by geothermal development. Scientific experts say that Yellowstone holds the greatest concentration of undisturbed phenomena. Proposals to commercially harness the region's wealth of naturally occurring steam and hot water continue to surface. "There need to be stronger safeguards in place," says Michael Scott of the Greater Yellowstone Coalition, a conservation group. "As the biotech industry explodes and new discoveries are made, the dividends of protection become more compelling."

Meanwhile, eight hundred miles south, Kerbo had made numerous trips to Washington on behalf of the Lechuguilla Cave Protection Act. "One of the things I have said all along is we've got to have good science or we can't make good decisions," former Park Service director James Ridenour tells me, reflecting back on the agonizing choice he had to make. "The issues with both bills were remarkably similar and had the same rationale in mind. With Yellowstone, one team of scientists went so far as to say they thought there was no problem with geothermal resource development near the park. But I told them that if they couldn't take the final step and guarantee to me that there were no risks at all—zero—to Old Faithful Geyser and the park's other treasures, then I couldn't support them, and that's why I took the stand not to allow drilling, which was not what the secretary [of the interior] wanted to hear. I told Secretary Lujan that if he wanted, he could overrule me, but my position was firm."

Preston T. Scott of the World Foundation for Environmental Development in Washington, D.C., an organization that brokers research arrangements involving intellectual property for biotech firms, says the parallels between Yellowstone's hot springs and Carlsbad's caves are undeniable—with one exception. Caves are immeasurably more fragile and thus more sensitive to incursion, be it an explorer collecting microbes or a drill pit puncturing the earth's strata.

~

Kerbo knew the debate over protection of Lechuguilla would be just as charged as the battle raging in Yellowstone. And it continues to be. His colleague and friend Jim Goodbar, a cave resource specialist with the BLM in Carlsbad, had serious reservations about what effect drilling by Yates, and possible full-field development, would have on the entire karstic ecosystem. His opinion was that no risk is acceptable if it means jeopardizing the integrity of the cave.

Goodbar is a wiry, ingratiating fellow and, like Kerbo, a family man and nationally respected authority on caves of the Carlsbad region. He meets me at the BLM district office in Carlsbad, and we set out into the desert in an agency pickup truck. The place we are headed is ground zero as far as Kerbo's career is concerned. Dark Canyon is a spot that galvanized the international caving community, environmentalists, and hundreds of citizens around the protection of America's greatest cave. And it placed Kerbo on his most precarious ledge of resource advocacy.

As we divert from the asphalt of the main highway and disappear into a circuit of bouncy jeep paths, Goodbar offers a crash course in the politics and natural history. The Roswell Resource Area manages 1.5 million acres in Eddie (where Carlsbad is located), Chaves, Lincoln, Roosevelt, Quay, Guadalupe, Curry, and DeBaca Counties. Karst formations underlie almost the entire southeast portion of New Mexico. In the Roswell Resource Area alone, he notes, there are nearly 250 known caves and perhaps as many more undiscovered. Caves in the region have yielded dinosaur bones, Indian remains and relics, and rare or endangered species. Two caves are on the national register of natural landmarks, and one is on the national register of historic place. Fort Stanton Cave, one of those on the register of natural landmarks, is the third-longest cave in New Mexico, with eight miles of surveyed passages, and contains a rare crystalline formation called "cave velvet" in addition to stalactites, stalagmites, and gypsum flowers. Feather Cave, listed on the national register of historic places, is where early Indians made a sun shrine and ornamented it with pictographs and petroglyphs.

Above ground is an unsightly spaghetti pattern of dirt roads that carve up the desert and lead to oil and gas head frames. The cluster of industrialization is conspicuously absent as we look out toward the park. "I believe the system of caves out there is priceless," Goodbar says. "If you look at the numbers, we've turned over far more acres of land to oil and gas leasing than to cave protection. I think that speaks for itself."

He and Kerbo were not alone in the fight. Many colleagues in the Park Service and BLM backed them up and assisted in making sure that science was not trumped by politics. Quietly, on the sidelines, Kerbo also received moral support from one of his early mentors, Jerry Trout, who today is the national cave coordinator for the Forest Service. "Ron and Jim saw the writing on the wall, that unless something was done to scrutinize the BLM's willingness to let oil and gas exploration occur over the top of Lechuguilla, the cave could lose," Trout explains one afternoon in Sierra Vista, Arizona, where his office is located. "They took risks, and the hammers of the agencies tried to come down on them."

Together Kerbo, Goodbar, and Trout were called "the three amigos" for bridging agency communication despite resistance from their superiors. "Jerry has experienced much personal sacrifice to protect these caves," Kerbo says. "He was one of the first proponents of a cave conservation ethic in the Guadalupe Mountains. He has come under controversy for his advocacy and was harassed by his agency so much that after he received a transfer to southern Arizona he suffered a heart attack."

Each of them—Kerbo, Goodbar, and Trout—has been accused at various times of demonstrating disloyalty to their agencies. "If you're just there to be a bureaucrat sitting on your duff, then you might as well go and sell shoes," Kerbo says. "I am very adamant that the Jerry Trouts and Jim Goodbars of the federal caving world are people whose hearts and souls are dedicated to preserving these places. Far from doing things to embarrass the agency, they are simply trying to carry out their mandates to the highest level of professionalism, which is not a comfortable position to be in."

Yates and a couple of other energy firms refused to back down. Kerbo put his neck out again by talking to the press, and eventually he was asked to testify before Congress. Hours after he returned to his office, he received a telephone call. A colleague told him that people in the local community were accusing him of "lobbying Congress." "It was subsequently communicated to me that the congressional delegation was in full support of the company's desire to drill," Kerbo explains. "They apparently didn't appreciate the fact that I was talking publicly about threats to Lechuguilla because it was creating inconveniences for the company. Apparently, they forgot it was the United States Congress that called me to testify, and I would hope that they would expect me to tell the truth."

As with the geothermal controversy in Yellowstone, Congress asked that a study, this time in the form of an environmental impact statement, be prepared by the BLM, in consultation with the USGS, to assess the risks of gas drilling. Part of the information that was gleaned became the backbone of the Lechuguilla Cave Protection Act.

After a backbreaking outpouring of international interest and much professional peril, Kerbo and thousands of cavers succeeded in getting the benchmark Lechuguilla Cave Protection Act shepherded through Congress to stop Yates, despite resistance from Lujan. On the basis of Kerbo's resolve, Park Service director James Ridenour, a Bush political appointee, refused to go along when fellow Republicans wanted him to soften the language of the act and, furthermore, to impose a gag order on Kerbo. Kerbo has also been protected by Ridenour's successors Roger Kennedy and Robert Stanton. "Ridenour was a down-the-line Republican except that he believed in true scientific understanding," says Morrow, who worked under Ridenour. "When Republicans wanted to be dismissive of that, Ridenour parted company with them. In that respect, Ron Kerbo was probably lucky, although it speaks to his knack for making cave protection such a compelling issue that others would join him in risking their own careers."

Ridenour, who today is a natural resource consultant and a lecturer at Indiana University, offers an insider's view. "One of the things I said all along is we've got to have good science or we can't make good decisions—even at times when science forced you into a decision you didn't want to make because emotions, in this case and at Yellowstone, which is remarkably similar, were going in another direction, in favor of development. Some of the scientific people went as far as they could go in saying there appeared to be no problem, but they wouldn't take that final step in saying with absolute assuredness there was no connection. I didn't then, and I still do not today, believe that even if there is a remote chance of damage occurring, it isn't worth the risk of allowing developers to possibly jeopardize Yellowstone's geysers or the caves at Carlsbad."

Ridenour acknowledges that Secretary of the Interior Lujan, a native son of New Mexico and a former Congressman, had a keen interest in helping Senator Domenici and Congressman Skeen accommodate the oil and gas industry. "There were very few times I can recall in my career, whether it was reporting to the governor of the state of Indiana or to my ultimate boss, being the president, that I ever felt the pressure more intensively to make a decision differently than what the science told me," he says. "I have seen situations in administrations at the state and federal level where I felt that was not the case. But once in a while you would get someone, perhaps a lower-ranked official with a political background and a base of pseudo-power, who might put the heat on you. There was some congressional pressure from time to time. There always is a fair amount of congressional or legislative-body pressure that comes from special interest lobbyists. It was the kind that I tried to resist because I felt the people I support, the experts on the ground, would support me."

Ultimately, in 1992, the Lechuguilla Cave Protection Act was signed into law by Bush. "We actually have a law to protect a cave that won't have any elevator, lights, or handrails going into it. That to me is a real high point. But now we have to take the next step toward official recognition of cave wilderness," Kerbo says.

The act withdrew minerals from development and places a moratorium on drilling south of the cave protection area. Congressman Skeen said at congressional hearings that the area smacks of being a buffer zone, normally a taboo topic, but Kerbo acknowledges that that is exactly what the act does: It creates a buffer against development but it does not stop the threat entirely.

Perhaps one of the best illustrations of sweetheart politics may be found in the aftermath of the Lechuguilla Cave Protection Act. Although many would say the act served the public interest by striking a compromise between development and environmental protection (resource development is still permitted on BLM land near the park), Yates and members of New Mexico's congressional delegation saw it as an opportunity for a private company to cash in at taxpayer expense. Because the act and the related Dark Canyon environmental impact statement say that drilling cannot occur directly on top of known karstic features, Yates claimed that the government's mitigation measures of forcing it to drill horizontally into the earth amounted to a federal taking of private property—even though the leasing of public lands for potential private mineral development is a privilege, not a right. Moreover, there was no certainty that Yates's wildcat wells would turn up any sizable find. That didn't stop the company from seeking $32 million for the "potential" revenue it lost, based upon figures prepared by the prodevelopment BLM and endorsed by Congressman Skeen and Senator Domenici. "The BLM has exaggerated the economic benefits likely to be derived from drilling into Dark Canyon," Jim Norton, Southwest regional director of the Wilderness Society, wrote in a letter to the director of the BLM's New Mexico state office. "Because only one in ten wildcat wells nationwide actually produces, the likelihood of a dry hole should be more rigorously evaluated. We are troubled that the BLM would assume that $32 million in gas will be generated for a lease that was sold for only a dollar an acre."

Eventually the figure was trimmed to $18 million and recently to less than $10 million, and finally to a fraction of that, but with strong support for a public payout from Skeen and Domenici. These are the same lawmakers, mind you, who have justified the gutting of federal land management agencies and environmental laws to theoretically save taxpayers money. But here they were willing to compensate a private company with a questionable claim. Profoundly ironic is the fact that the BLM knew as early as 1985 that potential conflicts loomed and yet, instead of delaying the issuance of drilling leases, went ahead and offered them to Yates, knowing that it could likely be a costly mistake.

"It's like the story told among truck drivers that when you run over a bull standing in the middle of the highway it suddenly becomes the farmer's prize-winning bull," Kerbo says. "That's the argument Yates made, that by establishing a zone of protection for caves, it tried to claim that the government had seized private property by usurping its right to drill. Of course, many people, including many geologists, considered it an exaggeration, which is why, despite the sympathies of the New Mexico congressional delegation, Yates's claim was denied."

Still, what seemed like the permanent shield of protection of the Lechuguilla Cave Protection Act has in the late 1990s turned out to be merely an obstacle for the oil and gas industry, which is being encouraged by the BLM to come back. Arguing that the Dark Canyon environmental impact statement applies only to Dark Canyon, agency officials have told industry officials that they will entertain new proposals from other companies with leases that existed prior to the creation of the protection act—which means the potential nightmare has started all over again and will likely languish well into the next century, unless a cave wilderness system settles it sooner. Kerbo points to the alleged value of the Yates well and the rush from other developers to try to exercise their claims knowing that even if they don't drill they may be able to walk away with cash from American taxpayers. "To me, it's strange the way the Yates figure wiggle-wobbled around, with the support of the congressional delegation," Kerbo says. "Rather than being accountable to all Americans, they seemed willing to try to cut the best deal for a private energy company. In my mind, the public needs to know, and the public has a right to know the truth, especially if they want to gamble with the caves. I've never cowered away from saying what I thought ought to be said, and I'm too old now to start."

Progress in educating the most hesitant of speleophobes is evolving, slowly. Senator Jeff Bingamon has sponsored legislation to make Carlsbad the official site of the National Cave and Karst Research Institute to coordinate the continued listing of publicly owned caves under the federal Cave Resources Protection Act. It will also provide scientific support for biotech research and monitoring of cave ecosystems. The bill carries the support of Congressman Skeen and Senator Domenici. Many say it might not have advanced without Kerbo's presence.

"Sometimes federal employees feel inhibited in their speech because they work for the government," Kerbo says. "My view is that as civil servants we are the government, we are the keepers of free speech. I've never believed in the practice of putting up all sorts of smoke screens or trying to cover up what's really going on for fear of upsetting the public or losing your job. I trust the larger American public to make the right decisions. I have never felt that going to work for the government should interfere with my First Amendment right to free speech or my pursuit of life, liberty, and the pursuit of happiness."

"Sometimes his demeanor may rub people the wrong way, but I think he has been a great benefit to the National Park Service," says Carlsbad Caverns superintendent Frank Deckert. "Kerbo is unflinching. As a manager, he knows my position and the political realities that we have to do with, but that shouldn't cause anyone to hesitate from raising concerns about threats to our resources. We realize we may get rolled politically, but people should not have to fear for their jobs. It may appear over the short term that managers are admonished, but over the long term, they will come out on top."

When Kerbo assesses the battles won and lost, he notes that a defining moment occurred on the day he left Carlsbad after he was promoted to take over the national cave coordinator post in Denver. The rancher who earlier had threatened his life approached Kerbo and his wife in a store. He turned to Kerbo's wife first: "You know I threatened to kill your husband once." He then looked Kerbo in the eye and added, "I'm sorry for what I did because I didn't know at the time what you were trying to do. Now I know better."

Influenced by Kerbo's determination to engender public appreciation, the rancher decided on his own to look into caves. Although he isn't a caver himself, he was bitten by the conservation bug, became involved with Carlsbad's Living Desert Museum, and sent in his dues for a membership in Bat Conservation International. The former adversary handed Kerbo a dollar and said to keep it in his wallet as a reminder of a person whose attitude he had changed.

"There's no question that in large measure Ron Kerbo changed the agency's and the public's attitude toward caves," Morrow says. "There was always a curious agency fascination in them from the standpoint of scientific inquiry, but primarily as display pieces. It wasn't until Kerbo came along, pushing and saying pay attention to these, that the federal government perked up. Often people think the battle he's fighting is one of opposition to development, but what he's fighting is a lack of understanding, which makes it more remarkable. Here is a guy who started with little education who is now educating the world."

Hearkening back to his first dive in the Bottomless Lakes four decades ago, Kerbo has never been more sure of his resolve. Wherever he goes, whether to lead an expedition to the other side of the globe in China, the Spirit World at Carlsbad, or the paneled rooms of senators and congressmen on Capitol Hill, another lucky charm travels with him. Tucked deeply into his briefcase or backpack is a ragged, dog-eared copy of the novel *Desert Solitaire*, and scrawled on the title page is a note from the book's author: "Ron, save them caves!" Signed "Ed Abbey."

Kerbo reads from the book often at public lectures he delivers around the country. He hasn't let Abbey down yet.

Riverkeeper

*The San Pedro River is the only river of
consequence that rises in Mexico and
flows north into the United States.*
—William Least Heat-Moon

BY BASIC INSTINCT, the hunters knew the behemoths would
come. They knew they had to. They knew there was no escaping the
reality of their environment. Patient, sentient, meditating in advance
of their dangerous encounter with the four-leggeds, they waited by
the side of a water hole shaded by oak and eucalyptus, sharpening
the churt points wrapped at the heads of their spears. As darkness
fell, the giant woolly beasts—their quarry—appeared, surprising the
hunters with a softness in their lurching, tremulous strides. They
seemed docile; the ambushers knew better. They had observed the
deadly utility of trunks, the crushing force of feet, the rage of jar-
ring tusks. All night they had waited in silence at the river. When
day came, they went slowly ahead.

Three million, six hundred fifty thousand sunrises later, Ben
Lomeli and I are scanning a distant wash that cradles the artifacts of
ancient human encampments and the remains of a mammoth. We
huff in the thin air, hiking atop the highest vertebra in the Huachuca
Mountains, and shift our attention from the northern valley to one
in the south. Turning from prehistory, we look through binoculars
across a North American version of the demilitarized zone. "If you
want to get a feel for the river," Lomeli says, pointing to the invisible international border with Mexico, "then you have to see where
it comes from and where it is going."

Far below us, sidewinding like a buzzworm, the San Pedro River
courses passively through the floor of the Chihuahuan Desert. Pushing northward, it leaves the womb of the Sierra Madre range in
Cananea and slithers green against a beige and dun backdrop. In relief the channel appears nondescript, a mirage boiling in scorching
heat. Soon a breeze breaks the stillness of dawn. Wind radiates the

warmth upward from the broad, tilted peneplain, carrying it over the ridgelines where raptors ride the thermals. For a brief moment our attention is transfixed, not by the surreal stream corridor but toward the sky. Sailing aloft in a turquoise garden of billowy cumulus is a hot-air blimp operated by the U.S. Drug Enforcement Agency. The ominous zeppelin floats in aerial surveillance of the frontier running east from the twin but separate towns of Nogales, splitting the border in two.

While the barbed wire on the ground and the blimp in the air have become ever-present reminders of the divisions between nations, the San Pedro River is a conduit that defies the fence and unites a common topography bonded by the location of water. Out there in the riparian jungle that requires aqua as the chief biological passport are game trails where mammoths wandered in to drink and where aboriginals waited five thousand years before Egyptians erected their pyramids to the pharaohs. It is the river that holds the record and tells their story. If we look hard enough, perhaps it will yield our reflection too.

Ben Lomeli's culture, a potent mingling of Old and New World tradition, is based on long-running relationships with rivers such as the San Pedro. In 1540 it was the San Pedro's sparkle that lured Francisco Vásquez de Coronado along this belt of arboreal shelter as his iron-clad soldiers sought refuge from the oppressive heat of the sun. Endeavoring in vain to locate the mythical Seven Cities of Gold, they left tracks in the sand here, and little else. The Spanish conquistadores would have been amazed to know that 450 years later the water in the river beside them looms as a commodity more controversial and priceless than any precious spoils plundered from native peoples.

"I still have hope," Lomeli says, his face pallid beneath a shock of black hair. "I wouldn't be here otherwise. My preference is to be a peacemaker, but sometimes you have to be a warrior first." Today there is no one who would deny Lomeli the title *warrior*. To save the river of his ancestors, the now former hydrologist with the U.S. Bureau of Land Management (BLM) is also seeking to clear his name. Although the history of the San Pedro is sculpted in a geological diary of dihedral bends, deep arroyos, beachheads of sediments, and even dinosaur bones, the path of its future, like Lomeli's, is less than certain.

Barring some miraculous reversal of political winds and, even more profoundly, a leveling off of human water consumption in southern Arizona, experts say the San Pedro could soon dry up. In blunter terms, the last great free-flowing river in the desert Southwest is in danger of becoming a ghost stream. Vanishing with it, ironically, would be a waterway the federal government considers a flagship of competent river management because it serves as a de facto refuge for five hundred vertebrate species of wildlife ranging from prolific numbers of neotropical birds to elusive jaguars. Lomeli says the appearance is an illusion, that the San Pedro is dying because of human avarice. He is viewed as a serious threat by profiteers who let him know that he was placing himself in danger. "I've been told in so many words that if I want to maintain my physical health it would be prudent to keep my mouth shut," Lomeli reveals, explaining the reason he sometimes carries a gun into the backcountry with him. "They wanted me to say there is enough water out there to last forever, that we can have out-of-control growth in Arizona and still have a river. I won't do it. I refuse to tell a lie."

Despite the high price exacted from Lomeli for his outspoken vigilance, he says the consequences of retreat are more severe than proceeding to the high ground of unemployment. The water battle along this river has relevance for every river valley in the American West that has not yet coped with shortages brought on by urban development and agricultural use. "The people will one day be looking back to these years, to this brief moment in time at the turn of a millennium, and either praise us for having had the wisdom to act or curse us for draining the river when there was still an opportunity to rescue it," Lomeli tells me. "The San Pedro isn't just Arizona's and Mexico's river. It's an international treasure and a test of our ability to avoid the same mistakes of the past. You hear it from the bureaucrats in Washington that what we need is the foresight to avoid environmental train wrecks brought on by our own hubris. Well, here is one barreling down the tracks."

In Arizona, challenging the stranglehold that water developers exert on natural resources is a little like disagreeing with the mafia, he tells me, instinctively folding his open palm across a holstered pistol. Here, an unspoken rule—and a clear pattern—of silencing is enforced against those who cross the powerful "water cartel" of developers, real estate dealers, ranchers, and irrigators. Lomeli acknowledges that he is hardheaded, obsessive, and relentless, but during his life he has witnessed the results of passive capitulation to water developers. Ninety percent of the original riparian corridors—the lifelines that nourish the desert—have vanished to make way for golf courses, swimming pools, exotic crops, cows, and a proliferation of retirement subdivisions. Nearly every kindred stream to the San Pedro is gone or disrupted by water diversion. Not since the start of the twentieth century has there been so much to lose in the span of a single river.

People can disparage the environmental effects of the North American Free Trade Agreement (NAFTA), feeding abject poverty with the maquiladora sweatshops to the south, but Mexico has given the United States a river of history, which the Yankees have squandered without repercussions. But the results are coming.

Lomeli and I have driven up Montezuma Pass in the cool, ruby-colored atmosphere of predawn. Reaching the wind-blown terminus of treeline, we pulled over and set out bushwhacking on foot above a little-known southern Arizona park called Coronado National Memorial. With snow above us and fresh coyote pawprints in the mud, we sloshed up the pitch until there was nowhere else in the Huachucas to climb.

According to the Nature Conservancy, which owns a handful of biological reserves in southeastern Arizona, the upper San Pedro is vaunted as one of the continent's thirteen "last great places." But the conservation group American Rivers also lists the San Pedro as one of the most endangered in North America. Born from melting snow and summer monsoons in the storied Sierra Madre (the "mother mountain") of Sonora, Mexico, the river descends more than a mile and a half in elevation before reaching its terminus at the Gila River near Winkelman, Arizona. From the San Pedro's banks have surfaced fossils, the spear points of antiquity, and the final remnants of desperate Apache encampments from a century ago. Geronimo and Cochise became legends near the San Pedro, and nearby, in Tombstone, is the OK Corral. Surpassing any of these human associations, however, the river has been a magnet for other kinds of organic life.

In the undammed span of 140-odd miles, the San Pedro binds together a mosaic of biological diversity that is largely unequaled on American soil. Birders cling to the bottomlands as a mecca because four hundred different species—more than half of the identified

array of birds in North America—are represented in the riparian
forests, blackbrush, mesquite-bosque, and associated upland scrub.
Funneling seasonally through the San Pedro are flyers that disperse
to every corner of the West. Were you to be blindfolded and set
down in the middle of the basin during peak months of avian migration and breeding, the chorus of songbirds would cause you to
mistake your surroundings for a tropical rainforest.

As I follow a maze of riverside game trails alone one afternoon
while hoping for a life-list sighting of rare green kingfishers and
yellow-billed cuckoos, the spoor of a dozen different four-legged animals, including coyotes and pumas, intersects my own. I wander behind them, made euphoric by the fragrant bloom of desert wildflowers. The San Pedro harbors at least twenty-four imperiled plants,
mammals, birds, reptiles, and amphibians protected under state or federal laws and that many more again under the endemic or rare cate-
gories. I am overcome by its primordial lushness, the sudden dense-
ness of brushy wilderness into which one can disappear. At night,
spreading a sleeping bag near the slow, meandering flow, I think of
the local equivalent of grizzly bears in my home state of Montana.
It's a cliché, but there are degrees of wildness in any landscape, the
most acute in places where an unarmed human might vie with an
animal at the top of the food chain.

Perhaps this essence of the river's remaining feralness is conveyed
in the dreams of conservation biologists who see the desert "jungle"
as a place where it might still be possible to restore jaguars and wolves
to prey upon javelina, deer, and pronghorn. That is, if the jaguars
aren't here already. Ranchers and scientists who have seen the tracks,
photographed the spotted wild cats, and examined the scat know that
during the 1980s the feline predators were recolonizing the old
haunts of Coronado.

The return of jaguars to the San Pedro ecosystem is an ambitious
vision, given that the corridor measures only half a dozen city blocks
across. Everything about the dense botanical profusion that provides
a haven—the spectrum of components ranging from microscopic
amoebas to black bears—clings to a tenuous pact that nature will
deliver liquid sustenance on schedule, as the seasonal pattern has un-
folded for millennia. Provide the water, and the animals will come.
Unfortunately, the same theorem holds for unsustainable numbers of
humans.

I won't kid you. The river isn't ruggedly wild in the sense of the common image of a river cascading through a remote, pristine gorge. The San Pedro's pastoral allure comes from its proximity to civilization. So subtly endearing is its effect that even Bruce Babbitt, former governor of Arizona and Bill Clinton's secretary of the interior, was handed a picture of the river by his late mother to hang on his office wall as a reminder of this gem in the vast vault of federal lands. "Look after this place," she told her son. "It means something to me; it should mean something to you."

But does it? Does Babbitt give a damn about the integrity—or in some cases, lack of integrity—of those hired to protect the river?

~

How the water filters through the landscape is Ben Lomeli's specialty, though his scientific expertise has been the bane of politicians and developers who inadvertently transformed him into the best-known dissident in the BLM. Lomeli's crime was telling the U.S. government that it shouldn't manage the San Pedro as it has the federal deficit or the Social Security program. A type B personality, Lomeli does not think of himself as a do-gooder. "This is a classic case of someone trying to do his job with intelligence and conviction. He's not radical. He's not a revolutionary. He's not an egomaniac. Although those in the Arizona water cartel would like to portray him as a firebrand environmentalist, he's just not that way," says Peter Galvin, cofounder of the Southwest Center for Biological Diversity (SCBD), an environmental watchdog group. "Ben's *just* a scientist," Galvin adds when we rendezvous over a beer. "If there is anything radical and revolutionary about him, it is that he still believes in letting scientific facts guide decisions because political science has been a failure. For saying that, he's been identified as an enemy of industry, and in Arizona that's the kiss of death, especially with an agency like the BLM that has kowtowed to industry's every whim."

The Southwest Center for Biological Diversity, led by environmentalist Robin Silver (who holds down a day job as an emergency-room physician in Phoenix), has taken aggressive positions on conservation issues avoided by mainstream organizations because of the political fallout. It has earned respect as well as a legendary reputation for promoting real conservation biology. Headquartered in Silver City, New Mexico, the SCBD led the much-publicized fight to save the Mt. Graham squirrel, and it has filed a battery of lawsuits to defend biological diversity. In a string of fifty lawsuits, SCBD holds the formidable record of winning 99 percent.

The outcome of old and impending lawsuits filed to protect the San Pedro—cases that also have implications for scientific whistle-blowers like Ben Lomeli—has potential repercussions for dozens of valleys and riverways in the West that face water shortages con-comitant with species declines caused by overuse of the resource. "Ben Lomeli," Galvin says, "is a hero who fell on his sword rather than be manipulated into a position of personal disgrace."

~

In contrast to most civil servants in federal land management agen-cies, Benjamin Lomeli cannot be castigated by locals as a ne'er-do-well outsider because he is, in the colloquial lexicon of the day, a true homeboy. He grew up down the highway in Nogales, Arizona, scarcely a two-minute walk across the border from Nogales, Mex-ico, where his extended family lives. He may have an Italian surname (pronounced *Loh-mah-LEE*), but his identity is rooted indelibly in Spanish, a language he often dreams and thinks in. His view of the land is like the river in that it reaches both sides of the border. Lomeli's father, Jesus, brought his boy often to southern Arizona rivers during crests of high water. He wanted Ben to experience the raw fury and roar of untamed rivers, their primordial value, having himself watched the Santa Cruz between Nogales and Tucson des-iccate and vanish since the 1950s. "We came to the rivers, and you could feel the energy. We would stand in utter amazement as cows and big trees were washed down the channel," Lomeli says. "At home my dad, my brother, and I built a model of the river, and he showed me how the water parts into braided channels and where the sediments settle in. He taught me that rivers were special and worthy of respect, that they had a purpose which far exceeded our ability to understand."

Every autumn father and sons returned at low water to wade the slow-moving pools and perennial stretches. They fished, watched wildlife, and swam. Those memories are what fueled Lomeli to make the study of water—hydrology—his passion in college after serving in the navy during the Vietnam era. His intuition and intensity—to say nothing of his ethnic heritage—led him to be identified as a ris-ing star in first the U.S. Forest Service and later the BLM. Lomeli comprehends what other people see as the San Pedro's sentient qualities, though he bristles at the suggestion that his own approach is "New Age." "Water runs through everything," he says. "It carries the memory of our ancestors and binds us to the land. It courses through our blood and gives substance to our own flesh. I consider the San Pedro to be the soul of the land in the Chihuahuan Desert. The water is what makes life here possible and desirable. Those who want to abuse it are fooling themselves if they think it is expendable."

Lomeli's bilingual background and cultural heritage have been used by federal agencies to establish a rapport with Mexican water users. What happens upstream in Mexico has direct consequences for Cochise County, one of the fastest-growing counties in one of the fastest-growing states in the nation. As Americans continue to squander their water reserves in the Southwest, there are deep-rooted fears in Sonora that gringos hypocritically will press to limit the consumption of their Mexican neighbors, who need the resources to elevate their own standard of living in the era of NAFTA. If Americans want Mexicans to respect the river, Lomeli notes, they need to lead by example.

Initially, in the late 1980s, that was exactly what the U.S. government planned to do. Recognizing the San Pedro's profound ecological, historical, and social importance, Congress in 1988 approved the purchase of two massive ranches that had come into existence as colonial Spanish land grants. With Ronald Reagan in the White House, the then Democrat-controlled House and Senate took the unprecedented action of creating the San Pedro River Riparian National Conservation Area and turned caretaking responsibilities for the novel fifty-six-thousand-acre preserve over to the BLM. The intent was to make the riparian reserve a national model for how to protect a linear liquid crown jewel. Its enabling legislation, signed into law by Reagan, poignantly instructed the BLM "to conserve, protect and enhance the riparian ecosystem." Its charter specifically compelled the agency to creatively conserve water.

In an ironic foreshadowing of later events, Reagan offered this quotation to the *Guardian,* a British newspaper, one year after retiring from the presidency: "Information is the oxygen of the modern age. It seeps through the walls topped by barbed wire. It wafts across the electrified borders." What Reagan said in reference to the Iron Curtain has been contradicted by government management of the San Pedro River, for in Lomeli's mind suppression of scientific information has become the greatest threat to the river's viability as a functioning natural system.

As the lead hydrologist for the San Pedro River Riparian National Conservation Area, Lomeli summed up the river's importance in an internal BLM report, later circulated to the public: "Riparian tributaries act as wildlife corridors between mountains, uplands, and the river by providing habitat continuity for diurnal species migrations. Small pools and near-surface water sources along these washes make excellent aquatic habitats. The vegetation provides cover, food, nesting and roosting areas. These corridors also provide habitat for many insects and reptiles which in turn serve as a base for the complete food chain," he wrote.

Painting a pristine depiction of the river, as I mentioned earlier, would be misleading. If we peer back over more than a century, the San Pedro has suffered from decades of various abuses but endured in spite of them. The cottonwoods and willows were felled and used as fuel; boom towns such as Charleston sprang up overnight and then were abandoned; miners scraped at the earth and deposited toxic tailings on the American and Mexican sides; water was diverted to neighboring ranches and farms; and cows overgrazed the watershed. Predators, including the jaguar, were mercilessly harassed and exterminated by bounty hunters, and native *cienegas*—desert marshes created by beaver—were systematically drained. Countless birds also vanished during spraying of DDT and habitat alteration by cattle. Of the thirteen native species of fish that evolved with the river, just two remain. Gone are five fish species now listed elsewhere as threatened or endangered—the desert pupfish, Gila topminnow, spikedace, loach minnow, and the Colorado River squawfish. Six other species are functionally extinct.

A more accurate assessment of the San Pedro is to say that the river is teetering on the brink of recovery and has the potential of being restored to its original grandeur. Such an option has been foreclosed upon in the vast majority of watersheds that feed the Colorado River system. Shortly after the BLM made the San Pedro a showcase, the agency won praise from environmentalists for initiating the bold, difficult step of pulling cattle off the river, sparking what wildlife officials say was a biological renaissance that proved that natural systems can rebound from the effects of overgrazing if given a chance. "After the BLM evicted cows and gravel scoops from the San Pedro River, everything looked good," wrote newspaper reporter Tony Davis in a story for the journal *High Country News*. "Thousands of young cottonwoods and willows began to flourish. Banks that had been barren grew so thick with sweet clover, ambrosia and grasses that they were difficult to hike. Bird populations skyrocketed. After just three years as a conservation area, BLM wildlife biologist David Krueper found that counts of song sparrows, summer tanagers and warblers had increased by up to 6,000 percent." Krueper, it should be noted, privately encouraged Lomeli to fight for the river, insisting that the two shared a mutual passion for ecological protection. Some have said that in the end, Krueper played the role of Judas.

When the gleam of the BLM's public relations triumph along the San Pedro began to fade, the euphoria proved to be ephemeral as the agency, in the face of resistance from developers, began waffling on protecting the most important element of its new preserve—the water. The benefits of keeping water in the San Pedro can be invisible to the hiker or hunter walking along the banks. The river corridor itself is a sponge that acts like an insurance policy during periods of drought because the vegetation helps hold moisture. That said, a riparian area cannot exist in the absence of a river, nor can a river be a river without water flowing between its banks. These assertions seem commonsensical, but it is revealing how quickly such obvious concepts can be mucked up by those who possess a different orthodoxy of water use. When the conservation area was created, the BLM (i.e., American taxpayers) bought six billion gallons' worth of annual water rights from farmers, water that ordinarily would be diverted from the river. The purchase was made to guarantee minimum flows, and the acquisition of water rights continues.

Yet, during the early 1990s, Lomeli and other experts realized that base flows were declining fast, indicating that far more water was being sucked from the basin than was being recharged. The evidence was found in the best of all indicators: the trees. The apparent culprits were Fort Huachuca, the city of Sierra Vista, and the Bella Vista Water Company, which together represent the only major human gauntlet the river must run once its crosses the border.

When western water law began to be written in the nineteenth century, the goal of those claiming dibs was to appropriate every available drop in the stream. The first non-Indian consumers were ranchers who jealously hoarded their shares under the "use it or lose it" doctrine. No one then, of course, was in a position to predict the dire consequences that would befall stream corridors throughout the Southwest from overappropriation. Early in the twentieth century farmers channeled off portions for irrigation, and before long fruit orchards sprouted in places where they would otherwise never grow. Then came subdivisions after the region was touted as the promised land for retirees and the infirm seeking a dry climate. By the time the population of Arizona started really booming in the years following World War II, the rising tally of ghost streams could no longer be ignored. Sucked bone dry, the baked riverbeds are a nightmarish vision of what the San Pedro could become.

Outside Tucson, the barren wash of the Santa Cruz is lined by the skeletons of dead trees. Smooth rocks that formed riffles in the current fifty years ago are bleached white from the sun. The flows that swam through this artery were pumped into the city for drinking water and to whet other, more opulent appetites. The people responsible for creating ghost rivers often were miles removed from the destruction and had no concept of the harm they caused. As Jesus Lomeli told his son, they don't hear the unspeakable void of songbirds or miss the therapeutic gurgling of a current. They have no idea that the price of lush golf-course fairways, water in their back-yard swimming pools, and thirty-minute showers is the evisceration of complex pieces of the landscape. The so-called sunbirds and their baby-boom heirs—who have imported a lifestyle requiring lavish consumption of water—have never incorporated water rationing into the cultural vocabulary because where they come from—Canada, the Midwest, and the Northeast—water exists in abundance.

In his seminal exposé, *Cadillac Desert*, which brilliantly divulged the nefarious politics of water, Marc Reisner described a general phenomenon that applies to the upper San Pedro watershed, now facing the same crises experienced decades ago in Phoenix and Tucson. "Not that the migrants had bothered to ask whether there was enough water before they loaded their belongings and drove west," Reisner wrote. "They simply came, no one could stop them. How they were to fill their pools and water their lawns was Arizona's problem. Arizona's solution was the same most other western states relied on: it began sucking its groundwater, the legacy of many millennia, as if tomorrow would never come."

That tomorrow isn't in the future any longer around Sierra Vista. "We have a biological meltdown in progress on the San Pedro and across the Southwest," Galvin of the Southwest Center for Biological Diversity noted one day after a walk along the river. The very same afternoon, Ben Lomeli was receiving a lecture from his superiors for too forcefully advocating water conservation to an ad hoc committee formed to examine water use. "It is criminal what Lomeli has been asked to do by his supervisors. In essence they have ordered him to stop doing his job and condone the draining of the river, which constitutes a breaking of the law—several laws, actually—the Federal Land Policy Management Act, the Endangered Species Act, the National Environmental Policy Act, and the Clean Water Act. Those are the legal codes, but worse yet is that the developers are violating the code of personal responsibility and ethics. The story of Ben Lomeli is the tribulations of a public servant caught in that dilemma, and that's how he should be judged. Do we as taxpayers want our employees beholden to us or to special interests?"

～

Back in the middle of the nineteenth century, Fort Huachuca was built to offer settlers protection against marauding Apaches. The U.S. Army holds title to some of the oldest recognized federal water rights on the river. As the single largest employer in southern Arizona (with more than 5,600 military personnel and almost six thousand civilians) and thus a massive water user, it is also a sacred cow. One of every three adults who reside in Cochise County works at Fort Huachuca. An economic pork-barrel juggernaut that brings $1.7 billion annually to the state, the fort long has been given carte blanche to use water as it sees fit, whether for military exercises, to grow exotic grasses on manicured lawns, or even to maintain the fairways on the golf course. Although the army deserves some credit for exploring ways that water can be conserved and recycled, it still unabashedly imposes a major drain on a resource. Thus, a paradox: Tax dollars are spent on the one hand to remove water from the San Pedro system for the operations at Fort Huachuca (under the jurisdiction of the Department of Defense), while on the other hand tax dollars are laid out by the BLM and Bureau of Indian Affairs (both agencies within the Department of the Interior) to keep water in the river. It is a classic example of government waste and bureaucratic counterproduction. Politicians have refused to touch it with a ten-foot pole. State representatives of the BLM have become their accomplices.

Fort Huachuca's most damaging impact on the San Pedro has been its role—along with the Bella Vista Water Company—in shamelessly promoting growth in Sierra Vista, eight miles away from the river. Until the mid-1950s the town of Sierra Vista didn't even exist. Today, projections by the Arizona Department of Economic Security show that the Sierra Vista–Fort Huachuca area will expand by 28 percent from the 1992 population of 33,725 to at least 43,168 in the year 2010. That means tens of millions of additional gallons of water will be needed—but where will it come from?

"For all its impressive engineering, modern water development has been governed by a fairly simple calculus: estimate the demand for water and then build a new supply to meet it," wrote Sandra Postel, director of the global Water Project in Cambridge, Massachusetts, and a regular contributor to the WorldWatch Institute's annual *State of the World Report,* where her comments appeared in 1996. "It [depending on alternative water] is an equation that ignores the complexities of the natural world, questions of human equity, concerns about other species, and the welfare of future generations. In a world of resource abundance, it may have served humanity adequately. But in a world of scarcity, it is a recipe for trouble."

Trouble is already brewing beneath the scenery flanking the San Pedro, and it is manifested as "cones of depression." To invoke an analogy, think of a cone of depression as a black hole beneath the surface of the ground, or in cruder terms a vacuum cleaner, siphoning off the aquifer and drawing down the overall water table. The larger a cone of depression grows, the more havoc it wreaks. Today the San Pedro is being attacked by several converging cones of depression that are expanding every year. It could be argued that BLM officials have looked the other way and tried to minimize concern over the river's decline at the behest of local developers.

Another irony is that conservationists were not the first to pinpoint the inaugural cone; rather, it was the military. In 1960 the Department of Defense commissioned a groundwater study and discovered a cone with its ground zero located beneath Fort Huachuca's perimeter fence. Although this cone originated in a quadrant of the aquifer well away from the San Pedro, by 1993 it had expanded to cover an area measuring a mile and a half by four miles and was on a course that would intersect the river. In 1998 several drains appeared to be encroaching from every direction.

Hydrological concepts can be confusing, but the water dynamics along the San Pedro are elementary. Water moves through the Chihuahuan Desert in three distinct zones—(1) the basin-fill alluvium (which serves as a massive subterranean reservoir), which is replenished by water coming off the mountains; (2) the river itself; and (3) a symbiotic flood plain between the basin-fill alluvium and the river. As a cone of depression widens, it reduces the water table. The flows of the San Pedro are dependent on both the runoff people see and the transference of water from the adjacent alluvium, which is unseen. With the overall levels of the aquifer being drafted off, the upper San Pedro has begun dying a slow death.

Because of expanding cones of depression due to virtually unbridled demand, the forecast has many ecologists worried. In 1993 the U.S. Department of the Interior hired consultant Catherine Kraeger-Rovey to reach an objective opinion about what Lomeli and others predicted as an end for the river. "This [a cone of depression beneath the town of Sierra Vista itself] gives me a rather bleak outlook for the San Pedro," Kraeger-Rovey wrote. "Even if Sierra Vista stopped pumping tomorrow, which of course will not happen, depletions [from the aquifer] would continue to increase for a while. Since the pumping will only increase, depletions will also increase and the ecosystem is going to be in real trouble."

In Arizona, groundwater (stored in the basin fill and flood plain) and surface water (in the river) historically have been treated as wholly separate entities available for exploitation, even though they are hydrologically connected. Lomeli says that allowing water to be taken simultaneously from the basin-fill alluvium and the river is like two people draining a small pond from opposite shores, both insisting that neither is having an impact on the other. In the case of the San Pedro, there are so many different forces extracting water from the system that it is a far smaller pond than people think. Representatives of the water cartel have denied the connection, although the overwhelming body of science reveals their folly and their twisting of the truth. "Science could discover and predict disaster, but agencies like the BLM [have] had a hard time reacting because they're straight jacketed by water law," wrote Tony Davis of the conflict in *High Country News*. If the BLM is not willing to defend its own model river, who will?

Complicating matters is the system of water allocation. Federal water law pertains to water physically in the river, while state laws provide access to the groundwater, and never the twain shall meet.

The double jurisdiction has resulted in the very same reserves being appropriated many times over. In fact, it has been asserted that the city of Sierra Vista and the Bella Vista Water Company—the two entities capitalizing most on the region's demographic boom—are pumping the aquifer and usurping the federal government's vital water reserves, which are necessary to protect the natural integrity of the river. It means that the six billion gallons' worth of costly water rights purchased by U.S. taxpayers to preserve in-stream flows may be coming out the taps of newly constructed condominiums sold by the real estate agents of Bella Vista. And this is where the story of Lomeli takes an ugly turn.

After building a thorough scientific base for his conclusions, Lomeli instructed his superiors that the riparian area is functioning on borrowed time, and the news spilled out to the media. The amount of development occurring around Sierra Vista has already led to lower flows in the river, and the dips show signs of acceleration. Lomeli laid out his concerns succinctly in a report titled "Hydrologic Summary, Water Rights Status, and Future Options for the San Pedro Riparian National Conservation Area." Hydrologists from other federal agencies commended him for the work. "The problem is not one of balancing the water budget for the upper basin," he wrote. "Concentrated overdrafting (by about twice the annual recharge), between the mountain-front recharge zone and the last remaining perennial reach of the river, is cause for concern."

He added that "many localized environmental impacts and economic restrictions will be encountered long before aquifer storage can be totally exploited." Diminishment and depletion of the base flows in the San Pedro is one of the first indications of overdrafting, leading to the extirpation of the riparian ecosystem. He continued, "The quality of regional groundwater can be expected to degrade as water tables continue to decline." In other words, Lomeli warned, the water being piped out of the ground is far outstripping nature's ability to replenish it through percolation, winter snowfall, and warm-weather rains. His frank assessment seized the attention of the water cartel because they knew it could incite widespread panic.

A concerted effort began to force Lomeli's silence. In Sierra Vista today, there are those such as Harold Vangilder who have grand plans for the little municipality, and he'll be damned if he'll tolerate saving water for bugs and trees if it means creating hardships for his fellow *Homo sapiens.* Vangilder, a former civilian worker at Fort Huachuca, was mayor pro tem of Sierra Vista when I spoke with him, and his antienvironmentalist ravings are well known and sincere. In public, he has boasted of declaring war on the environmental movement. When he speaks, his philosophies are laced with the predictability of a Rush Limbaugh antifederalist dittohead. Rotund, with a Limbaugh-like physique, his looks have been compared to those of the fictional 1970s television detective Sgt. Frank Cannon. Vangilder doesn't trust environmentalists, and he says that communities that invite them to become part of the planning process in managing limited resources do so at their own peril.

"All right, there may be five hundred species of wildlife found along the San Pedro. My response is, so what? What benefit do these animals have for humans? In my opinion we ought to interpret everything through the human perspective, not the animal perspective, and if a species is becoming endangered, I think we ought to ask ourselves if it is really worth the effort and the money to save it," he says.

Vangilder decries environmentalists because they say controlling growth is the only means of sparing the river. Groups such as the Southwest Center for Biological Diversity have indeed called for such radical measures as well as shutting down the fort, if necessary, to attack the impetus for future growth. "In my mind the real debate is not about water at all. Water is a tool in the debate, but the real issue is, do we smartly provide opportunities for human beings, or do we stop the spread of man? I believe the agenda of those in the environmental community is to stymie the aspirations of humans. It's a touchy-feely thing to them, a bunch of biological psychobabble. They want to defend Gaia against the storm troopers of destruction," Vangilder says with a laugh. "Yes, I think the San Pedro is a pleasant enough river in its proper context, but if it is supposedly one of the best rivers left in the Southwest, we're in a mess of shit. There are some people who want to save the damn river for the coyotes and the minnows. I want to save it so my wife and I can go down there and have a picnic. The only way the river is meaningful is if it is filtered through human experience. If I had to choose between the minnows in the river and the aspiration of humans, the minnows are dead. Nature has been selecting for species for a long time. It's called evolution, and part of the process is survival of the fittest. We're the ones who rule supreme, and if a plant or animal can't adapt to our needs, then it's too bad."

One fascinating element of Vangilder's attitude is that he actually has respect for Lomeli. "Ben is a hydrologist. I believe he believes what he says. I don't believe he is saying those things from an environmental or development perspective. I don't cast rocks at Ben Lomeli, but there are people who do. He becomes a lightning rod because he [was] a civil servant who allowed his reports to drift outside the channels of his superiors. I can tell you as a former civil servant myself that when it happened to me, the wrath of God came down from the heavens."

Lomeli realizes now that although he is adept at grasping the intricacies of water dynamics, he was naive about the flow of political power, particularly the connections of Judy Gignac. Gignac, the general manager of Bella Vista Water Company, has been more vocal than anyone else in trying to discredit Lomeli. Of course, her company's empire of water services and real estate has condemned as anathema the kind of conservation measures Lomeli endorses. Well connected to people in high places, she was appointed by former Arizona Governor Fife Symington III—now serving time in a federal prison for bank fraud—to sit on the Governor's Riparian Area Advisory Committee. As a former Cochise County supervisor, Gignac also serves an instrumental role in promoting Sierra Vista as a retirement paradise for senior citizens. And she helped get Symington elected. Not surprisingly, she long denied that a hydrological link existed between the water Bella Vista was pumping from the basin and the flows of the San Pedro—even when there were obvious signs of trouble. Admitting that the river draws its water from finite resources would force developers to accept limits to their ceaseless boosterism for water consumption and population growth.

In a testament to the influence of water companies, the Arizona Supreme Court ruled there was no legal basis for claiming a surface water–groundwater connection. The justices, not one of whom had a scientific background in hydrology, were swayed by arguments from attorneys for developers that the science is inexact, although report after report suggests otherwise. What the decision means is that before legitimate legal standing can be achieved for water conservation, a disaster must occur that establishes legal precedent and proves the developers wrong, at which time, of course, it will be too late. "We have a system that rewards users for wasting water instead of conserving it," Lomeli says, referring to the military, municipalities, water companies such as Bella Vista, Indian reservations, farmers, ranchers, and golf courses. "When you have that many different interests competing for a resource that is finite and shrinking, to preserve the consumptive status quo is being ignorant."

Lomeli has absorbed blame as a harbinger of bad news and a doomsayer, though his defenders say that he is simply amplifying empirical facts. Thirteen years after the army identified the first cone of depression, a water deficit was confirmed in 1973 by R. H. Roeske writing in the *Arizona Water Commission Bulletin;* and again in 1974 by the consulting firm Harshbarger and Associates, which drafted the "Report on Water Development in the Fort Huachuca Area, Arizona." These reports sparked the first water scare and forced land developers to admit they could not guarantee that a one-hundred-year supply of water existed in the basin. Pulling political strings, the water cartel in the twenty years following was successful in pushing a bill through the Arizona state legislature that no longer requires developers to inform home buyers that they may run out of water.

Meanwhile, growth continues, but, silently, so do the studies. In 1982 a cone of depression was identified by G. W. Freethy in a study completed for the U.S. Geological Survey; it was confirmed in a 1984 study for the city of Sierra Vista; and affirmed yet again in 1987. The mounting evidence continued in a study by a trio of scientists, F. Putman, K. Mitchell, and G. Bushner, in their report to the Arizona Department of Water Resources. A year after that report was published, Putman dispatched a memo on March 31, 1988, that warned, "Continued groundwater pumpage between 1986 and 2000 will mine an additional 208,000 acre-feet resulting in an estimated maximum groundwater decline of about six feet per year." He added, "In the year 2000 water levels may decline by 10 feet per year west of Hereford [which sits on the edge of the San Pedro], by about 25 feet west of Lewis Springs [on the river], and by 30 feet west of Charleston [also near the river]."

Another bombshell came in 1993. In a sobering statement that elicited fresh denials from the water cartel, Thomas Maddock, a respected professor of hydrology at the University of Arizona, said, "Pumping at the same rate [1988 levels] will dry up the river within 20 years [as base flows are lost]." To no one's surprise, Gignac emerged as the loyal spokeswoman for the opposition that attacked both Maddock's and Lomeli's charges as alarmist. Every time a new report emerges discussing cones of depression or other imminent

problems, she disputes it. One of her primary targets became
Lomeli's promotion of strict conservation as a solution; she argued
that that idea of rationing water was extreme. "There is absolutely
no reason to scare people half to death about water levels," Gignac
told a reporter for the *Arizona Daily Star.* "Ben is a good person and
he has some strongly-held beliefs. But when you purport to represent the position of an agency like the BLM, I think you need to be
cautious about what you say."

Lomeli has little doubt that Gignac initiated the grief he would
suffer. His supervisors at the BLM ordered him to refrain from speaking out unless what he said was cleared with them first. One BLM
official I spoke with, who asked to remain anonymous, said the gag
order can be traced back to Gignac. It was the start of four years of
threats and intimidation. I wanted to know for certain, so I called and
asked her point-blank. Gignac, who says she and Lomeli agree that
they approach the water issue from "different ends of the continuum," insists that Lomeli's allegations are overblown. "Ben ruffled a
few feathers; sure he did," she explains. "We got tired of seeing pho-
tos on the front page of the newspaper showing this young man
[Lomeli] standing by the river saying it was in trouble. The business
community got together and decided it had to fight back. I did talk
with Les Rosenkrance, the state director of the BLM, and I told him
what Ben was saying at public meetings while wearing a BLM uniform and making it clear we didn't agree with him. I don't have any
power over the BLM. What they did with Ben after that was purely
up to them. Ben gives me a lot of credit for getting things accomplished in different forms of retribution that really I had nothing to
do with." BLM insiders, who say their agency supervisors believe
they exist to serve people such as Gignac rather than the national interest in the river, believe Lomeli's treatment was intended to serve
as a warning that anyone who challenged exploding water use would
be destroyed professionally. It is telling that these people didn't want
their names mentioned for fear of retaliation from higher-level managers in the state BLM office.

Although several task forces have been set up to identify potential
solutions to water problems, initiatives have consistently been blunted
and substantive action delayed by the need to achieve "consensus."
Meetings have given way to more meetings, committees to subcommittees. The panels, stacked overwhelmingly with members representing the business community, were not fond of Lomeli's persistence

in advocating a strategy to arrest the cones of depression. Twice his BLM superiors pulled him from key task-force assignments on the Upper San Pedro Water Management Council, and the San Pedro Water Resources Association after water developers complained that his suggestions for mandatory conservation would cost them money. Lomeli sees the political maneuvering as a stalling tactic, and he charges the BLM with having lost any claim to the trust of the American public by deliberately pulling its own experts from decisionmaking bodies.

Galvin says what's so compelling about the persecution of Lomeli is the degree to which science has continually vindicated his position. The city of Sierra Vista hired a consulting firm for one study, on the premise that its hired guns would refute the other findings of Lomeli and others, but its own experts refused to dismiss the cone of depression now emerging within the city limits. "Lomeli's role has been to say the emperor has no clothes, and as a result the water developers wanted the BLM to try him for treason and have him exiled," Galvin said.

Weeks after Lomeli fell into disfavor with Gignac, the nightmare of his career commenced, and the man orchestrating it was Bill Civish, the BLM district manager directly overseeing the San Pedro Riparian National Conservation Area from offices in Safford. Civish called Lomeli in for the first of several verbal reprimands. "Civish was brought in from Washington to assuage the developers and control his own field personnel," Galvin says. "He's the archetypal BLM goon. He's there to quash any hint of dissent. If you think livestock is big business in the West, it is nothing compared to the power of the water industry. The money behind it puts it in the same league as oil and drugs. Billions of dollars are at stake. Ben is a threat because he challenges the status quo, which is business as usual and let another generation cope with the destruction this generation has caused." Civish's reputation for being dictatorial is not disputed by those on his staff. Shortly after he intervened at Gignac's request, Lomeli was threatened with reassignment to the bureaucratic equivalent of Siberia—the Kingman, Arizona, office; another threat was a forced transfer to Alaska. Civish claimed through a spokesman that the transfers were in Lomeli's "best interest." "He told me point-blank that it would just take a phone call from Judy Gignac or Gene Manring [the Cochise County supervisor] and I'd be transferred before I knew what hit me," Lomeli says. "It was as if he were on a power trip because he kept reminding me that he was in control, that if I didn't abide by the 'Civish rules' I would find myself in a place far away from the San Pedro."

Civish backpedaled when asked to explain his remarks: "It's a cliché. I said if we don't get our job done they're going to send us all to Alaska," he glibly told reporters. "No one else in the room took it seriously."

Actually, everyone else did see it as a threat, including Lomeli's direct supervisor Greg Yuncevich, who said that although the message appeared ambiguous, he understood keenly how Lomeli might interpret it. Civish denied that he employed any tactics of intimidation. Lomeli, however, had a silent ace in the hole that he had not yet played in the his-word-against-theirs confrontation. Fastidious in his note-taking, he had a habit of lugging a briefcase to all meetings, and inside, along with paper and pens, was a tape recorder. He took it to all public meetings to ensure he correctly interpreted what the public said, and on the day that Civish called him behind closed doors, he instinctively hit "record" with his thumb, then closed the briefcase and forgot about it. Lawyers who represent whistleblowers say that carrying a tape recorder, as Lomeli did, should be a tactical tool for dissidents. Get everything in writing and if a supervisor asks you to meet him in a back room with no witnesses, insist upon taping the conversations so that if a threat is made the supervisor can't deny it. Ironically, Lomeli had innocently begun recording meetings after his superiors told him it would be a good way to ensure that he accurately interpreted everything stated by the water developers.

In the wake of the tape revelation, BLM managers quickly embarked upon a different approach. Les Rosenkrance, then Arizona's state director for the BLM, suddenly insisted that Lomeli's "expertise" was needed elsewhere and that it made no sense to have a full-time hydrologist on the San Pedro, even though it was regarded as the agency's riverine equivalent of a national park. He offered Lomeli an alternative post, but Lomeli refused to be transferred, and as a result, Rosenkrance supported Civish's suggestion that he be placed on administrative leave to await termination. With nowhere else to turn, Lomeli enlisted the help of Jeff Ruch, a former attorney with the Government Accountability Project, a national whistleblower protection organization in Washington. Today Ruch is the executive director of Public Employees for Environmental Responsibility (PEER). Together, GAP and PEER brought Lomeli's plight to the attention of Jim Baca, then national director of the BLM. Baca was enraged by the agency's good-old-boy approach to conducting business.

By this time the press had stumbled upon the case, but reporters did not probe deeper. Based on what it saw, the *Arizona Daily Star* published an editorial in Lomeli's defense: "It's hard to believe a resource that's valuable because of its water, and threatened because of outside pressures on that water, doesn't need an on-site hydrologist. The San Pedro is an irreplaceable treasure. No matter whether it was because of politics or budget constraints, Lomeli's reassignment makes no sense. The San Pedro Riparian Conservation Area needs a dedicated hydrologist to oversee, monitor and defend its river."

Baca agreed and had a private meeting with Lomeli, which angered Rosenkrance and Civish, who attempted to present him as an alienated renegade. Baca found Lomeli's commitment to be not a liability but refreshing, and he issued a rare administrative order canceling any transfer. "Nobody is totally clean. Ben wasn't a saint, but then again, I don't want saints, I want honest people who do good work, and Ben's was very good," Baca tells me. "I stepped in because the bullying being done by Civish was just plain wrong, and Ben had support from independent scientists, environmentalists and water users such as ranchers." Whistleblower groups contend that Civish's actions breached ethical and legal codes of conduct.

Lomeli was momentarily spared. Yet only a few months later Baca himself was ousted by Bruce Babbitt. As Baca would soon learn, honesty is a dangerous virtue. He had delivered a speech before the U.S. Senate Subcommittee on Agricultural Research, Conservation, Forestry, and General Legislation, which, prior to the Republican takeover of Congress in 1994, fell under the purview of the Committee on Agriculture, Nutrition, and Forestry. A hearing was called to discuss the Clinton administration's plan for "ecosystem management" on public lands as part of an initiative launched by Vice President Al Gore to "reinvent government." The following is an excerpt of Baca's speech on Capitol Hill that got him into trouble.

The word ecosystem clearly implies some form of geographic delineation, one that crosses the traditional geopolitical boundaries by which we have managed our lands and resources. The backbone of our management approach will be the setting of common goals and developing consensus among diverse interests. These goals must be developed within the limits imposed by sustainability of natural systems if we are to ensure long-term viability of our resources and the economy.

The BLM views ecosystem management as the integration of ecological, economic, and social principles to manage lands and resources in a manner that safeguards long-term ecological sustainability. The primary goal of ecosystem management for the BLM is to develop management strategies that will maintain and restore the ecological integrity, productivity and biological diversity of public lands. Among other things, sustainable ecosystems provide high quality habitat for fish and wildlife; clean drinking water for communities; and economic and recreational opportunities. Our goal will be to implement management strategies to protect the integrity and diversity of ecosystems and to ensure economic, recreational, aesthetic, social, and cultural benefits from the land for present and future generations.

In the past the BLM's resource management placed emphasis on commodity production and the sale of natural resources. Management objectives were generally designed to expedite the development, extraction, and/or production of resources on public lands. Other uses and values such as wildlife and fish habitats, some recreational activities, cultural, scenic, and aesthetic resources were often viewed as adjuncts to more intensive uses.

The lack of the broad view encompassed by an ecosystem approach may have led to increased sedimentation in streams; less productive range land conditions; fragmented plant, animal, and fish habitats; and forest health problems. Population growth, increased use, and other factors, have also contributed to degradation of the public lands and caused significant declines in the distribution and populations of many native flora and fauna.

Many communities whose economies depend on public lands are affected because an ecosystem approach was not used. The declining timber and fishing industries of the Pacific Northwest, for example, demonstrate the economic repercussions and social displacement that can accompany ecosystem degradation. Conservation efforts on public lands make a critical difference to the stability of vulnerable plant and animal species and the stability of local economies.

Unfortunately, poor forest and range land health, degraded riparian areas, and inferior aquatic habitats often threaten species' viability, resource productivity, and ultimately, the overall sustainability of ecological systems. Because of such conditions and impacts to the public lands, we must take a holistic approach. Under ecosystem management, the BLM will manage the public lands to sustain viable ecological processes and functions. We intend to conserve, maintain, restore and enhance the ecological integrity of the land and its resources while providing for human values, products, and services and assuring ecological sustainability.

The water cartel and livestock industry interpreted those words—viewing the San Pedro as an ecosystem—as an attack on their livelihoods. Ranchers, miners, loggers, and other resource industrialists in the West took it the same way. Baca, who became a scapegoat, was forced out by Secretary of the Interior Bruce Babbitt after a handful of governors, including Arizona's Fife Symington III, complained of Baca's "activism." The administration waffled, then, retreating, handed Baca his pink slip, to the cheers of many rogue BLM employees, including some in the Arizona BLM office, who were committed to resource extraction rather than resource conservation.

With the shield of Baca gone, Lomeli was vulnerable and immediately he was issued a gag order by Civish and his public relations front man, Jess Juen, who told him to refrain from discussing water issues or from attending public meetings relating to the San Pedro's management. Civish and Juen confronted Lomeli directly: "Ben, you've become a lightning rod," Juen growled. "Not only have you become a lightning rod, but where lightning strikes once it can strike twice," Civish added. "And Ben, you know that if it strikes again, it's going to hurt real bad." This time, there was no mistaking the threat for what it was.

When the BLM has gotten itself into difficulties over water issues in Cochise County, Juen, a handsome, smooth talker, is often called to be the agency's spokesman, and when I phone he takes the questions instead of Civish. "Is Ben a hero, as the Southwest Center for Bilogical Diversity suggests?" I ask Juen.

"No, he isn't, not in my opinion," Juen replies. "No man is bigger than his agency. He is simply a hydrologist with training who's very emotionally attached to the river, which is neither bad nor good. That emotionalism, however, has blown a situation out of hand. What Ben does is heartfelt but emotional."

In response, Lomeli suggests that if BLM bureaucrats in cowboy boots—such as Civish and Juen—spent more time actually making emotional contact with their lands instead of isolating themselves in offices, they might have a different attitude. "If you put your feet on the ground, drink the water, and breathe the air, you're attached physically and emotionally to natural resources. Where could they send me on this planet where I wouldn't feel attached? It's almost as if these people are walking around in spacesuits to make such a statement. Of course I'm attached. It's my job. Every time people turn on their tap in Sierra Vista and Fort Huachuca, I hope they think about the aquifer and the river. But that's one of the problems everywhere in the desert, from L.A. to El Paso. We need people who consciously think about where the water comes from. It doesn't just magically materialize."

Greg Yuncevich awkwardly relates to Lomeli's orientation. More than any other person, Lomeli, he says, taught him about the river that he too grew up with as a local boy. "We feel there is plenty of water in the basin because it's a gigantic basin with a lot of capacity. However, the San Pedro is vein fed at the top, and if the water level drops below a certain threshold, the river is history," Yuncevich admits. "The cones of depression already are impacting the river today. It is urgent, but it was urgent ten years ago. I don't see a lot of people jumping on the bandwagon to make saving the river an issue. There is a huge public out there that has no idea what the threat is. Whatever we do, it may be too little, too late."

Yuncevich's candid fatalism is troubling to Lomeli, who says the BLM uses it as an excuse to do nothing, to discuss the importation of water, or to defer any action until there is a lawsuit. Yet at the same time there are proposals to build a multimillion-dollar visitor center on the San Pedro to educate visitors about the animal life that thrives in the riparian area. The BLM proposes this project while admitting internally that if the river dries up in ten years, the visitor center will overlook a true biological desert and be a monument to futility. When will the aquifer run dry? I ask Yuncevich, who demonstrated little backbone in defending Lomeli against Civish because of the urge for self-preservation.

"You're asking something that every hydrologist working out here over the last fifteen years has argued about. It could be five months or five thousand years," he says. "The thing is, we know that day is coming when there will be serious problems. If we can turn it around with the help of citizens, I believe we can resolve it ourselves. It's far better and more palpable to develop a San Pedro solution than to let the courts decide it for us, but the longer it is ignored, the less tolerable the solutions will be to those who deny there's a problem."

Yuncevich invokes the name of Charles Wilkinson as the guru of natural resource policy in the West, and Wilkinson's book *Crossing the Next Meridian* as the bible that explains why things need to change. Without question, Wilkinson, a law professor at the University of Colorado, is the preeminent authority on pinpointing the failed policies that have placed rivers like the San Pedro in dire straits.

"The unpleasant fact, as unpleasant for this writer as for any reader, is that we must come to grips with population growth," Wilkinson wrote in *Meridian*. "Our real choice comes down to this: Western communities can either take charge of the future by adopting some form of conscious management and direction, based on full and brightly etched visions of the future, and sustain the West's lands, waters, and way of life; or western communities can continue to abdicate—by allowing developers to charge ahead with few restraints—and surrender the distinctive qualities of the West within a few decades."

On the one hand, Yuncevich can identify with the writings of Wilkinson while on the other hand he helped to carry out the orders of reprimand against Lomeli, who gave scientific impetus to Wilkinson's words.

"When you see guys like Ben Lomeli, you realize how many of these employees are not speaking the truth," says Galvin. "It's a shame because the gutless bureaucrats have brought the government into disrepute. After the Oklahoma City bombing, you had militia groups talking about government ineptitude and oppression, but here is a textbook example. Distrust in government is occurring because of mealy-mouthed bureaucrats who cover up the truth, and it breeds paranoia."

~

If allowing the San Pedro to dry up in order to accommodate development seems outrageous, then the plan to rescue the riparian area is rife with even more absurdity. Currently a sorting-out of water rights is being done as part of the Gila River Water Adjudication, and although the San Pedro is among the first of several tributaries to be examined, estimates are that the process could take twenty years, which might be too late.

"The adjudication only addresses water rights, and it does not take into account beneficial uses insofar as trying to keep the river flowing," Gignac of Bella Vista Water Company notes happily. "If it is shown, and I believe it will be, that the legal water rights of the BLM are junior to other rights, then obviously the senior rights take precedent, and those users are not going to care if it dries up the river. I'm optimistic that a solution will be found, but it may be handed down through the courts. I will tell you this. Because of the elections in 1994 that gave Republicans control of Congress and changed the legislative composition of the Arizona legislature, the federal government coming down heavy-handed would not serve the issue well."

Predictably, another alternative has won the tacit endorsement of water developers and civic leaders in Sierra Vista. Instead of imposing serious restrictions on water pumping in the basin, water may one day be piped many miles into the Sierra Vista area from the Central Arizona Project (CAP) (i.e., the larger Colorado River) to augment flows in the San Pedro. In other words, robbing Peter to pay Paul and asking American taxpayers to subsidize the robbery. "It is Rube Goldberg logic elevated to the extreme," says Galvin. "We are allowing the natural river to be drained so that we can expensively pump outside water back in and call it good. But it's a farce. The real thrust of a solution should be teaching people how to live within their means. Unfortunately, the culture in Arizona is built upon the premise that it doesn't matter how much you live beyond your means because help will arrive from someplace else. Someday, perhaps sooner than everyone thinks, there won't be help to bail us out, and who will be left holding the bag?"

Every day in the vicinity of Sierra Vista and Fort Huachuca, at least two million gallons of water are, for the most part, wasted. Every spring and summer at high flow, much more water passes through the San Pedro than the river needs. During afternoon thundershowers, a tremendous volume of water runs off asphalt surfaces but is not captured. Lomeli believes a comprehensive conservation strategy of recycling, water retention, watershed improvement, effluent recharge, and enhancement of natural recharge could stave off a crisis by reducing the need to keep pumping high volumes from the aquifer. His ideas have rubbed off on people like Vangilder, but until the last drop is sucked, people and commerce come first. "People are going to continue to come here, if not to work then to retire, and it is our job to make sure they can have a drink. The truth of the matter is, humans are going to win out," Vangilder tells me. "The environmentalists say we are in denial down here, which is just plain bullshit. Some hydrologists out there believe we have enough water to last 1,500 years. We already are doing things to conserve water. I don't think you have to be a rocket scientist to realize we live in the desert."

Don Henderson, a farmer who represented the citizens' group Arid Resources in Danger (ARID), says Vangilder is in denial about being in denial and that even the modest proposals for conservation still place the aquifer in a deficit. ARID was among the groups in Sierra Vista that rallied behind Lomeli. "In the not too distant future, you're apt to have one major cone of depression under the river. Cones of depression don't move until they exhaust the local source of water, which means the river is going to die," says Henderson, who left Sierra Vista and moved to Kerrville, Texas, because he didn't want to wait around and have to cope with the inevitable. "People try to cloud the issue with statements that there is a lot of water in the ground. Yes, there is a lot of water there, and you can pump it for a long time, but look at Tucson. It had a lot of water and pumped it for a long time, and they wiped out the Santa Cruz. The demise of the San Pedro makes me feel lousy as hell because there are so few perennial rivers left in Arizona and none like this one."

According to Henderson, who recites statistics from the federal Bureau of Reclamation, it will cost between $60 and $100 million at minimum to divert water from the Central Arizona Project. He believes that plan—gaining support in the Arizona BLM office—will only exacerbate the crisis because it perpetuates a vicious cycle. Water budgets more development, which begets a greater demand for more water. Dale Pontius, who worked for the conservation group American Rivers, the group that named the San Pedro as one of the twenty most threatened rivers in North America, says there are solutions that allow for both modest growth and salvation of the San Pedro. "But nobody that I know wants to build a pipeline to extract CAP water," he says. "It is a self-defeating proposition if you let the river run dry and then pipe in water from elsewhere. I believe it will be an incentive for further growth."

With CAP water in mind, Civish had a cruel proposition for Lomeli: He could remain part of the BLM team on the San Pedro if he would publicly advocate the importation of CAP water as the best remedy. State BLM administrators know that Lomeli vigorously opposes such an action as expensive, wasteful, and an environmental travesty. "They told me they were going to create a flashy new federal position and make me a key player, but it would mean that I couldn't talk about conserving the San Pedro with natural solutions anymore. They gave me another gag order [after he rejected the proposal]. The government is very inventive at creating new committees, holding meetings, spending tax dollars, and laying out agendas that are designed never to get anything done. In the meantime, every day that the Bella Vista Water Company and the city of Sierra Vista attract more people, the San Pedro gets a little closer to going dry. They said, 'Ben, we're real sorry the resource is going to suffer, but that's the way it's going to be and we forbid you from talking to the media anymore.' I told them, 'When I was hired I took an oath to defend the laws and Constitution of the United States. One of those laws specifically commands the BLM to conserve, protect, and enhance the riparian ecosystem of the San Pedro. Without trying to protect the water, I would be in violation of my job.'"

Yuncevich sat between the proverbial rock and hard place. An Arizona native, he empathized with Lomeli, and shouldered enormous political pressure from Civish and Juen to reel Lomeli in. In turn, Civish was being pressured by Symington's office at the behest of Gignac and others in the water cartel. Yuncevich realized the waves that Lomeli had created when an unnamed Arizona congressman—later identified as Jim Kolbe of Tucson—weighed in on the issue. "I was driving him [the congressman] around, showing him the project [the national conservation riparian area] when he asked if there wasn't something that could be done to keep that Hispanic kid—Lomeli— quiet. He said Ben was a troublemaker and was ruffling up the feathers of [Kolbe's] constituents."

Yuncevich nodded to the congressman but promised nothing. Lomeli, he thought, didn't deserve to be harassed. "He's a damned good hydrologist who knows his stuff," Yuncevich says, privately admitting uneasiness about the role he had to assume. "Sometimes Ben has been too outspoken for his own good. He doesn't realize the way that things get done. While I don't agree with Ben taking matters into his own hands, I think what he is saying is right." Soon after the congressman's visit, Lomeli discovered why the BLM has gained a notorious reputation as a handmaid to industry. Not only was

Lomeli ordered to remain silent, he was also stripped of his scientific duties monitoring the river, had support personnel removed so he couldn't effectively do his job, and was told that if he attended any committee meetings pertaining to the river, even as a private citizen, he would be fired.

When Lomeli refused to lie low, the devoted family man and father of two children—whom he took to the San Pedro to admire the river—suddenly found himself facing trumped-up charges of sexual harassment and misusing a government vehicle. They were allegedly substantiated by biologist David Krueper (pronounced *creeper*), who had encouraged Lomeli to remain vigilant. Unbeknownst to Lomeli, Krueper was also a spy for Civish. A secretary who was loyal to Lomeli's superiors accused Lomeli of making lewd comments. Lomeli denies that he said anything; on the contrary, he said that given the pressure he had kept to himself and tried to conduct himself professionally. Lomeli's wife, Laura, stood by her husband, calling him "a person of honor," and said the things he was accused of were out of character. In an investigation that followed, several of his coworkers in the office said that they had witnessed none of the behavior attributed to Lomeli.

Tom Devine, an attorney with the Government Accountability Project, which has represented thousands of whistleblowers over the years, says the attack on Lomeli follows classic patterns. "The goal is to go well beyond merely defeating the whistleblower," Devine said before a House subcommittee exploring abuses of federal employees' First Amendment rights. "It is to prove that no one is safe. To do this, agencies seek to make stick the most outrageous charges possible. A dissenter renowned for being a gentleman may face sexual harassment charges. A soft-spoken, self-effacing individual will be branded as a loudmouthed egomaniac."

Civish and Juen called Lomeli into another closed-door meeting and demanded—if he wanted the heat to go away—that he be the BLM's expert witness supporting the importation of water from the Central Arizona Project. "They ordered me to say under oath that I support the expensive diversion of water so that developers would be justified in pumping the San Pedro dry. I told them I wouldn't do it. I don't care who I work for. I told them it was a disservice to me, to the BLM, to the San Pedro, and the taxpayers of the United States." Word of Lomeli's defiance spread throughout government

circles until it reached the attention of a national whistleblower organization that annually honors workers who risk everything to
speak the truth. For refusing to cower, Lomeli was honored with the
prestigious Cavallo Award, given to those who show "moral courage
in business and government." In the world of whistleblowers, it is the
equivalent of winning the Nobel Prize.

After Lomeli received the honor, Civish was furious. The morning
of Lomeli's return, Civish had a little surprise waiting. As soon as
Lomeli got out of his truck, several law enforcement officers searched
him and his belonging for a firearm, claiming that Lomeli represented a "threat to public safety." Even though he had been warned
to "watch his back" while working in the field. No gun was found,
but the tactic was clearly intended to humiliate the award-winning
hydrologist, to turn him into a pariah, to make him seem dangerous
to his colleagues, to teach him who was boss. The torment did not
stop there. Not long after, Lomeli was handed a reprimand for
allegedly making "demeaning remarks" to a secretary and his supervisors. Defeat the scientist as a means of discrediting the science. It
follows a familiar pattern of attacking the messenger.

Then something unplanned happened that caught Civish and
Juen off guard. In a strange twist, biologist Krueper and Yuncevich
both faced sexual harassment charges from other female workers.
Civish and Juen tried to sweep these cases under the rug, treating
them differently than the charge against Lomeli. Instead of pursuing
the cases with due diligence, Civish awarded Krueper a promotion
and gave Yuncevich a lateral transfer to Idaho.

Meanwhile, Lomeli was stripped entirely of any support staff, was
assigned to a desk job, and ultimately was set up for termination.
With the help of an attorney from the Government Accountability
Project, he filed a formal complaint through the Equal Employment
Opportunity Division of the BLM, which had no choice but to
launch an independent investigation. After the investigation was
completed, the agency refused to publicly release the findings of the
report, but an anonymous source told me that not only was Lomeli
exonerated of most charges (substantiated was the fact that he made
"demeaning remarks" to office workers seeking to alienate him) but
there was evidence of a bureaucratic conspiracy to punish him for
speaking out on behalf of the river. The investigation also corroborated the charges of sexual harassment brought against Krueper and

Yuncevich and the fact that their cases were clearly handled differently than Lomeli's.

"The thing to me that represents the hallmark of Ben's case was the early intervention of Jim Baca. Otherwise he would have been squashed right away and destroyed like so many other people," attorney Ruch says. "Because of Baca's personal interest, suddenly you had a combat biologist with connections. After Babbitt got rid of Baca, the BLM knew it couldn't act immediately to reverse what he had done, so it embarked upon a tactic with Ben that I call torture by a thousand paper cuts."

Former BLM director Baca, who in 1997 was elected mayor of the city of Albuquerque, New Mexico, says he has no doubt that Lomeli was being intimidated by superiors who "have sold their souls." "In terms of public land issues in the West, anytime you stand up to the traditional extractive industries and the newly arrived real estate development industries, you're going to get hit over the head pretty hard, which I know from personal experience," Baca says. "If nobody ever made a stand for what's right, we would be in a headlong race to environmental disaster. For Ben, there never has been an alternative. You either stay firm in your convictions and support your arguments with science, or you remain passive and lose the San Pedro. What would you do?"

Stripped of his professional duties, denied access to the river he loves, humiliated in the office, and enduring stress that had taken a toll on his wife and sons, Lomeli did what he had never thought possible: He resigned. Today he is a highly touted independent hydrologist working for an engineering consulting firm in Rio Rico, not far from the twin towns of Nogales along the U.S.-Mexican border where he was raised. A pending complaint with the BLM seeks disciplinary action against his superiors and compensation for years of abuse. Under normal circumstances, if he were just another government scientist with no supporters, Ben Lomeli would be working at a BLM outpost above the Arctic Circle or pushing papers in Kingman. But you still can find him on summer evenings walking the San Pedro with his two sons and teaching them that the river is a beautiful thing worthy of respect. Ruch believes the outcome of Lomeli's potential trial, if there is no BLM settlement, could be a benchmark. But what Lomeli wants most of all is to speak honestly and frankly, to apply his professional expertise toward protect-

ing the corridor that has attracted life to its banks all the way back
to the time of mammoths.

"To a certain extent Ben has emerged as a success story," Ruch of
PEER says. "His case has energized people and inspired other reformers. Ben made it possible for other ologists to speak out." But it
appears that there will be no cavalry riding over the hill either from
Washington or Phoenix, where the state office of the BLM is based.
Denise Meredith, the new director of the BLM's state office, who followed Rosenkrance, told Ruch before he represented Lomeli at initial hearings about his case, "Don't try and defend him. Save yourself
the embarrassment."

Baca says there is a thin green line that public employees must
walk between doing what's right and becoming martyrs at the ends
of their professional careers. "Ultimately, you can't win if there's no
courage in Washington," he notes. "Babbitt came into office vowing
to bring change and support those in the field making the hard decisions, but he has been a joke. He knows the politics of the San
Pedro, but where is he? It's really too bad because many, many people were counting on him, including me."

In the spring, after the snow melts and heavy rains push water into
the tributaries, swelling the San Pedro over its brim, Lomeli and his
sons make a pilgrimage. Like his father before him, he wants them
to see the force of a wild river before it disappears. At this moment,
the last great free-flowing river in the desert Southwest is in danger
of becoming a ghost stream. Within a mere generation, barring some
miraculous reversal of political winds and downturns in human consumption, the river will dry up. "If you want to get a feel for the
river," Ben Lomeli tells me as we look into Old Mexico, "then you
have to see where it comes from, and where it is going."

POSTSCRIPT: During the summer of 1998, the hydrologist dubbed
"Chicken Little" by his tormenters at the BLM received bittersweet
vindication. The Montreal-based Commission for Environmental
Cooperation, formed as an offshoot of NAFTA, released the findings
of a study showing that excessive ground-water pumping was indeed
killing the San Pedro corridor. "No longer can anyone doubt that
irrigation wells and private water companies serving fast-growing
Sierra Vista and Fort Huachuca are depleting the valley aquifer and
reducing river flows," declared an editorial in the *Arizona Daily Star*.
Predictably, water developers and "property rights" crusaders immediately dismissed the findings as evidence of a conspiracy to promote
one-world government.

Moonwalker

*In any organization there will always be
one person who knows what is going on.
This person must be fired.*

—Conway's Law

CONSIDER THE FOLLOWING proposition for career advancement:
You are an authority in your profession. You have been a dedicated
employee for three decades. You have won your firm wide recognition and awards of commendation from the outside world. Then one
day your boss approaches you with an option: You will be *allowed* to
keep your job, but your staying requires that another colleague, a person whom you've known intimately, toiled side by side with, and admired for much of your adult life, will have to lose her position and
be cast out in the street.

Do you adhere to personal honor, or pursue rational self-interest?
Do you show loyalty to the outfit, or do you quit? Do you remain
silent, accepting the Faustian bargain, or do you ask questions?

In the case of Howard Wilshire, a soils geologist with the U.S. Geological Survey (USGS), such a proposition was presented to him not
long ago in the form of an ultimatum. But here's an added wrinkle:
For him to keep his job, the person who would have faced instant
termination—like him a USGS scientist—happened to be his wife.

After thirty-four years of distinguished government service, Wilshire refused to accept the conditions of continued employment
crudely offered him, so he was fired by the Clinton administration.
The official story line is that his removal was the result of severe budget-cutting measures brought upon his agency by the conservative
Republicans now in control of Congress. However, the individual
expediting the layoff for the Democratic president was Secretary of
the Interior Bruce Babbitt, who oversees a number of federal bureaus, including the USGS.

In this so-called reduction in force, over five hundred government
scientists and dedicated staff members were laid off in the largest purge
in the history of the USGS, an agency founded by army Major John

Wesley Powell. The firings included Wilshire and several prominent scientists in the Geologic Division, a hallowed corps in the USGS involved in such controversial matters as measuring the impacts of off-road vehicles, assessing the value of minerals on federal lands being sought by private industry, and questioning the wisdom of opening the controversial Ward Valley nuclear dump site less than twenty-five miles west of the Colorado River in southern California.

Those in charge of orchestrating the pink-slip distribution, including Babbitt himself, will tell you to this day that the intent was purely benign, but for Wilshire, his colleagues, and environmentalist watchdogs in the desert, there is little doubt that the action was premeditated and motivated by politics. During an interview with the *Los Angeles Times* Wilshire referred to the Geologic Division as "the creative core of the USGS" and added, "We were the bad boys. ... They [the bureaucrats] got their revenge."

Today a silver-haired septuagenarian, Howard Wilshire is fit and Aristotelian in his wanderings. He still manages to load up a daypack with water jugs and set out on ten-mile hikes into the largest complex of sensitive desert in North America. A few weeks after the *Times* interview, he elaborated on why he was fired at his home in northern California as he and his wife, Jane Nielson, prepared to leave for the Mojave Desert, where his brilliant career first blossomed and eventually withered in the political heat. Feeling like a coyote being hassled by bounty hunters, he said of upper-level managers at the USGS, as well as interests connected with the industry that produces off-highway vehicles (OHVs), also known as off-road vehicles (ORVs), "They had been gunning for my hide for years, and finally they got me. But you'd think they could have been a little more coy."

To trace the circumstances that led to his ouster requires a bit of time travel, going back a quarter century to 1969. It was in the California desert at the end of a brutally scorching July day that Wilshire's epiphany—and his collision course with political science—rose with the moon. Three time zones away, midnight was fast approaching Cape Kennedy. Americans coast to coast, including Wilshire, had waited up late for the moment when contact finally arrived from space. Demure but giddy, Walter Cronkite appeared on television screens everywhere with a special bulletin. The aliens, he said in his familiar Orson Wellesian baritone, were landing. When such stellar events monopolize the headlines, we often forget about other quirky little discoveries, even those involving paradigm shifts. On July 20, 1969, at roughly the same moment that Apollo astronauts touched down on the moon, Wilshire was sitting beneath the stars in the Mojave Desert listening to a crackling portable radio. Leaning over to gently scoop a bit of crust from the sun-scoured ground northeast of Los Angeles, the then fortysomething geologist began thinking of possible parallels between his world and the lunar mysteries awaiting Apollo 11.

Over the next several months Wilshire pondered the comparisons often. Eventually he and his colleagues at the USGS offices in Menlo Park came to a remarkable conclusion. They theorized that it might take a million years before the virgin footprints of Neil Armstrong—and the rover tracks to follow—were erased from the face of the moon. If just a few celestial ORVs could chew semipermanent ruts there, Wilshire wondered, what were the ramifications for an earthly "moonscape" such as the Mojave? Because his own field work was concentrated there, Wilshire didn't have to look far to see, or hear, the possibilities. His desert base camps routinely were located in the middle of ORV nirvana. By the late 1960s this ocean of sand, reptiles, prickly pear, scrub, and lightly forested mountain valleys sprawling between southern California and the Great Basin had attracted hundreds of thousands of dune-buggy drivers and Evel Knievel wanna-bes saddled on dirt bikes. They were rapidly overtaking the desert, in the same way that jet-ski riders are congregating on the country's lakes and streams.

Fine-tuning his ears one evening to coyote serenades and the intermittent trills of songbirds, Wilshire was going through his field notes beside a campfire when the stillness was punctured by the throttles of twangy engines racing across the nearby valley bottom. The following morning, his tent and belongings coated in dust, he began noticing things he had previously ignored: obliterated shells of desert tortoises, swaths of crushed vegetation, rodents and snakes and lizards run over by mag wheels, beer cans and rubbish littering the high-dune complexes, and matted soils so snarled by tire grooves that they appeared almost sterile and devoid of life. Wilshire thought of the ecological barrenness of the moon.

"At the time, the popularity of off-road recreational vehicles was burgeoning, and I myself routinely drove off road through the desert in the course of my scientific work. I began to wonder what long-term effects my own activities, and the activities of others, would have on our nation's very sensitive arid lands," he testified two decades later before a congressional subcommittee investigating charges that he had committed scientific treason for taking an interest in the impact of ORVs.

Wilshire's first gesture thirty years ago was to stop driving off road himself. But what commenced as an innocent quest to collect empirical data on foot in epic hikes earned him the title of public enemy number one from the motorcycle arm of what has become today's Wise Use movement.

Though certainly not by his own design, this shy, grandfatherly rock hound has emerged as a scientific folk hero in some circles. With research as his sword, Wilshire has challenged those who would like nothing better than to surrender America's deserts to what noted University of Colorado law professor Charles Wilkinson calls "the lords of yesterday." The description refers to resource extractionists who had free rein over the West and monopolized public lands through corrupt politicians and shortsighted laws that reduced nature to a subordinate value. Wilshire has tried to restore balance to the resource protection versus plundering the earth debate.

"Howard Wilshire is a sage and a visionary," says Jayne Belnap, a veteran desert botanist who has conducted research for both the National Biological Service (now the Biological Services Division of USGS) and the National Park Service in Moab, Utah. "There are many scientists out there who have quietly cheered Howard's efforts and his willingness to take the heat on behalf of the rest of us. Although his years of service with the USGS have given him a tremendous amount of professional standing and respect, he has learned the hard way that the truth doesn't always prevail in the decisionmaking process of politicians, and the good guys rarely win."

Belnap offers this lesson from the well of her own personal experience: "The second you challenge authority as a government scientist, you learn that people will try to make your life pure misery, and you will only survive if your work is impeccable. That's why Howard is still around being a thorn in the side of those who have abused the desert." Pausing for a moment of reflection, she tells me, "The fact of the matter is that if the Wise Users decide to come after you, the first thing they do is label you a monster and attempt to make you seem extreme."

Is Howard Wilshire a radical, a conservative, or both? Decide for yourself.

~

At the Geologic Division of the USGS, a cohort of Wilshire who did not want his name used for fear of losing his job describes the senior scientist this way: "Howard comes from the old school of field men. He was a hotshot when he arrived on board in the late '50s, but so were all of his contemporaries. Like them, he was recruited to work here because the USGS naturally attracted the brightest and the best minds in field geology."

Being a hotshot then had a different connotation than it does now, he continues. "It meant paying your dues and establishing a solid reputation based upon reliable, consistent, peer-reviewed research that tends always to err on the conservative side of speculation. They don't make 'em like Wilshire anymore. Sure, there are plenty of smart young minds in the Survey today, but the new breed of geologists seems content to sit behind a desk running computer-model simulations and making high-tech graphics. They are proficient at virtual geology, but a lot of them understand little about how everything works in a landscape. Some of them seem willing to leave the Survey and sell their services to the highest bidder, which almost always is industry. Howard, on the other hand, well, let's just say he originated from a time when geologists had strong ethics and morals, when they liked nothing better than to get their hands dirty in the field, and quite frankly that's how the USGS got its worldwide reputation."

Born August 19, 1926, Wilshire cut his teeth on the desert floor of the Southwest, and his insights have led to a prolific number of important peer-reviewed scientific articles on the interworkings of dry basins. Where others have been smothered by intense heat or repelled by what they perceive as interminable wastelands, Wilshire has found inspiration. Though it may be taboo to admit it, given that objective science is not supposed to have a heart, Wilshire confesses that he is passionate about his laboratory. He seeks out the soothing, radiant shadows of desert dawns and dusks, the intricate stratigraphy that most folks can't see, and from that view he has taken notice of a specialized, nearly invisible carpet of organic richness.

However, if anyone has the background to appreciate the rewards of tapping America's rich deposits of natural gas, oil, and minerals—

and exploiting them for profit—it is Wilshire. The son of a petroleum geologist who helped map the oil patches of Oklahoma and Texas, he was taught as a boy that leading wildcatters to black gold was a noble profession. "My father believed the pursuit of knowledge was the highest course of action you could take because, in the end, the person with the most knowledge makes the best-informed decisions," he says after a week of field work in the Mojave. "In the oil business, that translated into money. In geology, those with knowledge on their side can avoid costly mistakes, which later come back to haunt them."

Taking a liking to his father's area of expertise, the younger Wilshire was perpetually distracted by the outdoors, so much so that he limped unspectacularly through high school but decided by college at the University of Oklahoma that he too would enter the earth sciences. He later received his Ph.D. from the University of California, Berkeley. It did not take long before he found himself on the fast track to landing a job with the USGS, a lofty institution that epitomized the tradition of scientific virtue in the New World. Before one attempts to draw a conclusion about Wilshire, it is important to understand the USGS mindset. For more than a century the USGS's motto has been "earth science in the public service." The legacy commenced in 1869—exactly a century before the Apollo moon landing—with a different kind of voyage, this one involving a trip down the uncharted Colorado River.

Leading the intrepid float was John Wesley Powell, the one-armed founder of the Survey and a Civil War veteran. Powell envisioned the then ad hoc agency as a distinctly American catalyst for geographical expeditions that would carry knowledge directly back to the president. As the architect of the agency, he insisted that the USGS be a civilian, not a military, force. Paramount among its tasks was completing exhaustive surveys, that is, inventories, of the nation's mineral resources on the frontier. Over the past 130-some years, the USGS role has broadened considerably, becoming synonymous with such tasks as determining where seismic faults lie, charting the magnitude of earthquakes, devising accurate topographical maps, drilling core samples to pinpoint the location of valuable minerals, monitoring geothermal phenomena, and studying the layout of watersheds. Of late it has incorporated a biological component, since geophysical elements of a landscape do not exist in isolation from the life inhabiting them.

The cornerstone of the agency's reliability has been its recruitment of top students from some of the best universities. Reports do not leave the USGS without being meticulously reviewed internally, and the agency has basked in its stuffy image, claiming that it is beyond political manipulation. The late Wallace Stegner articulated Powell's goal for the USGS in his classic work *Beyond the Hundredth Meridian: John Wesley Powell and the Second Opening of the West.* He referred to Powell as "the father of government bureaus far-reaching in their own effects and influential in the models they provided for other and later government agencies."

In Stegner's mind, Powell spoke to the notion of resource sustainability long before it would be popularized by Aldo Leopold; he set out to shape the USGS as a totemic overseer of the vault of resource wealth. Stegner wrote,

> His understanding of the West was not built on a dream or on the characteristic visions of his time, for on one side he was as practical as a plane table. The mythologies of the [1870s] and [1880s] had as little hold on him as the mythological tales of Hope or Paiute: he knew all about the human habit of referring sense impressions to wrong causes and without verification. His faith in science was a faith in the ultimate ability of men to isolate true—that is, verifiable—causes for phenomena. Also, he knew a good deal about the human habit of distorting facts for personal gain, and he fought western land interests and their political hatchet men for years, out of no motive but to see truth and science triumph and the greatest good come to the greatest number over the greatest period of time, according to the American gospels.

During this century it has been a foregone conclusion that a scientist with a Ph.D. and USGS credentials can command tremendous prestige in the private sector. And yet a large percentage of geologists hired into the USGS fraternity (for years it has been dominated by Caucasian males) remain there over the entire span of their careers. The joke often bandied about is that USGS scientists are as old as the fossils and ancient rocks they study. The ages of its corps of stodgy senior scientists range from forty to seventy-five. The senior corps is the primary reason why the USGS has unrivaled stature in the federal government. Wilshire himself has a kind, professorial air. "I've known Howard for many years as a geologist who has brought great insight to the ecology of the desert," attests Elden Hughes, a respected activist with the Sierra Club who was instrumental in helping to shepherd the recent California Desert Protection Act through Congress. "People admire Howard because he's a superb scientist, yes, but he's also quite adept at boiling down difficult scientific concepts into a language the lay public can understand. He calls things as they are."

This translation of facts, however, has met with disdain from several land management agencies because the more complex the problems facing the desert are, the easier it is to fool the public with deception and subterfuge, Hughes says. "Howard, in my opinion, has been a very important figure in bringing public attention to the very real threats confronting the Mojave and other desert lands." Even among the grand old deans who built the agency into an institution of respect, Wilshire commands admiration.

~

The late writer Edward Abbey, an agitator famous for being blunt, said that wilderness lands in the United States need neither a rational defense nor an economic justification to exist. They just need more defenders willing to heed a call to action. For Abbey, the spirit of those words assumed its profoundest meaning in the desert. Abbey was, after all, an admirer of Wilshire's meticulous work, and his friends say that work informed the writer's elegantly crafted tributes to the Southwest.

Reviled throughout the ages as godforsaken hellholes by some, embraced by others, deserts are the most abused land forms in our hemisphere. Just look at where the highest concentrations of endangered, threatened, and rare species of North America are clustered. The statistics point to a region stretching east to west from the Pacific Ocean to the Colorado Plateau and north to south from southern Idaho into Mexican Sonora. It's little wonder that these sinkholes of biodiversity are so prolific in number.

In one hundred years, America's deserts have been trampled incessantly by cattle hooves and ORVs, bombed and nuked by the military, disemboweled by the mining industry, drained by water developers, inundated by residential subdivisions, and, most recently in the 1990s, targeted by politicians as the ultimate graveyard for nuclear waste. This cumulative malevolent treatment troubled Abbey, who, though he was an agnostic, could not refrain from pointing out that in holy scripture it was to *a wilderness in the desert* that Moses, the keeper of the Ten Commandments, was exiled. Cast out to inhabit the infernal wasteland that many humans say is without beauty or redeeming value, Moses ultimately encountered the divine. The metaphor was not lost on Abbey, whose body rests today in an unmarked desert grave, nor does it escape Wilshire, who by the early 1970s realized that the Mojave had sustained the trenchant scars of a war zone.

Forgotten under the ORV tracks, military exercises, strip-mining, and expanding industrial infrastructure were shell-shocked plant and animal dwellers clinging to a thin layer of cryptogamic soil. Kindred counterparts to old-growth forests, cryptogamic communities are delicately stitched together by a specialized afghan of undisturbed crust. Although it measures only a few inches high, the fabric of fungi, mosses, lichens, and bacteria is a vital nutrient provider from which vascular plants and animal species reap sustenance. Connecting the blooming paloverde, yucca, mesquite, creosote bush, black brush, cacti, and burro-weed are rare perennial grasses. The cryptogamic layer is the biological foundation—the building block, if you will—that allows specialized organisms to survive in a hostile extreme realm. A single tire track can upset the balance because it loosens the matting of the desert floor and opens the door for the erosive forces of water and wind to take their toll. "Below that thin layer comprising the delicate organism known as soil is a planet as lifeless as the moon," Wilshire reflects, quoting G. V. Jacks and R. O. Whyte's 1939 book *Vanishing Lands*.

In 1942, within months of the United States entering World War II against the Nazis, a plan was hatched to fight General Erwin Rommel's panzer divisions in the deserts of North Africa. To prepare for the engagement, George Patton took his soldiers to train on 11.5 million acres of the Mojave. Like the tracks on the moon, the ruts made by Patton's tanks still are vivid, and so is the dearth of vegetation. Over a span of four decades, Wilshire watched the localized disintegration of the desert's basic floral species, including ocotillo *(Fouquieria splendens),* paloverde *(Cercidium floridum),* Joshua tree *(Yucca brevifolia),* and several species of cacti succulents that also are in serious decline.

"We already know the consequences of leaving disturbed land to natural revegetation. It doesn't work," Wilshire says. "I know because

I've seen it. In 1942, a number of three-hundred-meter strafing runs were pounded into the Mojave Mountains across the Colorado River from Needles, California, for aerial gunnery practice. Today the Joshua trees and ocotillo have not recovered and numbers of creosote bush are much reduced. This is just one place of many where we have turned the ecology into a moonscape."

Thirty years after Patton's departure, Wilshire looked at the blight exacted by the military and went back to the USGS with a proposal to study the effects of another army gathering in the sands—recreational ORVs. Although military exercises have the excuse of being an essential part of national defense, the federal Bureau of Land Management's (BLM) condoning of weekend warriors on motorcycles and three- and four-wheelers applies to much larger areas, and ostensibly, under national environmental laws, the impacts must be addressed through proper management.

Unfortunately, many BLM managers have abrogated their responsibilities in the face of fierce political pressure by giving the ORV industry free reign over much of the desert. And the ORV users may soon seize upon more of the landscape if the Republican-controlled Congress exercises its will to weaken environmental laws and move public lands into private ownership. Wilshire was among the first scientists who saw the Mojave as something other than a sacrifice area. "With the lunar experience in mind and having viewed the tracks from Patton's combat maneuvers, I proposed to the USGS that I undertake a study of the nature and life expectancy of human impacts on the desert," he says. "I honestly had no agenda going into it, because it seemed the agencies already had an agenda of their own."

The genesis of Wilshire's research happened to coincide with controversy. The BLM was in the process of reviewing environmental impacts relating to the mother of all ORV events—the famous Barstow–to–Las Vegas motorcycle race. The motor marathon attracted thousands of competitors and spectators who lined the course in the eastern Mojave. The scene was a carnival of swirling dirt and exhaust. After seven years of watching the event grow out of control, conservationists led by the Sierra Club demanded that the BLM come up with an environmental impact statement. Overlooking evidence that would support cancellation of the event, the BLM permitted the 1974 race to be run. Wilshire and a USGS colleague, John

Nakata, set out to assess and report on the physical impacts following the race. The methodology for the study was straightforward, and it exposed, for the first time, tangible problems with ORVs.

Despite assertions from race officials that riders adhered to the planned course and caused minimal earth disturbance, Wilshire discovered that veering off course was, in fact, rampant. He documented mile upon mile of shredded soil and plants as well as the effects of spinning tires that sent plumes of dust clouds into the air over eastern California and southern Nevada. According to his ongoing analysis, for every mile of travel on desert soil, a two-wheeled motorcycle with knobby or paddle-type tires displaces three-quarters of a ton of soil. The displacement by four-wheel-drive vehicles is even greater—between 3.3 and fifty tons of soil over every mile. All told, the three thousand riders who entered the Barstow-to-Vegas off-road race in 1974 kicked up an estimated six hundred tons of airborne particulates. The manmade dustbowl was damning enough, but the worst news for the ORV industry was yet to come.

Biologists assessing the postrace effects documented major declines in the numbers of resident mammals and reptiles. Among some species, the local populations were eight times less abundant than usual a full year after the race ended. Similar studies showed that ORVs drove away birds, trampled amphibians and reptiles, and caused harm to the sensitive hearing of small mammals. Perhaps most profound was the impact on desert tortoises—but more on that later.

Wilshire's findings and those of other field biologists were published in scientific journals. Representatives of the ORV industry were incensed and vigorously denied reports of the impacts of ORV use. Attempts at spin control made waves not only within the USGS and BLM but among certain congressmen whose districts included portions of California and Nevada, where the race generated millions of dollars in tourism as well as votes. Wilshire surfaced as a primary target when he proposed broader management scrutiny of ORVs, and a campaign was set in motion to discredit his work.

The matter was so controversial that then USGS National Director Vincent McKelvey in Virginia personally reviewed and approved the manuscript of Wilshire's report on the Barstow-to-Vegas race. Other studies on this subject and related issues ensued, building a compelling body of evidence. But it became clear that the findings of damaging effects and Wilshire's documentation that such effects would be very long lasting still were not sufficient to alter prosaic management policies on public lands that dated back to the age of manifest destiny. "The agencies chose to listen to the politicians rather than the scientists," Wilshire says. "That's when environmentalists, through no encouragement by us, picked up the ball."

The evidence may not have spurred the BLM to act, but there was no doubt that it would sway a judge or jurors in a court of law. Confronting the prospect of a lawsuit from the Sierra Club, which it almost certainly would lose, based upon violations of the National Environmental Policy Act, the BLM reluctantly halted the Barstow-to-Vegas race beginning in 1975. Almost overnight Wilshire was vilified by motorcycle lobbyists who blamed him for having the event shut down. Although he is hardly naive about the machinations of politics, Wilshire was stunned when he got wind that a bureaucratic deal apparently had been cut whereby the Barstow-to-Vegas race would be canceled in exchange for the BLM keeping open large spans of the desert as ORV "play areas"—even though agency officials knew many species would be harmed. The amount of acreage the BLM planned to make available to ORV users in the West dwarfed the huge amount already open to such use in the Mojave.

Wilshire says his own vaunted USGS collaborated with the BLM to downplay his findings because the data had implications for the management of other federal lands, including those in nearby national forests, where the ORV industry also wielded significant political sway. In an abrupt move, USGS officials decided internally, and against Wilshire's protests, that the agency would no longer commit resources to chronicling further ORV impacts. "The data that emerged from our research was compelling, too compelling to be ignored," Wilshire says. "I realized then that I had a difficult choice to make."

Without recompense from the government, Wilshire continued his studies of desert soils on weekends, and he spent hundreds of hours walking across the Mojave trying to better understand the complex nature of desert ecosystems and cryptogamic soils. The irony is that although the USGS chose to ignore his data, independent scientists praised him. Over the past twenty years he has written many peer-reviewed articles on the impacts of ORVs that have appeared in prestigious scientific journals, including the seminal report titled "Impacts and Management of Off-Road Vehicles: Report of the Committee on Environment and Policy" that was delivered to the Geological Society of America by Wilshire and seven other authors. Around the world, this paper is cited regularly as the definitive, irrefutable benchmark on the subject.

Not surprisingly, Wilshire's work and hundreds of independent studies by other scientists that have chronicled damage by ORVS are casually dismissed on flimsy evidence provided by the ORV industry. This situation is akin to what the tobacco industry did in denying the negative health effects of cigarette smoking and the addictiveness of nicotine. In fact, several studies paid for by motorcycle and ORV groups claim that damage to the environment has been exaggerated.

In the 1990s, the same members of Congress who receive hefty campaign contributions from the groups that have underwritten these reports use them as the basis for opening up more BLM lands to ORVs and expanded resource extraction. "Our congressional allies are now in control," boasts David Hess, chairman of the California Desert Coalition, a front for forty thousand ORV enthusiasts pushing for access to the last stable bastions of desert flora and fauna. Some GOP politicians and motorcycle lobbyists insist that the real villains are backpackers and horse packers—an assertion that Wilshire roundly disputes as preposterous.

"It is true that hikers and equestrians damage the natural landscape, but motorized vehicles have a much greater capability to cover ground," Wilshire wrote in an article for the ecological journal *Wild Earth*.

> The least surface disturbance is caused when vehicles are driven in a straight line on a dry surface. Under these conditions, typical medium-sized motorcycles impact the equivalent of one acre in 20 miles, and typical four-wheel-drive vehicles and three-wheel ORVs with balloon tires impact one acre in about six miles. By comparison, a typical hiker impacts one acre in about 40 miles. Measurements have not been made for modern large motorcycles and four-wheel [ORVs], which have become increasingly popular. The degree of impact is greatly exacerbated by the capability, especially of motorcycles, to negotiate steep, difficult terrain—precisely the land most susceptible to soil degradation and ensuring accelerated erosion. This is also the land most desired by many off-roaders because it is challenging.

As scientist David Sheridan, who wrote an authoritative report on ORVs for the California Council on Environmental Quality, stated insouciantly, "Even St. Francis of Assisi [the patron saint of wildlife] couldn't ride a motorcycle up a hill without damaging it."

~

The motorcycle and ORV lobby, flush with funding from Japanese-owned vehicle manufacturers, begs to disagree. A key strategist, Clark Collins, is executive director of the Blue Ribbon Coalition. The powerful advocate of off-road-vehicle use in the desert is also a vocal opponent of federal wilderness designation. The group has six thousand individual members and between five hundred and six hundred member organizations, including the 225,000-member American Motorcyclist Association (AMA). Collins has no love for Howard Wilshire.

"He's a real anti-OHV fanatic," Collins opines with resignation in his voice. "Both the Blue Ribbon Coalition and the AMA would say, 'Don't listen to him.' His research doesn't hold up, and he's clearly an activist with a mission." I ask Collins if the Blue Ribbon Coalition and the AMA possess the political clout, as Wilshire suggests, to get his work discredited and besmirch his reputation with the agency.

"We would certainly try. I'd like to think we have that kind of political influence. I do not see how political pressure could undermine the credibility of legitimate research."

To prove that his organization promotes Wise Use of public lands, Collins faxes me a copy of the coalition's Recreation Code of Ethics, which is accompanied by the motto, "Preserving our natural resources FOR the public instead of FROM the public." The credo includes the following points:

1. I will respect the rights of all recreationists to enjoy the beauty of the outdoors. I will respect public and private property.
2. I will park considerately, taking no more space than needed, without blocking other vehicles and without impeding access to trails.
3. I will keep to the right when meeting another recreationist. I will yield the right-of-way to traffic moving uphill.
4. I will slow down and use caution when approaching or over-taking another.
5. I will respect designated areas, trail-use signs, and established trails.

6. When stopping I will not block the trail.
7. I will not disturb wildlife. I will avoid areas posted for the protection of feeding wildlife.
8. I will pack out everything I packed in and will not litter.
9. I realize that my destination objective and travel speed should be determined by my equipment, ability, the terrain, weather, and the traffic on the trail. In case of an emergency, I will volunteer assistance.
10. I will not interfere with or harass others. I recognize that people judge all trail users by my actions.
11. Motorized trail users should pull off the trail and stop their engines when encountering horseback riders. It is also a good idea to take off your helmet and greet the riders.

Wilshire says the mantra looks impressive in writing, but in application it reads like a David Letterman Top 11 list of ways the OHV industry can co-opt federal land management agencies in order to abuse resources. He does not believe the breadth of abuse is necessarily deliberate, but in sensitive environments it cannot be avoided. Because of the sheer volume of ORV enthusiasts, the desert is being overwhelmed. And it takes only a handful of people riding "out of bounds" to wreak havoc. At the local district level, where both the BLM and the Forest Service have oversight responsibilities for ORVs, critics say that agency managers routinely underfund enforcement budgets. Furthermore, since federal agencies often rely upon supplemental funding provided by ORV-friendly states, local communities, and user groups, there is an implicit expectation of quid pro quo arrangements. Such arrangements provide a convenient excuse for land managers to look the other way as well as an opportunity to quietly accommodate ORV users, who often hold cultural sway in the communities where agency managers live. Another problem is that the agencies routinely transfer field personnel from district to district so that no one person is able to gauge profound environmental impacts over a length of time. With each successive wave of new managers, the effects increase incrementally.

Wilshire notes that there are also aesthetic impacts, which science has been unable to statistically quantify very well. Contrary to the aim of the top item on the Blue Ribbon Coalition's list, "I will respect the rights of all recreationists to enjoy the beauty of the outdoors," he says ORV users monopolize the landscape. Noise carries over long distances, puncturing the serenity and sense of solitude, which are rapidly becoming artifacts in the modern world. Lanes of motorized-bike paths slicing through the soil and brush detract from the tranquil virgin openness. Rooster tails of dust clouds sail across the backcountry like flagships of civilization that defeat the very essence of the desert's appeal. Can't there be a few places left where artificial forces do not conquer the setting?

Collins is convinced that Wilshire's emotional reflections have muddied his data and that by approaching the desert with a subjective bias he tarnishes his credibility. He characterizes Wilshire as a "crackpot" and a hired gun for environmentalists. He points to a 1995 General Accounting Office (GAO) investigation into the impacts of ORVs initiated by U.S. Representative Bruce Vento (D–Minnesota). The independent review was prompted by concerns that agencies were not fully complying with rules to regulate ORV use following the issuance of Executive Orders 11644 and 11989 in the 1970s. A report titled "Information on the Use and Impact of Off-Highway Vehicles" examined ORV use at eight locations on BLM and Forest Service lands in the West. "Everyone knows Congressman Vento is not a friend of ORVs," Collins says. "When GAO was putting together its analysis, Howard Wilshire took them out to show investigators the damage. Then they came and met with us and said after their tour with Wilshire that they wondered, 'Okay, what's the problem?' He was talking about things that have happened long in the past. I got a lot of satisfaction knowing they thought he was a nut case."

GAO investigators offered a different perspective in their report:

At all locations, off-highway vehicle use was being monitored casually rather than systematically, adverse effects were seldom being documented, and needed corrective actions remained to be prioritized. Although citations were being written for violations at all locations, enforcement was hampered by confusion over where and when restrictions applied." They added, "External and internal reviews have identified weaknesses in BLM's and the Forest Service's implementation of the executive orders on OHVs. In 1979, the Council on Environmental Quality concluded, in a report entitled "Off-road Vehicles on Public Land," that both BLM and the Forest Service have been slow to address damage from OHVs to soils, vegetation, wildlife, and watershed resources.

ORV lobbying groups insist that conditions have dramatically improved. Yet, the GAO report goes on, "Similarly, the Department of the Interior's Inspector General, in a 1991 report on BLM's activities, and the Forest Service, in a 1986 review of its OHV program and in an ongoing review, disclosed various deficiencies, such as incomplete inventories of routes open and closed to OHV use, inadequate mapping and posting of OHV routes, untimely resolution of conflicts between OHV users and other users of the lands, and limited monitoring of the effects of OHV use on natural and cultural resources."

~

The desert tortoise may well be the poster child for the kind of abuses inflicted upon the desert by ORVs. Not even St. Francis has been able to shield *Gopherus agassizii* from annihilation on much of the 6.2 million acres of critical habitat found in California, Nevada, and Utah. The Mojave stands out.

For travelers driving between Los Angeles and Las Vegas, Interstate 15 carves a rattlesnake pathway across the heart of the Mojave. From the ground in springtime, as far as the eye can see, the impression is one of interminable virgin wilderness coated by a bristly surface of Joshua trees, scrub, wildflowers, yucca, and cacti. Paradise, if you're a desert tortoise.

But when Kirk Waln, a herpetologist with the U.S. Fish and Wildlife Service, gazes out upon the same landscape, there is another view: "Don't be fooled by perception, because it could be a mirage." Much of the Mojave is not the pristine environment the American public thinks it is, yet this commonly held notion is one reason why desert tortoises—the senior citizens of the Southwest—are currently in a biological free fall over much of their northern geographical range. "I believe most folks would be surprised by the reality," Waln says. "When you're in the sky flying over in a plane you begin to understand how pervasive man's influence has been on the desert, and it's not a sight that bodes well for the tortoise. The desert isn't like the backcountry in other regions where habitat can bounce back. The effects here are cumulative and long term. Day in and day out, I see a steady stream of proposals to develop another part of the Mojave, and the sum of it all leads to one conclusion—habitat loss for the tortoise."

The tortoise is an indicator species that we can use to assess the overall health of the California desert, says Brian Huse, the Pacific regional representative for the National Parks and Conservation Association. "The precarious status of the tortoise warrants our attention now. If we allow the tortoise's name to be added to the list of extinct species, that in a real way indicates our willingness to accept the extinction of the rich ecology of the desert itself. Is this what we want? I think most people would say no."

Earlier in this century, settlers in southern California remarked in their journals how abundant the shelled reptiles were. Historically, desert tortoises lived from the northern end of the Mojave where it meets the Sierra Nevada range southward into the Colorado Desert of southern California, then eastward into Nevada, northern Arizona, and southwestern Utah. The animal is also found in the Sonoran Desert of Arizona and north-central Mexico.

Tortoises are the old salts of desert ecosystems. Their evolutionary roots go back perhaps three hundred million years to the beginning of the dinosaur age. Capable of reaching ages of over eighty years, they spend the winter months between November and March in hibernation. Being largely herbivorous, they exist on a diet of native desert grasses, herbaceous perennials, and forbs. They also rely upon burrows and a variety of scrub—typically creosote bush, Mojave yucca, burro-weed, and black brush—to shelter them from the sun and predators. To drink free water, they dig depressions in the soil and wait for rain to fill the natural bowls. Primitive-looking, with elephantine limbs and claws used for digging, they have proved their adeptness at surviving eons' worth of predators, climate changes, floods, drought, and disease, but the battery of impacts heaped upon them by humans over the past hundred years has threatened their continued persistence.

One major front of biological vulnerability is that by being slow to reach sexual maturity, tortoises do not breed and produce young until they enter their teens, and the offspring that do hatch from clutches of eggs suffer mortality rates as high as 99 percent. In some years predators such as badgers, kit foxes, coyotes, Gila monsters, and ravens take most of the eggs before they hatch. Few youngsters make it to adulthood, meaning that removing breeding adults from a population can cause ripple effects that are not recognized for dozens of years.

Although they are not large creatures, fleet of foot, or especially colorful, tortoises have an undeniable magnetic appeal to humans. For the first six to seven decades of this century, it was a well-known practice for Angelenos and dwellers of other desert cities to drive into the Mojave for a day of recreation and, if they came upon a tortoise, to take it home with them. A startling statistic is that federal wildlife officials now believe there are as many desert tortoises in the back yards of southern California residents as exist in the western Mojave. Hundreds of thousands are thought to be in captivity, but biologists say that many are actually "ticking time bombs" because they carry parasites or diseases that they acquired in civilization—afflictions such as upper respiratory disease that can decimate wild tortoise populations when captive tortoises are returned to their former homes. That, however, is just one threat among many that has killed thousands upon thousands of the animals in the last few years alone. One thought is that the tortoises are becoming more stressed by changes in their environment, and thus they are more open to catching diseases.

During the 1920s a study completed by field researchers turned up estimates of one thousand tortoises per square mile in parts of the western Mojave where today there are just twenty to fifty tortoises per square mile. In other areas of the western Mojave, populations have either vanished or been significantly reduced by urban and agricultural development. In 1990, due to dwindling numbers, accelerated destruction of habitat, poaching, and disease, desert tortoises in the Mojave were formally listed by the Fish and Wildlife Service as a threatened species under provisions of the Endangered Species Act. (A similar listing for tortoises was sought in Arizona's Sonoran Desert, but it was then deemed unwarranted.) The announcement in the Mojave created a flare-up in a contentious debate over how the desert should best be managed. For the moment, it appears that the Wise Use movement has gained the upper hand in a political tug-of-war.

Under terms of the Desert Tortoise (Mojave and Colorado Desert Populations) Recovery Plan approved by government agencies in four states, the key to maintaining a stable population of tortoises appears to be minimizing vehicular access, minimizing earth disturbance, and restricting human access. Four years after the tortoise was listed and a few months before the California Desert Protection Act was signed into law, the Fish and Wildlife Service published the recovery plan to serve as a blueprint for protecting tortoises on over six million acres of critical habitat containing the Mojave and Colorado Desert populations. The vast majority of acreage falls under the jurisdiction of the BLM, National Park Service, Department of Defense, and private property owners.

A reptile with a life span longer than most humans, the tortoise has the most to lose from efforts to open more of the Mojave to motorized recreation. Kristin Berry, a scientist with the USGS Biological Services Division, says a suite of impacts and budget cuts that have crippled research is closing in on the tortoise in both the West and East Mojave, where the animal may be making its final stand. Berry, whose data formed the basis for protecting the tortoise through the Endangered Species Act, considers herself a "combat biologist" who has been endlessly hounded by scientists hired by the ORV industry who try to discredit her work.

With scores of scientific papers to her credit and twenty-five years' worth of field experience, Berry is recognized as a leading national authority on tortoises. But she says that declining research budgets have gutted her monitoring programs and reduced her funding levels to less than she had in 1983. The net result is that politicians have effectively eliminated the ability of scientists to track emerging threats to tortoises and have ensured that management decisions will be made in the darkness of uncertainty. A haunting reminder, she says, is that the last time the scientific community was hamstrung by budget cuts—during the Reagan era—the fatal disease that attacks the upper respiratory tracts of tortoises first emerged but was not immediately detected because the field biologists were not there to identify it. Thousands upon thousands of tortoises perished.

Maybe the most disturbing summary of tortoise declines was made by law professor Charles Wilkinson, the foremost expert on western resource issues, who gleaned his conclusions from hundreds of scientific documents. In 1993 Wilkinson delivered an address titled "Translators for Those Who Cannot Speak: Scientists, Historians, Poets and the West's Endangered Animals" to a gathering at the Cinnabar Symposium, an annual conference put on by the Montana-based Cinnabar Foundation, which has been a major force in promoting discussion of western land issues. Wilkinson didn't mention Wilshire and Berry by name, but he praised the work of certain

brave government scientists and made no bones about describing
the enemy of the desert tortoise:

> The work of 300 million years of deep time has been nearly undone
> in a click of a moment. As with the salmon, the bulk of the decima-
> tion has been due to habitat destruction. Some has resulted from
> overgrazing of stock and from Las Vegas subdivisions built upon crit-
> ical habitat. The worst damage has been done by off-road vehicles.
> Most of the tortoise's diet is vegetative matter—desert wildflowers,
> the pads of the prickly pear, cactus flowers, and grasses—but the
> rampaging ORVs have rampantly destroyed the vegetation. The
> wheels break down the crytobiotic crust on the surface of the land,
> compacting it directly under the wheels and throwing it open for
> wind erosion next to the open wound of the track; this crust of sand
> is where new plants root.
>
> The ORV operators also kill some tortoises directly by running
> them over and sometimes shooting them. Their reckless, cross-
> country marauding drives out other animals who depend on the
> vegetation. Among other things this means that there is less animal
> scat and carrion, other sources of food for the tortoise. The ORV
> operators have been the main cause of another phenomenon. During
> the last several years, the Mojave has seen an explosion in the raven
> population. Ravens feed on turtle eggs and on young turtles after
> they are hatched. The cause of the influx of ravens, which is of criti-
> cal dimensions, is believed to be an upswing in the amount of human
> garbage in the desert.

Bruce Stein, a naturalist with the Nature Conservancy who studied plant communities in the Mojave, says that ORVs threaten
dozens of plant and animal species found nowhere else in the world.
In fact, according to the U.S. Fish and Wildlife Service, at least two
dozen native plant species and a dozen additional insects, reptiles,
amphibians, and rodents have been exterminated from high-use
ORV areas, particularly those in sand dunes.

Chris Schenk, a nationally recognized eolian geologist with the
USGS in Denver, has been studying sand-dune complexes for fifteen
years, particularly massifs of sand piled in the Southwest. Schenk believes that sand dunes are among the least understood ecosystems in
the world. And where there is a lack of understanding, there is an
invitation to abuse. Desert dunescapes historically have been maligned as worthless pieces of real estate. The worst abusers have been

ORV users and the military. Private landowners and developers complain about roving sand drifts overtaking their property, yet they fail to realize that their own activities may be hastening the process of desertification.

Although the classic high-activity dune fields are dynamic and ever changing, they represent only a small portion of the total sandscape, Schenk says. Dunes are actually anchored by inactive "sand sheets" on their perimeters. Not only are sand sheets the most productive places for wildlife and endemic plants but the vegetation, when left undisturbed, anchors the sand in place and keeps the desertification from spreading. When new roads and ORV paths, water development, or livestock grazing disrupt the sand sheets, the wind causes the dune complex to expand.

"Dunes play an important role because they are good indicators of global climate change," says Andrew Valdez, who was a staff geologist at Great Sand Dunes National Park in Colorado when I spoke with him. "During wet periods, sand is immobile, while during droughts it becomes active. If the planet warms as computer models predict, we might be able to decipher how other ecosystems will be affected by watching the behavior of dunes." One could easily argue that because dunes have taken a serious beating, the ecosystems around them have suffered an identical fate.

Scientists studying the Imperial and Kelso Dunes in Southern California have stated conclusively that over the years motorized vehicles have had a detrimental impact on flora and fauna. In defense of the BLM, which has management responsibilities for many of the largest dune fields in the West, it should be said that ORV users have seized de facto primacy by transforming their numbers into a powerful lobbying machine that federal land managers cannot ignore. Furthermore, environmentalists have a poor record of defending land managers who lock horns with the ORV industry and suffer the consequences.

Collins of the Blue Ribbon Coalition refers to environmental organizations such as the Sierra Club, Wilderness Society, and National Audubon Society as "hate groups." The Blue Ribbon Coalition has been instrumental in pressuring the BLM to refrain from protecting desert sand dunes as federal wilderness areas where motorized recreation is prohibited. Portraying scientists such as Howard Wilshire as the enemy, they depict dunes as nothing more than sandboxes for adults to blaze across on their dirt bikes. The notion of the desert having a scientific purpose is treated as anathema.

When the Biological Services Division of the USGS published its impressive compendium on imperiled species in a report titled "Our Living Resources," it said this about the tortoise: "The U.S. government treats the desert tortoise as an indicator or umbrella species to measure the health and well being of the ecosystems it inhabits. ... In summary, tortoise populations occurring in relatively undisturbed and remote areas with little vehicular access and low human visitation generally were stable, or exhibited lower rates of decline than tortoise populations in areas with high levels of disturbance, high vehicular access, and high human visitation."

Kristin Berry is philosophical. "When you tell people that if they want a species to be around for their grandchildren to see, it requires making decisions that look beyond their own lifetime, their eyes glaze over," she says. "We just don't think the same way the Europeans do about their cathedrals and art treasures. They take care of them from one generation to the next because stewardship is a tradition. When we think about our own treasures, we too have to consider that we are making decisions for posterity. We need to remind ourselves periodically that we are passing on something special that cannot be replaced.

"In the next ten years we will continue to observe populations going downward, but what we do over that time will determine the fate of the tortoise," Berry adds. "The recovery plan outlines the slow, steady progress we have to make. However, to get to a point where we can confidently say the tortoise is out of danger could take two hundred or three hundred years, which is a period of time that most people cannot relate to." Charles Wilkinson noted that "for three hundred million years, the desert tortoise was not hampered by its silence. Now is the time when we must translate for the tortoise." Howard Wilshire, like Berry, has been thrust into the role of translator.

Today, the ORV industry stands behind contentions that the body of scientific evidence is weak and disparate in documenting impacts. However, more than nine hundred articles have been published in scientific journals and other media confirming the destruction. "It can no longer be denied that vehicular use of natural terrain is severely damaging to soil, vegetation and wild animals," Wilshire wrote in an article that appeared in *Wild Earth*. "The land damages also are harmful to humans. Although ORV users sometimes form coalitions with [livestock] graziers and miners to protect their access to public lands, ORV use generally is incompatible with grazing, and mining interests commonly associate ORVs with trespass and vandalism."

Wilshire won no new friends in the Wise Use movement when he referred to cattle as "desert locusts." Cows are a serious concern, says the Sierra Club's Elden Hughes, mentioning efforts by U.S. Senator Pete Domenici of New Mexico that would give cattle primacy on federal BLM lands. "If in Texas it takes two acres of grass to sustain a cow and calf and in Georgia it takes about one acre, what do you think it takes in the Mojave?" Hughes asks. "On the very best allotment, it is three hundred acres per cow, and on the worst allotment it is three thousand acres. On the average it is six hundred, and there are thousands of cows denuding the desert of its grass. It was hell figuring out how many acres per cow because the BLM wouldn't tell us. They knew to the cow how many are supposed to be out there, but they won't say it because of political pressure. Those animals should not be there and Wilshire has been one who is not afraid to say so."

When Hughes, chairman of the Sierra Club's California Desert Committee, journeyed to Washington, D.C., in 1994 to watch Bill Clinton ink the epic California Desert Protection Act, he brought with him a goodwill ambassador that crawled across the president's desk—a young desert tortoise named Scotty. Hughes wanted Clinton to realize what was at stake.

"It took us 120 years to get into this mess of tortoise declines. It might take us a decade or two or much longer to get out, if we get out," he says. "Do the agencies have the power to get the job done? Sure. But do they have the will? I'm not so sure. When it comes down to actual implementation of the tortoise recovery plan, science is not leading the way. Because of politics and economic arguments, we are negotiating things that should not be negotiable. Science has already determined the minimum size of acceptable preserve areas. We as a conservation community need to make sure the welfare of the tortoise is put first on public lands where it hasn't been in the past."

He blames the BLM for developing a cozy relationship with resource developers. Ed Lorentzen, the threatened and endangered species coordinator in the BLM's California state office, says there is a difference of opinion over how imperiled the tortoise is. "There are different perspectives among different agency biologists," he says from his office in Sacramento. "In some areas the populations are doing well, and in other areas not as well." Lorentzen claims the magnitude of threats to the tortoise has been somewhat exaggerated, and he cites a scientific paper written by R. Bruce Bury and Paul Stephen Corn for the Biological Services Division of the USGS that questioned the data used by Berry. Calling the assertions that led to listing of the species speculative, they are skeptical of Berry's claims that habitat fragmentation has relegated tortoises to only island populations that exist at reduced densities.

"We don't have universal agreement on the methodology that was used to estimate densities and distribution of the species," Lorentzen says. "The paper written by Bury and Corn raises questions about the actual number of tortoises out there—that there might be more than previously thought." Lorentzen's comments are puzzling because a group of prominent government and independent scientists reviewed the body of evidence, looking at tortoise numbers—including the information from Bury and Corn—and concluded that large reserves were necessary to save the Mojave population. Bury and Corn say it is misleading for the BLM to use their paper as an excuse to promote desert development and expanded ORV use.

Responding to Lorentzen's assertions, Berry says the best gauges of tortoise health are the tortoises themselves. Go to some remote corners of the desert where they once thrived, and today the animals aren't there. Rough estimates are that there are anywhere from 200,000 to two million tortoises across the entire tortoise range—a fraction of that number in the Mojave—but as the Fish and Wildlife Service's Waln says, numbers reflect nothing but a snapshot in time. What's important is tracking the trends. Even the most optimistic scientists must admit that given growing population pressures, forecasts do not predict increases in tortoise densities. He says taking a Pollyannaish approach to tortoise conservation is dangerous.

"Some people said the same thing about the passenger pigeon before its numbers crashed," Waln says. "As it stands right now, the track record of agencies in managing for species viability over the long term has been poor to mixed. It's just the nature of how bureaucracies work and think. They operate on short-term funding and management cycles when conserving species requires taking a much broader view."

∽

Once upon a time, D. H. Lawrence looked toward the sky and had this thought: "When we describe the moon as dead, we are describing the deadness in ourselves. When we find space so hideously void, we are describing our own unbearable emptiness." Lawrence might have been sitting in the Mojave sipping refreshments with Wilshire.

Under reasonable circumstances, Wilshire's altruism and commitment to compiling a better baseline of scientific knowledge might have been appreciated, but in 1980 Ronald Reagan was elected president, and soon thereafter James Gaius Watt took the helm as secretary of the interior, commanding both the USGS and the BLM. Wilshire's rising status as a guru on ORV use had long infuriated lobbyists representing manufacturers of all-terrain vehicles, and they saw him as a major obstacle to their having free reign in the desert sands. "I was subsequently made aware that throughout the period preceding the 1980 change of administration, complaints had been registered against me by other government agencies," Wilshire told a congressional subcommittee convened to investigate charges that Reagan and Bush political appointees were seeking his ouster in violation of the Hatch Act, which protects public employees against intimidation. "Inquiries were made to senior USGS scientists by the director's office about how I presented my study results publicly."

Prior to the arrival of Reagan, the director of the USGS was satisfied that Wilshire neither misrepresented the facts nor embarrassed the agency, and no effort was made to muzzle him. "But this all changed," Wilshire told the congressional subcommittee, "with the change of administration in 1980, and my activities both on and off the job came under increasing attack from within and without the USGS administration. The challenges on my credibility have continued to this day."

In the worldview of Secretary of the Interior Watt, a born-again Christian, the Almighty created the world for humans to exploit, and it is the task of red-blooded American capitalists to give places like the Mojave a meaningful purpose. Watt swung open the gates of the desert to the mining industry, ranchers, and ORV groups, which had contributed generously to the election campaigns of Reagan and his political allies. Government statistics show that during the 1980s the number of desert species decimated by development, overgrazing of the range by livestock, and motorized recreation ballooned.

Prior to taking his cabinet post, Watt had been a founder of and prominent attorney with the Mountain States Legal Foundation, a bulwark for the Sagebrush Rebellion that favors the turning over of public BLM lands to states, which then could sell them off to private interests. Some have said the Sagebrush Rebellion was rekindled by the 1994 landslide at the polls that gave Republicans control of Congress.

Currently, such land-grab ambitions are revealed almost daily in proposals that would make 270 million acres of BLM lands—including most of the desert lands—available to the highest bidder. Prior to his forced resignation, Watt created a lasting legacy—that of intimidating government scientists who refused to slant field data to substantiate his political edicts. Allies of Wilshire believe that certain individuals with loose connections to the nascent Wise Use movement were lying in wait for the opportunity to flex their political muscle and destroy Wilshire's reputation once and for all.

Their first attempt came in 1987, when a friend at the USGS handed Wilshire a copy of a draft plan that called for expanding ORV use in the Eldorado National Forest, which borders the Mojave. Knowing of his expertise in desert soils, a local conservation group called Friends Aware of Wildlife Needs (FAWN) invited Wilshire to tour the Eldorado's Rock Creek area, where ORV use was proposed and endorsed by the Forest Service. Wilshire agreed to spend one Sunday afternoon on his own time at his own expense walking the Eldorado, but he made it clear he was not acting on behalf of the USGS. Besides, the USGS had no interest in documenting the negative geophysical effects of ORVS, so one would think Wilshire's actions represented no extracurricular conflict with his job.

Later, on plain white paper with no mention of his professional standing, he penned a letter to the Forest Service commenting on ways that the plan could be improved to protect natural resources. Slightly more than a year after Wilshire's comments as a private citizen were submitted to the Forest Service, Dallas Peck, the new director of the USGS, informed the senior scientist that he had violated the sacred USGS Organic Act and several federal conflict-of-interest regulations. The reason: Wilshire's observations had turned up in a lawsuit filed by FAWN to stop ORV use, and he had been subpoenaed to serve as an expert witness in the case.

To Peck and his successors at USGS, Wilshire's observations constituted grounds for a letter of reprimand that was placed in his personnel file, forced leave without pay, and possible dismissal. The disciplinary action had a unique source, for it started with a U.S. attorney who represented the Forest Service against litigation brought by FAWN. The lawyer accused Wilshire of, among other things, "breaching his duty of loyalty to the United States." Apparently, under the Reagan-Bush administration, exercising one's First Amendment rights as a private citizen—a liberty normally championed by the ORV industry in actions designed to overturn environmental regulations—was deemed acceptable only if it supported industry-backed positions. Otherwise, it was considered sedition.

"Ed Hastey, the BLM's California director, made multiple complaints to USGS headquarters to get me silenced, and the Department of Interior solicitor's office wanted my scalp," Wilshire says. "There's also the American Motorcyclist Association, the Blue Ribbon Coalition, the Justice Department, the Forest Service, and, of course, the upper management of the USGS."

Wilshire believes the multipronged attack proves that the government's real sympathies dwell not in the camp of science, as Vice President Al Gore and Secretary of the Interior Bruce Babbitt now assert, but with those trying to subvert it. Wilshire and Babbitt would clash again over the secretary's support of a plan to bury nuclear waste near the Colorado River.

As a result of the FAWN case, Wilshire found himself the target of Wise Use groups; he also came under fire from government attorneys raising questions about his "reputation." This move was perplexing, because even as the government pushed forward to silence him, Wilshire had already received, or been nominated for, the highest honors of his profession in government service. His field work earned him the Department of the Interior's prestigious Meritorious Service Award, and his peers nominated him for the Secretary [of the Interior's] Stewardship Award. However, Peck informed Wilshire that his nomination for the Stewardship Award was being withheld because of Wilshire's indirect association with environmentalists. "There didn't seem to be any one person orchestrating the trouble, and I can't name definite names of people in either the

USGS or industry that tried to destroy me, but it was coming from somewhere," Wilshire says. He points to hypocrisy: "When a USGS scientist presents and interprets research results [i.e., acts as an expert witness] in furtherance of the government's position, which helps developers, it is characterized by USGS as 'objective scientific support,' but when the same scientist presents and interprets research results that happen to contradict the government's and industry's position, it suddenly becomes prohibited advocacy. Surely such an official policy does more to undermine the integrity and impartiality of the USGS than anything any individual scientist could ever say or do."

Attorney Jeffrey Ross of the law firm Kathryn Burkett Dickson in San Francisco was hired to represent Wilshire after the federal government tried to ruin him. Ross noted that the attempted censuring of his client holds potential ramifications for millions of government employees, regardless of whether Democrats or Republicans are in power. The hidden meaning of the USGS positions is that a government agency, at its own discretion, can decide to arbitrarily discipline its employees for pursuing any activity outside the office with which a particular supervisor or politically connected lobbyist does not agree. Coincidentally, the desert environment that was so integral to Wilshire's day job also happened to be his passion on days off, Ross argued, pointing to persecution initiated by then USGS director Peck that continued throughout the 1990s. Was the USGS asserting that it could regulate what an employee did in his time off simply because someone did not agree with his activities?

"During his distinguished career, Dr. Wilshire has conducted original research in numerous substantive areas and has published more than [150] articles and books, many of them relating to the use and impacts of off-road vehicles," Ross wrote in a letter to USGS officials. "Never, in his 30-year career, has the scientific objectivity of his work ever been questioned, by anyone. Indeed, the USGS has expressly approved every one of his publications as satisfying the USGS's standards of objectivity and scientific merit. Needless to say, under these circumstances, Dr. Wilshire finds it both highly insulting and deeply disturbing that a non-scientist, wholly unfamiliar with any of his work or publications, would suggest in a written reprimand to be placed in Dr. Wilshire's file, that he is incapable of performing his professional responsibilities in an objective and competent manner."

In the FAWN matter, the "nonscientist" who had it in for Wilshire was Charles Kay, the Department of the Interior's principal deputy assistant secretary for policy, budget, and administration and a Republican political appointee. Kay dispatched a shrill letter to Wilshire stating essentially that he was guilty of violating the agency's Organic Act because he had conducted an official "survey" of the Eldorado without permission or cause from the USGS, and that he had engaged in the appearance of professional conflict of interest.

In Kay's opinion, which was written as if it might have been penned by an ORV lobbying group, Wilshire deserved to be disciplined because he "vociferously advocates a position that ORV use on arid public natural lands always is detrimental, and that Federal policy should be changed to reflect [his] conclusion." Here, Kay erroneously accused Wilshire of being in league with conservationists who support the complete banning of ORVs from public land. In fact, several of Wilshire's articles have been greeted with chagrin by some environmental groups because they actually have suggested methods by which ORV use and desert protection can coexist. "As [Kay's] assertion makes clear," Wilshire's lawyer Ross pointed out, "it is Mr. Kay—not Dr. Wilshire—who confuses science with advocacy. It is true that Dr. Wilshire's work, as well as the work of other scientists, has established that the use of ORVs on arid natural lands (whether public or private) causes certain identifiable forms of environmental damage, and that this damage is observable even where ORV use is relatively light. This is not, however, a 'position' which Dr. Wilshire 'advocates'; it is simply an undeniable fact, which Dr. Wilshire and others have responsibly reported in the scientific literature."

Ross noted that Wilshire's studies merely demonstrate that the arid landscape, like the moon, requires surprisingly long periods to heal from human disturbance. "Dr. Wilshire's contributions to this field have helped to shape policies of land use in arid areas, as well as to stimulate and focus further research," Ross added in a letter. "Dr. Wilshire's investigations of the effects of human activity on arid lands and his documentation of the sensitivity of the arid environment are a significant benefit to society as well as to science." Attorneys for the Government Accountability Project (GAP), a nonprofit organization dedicated to defending whistleblowers, elevated the case to national attention. In spite of attempts by the USGS to characterize Wilshire's plight as an "internal matter," GAP brought the case to the attention of congressmen overseeing the House Committee on Government

Operations (a committee that, certainly not coincidentally, has been abolished by the Republican-controlled Congress).

Thomas Devine, a lead GAP attorney, testified before Democrat Tom Lantos, a congressman from California who chaired the House Employment and Housing Subcommittee. "I think that the duty of loyalty issue [being discussed] today is very much on point here," Devine said. "The question is, loyalty to whom? Agencies equate loyalty to the United States with loyalty to the bureaucracy. That is wrong. Government workers are public servants. It is patriotic to challenge agencies, to uncover others' safety threats or lawlessness. Knowledgeable government scientists are a public resource, not bureaucratic property."

The subcommittee received an astounding seventy-five signed letters of support for Wilshire from his distinguished scientific colleagues at USGS, but some authors asked that their names not be released to their own agency for fear they would be summarily punished too. "During the past 20 years or so, we have witnessed a steadily increasing insinuation of the political process into ever lower levels of the Federal bureaucracy," one scientist wrote in discussing a document called "Administrative Digest 993," a USGS directive sent to all USGS scientists ordering them not to get involved with conservation groups outside the office. The directive was issued in large part as a means of justifying the disciplinary action against Wilshire and his alleged violations of the Organic Act. It warned USGS employees that "particular care should be taken by all employees to adhere to these restrictions in dealing with nonprofit organizations, such as the Sierra Club."

"AD 993 goes a long way toward furthering this process [politicizing science], and re-establishing an up-to-date, sophisticated form of patronage as a requirement of survival," another USGS employee observed. "If the purpose of AD 993 is to muzzle dissent, including technical dissent, it ranks as a neatly crafted document that will surely inhibit free and open discussion of a host of issues of concern." Added yet another senior scientist, "The present ground swell of resentment by senior scientists of the USGS against present management, from top to bottom, is unprecedented in my 37 years in the organization. Many of us feel that the Survey is rapidly becoming a remnant of the once proud and powerful scientific organization that is being crippled by the albatross of administration, whose personnel has increased by orders of magnitude during the last 15 years, while the scientific working staff has decreased. I hope that these sentiments will alert you to the fact that this outpouring of letters is not the usual gripe session, but an indication that something is rotten and rusted."

Wilshire ultimately was exonerated of all ethics charges, and his bosses at the USGS were verbally scolded by Congress for the tactics they had used against him in the ORV controversy. But Michael McCloskey, chairman of the Sierra Club, believes the Wilshire case points to a far deeper and more troublesome problem that has only worsened in the 1990s and involves a variety of issues. When USGS employees commit themselves to "science in the public service," it doesn't mean science to justify development at any cost but science to make informed decisions on whether development is in the public interest and not solely for the benefit of a narrow private interest, McCloskey told me.

"No one is arguing that federal employees ought to be able to operate publicly in contradiction to their official responsibilities, but an excessive anxiety about controlling such matters raises questions about the even-handedness of the effort," he later testified on Capitol Hill. "It strikes us that the record in this regard has been one-sided, and that indeed there is reason to believe that a double standard has been used. There seems to be an assumption that the U.S. Geological Survey, for instance, is supposed to help foster commercial mineral development, but yet involvement with environmental protection falls into a zone of impermissible conduct. While the director [of USGS] claims to want to protect the Survey's neutrality, the pattern of activity in reality suggests extreme bias."

McCloskey's next observation has a direct bearing on the proposed nuclear-waste dump in the Mojave's Ward Valley:

> For a long time the Survey has allowed USGS employees to tell the owner of a mineral property the unpublished results of its geological investigations and thus cause a mine to be opened, but apparently they cannot tell an environmental group anything about how a mine there might harm the environment. Unpublished maps can be given to miners, but apparently not to environmentalists. Unpublished data can be given oil companies in exchange for access to their drill core data, but apparently such information would not be given to environmentalists worried about pressure to drill in the Arctic [National]

Wildlife Refuge, not only because they don't have anything of value to exchange, but because they are on a 'dangerous group' list. Data developed with public funds by the USGS may cast doubt on the potential for oil development in the Arctic [National] Wildlife Refuge, but it is not available to environmentalists. Apparently USGS employees can join a party of oil company geologists on a prospecting trip through the Grand Canyon National Park, but they could not join environmentalists and advise them on a trip to look at the oil potential in the Arctic [National] Wildlife Refuge.

Finally, McCloskey noted, "Apparently USGS employees can visit coal mines to familiarize operators with new geological data, but cannot meet with environmentalists worried about reclamation problems. In fact, all sorts of arrangements exist with the USGS to promote interchanges with industry, as if the Survey is designed to be handmaid to it. ... One is left to conclude that neutrality and objectivity are not the real issues here, but rather that of maintaining a trusted clientele relationship with industry."

In the same episode that gave rise to the persecution of Wilshire, newspapers carried reports that a state wildlife biologist who testified that motorcycles would do serious harm to deer winter range in California's Eldorado National Forest was being maligned by his superiors. At the same time a woman who headed the local environmental group was fired from her job in a local restaurant after making public comments against ORVs, which is evidence of a climate of intimidation, McCloskey said.

The backroom style of the Reagan '80s is again de rigueur in Washington under a Democratic regime. Near the end of his congressional testimony in Washington, Wilshire was asked by U.S. Representative Lantos to assess the climate of his current working environment, and Wilshire said that politically motivated suppression, turned into an art form by James Watt, is still rampant.

"What you are saying, Dr. Wilshire, is that James Watt's legacy of suppressing employee dissent has not been mitigated in recent years?" Lantos asked curiously.

"That is correct," Wilshire responded. "It goes farther. And I believe this is the result of—actually it was put so beautifully by a 90-year-old former Survey member who said that we're still having our buttons pushed by the apparatchiks [a Russian term meaning minor Communist party functionaries] of the [Reagan] administration."

"Do you think, Dr. Wilshire, that the perception that the U.S. Geological Survey is trying to muzzle those employees who do not toe the agency line may in itself lead scientific organizations or the public to question the Survey's objectivity?" Lantos asked.

"I believe it already has," he said.

"Dr. Wilshire, how are we to have any meaningful debate on such issues as offshore oil drilling, nuclear waste disposal, global warming or, indeed, recreational use of off-road vehicles, if Federal employees run the risk of having their loyalty called into question simply because they happen to disagree with any administration's environmental or anti-environmental policies?"

Responding with the bluntness of Edward Abbey, Wilshire said, "That is why we need your help."

Today there's a grave being built below the surface of the Mojave Desert in a place called Ward Valley. The crypt will hold nuclear waste dumped straight into unlined trenches with no containment structure. Some argue that the facility may serve the dual tragic purpose of being a monument to human folly and an ecological tombstone.

Ward Valley is bounded by the famous Route 66 and Interstate 40 to the north and west. To the south is Interstate 10, connecting Phoenix with Los Angeles. To the east, demarcating the boundary between Arizona and California, is the Colorado River on the southward course that takes it to the Sea of Cortez after leaving the Grand Canyon and Lake Mead. The river passes alongside the Forest Mohave Indian Reservation, the town of Needles, California, the Chemeheuvi Valley Indian Reservation and the Colorado River Indian Tribes Reservation. It slices through the desert less than twenty-two miles from the proposed Ward Valley Radioactive Waste Facility.

By the time the dump is completed, it will hold "low-level" nuclear waste from reactors and other facilities for a quarter of a million years, and that's what troubles Howard Wilshire because nothing that humans have made has ever lasted a fraction that long, except maybe ruts on the moon. Wilshire, who has studied the geology of Ward Valley for two decades, believes the risks of a disaster lurking down the road are higher than proponents are willing to admit. "They are using a method that is illegal in many states and not used in any civilized country that I know of," he says. "Billions of dollars are at stake, and they loom as profits to the company operating the plant and, ultimately, in the cleanup costs that would be pushed off on the public."

His concerns focus on the possibility of radioactive agents reaching groundwater, or worse, leaking into the Colorado River, whose water is pumped to Los Angeles, sprayed across crops, and used by Native Americans living in the area. "The shallow graves at Ward Valley could accept as much as 700 pounds of plutonium, one of the most poisonous substances on earth with a half-life of 24,000 years. The assumption that we can isolate such radioactive materials from the biosphere reflects an ignorance of Earth history," wrote Philip Klasky, a member of the Ward Valley Coalition formed to fight the facility with a large assemblage of conservationists, sportsmen, Native Americans, and scientists. "It takes equal parts science and fantasy to envision what would be needed to guard substances that remain deadly beyond collective memory," he added. "Radionuclides such as plutonium, produced only in the last 50 years, will pose a threat to life for the next 12,000 human generations through periods of dramatic climatic and geologic changes and social and political upheaval. The level of witness and responsibility needed to safeguard these poisons through time requires a commitment unprecedented in human history."

Not long ago a federal district court judge removed legal hurdles allowing the private firm US Ecology to operate the facility once federal land administered by the BLM in the Mojave is deeded to the state of California by Secretary of the Interior Bruce Babbitt. The plan calls for US Ecology to receive four shipments of radioactive waste daily—from nuclear power stations, government agencies, medical institutions, academic institutions, and industrial firms—for thirty years; then the facility would be closed and oversight would rest with the state of California. The waste would be put in containers and buried under soil in unlined trenches thirty-five feet deep.

Almost eight hundred individuals submitted oral and written comments on the proposal, with the majority opposing the facility. Some of them noted how uncanny it has been that during the twentieth century, whenever planners choose to build waste facilities that are undesirable to wealthy urban and suburban residents, the plants often end up next to Indian reservations or in poor minority communities. This trend has spawned the study of "environmental justice," that is, the new grassroots movement in America that aims to stop landfills, incinerators, and waste facilities from being constructed in or near poor and minority neighborhoods.

"The Federal Land Policy and Management Act requires the Interior Secretary to ensure that federal lands transferred to other parties are properly used and protect the public interest. [The state of] California, on the other hand, is responsible for licensing and regulating the Ward Valley disposal facility according to the state's laws and regulations that are intended to adequately protect public health and safety. Where the respective responsibilities of Interior and the state overlap, if at all, has been an uncertain matter," wrote investigators from the General Accounting Office.

Where they overlap poignantly is that over the years, under both Republican and Democratic administrations in the White House, the BLM has transferred several tracts of desert land in the West to accommodate risky industrial uses, including several garbage dumps. There is a saying that "the BLM never met an industrial activity it didn't like." In this instance, California claims it has authority to issue an operating permit in accordance with the Atomic Energy Act of 1954, but given the scrutiny brought to bear by Wilshire and others, the Department of the Interior has second-guessed its involvement through the land transfer.

Both the state and US Ecology have sued the Department of the Interior to force it to transfer the land. "The task of developing new facilities for disposing of commercially generated low-level radioactive waste has proven more difficult than imagined when Congress gave states this responsibility 17 years ago," General Accounting Office investigators wrote in a 1997 report. "Because no state has yet developed a new facility the actions in a leading state, like California, are viewed as an indicator of whether the current national disposal policy can be successful."

According to the chairman and chief executive officer of US Ecology, Jack K. Lemley, the initial decision by California and Congress to permit the dump through a compact agreement with three other states shows that "the Ward Valley facility is fully protective of public health and the environment." That may be so, or it may not be, because a few days after a court ruling cleared the way for it to proceed, the USGS disclosed that high levels of radioactive tritium and carbon-14 were present in desert sands near another storage facility at Beatty, Nevada. Tritium, in fact, was found just ten feet above the water table.

"Before the discovery of contamination at Beatty, supporters of the proposed Ward Valley dump touted Beatty as analogous to Ward Valley, because both are located in arid lands and share similar geologic settings,"Wilshire wrote in a guest editorial published March 6, 1996, in the *San Francisco Chronicle*. "Supporters argued that Beatty, which was open for 30 years, provided proof that radioactive waste dumped at Ward Valley would not contaminate Ward Valley's ground water or the nearby Colorado River. Relying on Beatty and so-called 'state-of-the-art' computer models, they claimed that radioactive contaminants must move slowly, if at all, in desert soils."

Those claims were not only refuted by the leak; it also showed that waste can move laterally and rapidly through the soil, which confirmed Wilshire's fears. US Ecology operates four other low-level radioactive waste-disposal sites, and small amounts of radioactivity have been detected in groundwater at facilities in Sheffield, Illinois, and Maxey Flats, Kentucky. Both US Ecology and the state of California counter that the odds of nuclear material escaping at Ward Valley are very remote. In a1993 report, Wilshire and two USGS colleagues disagreed with the optimistic claims by federal and state government officials who touted the dump's alleged safeguards, some of them based on the company's commitment to provide voluntary monitoring. Furthermore, Wilshire has raised concerns about the potential threat to groundwater beneath Ward Valley, which was not even seriously considered in the initial studies used to approve the site.

All along, Wilshire made it clear that his critique of the Ward Valley site was being done as a private citizen, but his superiors at USGS were not happy with the level of his outspokenness and let it be known. As a result of a growing public outcry, Secretary of the Interior Babbitt asked a National Academy of Sciences (NAS) panel to review the merits of the dissenting scientists' research, concluding that inferior data had been used and additional tests were needed. Strangely, the NAS panel was never told about the leak at Beatty even though USGS researcher David Prudic, assigned basically to rubber-stamp approval, had had evidence of contamination for nearly a year prior to publication of the NAS's final report, which gave the project a lukewarm endorsement, but with the caveat that

further information was needed—again, without the data from
Beatty.

"Prudic's data showed that radioactive material had migrated several hundred feet from the dump to areas outside the Beatty facility
and through the soil to 357 feet below ground—just above the
groundwater table," Wilshire says. "Despite his newly obtained facts,
Prudic prepared a report for the NAS panel concluding that water
had migrated no more than a few feet into the ground at Beatty and
that no water would reach the water table either at Beatty or Ward
Valley for tens of thousands of years." It should be noted that two
members of the panel dissented with the final report, saying it is impossible to determine, for certain, that contaminants would not reach
groundwater. As Wilshire points out, the conclusions of the NAS majority are based on an assumption that current climatic and geologic
conditions will not change, that earthquake heaves will not open new
subterranean fissures, that torrential rainfall and thus percolation fifty,
one hundred, or two hundred years in the future will not significantly
increase despite events such as El Niño and global warming. "[The
waste dump's advocates] call us radical," Wilshire says, "but I believe
that we are being conservative. I feel an obligation to the voices that
are not being heard in this debate. We are just not willing to leave the
legacy of a poisoned earth to future generations."

Another of the voices not heard has been that of the desert tortoise. Making matters worse is the fact that Ward Valley is home to
some of the best habitat and one of the most stable populations of
tortoises left in the Mojave. Subpopulations elsewhere have been
fragmented by development. Rather than vigorously protecting the
habitat as demanded by law under the Endangered Species Act, the
U.S. Fish and Wildlife Service and the BLM have been pressured to
exempt the area to make way for nuclear-waste storage. Supporting
the habitat exemption was Congressmen Jerry Lewis, a California
Republican who has tried to abolish the newly created Mojave
Desert Preserve, proposed for national park status. Instead, Lewis
wants it to revert to the authority of the BLM so that it can be
opened to ORV use. An ideological compatriot of Lewis was the late
erstwhile singer Sonny Bono, unbelievably a California Republican
congressman from Palm Springs, who said society should continue to
mine and scrape the deserts for all they are worth. Bono's solution for
coping with the Endangered Species Act and the tortoise typified his
grasp of environmental issues. "Give them all a designated area and

then blow it up. I think we should put all of the endangered species in one place," he said, "and then blow 'em all up."

Wilshire has observed that this Bonoism is, on a piecemeal basis, more or less coming to pass. The Mojave, one of the greatest desert ecosystems on earth, has suffered a slow fracturing that will not ease anytime soon. ORVs, though significant enough by themselves, are joined by incursions of oil pipelines, military war games, megascale mines, and giant underground tunnels built to hold the nation's nuclear waste. Among the weekend motorhead crowd, serious discussion has even surfaced of bringing back the Barstow-to-Vegas race.

Here, in the debate over ecology and economics, Babbitt appeared to side with the latter on Ward Valley, suggesting that the NAS report "provides a qualified clean bill of health in relation to concerns about the site." Yet, in an abrupt turnaround because of Wilshire's vigilance and that of other scientific dissidents, the Clinton administration agreed to conduct long-overdue safety tests and to amend an admittedly deficient environmental impact statement. "There is a right way and a wrong way to make important public decisions," acknowledged Deputy Secretary of the Interior John Garamendi. "The right way is to seek, collect, and analyze pertinent scientific information before making a decision." In an internal Department of the Interior memo condemned by U.S. Senator Frank Murkowski (R-Alaska), a shameless proponent of the dump, Garamendi called California Governor Pete Wilson, who is championing the dump, "the venal toady of special interests."

"Public lands are owned by all of us," Wilshire says. "Merely because a company wishes to make a profit does not mean that public lands should be destroyed." Will the Mojave survive? Will this be the end of the line after three hundred million years for the desert tortoise because our society abandons it when protection is no longer convenient? Furthermore, is the proud legacy of the USGS coming to a close as it shuns one of its brightest and most dedicated scientists?

David Love, the USGS veteran hailed worldwide for his surface and substrata mapping, was the subject of author John McPhee's acclaimed book *Rising from the Plains* about the geology of the West. Love also was an influential force behind a public effort in the early 1990s to stop the government from burying nuclear waste in his home state of Wyoming. Love's outspoken stand did not tarnish his credibility one bit but rather brought reason into the debate. He knows the conscious decision Wilshire made to protect the public interest, and he dismisses assertions made by certain political appointees at USGS and by industry representatives that Wilshire has compromised his integrity.

"He is known for being independent, extremely competent, and very honest," says Love. "Whether Wilshire's contributions are appreciated and recognized depends upon with whom you are conversing. Those who disagree with him try to put him down and discredit him, but they are wrong. Dead wrong. He knows what he is talking about, but are we listening to him?"

~

Postscript: Again, suppose you are confronted with the dilemma handed to Wilshire. You can keep your job, but it means that your wife must lose hers. After thirty-four years of distinguished service with the USGS, Wilshire refused to make the choice his agency crudely handed him, so he was fired. "When they told me my only option for staying on was to bump my wife, it so pissed me off because it was such a transparent gimmick to get rid of me," he says. "I had made it clear that even though I held rank, I would not bump anyone younger than me or earlier in their career. I have had my opportunity with this agency; it is an agency I am quite fond of, but I also believe in the younger generation of geologists."

Because of his decision, his wife, Jane Nielson, a respected expert on desert geology, was able to keep her job while Wilshire lost his. So imagine that the same kind of treatment has just been meted out to you. Do you remain silent, accepting the Faustian bargain, or do you ask questions? Wilshire asked questions. After he cleaned out his office and desk, he went to the USGS administrative offices and searched through the documentation that justified his superiors' decision. The paper trail showed a deliberate attempt at manipulation. Just before Wilshire was planning to go public with the revelation and the news reached the Department of the Interior, ever worried about damage control of public perceptions, he suddenly received word that management had reconsidered its proposal. He could have his job back. He accepted, but then retired because of the hostile work environment.

"I've been doing a lot of thinking about how the agency needs to change in order to rescue itself from oblivion," he tells me. " I believe in the purpose of the USGS, but those working to suppress science may yet kill it. I haven't given up hope, and I realize that I do not need to work for the organization in order to receive satisfaction from trying to save it."

Once upon a time, Howard Wilshire imagined spending the rest of his days as a civil servant who would have to be carried dead from his office, like so many of the other valuable fossils in his rank. These days he spends an unexpectedly early retirement wandering the Mojave. "When the stakes are so high for so many people, it is appropriate that we take the time needed to act carefully," he says. "We are fortunate that maybe science still has a chance to win out over politics, but I'm not so sure it will."

It seems ironic and telling that *Homo sapiens* would have to travel to the moon to grasp the delicacy of their own biosphere. Whenever there is a big white glow over the cooling arid sands, Wilshire remembers the evening when aliens landed and humans were able to trumpet their progress to the heavens. We went all that way, and we still treat the desert as if it were the moon.

In the mind of David Love, Wilshire's departure is America's loss. A rock hound with the highest intentions, Wilshire looked to the heavens for answers but had his feet planted firmly on terra firma.

Epilogue
Defending the Defenders

THERE ARE MANY CITIZENS in America today who believe our system of government is at a crucial crossroads and that the future of democracy itself may hang in the balance. They see corrupt, intransigent politicians holding public office, public servants who have sold their souls to private interests, and a general atmosphere of quickly eroding free speech.

Although a groundswell of grassroots efforts has begun to reform the way government does business, few efforts have managed to actually penetrate the bureaucratic armor of resistance. Three public interest groups that have had many successes are Public Employees for Environmental Responsibility (PEER), Forest Service Employees for Environmental Ethics (FSEEE), and the granddaddy of them all, the Government Accountability Project (GAP).

For workers who suffer suppression in the workplace, this question is often asked: "Where can they take their concerns?" Below are three outlets dedicated to preserving and protecting the First Amendment right to free speech and other constitutional liberties under the law. Here in their own words are leaders of the three whistleblower organizations explaining how agencies can be more accountable to the environment and American citizens.

Protecting Employees Who Protect the Environment: The PEER Method
Jeffrey Ruch, executive director, Public Employees for Environmental Responsibility

After reading these stories of bureaucratic courage, the question naturally arises as to whether these struggles are inevitable; if so, then any employee should expect to pay a steep price for breaking ranks. The main goal of Public Employees for Environmental Responsibility is to establish that the exhibition of integrity within public resource agencies does not require professional suicide.

We at PEER truly believe that in unity there is strength. Isolation of the whistleblower is generally the principal tactic of the miscreant bureaucracy precisely because that isolation makes it relatively easy to kill the messenger. It is much harder to kill the messenger if the messenger is not alone. And if the identity of the messenger is unknown, then all that is left is the message—which is precisely where the debate should be. That is exactly why PEER serves as a vehicle for anonymous activism, so that concerned professionals can police the conduct of their own agencies without being victimized in the process.

No "Down Side" for Malfeasance

Public land management and pollution control agencies in this country are politically controlled as a function of our system of government. Even on issues that are supposed to be decided exclusively on scientific or technical grounds, the insulation from political influence is usually tissue-thin. PEER believes that the same political forces that pervert agency performance can be used to reform it.

One pattern that emerges from a review of environmental whistleblower stories is that the manager who tries to suppress truth or to violate the law almost never suffers negative career consequences. On the contrary, the harassers are usually rewarded or promoted because they defended the bureaucracy against the threat of internal dissent. PEER is dedicated to reversing this pattern by using the media and access to political decisionmakers to create a down side for agency misconduct. When PEER files a criminal complaint against an agency manager for filing a false official certification over the objections of his technical staff whose data was changed or disregarded, then PEER raises the prospect of direct personal liability for that manager. Like any schoolyard bully, if the manager believes that he will have his hand slapped (or chopped off) for antienvironmental malfeasance, then the manager will back down and allow his or her employees to do their jobs without interference.

Transparency

Public employees are the best, and often the most credible, witnesses of the actual internal operations of their agencies. PEER tries to harness the credibility, expertise, and brain power of the public's servants to "out" the agency's true record, placing that record in the sunshine for all to see. If any order or memo issued within an agency can end up on the front page of the newspaper the next day without agency management knowing how it got there, that fact alone changes how the agency does business. The reality of this constant internal scrutiny prevents an agency from even attempting to erect a false front.

PEER regards conscientious public employees as vital public resources whose survival depends upon a healthy ecosystem. A healthy agency ecosystem requires transparency. Only the employees themselves can dispel the bureaucratic murkiness so that the public at large can actually track how the public's business is being done. Without this public knowledge, individual whistleblowers will not be able to spread the word beyond their own cubicles.

Freedom of Association

What surprises most whistleblowers is the discovery that they are not alone. Most conscientious public employees do not spend their time "networking" or maneuvering for position within the agency, so their support structure is often limited. The function of PEER is to provide a support structure for employees who are trying to serve the public and to provide a safe vehicle for employees so that they can continue to serve the public when their agency does not. Because conscientious employees are vital public resources, each time a whistleblower is forced to resign the public suffers an irreplaceable loss. PEER seeks to couple the employee's First Amendment freedom of speech with the same First Amendment's freedom of association in order to prevent those losses.

Many of the employees profiled in this important volume are pioneers who have cleared the path for others behind them. PEER's job is to make sure the path these courageous individuals have blazed remains open.

Contact PEER at :
2001 S Street, NW, Suite 570
Washington, DC 20009
Telephone: (202) 265-PEER (7337)
E-mail: info@peer.org
Web site: http://www.peer.org

Reforming Government from the Inside out:
Forest Service Employees for Environmental Ethics
Matt Rasmussen, editor, the Inner Voice

Back in 1989, a remarkable movement blossomed within the ranks of an entrenched federal bureaucracy. A handful of U.S. Forest Service resource professionals joined forces to proclaim loudly and publicly that something had gone terribly wrong with their agency. They said the Forest Service had betrayed the public trust by favoring big-industry timber interests over the interests of the public at large. They said the agency had lost credibility as a responsible steward of the land. Above all, they said things must change. Then they set out to do just that, from the inside out.

Things have indeed changed since Jeff DeBonis, a timber-sale planner on Oregon's Willamette National Forest, founded the Association of Forest Service Employees for Environmental Ethics (AFSEEE). The amount of timber harvested from national forests has dropped from an annual peak of twelve billion board feet in the 1980s to less than four billion board feet today. In many circles it has become acceptable—even fashionable—to talk about ending road subsidies for timber companies, or halting commercial timber harvesting on public lands altogether.

What prompted this change? Ascribing credit is a tricky game. Certainly whistleblowers such as DeBonis can claim a good portion of the credit, as can the thousands of Forest Service employees who have joined or supported AFSEEE (now FSEEE) since 1989. But so can activists outside the agency who used the courts to drag the Forest Service—often kicking and screaming—into a new era. And so can millions of Americans across the country who directly or indirectly let it be known that they were not happy with the way the so-called experts were managing their lands. In fact, change came from an intricate symbiosis of mutually supporting forces.

Change continues today, and it's sorely needed. Forest Service managers still persecute whistleblowers for committing what the agency's old guard considers the ultimate sin: publicly airing dirty laundry. The agency still operates under the terms of an arcane budgetary system that encourages timber sales even when they lose millions of taxpayer dollars. The Forest Service has a long way to go before it can truly claim to follow a sustainable-resource ethic. Many critics of the agency wonder whether it will ever get there. In the old days, the Forest Service maintained a haughty independence from the rough-and-tumble pressures of politics—an independence it enjoyed because of its reputation of expertise. That independence is gone, leaving the Forest Service vulnerable to intense pressure from Congress and the presidency. Forces across the political spectrum believe the time has come to scrap the Forest Service altogether and start anew.

For those who are dedicated to bringing sustainable management to national forests, the demise of the Forest Service is a dangerous notion. Whatever happens to the agency in coming years, one thing is certain—some entity will be in charge of managing the 191 million acres in the national forest system. Perhaps that entity will be an enlightened new agency that works for ecologically responsible management. Or perhaps it will be a hodgepodge of local interests that share the exploitative vision of powerful conservative legislators such as Larry Craig of Idaho or Alaska's Don Young. Given the wild swings of political fortune, that's probably not a dice roll that conservationists want to encourage.

Meanwhile, the Forest Service, imperfect as it is, remains in place, and the battle over the agency's soul continues. There is plenty of reason for optimism. Managers with values forged in the dark days of unchallenged exploitation are fading away. Hundreds of bright employees are sprinkled throughout the agency, working quietly—and not so quietly—for reform. Perhaps even more important, a rough consensus seems to be forming among society at large that there are attributes of the national forests that are more valuable than timber sales, grazing permits, and road networks.

The work of reform-minded Forest Service employees, including those who are members of FSEEE and those featured in this book, is a crucial element in the effort to change the agency. But true change also comes from the outside—from broad societal shifts that manifest themselves at the ballot box, in letters to editors, and at town hall meetings. Surveys show that most Americans share a core of basic environmental values, and that sustainable forest management is near the top of their list of concerns.

Ultimately, meaningful Forest Service reform—and the success and welfare of those who are working for change inside the agency—depends on the ability to more fully cultivate those core

societal values, bringing the powerful force of the American center
to bear on those who hold sway over the nation's public forests.

Contact FSEEE at:

P.O. Box 11615

Eugene, OR 97440

Telephone: (541) 484-2692

E-mail: afseee@afseee.org

Web site: http://www.afseee.org

Bridging the GAP of Accountability in the New American Culture War

Louis Clark, executive director, Government Accountability Project

We are presently in the midst of a corporate culture war being waged
on our society and environment. As an accomplice, government at all
levels has failed to hold corporations accountable for their actions by
not demanding that they change their institutional culture to meet
basic social responsibilities to the land and its inhabitants.

Community health and environmental protection, for example,
are hostage to corporate misinformation campaigns that take advantage of legitimate public concerns, such as jobs, and then put a spin
on them. Government regulations to ensure higher standards of corporate behavior are subsequently demeaned as "bureaucratic interference" and "red tape," even when they prove effective.

The nation's security program, a.k.a. the military, looks increasingly like a giant entitlement program for megacorporations to pioneer idiotic schemes such as Star Wars and "stealth" bombers that fail
to function in the rain. Internationally, the U.S. government has become a "chamber of commerce" for multinational private interests as
concerns about inhumane labor conditions yield to the demands of
trade and the latest quarterly profit margin. Often the biggest loser is
the environment when government cedes its power to companies
whose leaders are not elected by the people, whose raids on natural
resources are not driven by principles of long-term stewardship, and
whose priority is answering to corporate boardrooms rather than
ecological communities of which our species is a part.

As bleak as this picture may appear, there are signs of hope. Buried
in the fabric of every human institution are individuals of conscience

who will do the right thing, despite the risks. In the tradition of Daniel Ellsberg of Pentagon Papers fame and Karen Silkwood, who exposed the crimes of Kerr-McGee nuclear corporation, they are the whistleblowers in government and industry who speak out in the public's interest. Often outside the public's view, these courageous employees act quietly to stop every imaginable corporate crime, sometimes committed with the tacit endorsement of decisionmakers in their own agencies. They block grocery-store chains from packaging and selling rotten meat at gourmet prices. They expose defense firms that use government equipment for private gain. They shut down private hazardous-waste incinerators that spew plumes of unburned toxins at will. And they prevent timber barons from logging the last stands of old-growth forests.

I personally have witnessed how the power of honest employees—armed with damaging information about corporate and government abuses—to demand accountability is often underestimated. Most powerful corporations must still, ultimately, answer to an outraged public if they want to keep selling their products. Millions upon millions of dollars in corporate advertising can be defeated with the broadcast on national television of a single hard-hitting investigative story about corporate wrongdoing. But to be effective as the public's eyes and ears, whistleblowers need guidance and support. There is a continuing need for effective whistleblower protections that allow the brave and conscientious to fully air their substantive concerns without fear of reprisal.

Public attacks on questionable corporate practices and government involvement have led some companies to seek alternative dispute resolution processes in an effort to reform. The most innovative model is the Hanford Joint Council on Employee Disputes, created for the Hanford nuclear facility in Washington state. On the council sit company representatives, a whistleblower, public interest activists, and neutral third parties. The council is entirely independent of any corporation or government agency. After reviewing a situation, it presents recommendations to Hanford management about alleged whistleblower reprisals and the substantive concerns that they raise. The company has the power to reject the council's findings, but it has agreed in advance not to do so unless the recommendations would require the company to violate the law.

Another model is embodied by the federal government's Commission on Research Integrity. The commission has suggested that companies with government research grants be required to recognize certain basic whistleblower rights and adopt mechanisms that will allow for their full realization. This whistleblower "Bill of Rights" includes the right to speak out about scientific misconduct, freedom from reprisal, and the ability of whistleblowers to participate in the investigation of their concerns. Unfortunately it has not stopped abuse.

Less effective, but still significant, are the growing numbers of "employee concerns offices" within corporations and support groups springing up inside government agencies. To be successful, these efforts must be independent of the corporate and bureaucratic management structure; they must report directly to the highest authority within a company or office. The idea is that whereas grassroots change starts at the bottom, true leadership to recognize the value of listening to the rank and file must be present at the top.

As effective mechanisms for reviewing whistleblower claims and ending reprisals are gradually put into place, standard operating procedures within corporations as well as federal and state agencies can begin to change in ways that benefit us all. And when these reform measures fail, the setback provides a vital measure of how far we must go in the continuing effort to create a more ethical culture within the workplace. Government and corporate employees around the country are making their concerns known. The real questions are, will those voices be heard, and can we as a nation survive in the next millennium if they are not?

Contact GAP at:
1612 K Street, NW, Suite 400
Washington, DC 20006
Telephone (202) 408-0034
E-mail: gap@whistleblower.org
Web site: http://www.accessone.com/gap/index.htm

Bibliography

Activities Outside Park Borders Have Caused Damage To Resources and Will Likely Cause More. A report prepared by the U.S. General Accounting Office to the House Subcommittee on National Parks, Forests and Public Lands, under the jurisdiction of the House Committee on Natural Resources, January 1994.

An Assessment of Forest Ecosystem Health in the Southwest. 1997. Rocky Mountain Forest and Range Experiment Station, Southwestern Region, USDA Forest Service General Technical Report RM-GTR-295.

A Sense of Place: Issues, Attitudes and Resources in the Yellowstone to Yukon Bioregion. Summary of the Interim Draft Prepared for the Y2Y Connections Conference, October 1997.

Atencio, Ernie, and Paul Larmer. "Arizona BLM punishes 'bad bureaucrat.'" *High Country News*, April 5, 1993.

"Babbitt signs pacts to protect Western spotted frog." *The Associated Press*, April 3, 1998.

Baca, Jim. Testimony by the Director of the Bureau of Land Management before the Subcommittee on Agricultural Research, Conservation, Forestry, and General Legislation, Committee on Agriculture, Nutrition, and Forestry, United States Senate Oversight Hearings on Ecosystem Management, November 9, 1993.

Badaracco, R.J. "ORVs: Often Rough on Visitors." *National Parks and Recreation*, September 1976.

Barbato, Joseph, and Lisa Weinerman. 1994. *Heart of the Land: Great Essays on the Last Great Places.* Published by Pantheon (New York) for The Nature Conservancy.

Barker, Rocky. "Leadership is the Main Issue in Grizzly Bear Fight." *Idaho Falls Post-Register*, January 8, 1995.

Barnes, G.G., J.K. Nakata, H.G. Wilshire. Origin of Mojave Desert Dust Storms Photographed From Space on January 1, 1973. Paper titled "Desert Dust: Origin, Characteristics, and Effect on Man." Geological Society of America Special Paper 186, 1981.

Belnap, Jayne. "Microphytic Crusts: 'Topsoil of the Desert.'" *Permaculture Drylands Journal*, Spring 1990.

Barnett, John. 1981. *Carlsbad Caverns National Park: Silent Chambers, Timeless Beauty.* Published by Carlsbad Caverns/Guadalupe Mountains Association, Carlsbad, New Mexico.

Benton, R., K. Berry, M. Coffeen, R. Haley, B. Hardenbrook, J. Payne, C. Pregler, C. Schwalbe, and S. Slone. Proposed Desert Tortoise Research Rangewide Funding Needs. Unpublished report. Bureau of Land Management, Riverside, California.

Berry, Kristin. (Two dozen reports on the desert tortoise published between 1973 and 1996).

"Bill Would Halt Drilling Near Cave." *Albuquerque Journal*, May 7, 1993.

"BLM Hydrologist Fights Another Silencing Attempt." *PEEReview*, newsletter of Public Employees for Environmental Responsibility, Washington, D.C., Fall 1993.

Bondello, M.C. 1976. The Effects of High-intensity Motorcycle Sounds on the Accoustical Sensitivity of the Desert Iguana, Dipsosaurus Dorsalis. M.S. Thesis, California State University, Fullerton, California.

Brattstrom, B.H., and M.C. Bondello. 1983. "Effects of off-road vehicle noise on desert vertebrates." pp. 167-221. *Environmental Effects of Off-Road Vehicles: Impacts and Management in Arid Regions*. R.H. Webb and H.G. Wilshire, editors. Springer-Verlag, New York.

Bury, R.B. 1978. Desert tortoises and off-road vehicles: do they mix? p. 126. Editors: M. Trotter and C.G. Jackson, Jr. Appeared in Proceedings of the 1978 Desert Tortoise Council Symposium, Las Vegas, Nevada.

Bury, R.B., and T.C. Esque. 1988. Ecology and Conservation of Desert Tortoise: Comparative Research Study in the Tristate Regions (AZ-NV-UT). Unpublished draft report. National Ecology Research Center, U.S. Fish and Wildlife Service, Fort Collins, Colorado.

Bury, R.B., S.D. Busack, and R.A. Luckenbach. 1977. Effects of Off-road Vehicles on Vertebrates in the California Desert. U.S. Department of the Interior, Wildlife Research Report 8, Washington, D.C.

Cahill, Tim. "Charting the Splendors of Lechuguilla Cave." *National Geographic*, March 1991.

Caring for our Natural Community: Threatened, Endangered, and Sensitive Species Program, Region 1, U.S. Forest Service. Published by the U.S. Department of Agriculture, 1989.

Carlsbad Caverns National Park Final General Management Plan/Environmental Impact Statement. Published by the U.S. Department of Interior.

Carlsbad/Roswell Resource Areas Draft Resource Management Plan. Roswell District Office, U.S. Bureau of Land Management. Published by the U.S. Department of Interior, September 1994.

Carpenter, Betsy and Lisa Busch. "Subterranean blues: Caverns are an uncharted, and increasingly threatened, wilderness." *U.S. News and World Report*, November 22, 1993.

Carson, Rachel L. 1962. *Silent Spring* (Foreword 1987 by Paul Brooks) Houghton Mifflin Co., Boston.

Congressional Quarterly. 1983. *The Battle for Natural Resources.* Congressional Quarterly Inc., Washington, D.C.

Conservation Assessment for Insland Cutthroat Trout: Distribution, Status and Habitat Management Implications. 1996. Prepared by USDA Forest Service's Northern, Rocky Mountain, Intermountain and Southwestern Region.

Crisman, Bob. "Following the Money Underground." Op Ed piece written by Bob Crisman, management assistant, Carlsbad Caverns National Park, 1994.

Dark Canyon Environmental Impact Statement, Draft, 1992. U.S. Department of the Interior, Bureau of Land Management.

Dark Canyon Final Environmental Impact Statement Record of Decision. 1994. U.S. Department of the Interior, Bureau of Land Management.

Depositions taken by attorney Richard Condit, attorney with the Government Accountability Project representing Jeff van Ee in van Ee's case against the U.S. Environmental Protection Agency. Case was heard by the U.S. Merit Systems Projection Board. From March 11, 1992 to present.

Doak, Daniel F. "Source-Sink Models and the Problem of Habitat Degradation: General Models and Applications to the Yellowstone Grizzly." *Conservation Biology,* December 1995.

Dolak, Diane. "BLM worker retains job following appeal." *Sierra Vista Herald/ Bisbeee Review,* August 9, 1993.

Draft Proceedings of the East Mojave Desert Symposium at the University of California, Riverside. 1992. Published by the Los Angeles County Museum in 1995.

Drost, Charles A., and Gary M. Fellers. "Collapse of a Regional Frog Fauna in the Yosemite Area of the California Sierra Nevada, USA." *Conservation Biology,* April 1996.

Endangered and Threatened Wildlife and Plants; Proposed Determination of Critical Habitat for the Mojave Population of the Desert Tortoise; Proposed Rule. Department of the Interior–Fish and Wildlife Service. Published in the Federal Register. Monday, August 30, 1993.

Endangered Species: Factors Associated with Delayed Listing Decisions. U.S. General Accounting Office Report, August 1993.

Environmental Effects of Off-Road Vehicles. 1983. Edited by R.H. Webb and H.G. Wilshire. Springer-Verlag, New York.

Environmental Protection Agency Investigative Report prepared by the Assistant Inspector General for Investigations into conduct of Jeff van Ee. Agency document entered as exhibit document February 11, 1992.

"EPA: Merit Board Cancels Reprimand of Agency Employee Over Conflict Charge" (no author). *The Bureau of National Affairs,* March 1, 1995.

Espinosa, F. Al Jr., John J. Rhodes and Dale A. McCullough. 1997. "The Failure of Existing Plans to Protect Salmon Habitat in the Clearwater National Forest in Idaho." *Journal of Environmental Management,* Vol. 49, pp. 205–230.

"Exploration of Lechuguilla Cave." Special Issue *National Speleological Society News*, October 1988.

Federal Lands: Information on the Use and Impact of off-Highway Vehicles. U.S. General Accounting Office Report, August 1995.

Fenton, M. Brock. "Bat biodiversity." Published in *Global Diversity*, a journal of the Canadian Museum of Nature, Summer 1993.

First Amendment Rights of Federal Workers. A Hearing Before the Employment and Housing Subcommittee of the Committee on Government Operations, U.S. House of Representatives, February 14, 1990. Minutes published by U.S. Government Printing Office, Washington, D.C.

Flather, Curtis H., Linda A. Joyce, Carol A. Bloomgarden. 1994. Species Endangerment Patterns in the United States. Rocky Mountain Forest and Range Experiment Station. USDA Forest Service General Technical Report RM-241.

Forest Service: Actions Needed to Ensure That Salvage Sale Fund is Adequately Managed. U.S. General Accounting Office Report, September 1997.

Forest Service Decisionmaking: A Framework for Improving Performance. U.S. General Accounting Office Report, April 1997.

Forest Service Decisionmaking: Greater Clarity Needed on Mission Priorities. Statement of Barry T. Hill, associate director of the Energy, Resources, and Science Issues, Resources, Community, and Economic Development Division, U.S. General Accounting Office, before the Subcommittee on Forests and Public Lands Management, Committee on Energy and Natural Resources, U.S. Senate, February 1997.

Glazer, Myron Peretz, and Penina Migdal Glazer. 1989. *The Whistleblowers*. Basic Books, Inc., New York.

Glover, Jim. "Journey to the Underworld to find albino crayfish, moonmilk crystals, and subterranean rivers." *National Parks*, May/June 1985.

Greater Yellowstone Ecosystem: An Analysis of Data Submitted by Federal and State Agencies. 1987. Report prepared by the Congressional Research Service for the Subcommittee on Public Lands and the Subcommittee on National Parks and Recreation of the Committee on Interior and Insular Affairs, U.S. House of Representatives.

Grizzly Science: Grizzly Bear Biology in the Greater Yellowstone. 1997. Published by Public Employees for Environmental Responsibility in association with the Government Accountability Project.

Haroldson, M., and D. Mattson. 1985. Response of grizzly bears to backcountry human use in Yellowstone National Park. U.S. Department of the Interior, National Park Service, Interagency Grizzly Bear Study Team Report.

Harting, A.L., Jr. 1985. Relationships between activity patterns and foraging strategies of Yellowstone grizzly bears. M.S. Thesis, Montana State University, Bozeman.

Hawken, Paul. 1993. *The Ecology of Commerce*. HarperCollins Publishers, New York.

Heisler, Karen, and B.M. Pavlik. Construction of a Bibliographic Database on Off-Highway Vehicles Emphasizing Impact, Recovery and Restoration. State of California Department of Parks and Recreation. 1990.

Helvarg, David. 1994. *The War Against the Greens*. Sierra Club Books, San Francisco.

Herrero, Stephen. 1985. *Bear attacks: their causes and avoidance*. Nick Lyons Books, New York.

Hill, K.E. "Hydrologist at odds with BLM." *Sierra Vista Herald/Bisbee Review*, May 27, 1993.

Hoffman, Andrew J., Max H. Bazerman, and Steven L. Yaffee. "Balancing Business Interests and Endangered Species Protection." *Sloan Management Review*, Fall 1997.

"Human Causes of Accelerated Wind Erosion in California's Deserts." Thresholds in Geomorphology. 1980. Allen & Unwin, London.

Hydrological Studies on San Pedro River (30 reports) published since mid-1950s.

Ibarra, Ignacio. "BLM seeking to transfer outspoken hydrologist." *The Arizona Daily Star*, May 10, 1993.

———. "Hydrologist keeps BLM job but says he's of San Pedro." *The Arizona Daily Star*, August 3, 1993.

Impacts to Jeff van Ee on the Letter of Reprimand from EPA and Related Matters, 1990 to present. Prepared by van Ee to explain impacts of disciplinary action on professional and private life for court background information.

Inner Voice (Special issue on whistleblowing) newsletter of the Association of Forest Service Employees for Environmental Ethics (no date). Volume 3, Number 4. Association of Forest Service Employees for Environmental Ethics, Eugene, Oregon.

Jagnow, David. Memo sent to cavers by David Jagnow, geologist and Pajarito Grotto Conservation Chairman on controversy over efforts to remove the Carlsbad Caverns Underground Lunchroom, March 4, 1994.

Jeffrey van Ee v. U.S. Environmental Protection Agency and the U.S. Office of Government Ethics. Complaint for Declaratory and Injunctive Relief. Filed November 9, 1985.

Keeping the Grizzly Bear in the American West, An Alternative Recovery Plan. Published by The Wilderness Society, 1992.

Kerbo, Ronal C. 1981. Caves. Childrens Press, Chicago.

Kimball, Rene. "Lechuguilla Cave Proposals Curb Drilling." *Albuquerque Journal*, May 25, 1993.

Lambright, Teresa. "Cavers support lunchroom closure." *Carlsbad Current-Argus*, April 14, 1994.

_____. "Skeen: Amendment saves Caverns Lunchroom." *Carlsbad Current-Argus*, June 18, 1994.

Land Management Agencies: Information on Selected Administrative Policies and Practices. U.S. General Accounting Office Report to the Chairman, Committee on Appropriations, U.S. Senate, February 1997.

Lechuguilla Cave Briefing Paper. 1989. Prepared by Carlsbad Caverns National Park.

Lechuguilla Cave Public Law 103-169. Bill permanently withdrawing area near Carlsbad Caverns National Park from oil and gas drilling. Copy of bill signed into law by President Clinton, December 2, 1993.

Leopold, Aldo. 1949. *A Sand County Almanac*. Oxford University Press.

Lomeli, Ben. Hydrologic Summary, Water Rights, Status, and Future Options for the San Pedro National Conservation Area. Completed for the United States Department of the Interior, Bureau of Land Management, June 1993.

Mace, R., K. Aune, W. Kasworm, R. Klaver, and J. Claar. 1987. "Incidence of human conflicts by research bears." *Wildlife Society Bulletin* 15:170-173.

Management Recommendations for the Northern Goshawk in the Southwestern United States. 1992. Rocky Mountain Forest and Range Experiment Station, USDA Forest Service, General Technical Report RM-217.

Manning, Mary. "EPA whistleblower scores 'bittersweet' victory." *Las Vegas Sun*, Wednesday March 1, 1995.

Mattson, David J. Sensitivity of Grizzly Bear Indices to Long-Term Change in Habitat Support Capability. 1990. Prepared for Interagency Grizzly Bear Study Team.

_____. 1987. Habitat dynamics and their relationship to biological parameters of the Yellowstone grizzly bear, 1977-83. Progress report. U.S. National Park Service Interagency Grizzly Bear Study Team Report.

_____. Background and Proposed Standards for Managing Grizzly Bear Habitat Security in the Yellowstone Ecosystem. Published through the Cooperative Park Studies Unit, College of Forestry, Wildlife and Range Sciences, University of Idaho, Moscow.

_____. Human Impacts on Bear Habitat Use. International Conference on Bear Resources and Management.

_____. Exchange of interoffice memoranda between Mattson and Richard R. Knight, team leader of the Interagency Grizzly Bear Study Team during 1993.

Mattson, David J., and Richard R. Knight, 1991. Effects of access on human-caused mortality of Yellowstone grizzly bears. U.S. Department of the Interior, National Park Service, Interagency Grizzly Bear Study Team Report.

_____. 1992. Spring bear use of ungulates in the Firehole River drainage of Yellowstone National Park. In federal report *Wolves for Yellowstone* edited by J.D. Varley and W.G. Brewster. Published in a report to the United States

Congress. Vol. IV Research and Analysis. National Park Service. Yellowstone National Park, Wyoming.

Mattson, David J., Bonnie M. Blanchard, and Richard R. Knight. "Yellowstone Grizzly Bear Mortality, Human Habituation, and Whitebark Pine Seed Crops." *Journal of Wildlife Management*, 1992.

Mattson, David J., and Gerald R. Wright. Assessing Status and Trend of Grizzly Bear Populations in the Contiguous United States. Draft report, 1994.

Mattson, David J. and Craig Pease. Draft copy of report "Behaviorally-structured demography of the Yellowstone grizzly bear population." May 1993.

Mattson, David J., Stephen Herrero, Gerald R. Wright, and Craig M. Pease. "Science and Management of Rocky Mountain Grizzly Bears." *Conservation Biology*, August 1996.

Mattson, David J., and M.M. Reid, 1991. "Conservation of the Yellowstone Grizzly Bear." *Conservation Biology*, Volume 5, No. 3.

Mattson, David J. and Bonnie M. Blanchard. 1987. The effects of developments and primary roads on grizzly bear habitat use in Yellowstone National Park, Wyoming. Part of proceedings from International Conference on Bear Resources and Management.

McKibben, Bill. 1989. *The End of Nature*. Random House, New York.

McPhee, John. 1986. *Rising From the Plains*. Farrar Strauss Giroux, New York.

Metzer, S.K., D.V. Prose, and H.G. Wilshire. "Effects of Substrate Disturbance on Secondary Plant Succession; Mojave Desert, California." *Journal of Applied Ecology*, v. 24, 1987.

Mills, Enos. 1909. *Wild Life on the Rockies*. Houghton Mifflin, Boston.

Minutes of the Oversight Hearing on Whistleblower Protection and the Office of the Special Counsel. Testimony before the Subcommittee on Civil Service, Post Office and Civil Service Committee, U.S. House of Representatives, March 31, 1993.

National Forest Planning: A Conservationist's Guide. 1993. Published by The Wilderness Society, Sierra Club, National Audubon Society, Natural Resources Defense Council and National Wildlife Federation.

National Parks: Park Service Needs Better Information to Preserve and Protect Resources. Testimony submitted before the Subcommittee on National Parks and Public Lands, Committee on Resources, U.S. House of Representatives, February 27, 1997.

Negri, Sam. "The San Pedro Riparian Area." *Arizona Highways*, April 1989.

Newmark, William D. 1995. "Legal and Biotic Boundaries of Western North American National Parks: A Problem of Congruence." *Biological Conservation*, Issue 33.

Noss, Reed F., Edward T. LaRoe III, and Michael J. Scott. 1995. Draft copy of Biological Report 28, Endangered Ecosystems of the United States: A Preliminary Assessment of Loss and Degradation. Prepared for the U.S. Department of Interior, National Biological Service.

Osechsner, Marynell. Testimony of grizzly bear biologist before the House Government Operations Subcommittee on Environment, Energy, and Natural Resources, March 31, 1992.

Our Living Resources, A Report to the Nation on the Distribution, Abundance, and Health of U.S. Plants, Animals, and Ecosystems. 1995. U.S. Department of the Interior—National Biological Service. Published by the U.S. Government Printing Office, Washington, D.C.

Parker, Richard. "Skeen Wins Great Lunchroom Battle—At Least for Now." *Albuquerque Journal*, September 11, 1994.

Park Service: Managing for Results Could Strengthen Accountability. U.S. General Accounting Office Report, April 1997.

Pease, Craig. October 7, 1992, letter to federal grizzly bear recovery coordinator Chris Servheen on flaws pertaining to the Grizzly Bear Recovery Plan.

Pezeshki, Charles. 1998. *Wild to the Last: Environmental Conflict in the Clearwater Country.* Washington State University Press, Pullman.

Pinchot, Gifford. 1947. *Breaking New Ground.* Harcourt, Brace and Co., New York.

Principle Laws Relating To Forest Service Activities. 1983. United States Department of Agriculture. Published by the U.S. Government Printing Office, Washington, D.C.

Prose, D.V. Map showing Areas of Visible Land Disturbances Caused by Two Military Training Operations in the Mojave Desert, California. U.S. Geological Survey Map MF–1855, 1986.

Protecting the Resource: Land Conservation and the Future of America's Drinking Water. 1997. Report published by the Trust for Public Land, San Francisco.

Quammen, David. 1996. *The Song of the Dodo: Island Biogeography in an Age of Extinctions.* Scribner, New York.

Radioactive Waste: Interior's Continuing Review of the Proposed Transfer of the Ward Valley Waste Site. U.S. General Accounting Office Report, July 1997.

Reinhart, D.P., and D.J. Mattson. 1990. Bear use of cutthroat trout spawning streams in Yellowstone National Park. International Conference on Bear Resources and Management. 8:343-350.

Reisner, M. 1986. *Cadillac Desert.* Viking Penguin, New York.

Rieman, Bruce E., and John D. McIntyre. 1993. Demographic and Habitat Requirements for Conservation of Bull Trout. Intermountain Research Station, USDA Forest Service General Technical Report INT-302.

Roberts, David. "Caving comes into its golden age: a New Mexico marvel." *Smithsonian*, November 1988.

Roth, John. "Preserving Biodiversity in Caves." *Wild Earth*, Fall 1993.

Sahagun, Louis. "Protecting buried treasures: New federal rules are planned for threatened caves." (Originally appeared in the L.A. Times). Published in the *Minneapolis Star Tribune*, June 1, 1993.

"San Pedro: There's no good reason to reassign Lomeli." Editorial in the *Arizona Daily Star*, March 11, 1994.

Schleyer, B.O., Jonkel, J.J., Rhodes, K.G., and Dunbar, D.M. 1984. The effects of nonmotorized recreation on grizzly bear behavior and habitat use. U.S. Department of the Interior National Park Service Interagency Grizzly Bear Study Team Report.

Schullery, Paul. 1992. *The Bears of Yellowstone*. High Plains Publishing Company, Inc. Worland, Wyoming.

Science and the National Parks. 1992. National Research Council. Published by the National Academy Press, Washington, D.C.

Scott, Norman (Editor). 1982. Herpetological Communities: A Symposium of the Society for the Study of Amphibians and Reptiles and the Herpetologists League, August 1977. Wildlife Research Report 13. United States Department of Interior, Fish and Wildlife Service. Washington, D.C.

Sellars, Richard West. 1997. *Preserving Nature in the National Parks, A History*. Yale University Press, New Haven.

Servheen, Chris. 1989. The status and conservation of the bears of the world. International Conference on Bear Resources and Management. Monograph Series 2:1-32.

_____. Grizzly Bear Recovery Plan. U.S. Fish and Wildlife Service. 1992 Draft and subsequent updates.

_____. Response to Issues Raised Concerning the Grizzly Bear Recovery Plan: A Response from the U.S. Fish and Wildlife Service and the Interagency Grizzly Bear Committee, January 1994.

Sheridan, David. 1979. Off-Road Vehicles on Public Land, Council on Environmental Quality Report.

Snedden, Lois. "Jeff van Ee: Citizen Activist/EPA Target." *The Toiyabe Trails*, newsletter of the Toiyabe Chapter of the Sierra Club, February–March 1992.

Songbird Ecology in Southwestern Ponderosa Pine Forests: A Literature Review. Rocky Mountain Forest and Range Experiment Station, USDA Forest Service General Technical Report RM-GTR-292.

State of the World. Years 1988–1998. Worldwatch Institute Report on Progress Toward a Sustainable Society. W.W. Norton and Co., New York.

Stegner, Wallace. 1962. *Beyond the Hundredth Meridian: John Wesley Powell and the Second Opening of the West*. University of Nebraska Press.

Steiger, J.W., R.H. Webb, and H.G. Wilshire. 1986. "Recovery of Compacted Soils in Mojave Desert Ghost Towns." *Soil Science Society of America Journal*, v. 50.

Stolzenburg, William. "Links to the Underworld." *Nature Conservancy*, May/June 1995.

"Study of space leads team to Carlsbad cave." *The New Mexican*, April 24, 1994.

Stuever, Hank. "Subterranean Matters of Taste: Examining the culture clash of Carlsbad Caverns' underground lunchroom." *Albuquerque Tribune*, April 11, 1994.

Taxpayer's Double Burden. 1993. Report published by The Wilderness Society and the Environmental Defense Fund on $1 billion in annual subsidies of water development, grazing, off-road vehicle recreation, and other development and the millions of dollars taxpayers spend again to recover species harmed by those activities.

Taylor, Michael Ray. "Lechuguilla Cave: Daring and Danger in a World of Delicate Beauty." *Audubon*, September/October 1991.

Thuermer, Angus M. Jr. "Ranchers Target Rules That Protect Grizzlies: Group wants to see griz hunting resumed." *Jackson Hole News*, December 18, 1996.

Udall, Stewart Lee. "In Coronado's Footsteps." *Arizona Highways*, April 1984.

Underground Concession, Carlsbad Caverns National Park Environmental Assessment 1993.

Varley, John. "Holding on to Yellowstone's Grizzlies: A Parting Chat with a 24-year Veteran of Yellowstone's Grizzly Bear Wars." *Yellowstone Science* Volume 6, Number 1, Winter 1988.

"Wallop glad about Baca." Press release from from U.S. Senator Malcolm Wallop, a Wyoming Republican on the news that Interior Secretary Bruce Babbitt had fired Jim Baca, national director of the federal Bureau of Land Management, January 28, 1994.

Weaver, J., R. Escano, D.J. Mattson, T. Puchlerz, and D. Despain. 1986. A cumulative effects model for grizzly bear management in the Yellowstone ecosystem. Proceedings of the Grizzly Bear Habitat Symposium. United States Department of Agriculture.

Weaver, John L., Paul C. Paquet, and Leonard F. Ruggiero. "Resilience and Conservation of Large Carnivores in the Rocky Mountains." *Conservation Biology*, August 1996.

Webb, R.H. and H.G. Wilshire. "Recovery of Soils and Vegetation in a Mojave Desert Ghost Town, Nevada, U.S.A." *Journal of Arid Environments*, v. 3.

Wilkinson, Charles F. 1992. *The Eagle Bird: Mapping a New West*. Pantheon Books, New York.

_____. 1992. *Crossing the Next Meridian: Land, Water, and the Future of the West*. Island Press, Washington, D.C.

Willcox, Louisa. "Grizzly Bears and Wildlands." Article published in fall 1996 newsletter of *Wild Forever*, collaborative grizzly bear conservation project of the Greater Yellowstone Coalition, Sierra Club, Wilderness Society, and Great Bear Foundation.

Wilshire, Howard. "The Wheeled Locusts." *Wild Earth*, Spring 1992.

Index